THE UNITED ARAB EMIRATES

Led by Dubai and Abu Dhabi, the UAE has become deeply embedded in the contemporary system of international power, politics, and policymaking. Only an independent state since 1971, the seven emirates that constitute the UAE represent not only the most successful Arab federal experiment but also the most durable. However, the 2008 financial crisis and its aftermath underscored the continuing imbalance between Abu Dhabi and Dubai and the five northern emirates. Meanwhile, the post-2011 security crackdown revealed the acute sensitivity of officials in Abu Dhabi to social inequalities and economic disparities across the federation.

The *United Arab Emirates: Power, Politics, and Policymaking* charts the various processes of state formation and political and economic development that have enabled the UAE to emerge as a significant regional power and major player in the post–Arab Spring reordering of Middle East and North African politics, as well as the closest partner of the US in military and security affairs in the region. It also explores the seamier underside of that growth in terms of the condition of migrant workers, recent interventions in Libya and Yemen, and, lately, one of the highest rates of political prisoners per capita in the world. The book concludes with a discussion of the likely policy challenges that the UAE will face in coming years, especially as it moves towards its fiftieth anniversary in 2021.

Providing a comprehensive and accessible assessment of the UAE, this book will be a vital resource for students and scholars of International Relations and Middle East Studies, as well as non-specialists with an interest in the United Arab Emirates and its global position.

Kristian Coates Ulrichsen is the Fellow for the Middle East at Rice University's Baker Institute for Public Policy.

THE CONTEMPORARY MIDDLE EAST

Edited by Professor Anoushiravan Ehteshami, Institute for Middle Eastern and Islamic Studies, University of Durham

For well over a century now the Middle East and North Africa countries have formed a central plank of the international system. The *Contemporary Middle East Series* provides the first systematic attempt at studying the key actors of this dynamic, complex, and strategically important region. Using an innovative common format – which in each case study provides an easily-digestible analysis of the origins of the state, its contemporary politics, economics and international relations – prominent Middle East experts have been brought together to write definitive studies of the MENA region's key countries.

Books in the series:

Saudi Arabia
Tim Niblock

Jordan
A Hashemite legacy
2nd Edition
Beverley Milton-Edwards and Peter Hinchcliffe

Morocco
Challenges to tradition and modernity
James N. Sater

Tunisia
Stability and reform in the modern Maghreb
Christopher Alexander

Libya
Continuity and change
Ronald Bruce St John

Lebanon
The politics of a penetrated society
Tom Najem

Libya
Continuity and change
2nd edition
Ronald Bruce St John

Morocco
Challenges to tradition and modernity
2nd edition
James N. Sater

Tunisia
From stability to revolution in the Maghreb
2nd edition
Christopher Alexander

The United Arab Emirates
Power, politics, and policymaking
Kristian Coates Ulrichsen

Iran
Stuck in transition
Anoushiravan Ehteshami

THE UNITED ARAB EMIRATES

Power, Politics, and Policymaking

Kristian Coates Ulrichsen

Routledge
Taylor & Francis Group

LONDON AND NEW YORK

First published 2017
by Routledge
2 Park Square, Milton Park, Abingdon, Oxon OX14 4RN

and by Routledge
711 Third Avenue, New York, NY 10017

Routledge is an imprint of the Taylor & Francis Group, an informa business

© 2017 Kristian Coates Ulrichsen

British Library Cataloguing in Publication Data
A catalogue record for this book is available from the British Library

Library of Congress Cataloging in Publication Data
A catalog record for this book has been requested

ISBN: 978-1-138-81364-9 (hbk)
ISBN: 978-1-138-81365-6 (pbk)
ISBN: 978-1-315-74802-3 (ebk)

Typeset in Bembo
by Taylor & Francis Books

CONTENTS

LIST OF TABLES

ACKNOWLEDGMENTS

I would like to thank Professor Anoushiravan Ehteshami for commissioning this book and my editors at Routledge for their patience and assistance. Writing a book is both a solitary task and a collective endeavor that could not happen without the support of friends and family as well as the many academic and other colleagues whose research and insight I have benefited enormously from. Particular gratitude goes to my wife, my brother, and, not least, my parents, to whom I dedicate this book.

ABBREVIATIONS

ADCO	Abu Dhabi Company for Onshore Oil Operations
ADD	Abu Dhabi Dialogue
ADDF	Abu Dhabi Defense Force
ADEC	Abu Dhabi Executive Council
ADF	Australian Defence Force
ADFD	Abu Dhabi Fund for Development
ADIC	Abu Dhabi Investment Council
AdGas	Abu Dhabi Gas Liquefaction Company
ADGM	Abu Dhabi Global Market
ADIA	Abu Dhabi Investment Authority
ADMA	Abu Dhabi Marine Areas
ADMA-OPCO	Abu Dhabi Marine Operating Company
ADNOC	Abu Dhabi National Oil Company
ADOC	Abu Dhabi Oil Company
ADPC	Abu Dhabi Petroleum Company
ADUG	Abu Dhabi United Group for Development and Investment
AGSIW	Arab Gulf States Institute in Washington
AIIB	Asian Infrastructure Investment Bank
APOC	Anglo Persian Oil Company
AQAP	Al Qaeda in the Arabian Peninsula
BBME	British Bank of the Middle East
BCE	Before Christian Era
BCCI	Bank of Credit and Commerce International
BIT	Bilateral Investment Treaty
BOAC	British Overseas Airways Corporation
BP	British Petroleum
CEO	Chief Executive Officer

CFIUS	Committee on Foreign Investment in the United States
CIO	Central Informatics Organization
CNIA	Critical National Infrastructure Authority (Abu Dhabi)
DDF	Dubai Defense Force
DDW	Dubai DryDocks World
DFF	Dubai Foundation for the Future
DFSA	Dubai Financial Services Authority
DFSF	Dubai Financial Support Fund
DIAC	Dubai International Academic City
DIFC	Dubai International Financial Center
DIFX	Dubai International Financial Exchange
DKV	Dubai Knowledge Village
DMCA	Dubai Maritime City Authority
DPC	Dubai Petroleum Company
EAA	Executive Affairs Authority (Abu Dhabi)
EAIG	Emirates Advanced Investment Group
EDIC	Emirates Defense Industries Company
EGA	Emirates Global Academy
EM	Emerging Market
EMAC	Emirates Marine Arbitration Center
ENEC	Emirates Nuclear Energy Corporation
FATF	Financial Action Task Force
FCO	Foreign and Commonwealth Office (United Kingdom)
FIFA	Federation of International Football Associations
FIU	Financial Intelligence Unit
FNC	Federal National Council
FOAA	Fujairah Offshore Anchorage Area
FSA	Financial Services Authority (United Kingdom)
FSC	Federal Supreme Council
GASCO	Abu Dhabi Gas Industries Limited Company
GATT	General Agreement on Tariffs and Trade
GAVI	Global Alliance for Vaccines and Immunization
GCC	Gulf Cooperation Council
GDP	Gross Domestic Product
GFMD	Global Forum on Migration and Development
GHQ	General Headquarters
GLAC	Gulf Labor Artist Coalition
GNC	General National Congress (Libya)
GRE	Government-Related Enterprise
HoR	House of Representatives (Libya)
HMG	His/Her Majesty's Government
HMS	His/Her Majesty's Ship
HMSDC	Harvard Medical School Dubai Center
HRW	Human Rights Watch

IAEA	International Atomic Energy Agency
ICI	Istanbul Cooperation Initiative
ICJ	International Commission of Jurists
ILO	International Labor Organization
IMF	International Monetary Fund
IOM	International Office of Migration
IONS	Indian Ocean Naval Symposium
IPIC	International Petroleum Investment Corporation
IRA	Independent Regulatory Agency
IRENA	International Renewable Energy Agency
ISIS	Islamic State of Iraq and al-Shams
JODCO	Japan Oil Development Company
KEPCO	Korea Electric Power Corporation
KFOR	Kosovo Force
KNOC	Korea National Oil Corporation
LNG	Liquefied Natural Gas
LSE	London School of Economics and Political Science
MBR	Mohammed bin Rashid Al Maktoum
MBZ	Mohammed bin Zayed Al Nahyan
MEDRC	Middle East Desalination Research Center
MEED	Middle East Economic Digest
MEPI	Middle East Partnership Initiative (US State Department)
MIST	Masdar Institute of Science and Technology
MIT	Massachusetts Institute of Technology
MITI	Ministry of Trade and Industry (Japan)
MOU	Memorandum of Understanding
MSCI	Morgan Stanley Capital International
NATO	North Atlantic Treaty Organization
NEC	National Election Committee
NIOC	National Iranian Oil Company
NTC	National Transitional Council (Libya)
NYUAD	New York University Abu Dhabi
OBAD	Office of the Brand of Abu Dhabi
OBU	Offshore Banking Unit
OECD	Organization for Economic Cooperation and Development
OEM	Original Equipment Manufacturer
OPEC	Organization of Petroleum Exporting Countries
PPP	Purchasing Power Parity
QFC	Qatar Financial Center
QFCRA	Qatar Financial Center Regulatory Authority
RAK	Ras al-Khaimah
RDIF	Russia Direct Investment Fund
RUSI	Royal United Services Institute (London)
SCAF	Supreme Council of the Armed Forces (Egypt)

SDR	Special Drawing Rights
SEWA	Sharjah Electricity and Water Authority
SFC	Supreme Fiscal Committee (Dubai)
SGX	Singapore Exchange
SWF	Sovereign Wealth Fund
SPC	Supreme Petroleum Council
TEPCO	Tokyo Electric Power Company
TDIC	Tourism Development and Investment Company
UAE	United Arab Emirates
UAQ	Umm al-Quwain
UAR	United Arab Republic
UDF	Union Defense Force
UN	United Nations
UNESCO	United Nations Educational, Scientific and Cultural Organization
WGES	World Green Energy Summit
WIPO	World Intellectual Property Organization
WTO	World Trade Organization
ZADCO	Zakum Development Company

1

INTRODUCTION

Led by Dubai and Abu Dhabi, the United Arab Emirates (UAE) has become deeply embedded in the contemporary system of international power, politics, and policymaking. In possession of the seventh-largest oil reserves in the world and strategically located at the southern end of the Gulf, the UAE has developed a global footprint in trade, financial flows, aviation, and logistics, as well as a trans-regional significance in labor migration and remittance flows. Long tied to the Global South through the generous provision of overseas development assistance, in the 2000s the UAE began to participate actively in the broader rebalancing of geo-economic power between West and East. Moreover, as a founder and active member of the six-nation Gulf Cooperation Council (GCC) and an integral cog in the regional security architecture of the Gulf, the UAE has, since 2011, engaged heavily with states impacted by the upheaval unleashed by the "Arab Spring."

This book charts the processes of historical and state formation and political and economic development that have framed the rapid emergence of the UAE as a regional power with truly international reach. Only an independent state since 1971, the seven emirates that together constitute the UAE represent not only the most successful Arab federal initiative but also the most durable. An incremental pattern of nation-building has gradually grafted a common Emirati identity onto the seven emirates that, over time, has taken deep root, although differences do persist both in political outlook and economic prospect. Moreover, the impact of the 2008–2009 financial crisis and its aftermath illustrated continuing imbalances between Abu Dhabi – home to 90 percent of UAE oil reserves, Dubai, and the five smaller northern emirates. Meanwhile, the post-2011 domestic security crack-down that targeted members of an Islamist group affiliated with the Muslim Brotherhood highlighted the sensitivity of senior officials in Abu Dhabi to the potential for politicization of social and economic disparities across the federation even as the UAE emerged at the forefront of regional attempts to shape the direction of post–Arab Spring transitions in North Africa.

An extensive literature has developed around the emergence and growth of the UAE. Early volumes in the 1970s and 1980s constitute significant historical sources informed by participant accounts of many of the initial processes of state-formation and subsequent consolidation. Donald Hawley, a British diplomat who served as Political Agent in Dubai from 1958 to 1962, penned a historical account of the Trucial States that appeared in 1970, the year before the creation of the UAE itself.[1] Seventeen years later, Abdullah Omran Taryam published a detailed history of the formation and formative years of the UAE that drew heavily on his own experiences in the first Cabinets of the UAE (as Minister of Education and Minister of Justice) and remains one of the most important first-hand accounts of the period available in English. Taryam's work constitutes an indispensable guide to the troubled early years of the federation when its later durability was by no means assured, or even predicted.[2]

Other important early works on the UAE by Mohammed Morsy Abdullah,[3] Ali Mohammed Khalifa,[4] and Rosemarie Said Zahlan[5] were followed in the 1980s by Malcolm Peck[6] before a surge of publications in the 2000s that included a detailed volume edited by Ibrahim al-Abed and Peter Hellyer,[7] Frauke Heard-Bey's voluminous study of the UAE,[8] Christopher Davidson's trio of books,[9] and Jim Krane's highly accessible study of Dubai's meteoric rise.[10] More specific volumes on diverse aspects of UAE policy include Hassan Hamdan al-Alkim on foreign policy,[11] Khalid Almezaini on foreign aid,[12] Hendrik van der Meulen[13] and Andrea Rugh[14] on the role of kinship ties and the political culture of leadership respectively, Karen Young on the political economy of, and formal–informal linkages in, energy, finance, and security,[15] Ahmed Kanna[16] on the intersection of cultural and political forces in the shaping of Dubai, works by Syed Ali,[17] Pardis Mahdavi,[18] and Neha Vora[19] on migrant labor, and Michael Herb's important comparative analysis of economic, political, and business development in the UAE and Kuwait,[20] to list but a few.

The United Arab Emirates: Power, Politics, and Policymaking offers a full and frank assessment of the UAE in historical and comparative perspective, political and security orientation, and economic globalization. The book adopts a comprehensive approach that covers, among others, the fields of political science and comparative politics, economics, the theory and practice of globalization, aspects of international relations and international political economy, and security studies. Further, the book strikes a balance between narrative and analysis in order to document both the factors that have propelled the UAE to regional and international prominence as well as the underside of that growth. Along with GCC neighbor Qatar, the rise of the UAE has challenged the existing academic literature on the role of small states in the international system. Opportunities for small states to make their voice heard have proliferated in today's intensely globalized environment where concepts of *power* and *influence* are projected through multiple channels and are less reliant on territorial or population size than ever before. With the UAE having become a major player in the post–Arab Spring reordering of

Middle East and North African politics, and remaining the closest Arab partner of the US both in military and in security affairs, an analysis of the factors that propelled the UAE to this position is both relevant and opportune.

Key Themes

A number of key themes outline the intellectual and analytical core of this book. Together, these themes help to outline how the political and economic challenges that faced the new federation of United Arab Emirates in the 1970s and 1980s were overcome and subsequently paved the way for the liberalization and internationalization of the political economy of the UAE in the 1990s and 2000s. The first is the blend of traditional and charismatic political authority exercised during the early years of the federation by Sheikh Zayed bin Sultan Al Nahyan, the Ruler of Abu Dhabi between 1966 and 2004, and Sheikh Rashid bin Saeed Al Maktoum, the Ruler of Dubai from 1958 to 1990. The relationship between the two leaders was not without tension during the formative years of the UAE, particularly when their opposing positions over the degree of centralization within the young federation precipitated a constitutional crisis in 1976 that lasted until 1979.[21] This notwithstanding, Sheikh Zayed and Sheikh Rashid succeeded in maintaining and updating political order in the face of the transformative period of socio-economic change that accompanied the onset of the oil era and the passage to statehood in the 1960s and 1970s.

The importance of personalized top-down leadership was magnified by the difficult and, at times, fractious task of aligning policies and expectations among the seven constituent emirates – and their individual rulers – which finally cohered on February 10, 1972, when Ras al-Khaimah joined the union of the other six former Trucial States that had been proclaimed on December 2, 1971.[22] The success of the federation was far from preordained in 1971 and its subsequent durability contrasted sharply with nearly all of the other federal "experiments," such as the short-lived Federation of South Arabia, that dotted the Arab political landscape around that time. In December 2011, the lavish celebrations of the fortieth anniversary of the UAE's founding illustrated the extent to which an initially top-down program of nation-building gradually was grafted, at times uneasily, onto the individual narratives and "localisms" of the constituent emirates to impart a distinctive "Emirati" national identity.[23] More than a decade after his death, aged 86, in November 2004, Sheikh Zayed remains revered, even mythologized, throughout the UAE as the nation's "founding father," and an aspirational standard of reference for all public figures in the country.

The gradual creation of "national" (i.e. federal) institutions provides an illustration of the second element to consider when analyzing the formation and subsequent evolution of the UAE, which is that the federation is a collection of seven constituent emirates with individual ruling families and interests that have gone through periods both of convergence and divergence. Indeed, writing in 1997, shortly after the UAE commemorated its quarter-century, US diplomat Hendrik van der Muelen observed that "tribal and kinship considerations dominate the internal struggle for political power in the UAE" both at the federal and constituent emirate levels.[24] The process of state formation and nation-building in the UAE therefore is as much one of identifying and strengthening the integrative mechanisms among the seven emirates as it is about transforming "traditional" patterns of tribal legitimacy into political and bureaucratic institutions. What is today the UAE is a symbiosis of the principle of hereditary rule alongside sophisticated areas of integration into global economic structures, as well as the translation of the initial charismatic political authority of the nation's founders into a "legal-rational" bureaucratic, albeit authoritarian in places, form of rule.

Tables 1.1 and 1.2 illustrate the disparities in territorial size and list the ruling families of each of the seven emirates that constitute the UAE (an additional "emirate," Kalba, received British recognition as a separate Trucial State in 1937 but this proved short-lived and in 1951 Kalba was reincorporated into Sharjah). The emirate of Abu Dhabi is dominant within the UAE both in terms of land mass and oil reserves and accounted for some 95 percent of total UAE crude oil production of about 2.9 million barrels per day in 2014.[25] Notably, it was Abu Dhabi as an individual sheikhdom that joined the Organization of Petroleum Exporting Countries (OPEC) in 1967, four years before the creation of the UAE and the transfer of membership to the federation.[26] Abu Dhabi was initially represented at OPEC by a former Iraqi government minister, Nadim Pachachi, who was appointed an Advisor on Oil Affairs in the sheikhdom.[27]

Far smaller in size and energy resources, and partially as a result of its own oil production having peaked at 410,000 barrels per day in 1991 before falling sharply to 170,000 barrels per day by 1999,[28] Dubai became an early-mover in economic diversification and infrastructural and industrial development in the 1990s. The success of the "Dubai model" of development enabled the emirate to surpass Abu Dhabi in scope and scale of economic ambition in the 2000s before the impact of the global financial crisis of 2008–2009 brought a temporary slowdown to a decade of freewheeling growth.[29]

Far smaller quantities of petroleum are located in Sharjah and Ras al-Khaimah, while Fujairah developed a niche in oil refining, bunkering and storage, and, since 2012, as the terminus of a pipeline from Abu Dhabi bypassing the Strait of Hormuz.[30] The other emirates also signed oil concessions in the 1960s that led to the drilling of experimental wells, but without success in Ajman and Umm al-Quwain.[31]

Abu Dhabi and Dubai constitute therefore the two poles of political and economic gravity in the UAE. In 2013, the Gross Domestic Product (GDP) of Abu Dhabi was 672,668 million Dirhams, just over twice the size of Dubai's GDP of 325,687 million Dirhams.[32] By convention, the Ruler of Abu Dhabi has held the post of President of the UAE, albeit subject to election by the Federal Supreme Council every five years, while the position of Prime Minister has been held by the Ruler of Dubai. Abu Dhabi also was allocated six Cabinet portfolios upon independence in 1971, including the key ministries of foreign affairs, interior, and information. Three important ministries were apportioned to Dubai (defense,

TABLE 1.1 List of Emirates by Territorial Size

Emirate	Land Mass (square miles)
Abu Dhabi	26,000
Dubai	1500
Sharjah	1000
Ras al-Khaimah	650
Fujairah	450
Umm al-Quwain	292
Ajman	100

Source: information compiled by Kristian Coates Ulrichsen.

TABLE 1.2 Ruling Families of the UAE

Emirate	Ruling Family	Ruler (2015)
Abu Dhabi	Al Nahyan	Sheikh Khalifa bin Zayed Al Nahyan
Dubai	Al Maktoum	Sheikh Mohammed bin Rashid Al Maktoum
Ras al-Khaimah	Al Qasimi	Sheikh Saud bin Saqr Al Qasimi
Sharjah	Al Qasimi	Sheikh Dr. Sultan bin Mohammed Al Qasimi
Ajman	Al Nuaimi	Sheikh Humaid bin Rashid Al Nuaimi
Fujairah	Al Sharqi	Sheikh Hamad bin Mohammed Al Sharqi
Umm al-Quwain	Al Mu'alla	Sheikh Saud bin Rashid Al Mu'alla

Source: information compiled by Kristian Coates Ulrichsen.

finance, and economy and industry) while Sharjah also received three, lesser-ranking, posts, with the remainder divided among Ajman, Fujairah, Ras al-Khaimah, and Umm al-Quwain.[33]

The character and composition of Emirati institutions such as the Federal Supreme Council (FSC), which consists of the seven individual Rulers and constitutes the highest executive and legislative authority in the UAE, and the Federal National Council (FNC), also reflect an apportionment by emirate size. Thus, while Abu Dhabi and Dubai each have eight seats in the FNC, six are allotted to Ras al-Khaimah and Sharjah, and four each to the emirates of Ajman, Fujairah, and Umm al-Quwain.[34] Meanwhile, Emirati academic Khalid Almezaini notes that, in the Federal Supreme Council, "each ruler has a single vote and procedural matters are determined by a simple majority vote, but substantive issues require the concurrence of both Abu Dhabi and Dubai."[35]

The separation of powers between federal and emirate-level institutions was covered in Articles 2 and 3 of the Constitution drawn up on a temporary basis in 1971 and made permanent in 1996. Whereas Article 2 stated that "The Union shall exercise sovereignty in matters assigned to it in accordance with this Constitution," Article 3 added that "The member Emirates shall exercise sovereignty over their own territories and territorial waters in all matters not within the jurisdiction of the Union as assigned in this Constitution."[36] Article 120 assigned to the federal government responsibility for nineteen issues, including foreign affairs, defense and security, law and order, finances, education, and public health. Interestingly, Article 9 stipulated that Abu Dhabi was only to become the "provisional headquarters" of the federation pending construction of a new capital, Al Karama, on the borders of Abu Dhabi and Dubai.[37] Vestiges of the founders' aspirations for Al Karama, which was to have been built within seven years of the signing of the UAE constitution, can still be seen in the UAE's telephone dialing code, which begins at '02' for Abu Dhabi (which became the permanent capital of the UAE in 1994) as "01" was earmarked for the new city that was never built.[38]

The points listed above – the importance of personalized leadership and the creation of national institutions – intersect in the networks of personal relationships between and among the ruling families of the seven constituent emirates. Such interpersonal ties have been examined in depth by Andrea Rugh in her study of the *political culture* of leadership in the UAE and in a context where governance is based both on personal relations and formal institutions.[39] Dynastic marriages among the members of the seven ruling families and with influential (non-ruling) merchant families illustrate the enduring importance of personalized connections that persist alongside (and sometimes complicate) the formal mechanisms of bureaucratic institutionalization. As one example of many, Rugh described the dense network of familial ties of Sheikh Humaid bin Rashid Al Nuaimi, ruler of Ajman since his father's death in September 1981:

> Counting his wives, mother, and grandmother, Sheikh Humaid is linked to wealthy merchant families [such as the al-Ghurair], the critical Bani Qitab, the Nahyans (albeit from a section that is not in favor), and the Rulers of RAK [Ras al-Khaimah], UAQ [Umm al-Quwain], and the Bu Falasa of Dubai. In addition, his sister married the Ruler of Fujairah, and her son is now ruler there. One could not be better positioned from the point of view of marriage relations to form political alliances with all parties in the area.[40]

One of the most prominent recent dynastic connections has been the 2005 marriage of Sheikha Manal bint Mohammed Al Maktoum, the daughter (and eldest child) of Sheikh Mohammed bin Rashid Al Maktoum, the Ruler of Dubai, to Sheikh Mansour bin Zayed Al Nayhan of Abu Dhabi (and, as of 2015, the UAE Deputy Prime Minister and Minister of Presidential Affairs). Others include the 2009 wedding of the Crown Prince of Fujairah and a younger daughter of the Ruler of Dubai as well as the 2012 marriage between the Crown Prince of Umm al-Quwain and a daughter of the ruling family of Ras al-Khaimah, while the current Ruler of Umm al-Quwain, Sheikh Saud bin Rashid Al Mualla, is married to a daughter of the late Ruler of Ras al-Khaimah, Sheikh Saqr bin Mohammed Al Qassimi.[41]

More relevant to policy is the strong personal bond that is said to have formed between Sheikh Mohammed bin Zayed Al Nahyan, the Crown Prince of Abu Dhabi, and the Ruler of Dubai and Prime Minister of the UAE, Sheikh Mohammed bin Rashid Al Maktoum. "MBZ" and "MBR" are, in 2015, seen as the architects of, respectively, the political and economic emergence of the UAE as a regional and international power. The roots of their close personal and professional relationship extend well before the accession of Mohammed bin Zayed as Abu Dhabi Crown Prince in November 2004 and Mohammed bin Rashid as Ruler of Dubai in January 2006, and were forged after MBZ's appointment as Chief of Staff of the UAE Armed Forces in January 1993, after which he worked closely with MBR, the UAE's Defense Minister since 1971.[42] The connection between the two men has acted to ensure that the policy leadership in Abu Dhabi and Dubai has overcome periodic obstacles and points of friction, such as during the debt crisis that rocked Dubai in 2008–2009 and required an injection of funds from Abu Dhabi, and has provided an enduring backbone to federal affairs.

Closely related to the personalization of key decision making among elites in the UAE is the dense network of interpersonal relationships that form the cornerstone of the large family conglomerates that dominate the Emirati business landscape (as they also do in other Gulf States). The fortunes of merchant families have, for generations, been intertwined with those of the ruling families in each of the Gulf States. Whereas merchant families on occasion possessed greater economic and financial resources than ruling families during the formative, pre-oil era of development in the Gulf sheikhdoms, Jill Crystal has noted how the advent of the oil era resulted in a political and economic tradeoff between rulers and merchants whereby "merchants renounced their historical claim to participate in decision making, [and] in exchange the rulers guaranteed them a large share of the oil revenues."[43] Such a political and economic tradeoff meant that business elites in the UAE, as in other Gulf States, followed a highly distinctive pattern of development. Cut out by the ruling family/government from direct ownership or control of the energy sector, prominent merchants pursued business opportunities in other industries that were either derivative to the oil sector or were initiated with state assistance from accrued oil revenues. Over time, as J.E. Peterson has documented, the most successful family businesses transformed into diversified conglomerates as they expanded both horizontally and vertically and often cemented their ties to ruling families through intermarriage.[44]

The most significant mechanism linking the "state-business" elite over the past half-century has been the assignment by ruling elites of "agency rights." This was a way of permitting the merchant elites to pursue business opportunities in other industries and sectors. It was, also, an opportunity for the ruling family to obtain and reward the loyalty of the economic and business elites by granting or revoking the licenses for concessions to import goods or operate "local franchises" as they arose. A new "ruling bargain" evolved whereby merchant families close to senior decision makers were granted the most lucrative franchise concessions, both as a way of ensuring their loyalty and giving them an economic stake in the status quo. Both the agency and the sponsorship system provided ample opportunities for local middlemen to profit from business relationships; the difference between them was that whereas foreign companies needed an agent to export to the Gulf States, a sponsor was required if a company wished to operate locally.[45]

Khalid Almezaini has estimated that "traditional merchant families" still "constitute over 90 percent of the private companies" in the UAE and continue to enjoy "strong business partnerships" with the ruling families of the seven emirates.[46] Leading merchants were instrumental in the early creation of the banking and finance industry, with representatives of most of the leading merchant families featuring on the boards of directors of banks such as Emirates Bank, and Mashreq Bank, one of the largest in the country, linked to the prominent al-Ghurair family.[47] Indeed, the trajectory of the Al Ghurair group illustrates the close overlap among commerce, governance, and technocratic leadership in the contemporary UAE, beginning with one of the founders of the group, Saif Ahmad al-Ghurair, who served also a close adviser to Sheikh Zayed and as the Chairman of bodies such as the Dubai Chamber of Commerce and Industry, and continuing with his nephew, Abdul Aziz al-Ghurair who, in addition to his duties as CEO of Mashreq Bank, has headed the Family Business Network, which aims to modernize family businesses across the Gulf Cooperation Council (GCC), and the Emirates Banks Association, and who between 2007 and 2011 served as the Speaker of the FNC before becoming Chairman of the Dubai International Financial Centre (DIFC) Authority Board of Directors from 2012 until 2014.

A further key characteristic of the modern history of the UAE is the sheer rapidity with which the processes of state formation and institutional consolidation have taken place. In little more than two generations, unprecedented socio-economic (if not political) change has transformed the coastal Gulf sheikhdoms from British protected states into key players in the twenty-first-century global economy. This means that some of the most remarkable and all-encompassing socio-economic transformations in recorded history have been distilled into the space of a single human lifetime. Julian Walker, a young British official posted to the Trucial States (as they then were) in the 1950s, recalled in 1994 his travels to inland communities during that decade:

> In a world of raiding parties every stranger was suspect. Shots would often greet one's approach to a village. Only if one was patently no threat, walking ahead of one's Land Rover and obviously unarmed, or came in the company of friendly tribesmen, would the traditions of hospitality and curiosity prevail over fear. Often I was warned off. In some cases I came with the wrong companions and was detained and threatened.[48]

Far from representing a colonial-era official looking back, Walker's experiences came less than a decade after Abu Dhabi and Dubai had gone to war with each other in a brief yet bloody encounter that left dozens of tribesmen dead.

Writing in 1995 in *Rags to Riches: A Story of Abu Dhabi*, the prominent Emirati businessman Mohammed al-Fahim described the circumstances of his 1950s childhood as a place where:

> the permanent and seasonal residents of Abu Dhabi island still lived in barasti huts built of palm fronds harvested from the date trees. The exceptions were a few wealthier residents and the ruling family who lived in earth or clay houses ... The houses were clustered together for security, companionship, and warmth during the cooler months.[49]

Al-Fahim added that "the changes that have taken place throughout the Emirates over the past three decades have been incredible, difficult to believe even for those who have seen them with their own eyes."[50] In a similar vein, Khabeer Khan, a Pakistani advisor recruited by Sheikh Zayed to work on agricultural development, described his first arrival in Abu Dhabi in 1962 as "like stepping back into the Stone Age."[51] Khan recalled his initial impressions when flying into Abu Dhabi thus:

> "Oh my God, we've crash landed!" I'm afraid this was my first thought as the small commuter plane of Gulf Aviation hit the ground. It took a while to realise that we had actually landed at Abu Dhabi. This was because looking out of the window upon landing just showed gravel on the ground and no tarmac, no runway as one was accustomed to seeing at airports ... Stepping out, there was little semblance of an airport; no terminal building, just a shade by the wayside in what appeared to be total wilderness ... A red and white Abu Dhabi flag hoisted upon a pole was the only indication that this was indeed Abu Dhabi. A lone date palm standing tall at a distance was the only welcome sign.[52]

In the early 1960s, Abu Dhabi was a small coastal settlement of about 4,000 inhabitants that lacked basic infrastructure such as electricity or running water, while Dubai was the only large town in the Trucial States capable of supporting much more than a subsistence economy.[53] Indeed, it was only in 1968 that cities such as Al Ain were supplied with electricity for the first time.[54]

On a comparative level, the rise of the UAE poses questions as to the extent to which the country can be classified as a small state and how it fits into the academic literature on small state theory. Comparisons are often drawn between the UAE and neighboring Qatar and Kuwait as examples of extreme resource-rich states that constitute a sub-genre of their own in the broader "rentier state" literature. In his analysis of the political economy of rentierism, the Doha-based academic Mehran Kamrava has observed a number of similarities between Qatar and the UAE. In both countries the state has been able to use its massive wealth to enhance its instruments of control – through either patronage, or surveillance and coercion – or both, and has developed a variety of highly effective, often very polished regime maintenance mechanisms … in both Qatar and the wealthier emirates of the UAE, notably Dubai and Abu Dhabi, state actors often have to temper their enthusiasm for rapid change and modernization with attention to the sensibilities of more conservative prominent families … [55]

Michael Herb also has compared and contrasted the differing trajectories of political and economic development in Kuwait and the UAE. Herb has noted that the UAE and Kuwait have much in common and, moreover, that their "many similarities make these two countries excellent cases for understanding the effect of variation in the level of political participation on economic development."[56] And yet, there are significant features that distinguish the UAE not only from its GCC neighbors but also from other examples of "small states" across the world. Aside from the federal nature of the UAE that means that policymaking is filtered through multiple layers of authority not replicated elsewhere in the Gulf, there are statistical differences between the UAE and its neighbors and other states the country is sometimes compared with, as illustrated in Table 1.3.

From the table it is readily apparent that the UAE far outstrips Kuwait and especially Qatar both in terms of size and population while, paradoxically, the GDP per capita is higher in the latter two countries than it is in the UAE itself. The lower GDP per capita reflects the wealth differential among the seven emirates and, particularly, the sharp divide between resource-rich Abu Dhabi, affluent Dubai, and the five Northern Emirates. The UAE thus has greater disparities in wealth and development among its own nationals than exist in Kuwait and Qatar even as, in all three states, citizens are outnumbered by expatriates. Indeed, it is the scale of the "demographic imbalance" whereby non-nationals now constitute close to 90 percent of the total population of Abu Dhabi, Dubai, and Qatar that offers the clearest point of comparison, especially to outside observers.[57]

TABLE 1.3 Selected Statistical Indicators for Small States

Country	Territorial Size	Population	GDP	GDP per capita (PPP)
UAE	83,600 sq. km.	9,445,625 (UN)	US$599.8bn	US$64,500
Kuwait	17,818 sq. km.	2,788,534	US$284bn	US$71,000
Qatar	11,586 sq. km.	2,194,817 (2015)	US$320.5bn	US$143,400
Norway	323,802 sq. km.	5,207,689 (2015)	US$500.2bn	US$$66,900
Singapore	697 sq. km.	5,674,472 (2015)	US$445.2bn	US$82,800

Source: adapted by Kristian Coates Ulrichsen from the CIA World Factbook. All figures are for 2014 unless otherwise indicated.

In addition to having a far larger population and territorial size than those neighboring states to which the UAE often is compared, the country additionally has exhibited a greater set of capabilities in its engagement with the international system than commonly ascribed in classical international relations theory, which has tended to view "small states" as relatively weak and having only a limited role in the international system. In *Small States in World Politics: Explaining Foreign Policy Behavior*, Jeanne Hey argued that the majority of small states:

> exhibit a low level of participation in world affairs, limit their behavior to their immediate geographic arena, employ diplomatic and economic foreign policy instruments as opposed to military instruments, and rely on superpowers for protection, partnerships, and resources.[58]

In a study of Kuwait published in 1991, Mary Ann Tetreault raised a number of conceptual questions that remain pertinent to the study of small states a quarter-century later:

> The study of small states is filled with theoretical and substantive problems. What is a small state? How much can it do by itself to ensure its own security? Can its foreign policy ever be "voluntary" – that is, initiated by the small state and centered on its own interests – or is it, by necessity, dictated by the structure of the international system, the interests of dominant states, or a combination of these factors?

As the chapters in this book illustrate, however, policymakers in the UAE have been able to project and leverage a far higher degree of power and influence than predicted in the literature, and across a considerable array of sectors that have made the country a regional actor with truly global reach. Moreover, since the 1990s, officials in Dubai and Abu Dhabi have projected the "harder" elements of force alongside the "softer" focus on diplomacy and foreign aid that characterized other Gulf States such as Kuwait, Qatar, and, to an extent, Saudi Arabia. The regular use of military force in support of multilateral (United States–led) operations in the 1990s and 2000s marked the UAE as distinct from regional neighbors. The UAE participated in every US-led military operation in the "Broader Middle East" region after 1990 – Somalia, Kosovo, Libya, Afghanistan, and the air campaign against the Islamic State of Iraq and Syria – with the sole exception of George W. Bush's controversial invasion of Iraq in 2003. This culminated in the UAE's muscular response to rolling back Islamist gains in Arab Spring transition states and, in 2015, in the forceful military intervention in Yemen, as later chapters in this book make clear.

Structure of the Book

Following this introductory chapter, Chapter Two examines the processes of historical development that shaped state formation in the seven emirates, also known for much of the nineteenth and twentieth centuries as the Trucial States, which became the UAE in December 1971. The chapter focuses on the century and a half between the signing of the General Maritime Treaty with the British Empire in 1820 and the beginning of the oil era in the Trucial States (primarily in Abu Dhabi and Dubai) in the mid-1960s. Sections covered in the chapter explore the strategies for regional influence among the leading local sheikhs of the southern Gulf, the growth of the emirates of Abu Dhabi and Dubai as well as their ruling dynasties, the Al Nahyan and the Al Maktoum, the eclipse of the maritime power of the *Qawasim* in Ras al-Khaimah and Sharjah, as well as the politics of protection that came to characterize the relationship between the Trucial States and the United Kingdom. The chapter ends with the discovery of oil and the challenges of fixing both internal (inter-emirate) boundaries and external borders as the granting of oil concessions required the drawing up and formalization of sometimes-competing territorial claims.

Chapter Three turns to the evolution of political structures in the UAE during the quarter-century that spanned the formation of the UAE and covers the opening two decades of independence until 1990 as well as the growth and political evolution of representative institutions such as the FNC. It begins with the negotiations that culminated in the formation of a seven-emirate federation as opposed to British plans for a nine-member Union of Arab Emirates that would have included Bahrain and Qatar as part of an intended British counterweight to the hegemonic influence of Saudi Arabia. Against the backdrop of significant turbulence in regional affairs with the Islamic Revolution in Iran in 1979 and the eight-year Iran–Iraq War between 1980 and 1988, the new federation had to navigate a challenging domestic environment while also managing rapid urbanization and keeping ahead of unprecedented socio-economic changes. Particular difficulties arose in resolving tensions among individual emirates and in balancing responsibilities between the emirate and federal levels, as deep-rooted differences over a federal constitution and a unified defense force came repeatedly to the fore while the Iran–Iraq War split the federation down the middle as individual emirates backed different sides. And yet, during these formative years, the federation endured, marking it as distinct from almost all other regional federal experiments that rose and fell in the 1960s and 1970s.

The economic factors that underpinned the UAE's move into the global arena in the 1990s and 2000s form the focal point of Chapter Four. As the UAE transitioned into a new era of political leadership as the generation of founding sheikhs passed away and power passed – relatively smoothly – to a younger generation of rulers, the new leadership in Dubai took the lead in creating innovative and specialized zones of economic activity that marked the emirate as a pioneer in economic liberalization across the Gulf. These moves built upon incipient measures taken in the 1970s and 1980s that positioned Dubai as a regional infrastructural hub already by 1990 but were qualitatively and quantitatively different both in scope and in scale and were designed to accelerate the transition of Dubai into a post-oil economy. While Abu Dhabi subsequently borrowed from several aspects of the "Dubai model" to guide its own strategy of economic diversification, the chapter explores the commonalities and differences between Abu Dhabi and Dubai in areas such as energy policy and sovereign wealth investment, while the chapter closes with a look at the growth of global brands in UAE aviation and the emphasis going forward on innovation. An underlying theme that links this chapter with those on politics and international relations is the growth of a globally focused economy based on neo-traditional political lines.

With the deaths of Sheikh Zayed in November 2004 and Sheikh Maktoum in January 2006, the present leaders (as of mid-2016) of Abu Dhabi and Dubai came to power. Their emergence coincided with the long upward trend in international oil prices and Chapter Five charts how the new leadership in the UAE leveraged the country's reserves of oil and accumulation of capital to take full advantage of the new regional and international opportunities that opened up in the 2000s. The chapter explores the succession of developments that transformed the UAE into an international player during this period and analyzes how the country became a more proactive player in evolving structures of global governance using a mixture of "soft" and "smart" power. A case-study of the Abu Dhabi United Group takeover of Manchester City FC and the subsequent regeneration of parts of Manchester illustrates this more nuanced projection of influence at work.

Chapter Six examines the impact of the Arab Spring on the UAE. The sudden outbreak of political upheaval in North Africa and in Syria ought not to have had major domestic implications for the UAE but it revealed a deep-rooted antipathy among officials in Abu Dhabi at the potential empowerment of the Muslim Brotherhood across the region. In particular, the rise of the Muslim Brotherhood to power in Tunisia and in Egypt in 2011–2012 was followed by a comprehensive security crackdown that targeted Islamists within the UAE amid a broader restriction of spaces for debate and dissent. Led by Abu Dhabi, policymakers in the UAE additionally developed a proactive and assertive approach to regional issues characterized by an unprecedented use of hard military power in Libya and Yemen and the backing given to non-Islamist forces in other Arab Spring transition states such as Egypt. Furthermore, the military campaigns against the so-called Islamic State of Iraq and al-Shams (ISIS) and against Houthi militants in Yemen that began in 2014 and 2015, respectively, involved the UAE in the unprecedented application of the use of hard military power, particularly in Yemen, and resulted in equally unprecedented casualty levels.

The final chapter in this book provides a forward look at the likely policy challenges that the UAE will face under the leadership of Sheikh Mohammed bin Zayed and as the federation moves toward marking its fiftieth anniversary in 2021 with the organization of Expo 2020 in Dubai and a series of other high profile events that include a planned Emirates Mission to Mars. That these events – global in scope and ambition – may well take place against the backdrop of a prolonged period of lower oil prices that introduce new pressures on domestic economic – and potentially political – structures epitomizes, in many ways, the analysis in this book of the varied yet intertwined forces that have shaped, and will continue to shape, the UAE.

Notes

1 Donald Hawley, *The Trucial States* (London: George Allen & Unwin, 1970).
2 Abdullah Omran Taryam, *The Establishment of the United Arab Emirates, 1950–1985* (London: Croon Helm, 1987).
3 Mohammed Morsy Abdullah, *The United Arab Emirates: A Modern History* (London: Croon Helm, 1978).
4 Ali Mohammed Khalifa, *The United Arab Emirates: Unity in Fragmentation* (London: Croon Helm, 1979).
5 Rosemarie Said Zahlan, *The Origins of the United Arab Emirates: A Political and Social History of the Trucial States* (London: Macmillan, 1978).
6 Malcolm Peck, *The United Arab Emirates: A Venture in Unity* (Boulder, CO: Westview Press, 1986).
7 Ibrahim al Abed and Peter Hellyer (eds), *United Arab Emirates: A New Perspective* (London: Trident Press, 2001).
8 Frauke Heard-Bey, *From Trucial States to United Arab Emirates* (Dubai: Motivate Publishing, 2007).
9 Christopher Davidson, *The United Arab Emirates: A Study in Survival* (London: Lynne Rienner, 2006); *Dubai: The Vulnerability of Success* (London: Hurst & Co, 2008); *Abu Dhabi: Oil and Beyond* (London: Hurst & Co, 2009).
10 Jim Krane, Dubai: *The Story of the World's Fastest City* (New York: St Martin's Press, 2009).
11 Hassan Hamdan al-Alkim, *The Foreign Policy of the United Arab Emirates* (London: Saqi Books, 1989).
12 Khalid Almezaini, *The UAE and Foreign Policy: Foreign Aid, Identities and Interests* (Abingdon: Routledge, 2012).
13 Hendrik van der Meulen, "The Role of Tribal and Kinship Ties in the Politics of the United Arab Emirates," Ph.D. thesis presented to the *Fletcher School of Law and Diplomacy*, May 1997.
14 Andrea Rugh, *The Political Culture of Leadership in the United Arab Emirates* (New York: Palgrave Macmillan, 2007).
15 Karen Young, *The Political Economy of Energy, Finance and Security in the United Arab Emirates: Between the Majlis and the Market* (New York: Palgrave Macmillan, 2014).
16 Ahmed Kanna, *Dubai: the City as Corporation* (Minneapolis, MN: University of Minnesota Press, 2011).
17 Syed Ali, *Dubai: Gilded Cage* (New Haven, CT: Yale University Press, 2010).
18 Pardis Mahdavi, *Gridlock: Labor, Migration, and Human Trafficking in Dubai* (Stanford, CA: Stanford University Press, 2011).
19 Neha Vora, *Impossible Citizens: Dubai's Indian Diaspora* (Durham, NC: Duke University Press, 2013).
20 Michael Herb, *The Wages of Oil: Parliaments and Economic Development in Kuwait and the UAE* (Ithaca, NY: Cornell University Press, 2014).
21 Frauke Heard-Bey, "The United Arab Emirates: Statehood and Nation-Building in a Traditional Society," *Middle East Journal*, 59(3), 2005, p. 364.
22 Ibrahim al Abed, "The Historical Background and Constitutional Basis to the Federation," in Ibrahim al Abed and Peter Hellyer (eds), *United Arab Emirates: A New Perspective* (London: Trident Press, 2001), p. 133.
23 Neil Partrick, "Nationalism in the Gulf States," in David Held and Kristian Ulrichsen (eds), *The Transformation of the Gulf: Politics, Economics and the Global Order* (Abingdon: Routledge, 2012), p. 54.
24 Van der Meulen, *Tribal and Kinship Ties*, p. 7.
25 Tamsin Carlisle, "Abu Dhabi's Upstream Oil Sector Shifts Gears Subtly," *Platts*, December 2, 2014.
26 "United Arab Emirates: International Energy Data and Analysis," *US Energy Information Administration*, May 18, 2015.

27 Hawley, *Trucial States*, p. 222.
28 Gerald Butt, "Oil and Gas in the UAE," in Ibrahim al Abed and Peter Hellyer (eds), *United Arab Emirates: A New Perspective* (London: Trident Press, 2001), p. 237.
29 Christopher Davidson, "The Dubai Model: Diversification and Slowdown," in Mehran Kamrava (ed.), *The Political Economy of the Persian Gulf* (London: Hurst & Co, 2012), pp. 196–199.
30 "Habshan-Fujairah Pipeline Inaugurated Today," *Gulf News*, July 16, 2012.
31 Hawley, *Trucial States*, p. 222.
32 "'Abu Dhabi: Selected Economic Indicators' and 'Dubai: Selected Economic Indicators'," in *Gulf States Newsletter*, 39(984), January 8, 2015, p. 24.
33 J.E. Peterson, "The Future of Federalism in the United Arab Emirates," in H. Richard Sindelar III and J.E. Peterson (eds), *Crosscurrents in the Gulf: Arab Regional and Global Interests* (London: Routledge, 1988), p. 208.
34 Peck, *Venture in Unity*, p. 123.
35 Almezaini, *UAE and Foreign Policy*, p. 32.
36 *Text of the United Arab Emirates Constitution of 1971 with Amendments through 2004*, available at constituteproject.org (accessed July 15, 2015).
37 Ibid.
38 Mishaal al-Gergawi, "Emirates plus Etihad Equals Neo-Federal UAE," *Gulf News*, December 13, 2009.
39 Rugh, *Political Culture of Leadership*, pp. 220–221.
40 Ibid. p. 176.
41 Information compiled from family trees of the seven ruling families of the United Arab Emirates contained in Issue 1000 of *Gulf States News*, 39, September 17, 2015.
42 "MBR's Accession Injects a New Dynamic into Dubai/Abu Dhabi Ties," *Gulf States Newsletter*, 30(773), January 13, 2006, p. 6.
43 Jill Crystal, *Oil and Politics in the Gulf: Rulers and Merchants in Kuwait and Qatar* (Cambridge: Cambridge University Press, 1990), pp. 1–2.
44 J.E. Peterson, "Rulers, Merchants, and Shaykhs in Gulf Politics: The Function of Family Networks," in Alanoud Alsharekh (ed.), *The Gulf Family: Kinship Policies and Modernity* (London: Saqi Books, 2007), p. 30.
45 Giacomo Luciani, "From Private Sector to National Bourgeoisie: Saudi Arabian Business," in Paul Aarts and Gerd Nonneman (eds), *Saudi Arabia in the Balance: Political Economy, Society, Foreign Affairs* (London: Hurst & Co, 2005), p. 151.
46 Khalid Almezaini, "Private Sector Actors in the UAE and their Role in the Process of Economic and Political Reform," in Steffen Hertog, Giacomo Luciani, and Marc Valeri (eds), *Business Politics in the Middle East* (London: Hurst & Co, 2013), p. 58.
47 Almezaini, *Private Sector Actors*, p. 58.
48 Julian Walker, "Practical Problems of Boundary Delimitation in Arabia: the Case of the United Arab Emirates," in Richard Schofield (ed.), *Territorial Foundations of the Gulf States* (New York: St Martin's Press, 1994), p. 112.
49 Mohammed al-Fahim, *From Rags to Riches: a Story of Abu Dhabi* (London: London Center of Arab Studies, 1995), p. 55.
50 Ibid., p. 15.
51 Abdul Hafeez Yawar Khan Al Yousefi, "50 Years in Al Ain Oasis – Memoirs of Khabeer Khan," *Liwa: Journal of the National Centre for Documentation and Research*, 5(9), 2013, p. 57.
52 Ibid., p. 58.
53 Jayanti Maitra and Afra al-Hajji, *Qasr Al-Hosn: The History of the Rulers of Abu Dhabi, 1793–1966* (Abu Dhabi: Center for Documentation and Research, 2001), pp. 248–149.
54 Fred Lawson and Hasan al-Naboodah, "Heritage and Cultural Nationalism in the United Arab Emirates," in Alanoud Alsharekh and Robert Springborg (eds), *Popular Culture and Political Identity in the Arab Gulf States* (London: Saqi Books, 2008), p. 18.

55 Mehran Kamrava, "The Political Economy of Rentierism in the Persian Gulf," in Mehran Kamrava (ed.), *The Political Economy of the Persian Gulf* (London: Hurst & Co, 2012), p. 62.
56 Michael Herb, "A Nation of Bureaucrats: Political Participation and Economic Diversification in Kuwait and the United Arab Emirates," *International Journal of Middle East Studies*, 41(3), 2009, pp. 375–376.
57 Cf. Onn Winckler, "Labor and Liberalization: The Decline of the GCC Rentier System," in Joshua Teitelbaum (ed.), *Political Liberalization in the Persian Gulf* (London: Hurst & Co, 2009), pp. 59–85.
58 Jeanne Hey, *Small States in World Politics: Explaining Foreign Policy Behavior* (Boulder, CO: Lynne Rienner, 2003), p. 5.

2

STATE FORMATION

In the harsh conditions of the pre-oil political economy on the Arabian Peninsula, a relationship of mutual dependence grew up around the provision of stable and secure market conditions from which both ruling and merchant families derived material benefit. This produced a set of political and social arrangements that emphasized the principles of consultative rule and the linkage of governing "stakeholders" through social institutions such as marriage and the *majlis* (council). Ruling families needed to coexist alongside prominent families and merchants, and not infrequently relied on them for economic and financial assistance.[1] The exercise of political authority during this period was, in the words of James Onley and Sulayman Khalaf, "characterized by frailty, vulnerability, and precariousness." Further, the scarcities of the pre-oil economy sharpened competition between the tribes and their rulers for control over local resources such as pearling, shipping, and trading activities. However, they also imposed limitations on the leading families' legitimacy to rule as the option of tribal withdrawal was available as a last resort, as happened in 1833 when a section of the Bani Yas relocated from Abu Dhabi to Dubai.[2]

Processes of state formation in the coastal emirates of the Arabian Peninsula reveal a dynamic interplay among competing tribal influences, land and maritime powers, and the projection of external interests. Similarly, the "transformation of tribes into a nation" in the twentieth century involved the harmonization and coordination of tribal interests and the creation of broader, national, concepts of legitimate political authority.[3] This combination of internal and external influence has been particularly pronounced in the UAE. The Qawasim (al-Qasimi) tribal confederation rose to regional prominence during the eighteenth century and projected their maritime power throughout the Gulf. At around the same time, the Bani Yas tribal confederation emerged as the primary land-based power in the oasis region of Liwa and during the nineteenth century extended and consolidated their control over Abu Dhabi and (through a sub-branch) Dubai.[4] This was part of a more general trend across the Arabian Peninsula during the nineteenth century as political power began to coalesce around control of maritime trade and pearl diving and the emerging coastal settlements gradually began to exert control over the tribes of the hinterland.[5]

Beginning in 1809 and continuing in 1819, British naval power subdued first the Qawasim stronghold of Ras al-Khaimah and established later, between 1820 and 1853, a patchwork of agreements with paramount local sheikhs that extended protected status to the coastal sheikhdoms of the Gulf and brought them into the sphere of Britain's "sub-imperial" system based in (British-ruled) India (until Indian independence in 1947 whereupon responsibility for the protected states in the Gulf was transferred from the Government of India in Delhi to the British Government and the Foreign Office in London). British recognition strengthened the standing of the coastal sheikhdoms and, as James Onley and Sulayman Khalaf have illustrated, "also helped to empower most of them to dominate the independent rulers and tribal leaders of the interior."[6] While British protection formalized and elevated the roles of the ruling families in each sheikhdom, the case of the UAE differed from other British-protected states in Bahrain, Kuwait, and Qatar as state-building required the alignment of seven different and, at various times, fiercely independent rulers.[7]

Historical Origins

Both the Arabian and Persian shores of the Gulf and its hinterland have been an inter-regional crossroads for centuries. Powerful processes of settlement and exchange tied the area into a cosmopolitan network of inter-regional trade and migration. Such social and commercial links extend back into antiquity and the pre-Islamic era. Archaeological discoveries of imported Persian ceramics and seals at many sites in modern-day Kuwait and Bahrain indicate the presence of thriving traffic between the two coasts of the Gulf as far back as the third millennium BCE. Such was the density of commercial connections and the fluidity of movement between the Arabian and Persian littorals that one anthropologist has asserted persuasively that the coastal communities had more in common with each other than with the inland towns and cities in Arabia and Persia such as Riyadh or Teheran.[8]

What is today the UAE has been the site of human settlement for about seven thousand years. Shards of pottery from Mesopotamia have been discovered at coastal archaeological sites in the UAE, as they have at similar coastal sites elsewhere on the Arabian Peninsula. These shards have been dated to the fifth millennium BCE and provide early evidence of contact with regional powers through trade, although comparatively little is known about the identity of the actual inhabitants of the southern Gulf, and the first discoveries predate by about two thousand years the oldest tombs excavated at Jebel Hafit (near Al Ain) and Jebel al-Emalah.[9] One of the oldest known settlements at Tell Abraq, nestled astride the modern-day emirates of Sharjah and Umm al-Quwain, became a node in regional trade routes with the ancient civilization at Dilmun (centered on present-day Bahrain) as well as with Mesopotamia itself. Other zones of early settlement were the fertile areas around the Hajar Mountain range and the al Ain oasis.[10]

Patterns of tribal migration into the southeastern flank of the Arabian Peninsula probably occurred in the pre-Islamic period around the third century AD. During this period, the coastal area of what is today the UAE was labelled "al-Bahrayn" by Arab geographers although it was also known as "al-Shamal" (the North) in Oman.[11] In the seventh century AD, Islam united the disparate tribal confederations scattered across the Arabian Peninsula and brought them under Arab Muslim rule.[12] By the eighth century AD, Julfar (in Ras al-Khaimah) had emerged as a significant port in the lower Gulf and an important transit node in the trade route to al Ain and for the export of pearls to Hormuz in Persia and as far afield as Bombay and Zanzibar.[13] Further significant inflows of migrants occurred some three hundred years later, in the eleventh century AD although the region of Greater Oman was subsequently the site of prolonged internal strife that lasted until 1624.[14]

In the eighteenth century, the Qawasim tribal confederation, branches of which today constitute the ruling Al Qasimi families of Ras al-Khaimah and Sharjah, developed into a regional maritime power with control of territory on both the Arabian and Persian coastlines of the Gulf. By the end of the eighteenth century, the Qawasim were the leading power in the southern Gulf and a tacit alliance with Wahhabi forces in the first Saudi state (1744–1818) amplified further their power and influence.[15] Following several previous attempts to secure a Persian foothold, in 1779 the Qawasim succeeded in assuming control of the coastal town of Lingah and installing as commander an Al Qasimi sheikh. The Qawasim maintained control of Lingah for nearly a century, until 1887, while their control of three islands in the Strait of Hormuz (Abu Musa and the Greater and Lesser Tunbs) outlasted the loss of Lingah and later became a source of considerable tension in Iranian–UAE relations after the Shah of Iran seized the islands from Ras al-Khaimah and Sharjah in November 1971.[16]

Their presence on both sides of the coastline of the Gulf and of its entrance into the Arabian Sea (and from there, the Indian Ocean) ensured the Qawasim became dominant figures in regional trade patterns. Indeed, a substantial proportion of Qawasim revenues came from tolls levied on all shipping that entered or exited the Gulf through the Strait of Hormuz.[17] Regional prominence also brought the Qawasim into conflict with other regional and international actors, particularly Oman and the British Empire but also as far northward in the Gulf as Kuwait.[18] This trajectory was at its most pronounced during the long rule of Sheikh Sultan bin Saqr Al Qasimi between 1803 and 1866. During the early years of Sheikh Sultan's rule, the Qawasim dominated the rugged coastline of the southern Gulf and challenged the maritime supremacy both of the Omanis and the British, as described in further detail below. However, the Qawasim also provided a strong buffer against the expansion of Wahhabi political and religious influence into what is today Oman and the UAE, their tacit alignment with Wahhabi forces notwithstanding.[19]

The Bani Yas tribal confederation, from whom the present ruling families of Abu Dhabi and Dubai are drawn, originated in the Najd region of central Arabia (modern Saudi Arabia) and established a power base in the Liwa oasis region (southwest of Abu Dhabi city) during the sixteenth century AD. The Bani Yas therefore are distinct from the ruling families of Bahrain, Kuwait, and Saudi Arabia, which trace their lineage to the ancient 'Anaza tribal confederation.[20] The villages dotted around the string of oases that arced about 100 kilometers from east to west subsequently became "the center for the economic and social life of the Bani Yas" and its multiple tribal sections and sub-sections.[21] During the course of the eighteenth century, power within the Bani Yas coalesced around a respected elder, Falah, and his son, Nahyan, who became the first of the Al Bu Falah sheikhs and the founder of the Al Nahyan line. A separate sub-section of the Bani Yas, the Al Bu Falasah, split from the Al Bu Falah in 1833, established themselves further north up the coastline at Dubai, where they constituted the ruling Al Maktoum line.[22]

In 1793, members of the Bani Yas migrated from the Liwa oasis region to the island of Abu Dhabi that lay just offshore the Arabian Peninsula coastline. Water had been discovered on the island, whose name means "Father of the Gazelle" thirty-two years previously, in 1761. Benefiting from a strategically defendable location from coastal attack and in proximity to rich pearling beds, the island became the seat of Al Nahyan rule and a watchtower was built on the mainland at Maqta.[23] During the nineteenth century, the watchtower was expanded into the Qasr al-Hosn compound and provided the Al Nahyan with "a symbol of power and a refuge in times of strife" (the fort today houses the National Center for Documentation and Research).[24]

Successive waves of additional migration occurred as the Bani Yas cemented their position and gained the support of two major local tribes, the Manasir (al-Mansuri) and the Dhawahir (al-Dhaheri). Further inland, the second major oasis region in modern-day UAE (in addition to Liwa) at Buraimi (al Ain), became the site of repeated struggles between the Bani Yas and Wahhabi forces operating from central Arabia until the Wahhabis were finally ejected in 1869.[25] With the Wahhabi threat to the Bani Yas having receded, Abu Dhabi embarked upon a period of political and economic consolidation under the leadership of Sheikh Zayed bin Khalifa Al Nahyan, known also as "Zayed the Great," who ruled from 1855 until 1909.[26]

Dubai was a small fishing village about 120 kilometers farther up the northern coastline that was probably first inhabited at some point during the eighteenth century. In 1822, a British naval surveyor visited Dubai and found a settlement of about 1,000 people living in thatched or mud huts clustered around a central fort and three watchtowers.[27] The village was a dependency of Abu Dhabi when, in 1833, between 800 and 1,000 members of the abovementioned Al Bu Falasah section of the Bani Yas seceded from Abu Dhabi following a disagreement with the Al Bu Falah section. The dispute revolved around the fallout from the death of the paramount and popular leader of the Al Bu Falah, Sheikh Tahnun bin Shakhbut Al Nahyan, at the hands of two of his half-brothers. Members of the

Al Bu Falasah section of the Bani Yas, led by Maktoum bin Buti and his uncle, 'Ubeid bin Said Al Falasi, left Abu Dhabi in opposition to the internecine fighting and settled in Dubai. Maktoum bin Buti shared power initially with 'Ubeid bin Said but after the latter died in 1836 he ruled alone until his own death in 1852, and established the eponymous dynastic line that continues to rule in Dubai today.[28]

In its early years as the seat of Al Maktoum power, Dubai was located precariously along a tribal front-line between the confederacies of the Bani Yas, from whom the Al Maktoum had effectively seceded, and the Qawasim in Sharjah, just opposite the creek from Dubai. On several occasions in the late 1830s, tensions between the Bani Yas and the Qawasim threatened to draw Dubai into a regional conflict. However, by 1845, the hitherto strained relations between Dubai and Abu Dhabi had improved significantly while the threat to Dubai from the Qawasim also receded.[29] The greater political and economic stability afforded Dubai the space to develop commercially and benefit from its advantageous location astride a wide creek and natural harbor. Already by the 1840s the Dubai *suq* (market) hosted more than forty shops and 100 traders as the town grew rapidly into a trading entrepôt for the southern Gulf.[30] Later in the nineteenth century and in the early years of the twentieth century, Dubai also profited greatly from an influx of Persian and Arab merchants from the port of Lingah on the Persian coastline of the Gulf following the imposition of high taxation and greater regulation from Teheran in the years after the Persians regained control of the city from the Qawasim. The newcomers brought with them their business and shipping networks and their links with trading associates in India who linked Gulf merchants to markets and clients worldwide. Emirati historian Fatma al-Sayegh has noted how this "drain of expertise from Lingah to Dubai was to be the foundation for the latter's strong commercial growth after 1903."[31]

Britain and the Politics of Protection

British interests in the Gulf were both commercial and strategic. These revolved around the need to secure the maritime approaches to India, the "jewel in the crown of the British Empire,"[32] as well as the need to quell what British officials regarded as acts of maritime piracy in Gulf waters. The political economy of India increasingly became linked to strategic developments in the Middle East that revolved around the evolution of an Anglo-Indian "sub-imperial system" over the coastal sheikhdoms in the Gulf. This developed over the course of a "century of commerce and diplomacy" that peaked in the nineteenth century although it had its roots in the formation of the East India Company in London in 1600. The East India Company rapidly established its first factories in the Gulf at Isfahan, Shiraz, and Jask in Persia between 1617 and 1618, and a commercial headquarters and political agency at Bandar Abbas, also in Persia, in 1622. Just over a century later, in 1723, the political agency was transferred from Bandar Abbas to Basra, in Mesopotamia, after a period of political upheaval and commercial decline in Persia.[33]

The attempted imposition in 1797 of tolls on British maritime vessels – which refused to acknowledge or pay them – ratcheted up the tension between the British and the Qawasim and led to a number of raids by the Qawasim on British ships. In response, British officials in the Government of India in Bombay provocatively described the tolling and raiding as "piracy" and vowed to take military action to quell them.[34] Nearly two centuries later, the Ruler of Sharjah, Sheikh Dr. Sultan bin Mohammed Al Qasimi challenged and dissected these accusations in his Ph.D. dissertation and subsequent book, *The Myth of Arab Piracy in the Gulf.*[35] This notwithstanding, British concerns increased still further in the early 1800s when Qawasim dhows began expanding their zone of activity by attacking vessels off the northwest coast of India. The first such attack is believed to have occurred in September or October 1805 while a fresh spate of incidents took place in late 1808 and early 1809 off Karachi and Cutch.[36]

Following the attacks on British Indian shipping, the East India Company urged the British Government in London to deploy units of the Royal Navy to the Gulf amid projections that the Qawasim fleet amounted to more than 800 dhows and up to 25,000 men.[37] A squadron of ten ships led by the frigates HMS Caroline and HMS Chiffone and accompanied by eight warships from the Bombay Marine and additional vessels provided by the Sultan of Muscat proceeded to besiege the Qawasim capital at Ras al-Khaimah in November 1809. Led by Commodore John Wainwright, the fleet mounted sudden raids on the Qawasim strongholds at Ras al-Khaimah, where they also stormed the Sheikh's palace, and Lingah and destroyed dozens of dhows and other ships before they returned to Bombay in January 1810.[38]

From the British perspective, the assaults on Ras al-Khaimah and Lingah and the partial destruction of the Qawasim fleet brought only temporary respite. By 1813, more incidents at sea were being reported in the Indian Ocean and within a couple of years their frequency – and proximity to the northwestern Indian shoreline – was once again at pre-1809 levels. The 1813 incident was notable for having taken place within the purportedly safe confines of Karachi's harbor while eleven vessels were raided within a two-week period in January 1817 alone.[39] As a result, a second naval expedition was assembled in Bombay, and in November 1819 a force consisting of three Royal Navy frigates, six warships, and troop transports carrying some 3,000 men set sail for the Gulf, reinforced again, as in 1809, by the Sultan of Muscat. On December 2, Major General Sir William Grant-Keir's force besieged Ras al-Khaimah for six days, razed the town and left 1,200 British and Indian soldiers behind to prevent its recapture by the Qawasim, and sank 184 ships in their assault on Ras al-Khaimah and other fortified harbors at Ajman and Umm al-Quwain.[40]

The events of 1809 and the decade that followed were to be pivotal to the later evolution of political and security policy in the Gulf for they placed Great Britain (and British India) at the heart of considerations of Gulf security and stability. This occurred through the formalization of two principles – external intervention in regional affairs and the politics of protection to local allies – that would play a defining role in structuring the relationship of the Trucial States and other Gulf sheikhdoms with British and, latterly, American partners throughout the nineteenth and twentieth centuries. At the same time as the 1809 naval bombardment of Ras al-Khaimah and Lingah, British officials also extended, for the first time, their protection to a local ruler – the Sultan of Muscat, with whom they had signed in 1798 a treaty of friendship.[41] Ten years later, the principle of external intervention was pronounced officially as the Governor of Bombay, Mountstuart Elphinstone, informed the Governor-General of India, the Marquess of Hastings of his intention to "station as large a marine force in the Gulf as we can spare" after the conclusion of the punitive strike on Ras al-Khaimah in 1819.[42]

Immediately after the conclusion of the December 1819 naval expedition to the Gulf, British officials imposed a General Treaty of Maritime Peace. The General Treaty was signed on January 8, 1820 by Grant-Keir on behalf of the East India Company and the local rulers of what became the Trucial States. Article 1 stipulated the "cessation of plunder and piracy by land and sea" while Articles 6 and 10 authorized the British to function as a maritime policeman to ensure compliance and settle any disputes arising in Gulf waters.[43] In 1821, the Government of Bombay established the Gulf Squadron consisting of between five and seven ships of the Bombay Marine (renamed the Indian Navy in 1830) and created the Gulf Residency system of Political Agents and Political Officers to enforce the General Treaty.[44] A British garrison was set up alongside the first Political Agency on the island of Qishm in the Strait of Hormuz. However, appalling rates of sickness forced the abandonment of the island just two years later, in 1822, whereupon the Lower Gulf Agency was renamed the Political Residency and moved to Bushehr, in Persia, where it remained until it was transferred in 1946 to Bahrain.[45]

Political and security relations between the Trucial rulers and the British deepened again in 1835 following a meeting between Sheikh Sultan bin Saqr Al Qasimi of Ras al-Khaimah, Sheikh Shakhbut Al Nahyan of Abu Dhabi, Sheikh Ubeid bin Said Al Maktoum of Dubai, and Sheikh Rashid bin Humaid Al Nuaimi of Ajman with the acting British Resident, Lieutenant Samuel Hennell. On May 21, 1835, the three rulers (with the fourth present, Sheikh Shakhbut of Abu Dhabi, being the sitting ruler's father and representative) signed a Maritime Truce that aimed to bring to an end the sporadic maritime skirmishes that the 1820 General Treaty had failed to completely eradicate. The Maritime Truce extended British protection to Abu Dhabi, Ajman, Dubai, Ras al-Khaimah and Sharjah as well as Qawasim-controlled Lingah. Although initially only six months in duration (to cover the pearling season), the truce was renewed and extended to cover Umm al-Quwain in 1836 (Fujairah did not secure British recognition as a Trucial State until 1952). In 1843, the truce was extended for ten years while in 1853 it was extended into perpetuity with the signing of the Perpetual Maritime Truce by the rulers of the Trucial States.[46]

Under the terms of the Maritime Truce, British policy was focused primarily on the maintenance of maritime security and the suppression of acts of "piracy" at sea and relative non-involvement in internal affairs in the protected sheikhdoms.

Onley has calculated that, between 1805 and 1861, the British Residency received 98 requests for protection from Trucial States' rulers (in addition to twenty-one requests from Bahrain, twelve from Oman, and one from Kuwait).[47] Such an agreement facilitated the consolidation of domestic power by the ruling sheikhs in each emirate as they extended their control over tribes and regions inland. This occurred particularly forcefully in Abu Dhabi during the long rule between 1855 and 1909 of Sheikh Zayed bin Khalifa Al Nahyan. During this period, Zayed presided over an extended spell of political stability, consolidated Al Nahyan control over the Buraimi oasis region in the face of Wahhabi contestation, and transformed Abu Dhabi into a regional power possessing the largest pearling fleet (of over 400 boats) in the Gulf.[48]

As British interests in the Gulf and the wider West Asian region came under pressure from international competition in the late nineteenth century, the strategic value to London of Britain's relationship with the Trucial States increased further. British anxieties about French and Russian (and, after 1900, German) designs on the Gulf triggered attempts to bring the coastal sheikhdoms even further into Britain's sphere of influence. Hence, in March 1892, Britain concluded an Exclusive Agreement with the rulers of the six Trucial States (Abu Dhabi, Ajman, Dubai, Sharjah, Ras al-Khaimah, and Umm al-Quwain.) The Exclusive Agreement granted Britain complete control over all forms of foreign affairs as the Trucial rulers pledged not to host residents of other governments or to "cede, sell, mortgage or otherwise give for occupation any part of [their] territory except to the British Government."[49] The move to exclude non-British economic interests required closer British scrutiny of internal affairs, and caused friction in the 1920s and 1930s over the issue of granting petroleum concessions as British officials impelled the Trucial rulers to not give any concession to companies not supported by the British Government.[50]

Writing in her 1978 social and political history of the Trucial States, Rosemarie Said Zahlan suggested that the 1892 Exclusive Agreement had a profound impact on subsequent political and economic development in the seven sheikhdoms:

> The binding clauses of the 1892 agreements meant that the shaykdoms lived in almost complete isolation. As time passed, they became more introverted and effectively more remote, having little interest in the outside world. The British authorities guarded the area with a jealous eye, and during the inter-war period no foreigner was granted a visa to visit the Coast … [51]

Set against this trajectory of conservativism, other analyses have called attention to what Mohammed Morsy Abdullah has labelled a "cultural awakening" that took place among the Trucial States in the 1920s. This occurred in Dubai and Sharjah, in particular, through integration into the wider trans-regional shipping and logistical services such as the Bombay shipping route (which called at Dubai after 1903) and the overland mail service to Syria, which launched in 1924.[52] These moves contributed to a flourishing network of books, newspapers, and literary magazines while the Arab community in Bombay owned a printing press that further supplied publications to readers across the Trucial States.[53] Sharjah led the way in intellectual advancement during the interwar years as local scholars created the first private (and later public) library in the Trucial States and launched newspapers in the late 1920s and early 1930s, such as *Sawt al-Asafeer*, that frequently adopted editorial positions critical of British policy. One local scholar, Ibrahim bin Muhammad al-Midfa, was especially influential, as he worked as an advisor to the Ruler of Sharjah (who himself kept a private library that evolved into Sharjah's first public library, and whose support of education, culture, and the arts has lived on among his successors as Ruler) and "wielded immense influence in Sharjah's educated circles, for whom he made available the *majlis* of his house as a place for reading and for literary and political discussion."[54]

The pinnacle of Britain's search for paramountcy in the Gulf came with two set-piece events in 1903. On May 5, the British Foreign Secretary, Lord Lansdowne, used a House of Lords debate on *Great Britain and the Persian Gulf* to make an official statement of Britain's policy in the region. Lansdowne was a former Viceroy of India (1888–1894) and his policy reflected the considerable commercial and strategic value that successive generations of imperial administrators attached to the Gulf. Lansdowne began by stating that "our policy should be directed in the first place to promote and protect British trade in those waters." He went on to add that the British Government "should regard the establishment of a naval base, or of a fortified port, in the Persian Gulf by any other Power as a very grave menace to British interests, and we should certainly resist it with all the means at our disposal."[55] This represented what one British historian has labelled "a sort of Monroe Doctrine for the Persian Gulf."[56]

Six months after Lansdowne's proclamation of British primacy in the Gulf, the then Viceroy of India, Lord Curzon, embarked on a grand tour of the region that Lansdowne labeled dismissively as "Curzon's prancings in the Persian puddle."[57] Curzon sailed in RIMS Hardinge and was accompanied by HMS Argonaut, a cruiser that was, at that point, the largest ship ever to enter the Gulf, together with a steamer, and six other naval vessels. His visit to the Gulf was intended as a powerful show of strength aimed both at local rulers and international (German and Russian) rivals. Curzon stopped at Muscat, Bahrain, and Kuwait, where his stately progress was interrupted only briefly by "a scene of wild confusion, with several thousand Arab escorts, many firing into the air," which pitched Arthur Hardinge, the British Minister to Persia "over his horse's head before the assembled tribesmen."[58] In a set-piece speech to local rulers, Curzon stated bombastically that "We are not going to throw away this century of costly and triumphant enterprise … The peace of these waters must still be maintained; your independence will continue to be upheld, and the British Government must remain supreme."[59]

Such zealous statements by senior British policymakers obscured the fact that, on the ground, the actual terms of the agreements between Britain and the Gulf sheikhdoms that structured the nature of the bilateral relationship for more than a century were vague and relatively undefined. In her analysis of the structural foundations of the British relationship with the Gulf sheikhdoms, German scholar Helene von Bismarck has argued persuasively that "[The] development of the legal connection between Britain and the Gulf States was deeply influenced by the flexibility and the pragmatism that characterized British imperial expansion in the eighteenth and nineteenth centuries."[60] Writing at the conclusion of his long and distinguished diplomatic career which included a stint as Political Agent in Dubai between 1964 and 1966, Glencairn Balfour Paul noted that "attempts by jurists to define the nature of a British Protected State have a somewhat ex post facto look" as "Britain may be said to have made up the rules of the game as she went along, with the result that no-one really knew what they were."[61] Balfour Paul acknowledged also the enduring strength of the legacy of memories of British actions during their long, if disjointed, period of paramountcy in the Trucial States when he recounted how, in the 1960s, the Ruler of Fujairah, Sheikh Mohammed bin Hamad Al Sharqi (whom Balfour Paul had nicknamed "Fudge") requested a 144-gun salute on a trip to the United Kingdom. When Balfour Paul asked why the ruler had picked that number, Sheikh Mohammed responded: "Because that was the number of shells fired by the Royal Navy at my father's fort in 1907. You can still see many of them in its walls."[62]

Pre-Oil Political Economy

In 1904, as part of a Government of India attempt to produce a standard reference work on the Gulf following the Viceroy of India's visit and proclamation of a British "Monroe Doctrine" in the region the previous year, John Gordon ("JG") Lorimer visited Sharjah and collected records that provide a snapshot of the Trucial States at the turn of the twentieth century. Lorimer's six-volume Gazetteer of the Persian Gulf, Oman, and Central Arabia comprised more than 5,000 pages and initially was published as a secret document by the Government of India between 1908 and 1915. In addition to describing how in Abu Dhabi he saw "no cultivation except a little of dates [and] no trade worthy of mention outside the town,"[63] Lorimer also compiled detailed population figures for each of the Trucial States. Dividing the inhabitants of the Trucial States into forty-four tribes (with additional sub-tribes and sub-sections), Lorimer calculated the population of the Trucial States as approximately 80,000.[64] By far the largest share of the overall population lay in Sharjah (for which Lorimer included Ras al-Khaimah and Fujairah) with 45,000 inhabitants, followed by Abu Dhabi (11,000), Dubai (10,000), Umm al-Quwain (5000), and Ajman (750), in addition to about 8,000 nomadic Bedouin who were not settled year-round in the Trucial States.[65]

Fishing and pearling dominated the harsh pre-oil economy and these primarily subsistence forms of economic activity provided the major source of income for most communities until at least the 1930s. Pearl diving, in particular, was highly segmented with slaves often diving for the pearls and the wealthy pearl merchants constituting a powerful landholding class of their own.[66] Revenue from the taxes imposed on the pearling fleets and the trade that passed through the customs houses constituted the bulk of the rulers' income and, as their collection was sub-contracted to local merchants, consequently "strengthened the influence of the merchants and gave them power within the ruling order."[67] Small-scale agriculture was concentrated around the Liwa and Buraimi oasis regions where farmers grew wheat in the winter and harvested their date-palm groves in the summer.[68] The date-palm groves were irrigated by an ancient and intricate system of gravity-fed irrigation channels known as *aflaj* (sing. *falaj*). In 2011, the extensive and well-preserved *aflaj* network received the highest global recognition with the inscription of Al Ain (the city on the UAE side of the Buraimi oasis) on the UNESCO World Heritage List.[69]

Within this tapestry, ruling families emerged in each of the sheikhdoms. Hendrik van der Meulen, a career United States Foreign Service Officer who wrote his doctoral thesis on the role of tribal and kinship ties in the UAE following a period of service in Abu Dhabi as First Secretary at the US Embassy between 1993 and 1996, observed that:

> The ruling families were those which had become the strongest and most prestigious in terms of martial skills and success in forging political marriage alliances, and by gaining control of economic resources with which they could support their followers ... The personal role of the ruler and the members of the ruling families was and remains paramount in the UAE. Rulers were chosen by the ruling families, in consultation with notables from leading tribes, based on their qualities of intelligence, martial skills, political acumen, piety, good character, and generosity.[70]

The importance of leadership in the ruler was paramount and meant that succession most often was determined by informal (and, on occasion, formal) consensus among senior ruling family members rather than through primogeniture. In their study of sheikhly authority in the pre-oil Gulf, Sulayman Khalaf and James Onley observe that the exercise of power was "frail, vulnerable, and precarious" as:

> The ruling family, for instance, was both the source of the ruler's hereditary legitimacy and strength, and a constant constraint on his rulership; it supported him against the merchants and tribes, but it produced his strongest rivals ... To maintain their rulerships and the wellbeing of their shaikhdoms, the rulers had to engage in a never-ending juggling act ... constantly observing, assessing, balancing and rebalancing situations; forever negotiating and renegotiating the various options available to them at any one moment ... [71]

Similarly, in her seminal work, *The Making of the Modern Gulf States*, Rosemarie Said Zahlan noted that, while in principle the individual rulers held absolute power:

> they generally consulted a small, informal council (*majlis*) according to the Islamic principle of *shura* (consultation). The concept of shura was essential to

the administration of authority ... The administrative infrastructure was very limited, and the functions of government varied from place to place. But the rulers remained accessible to their people: they gave daily audiences of several hours; they heard petitions and acted on them; they also gave judgements on personal and commercial disputes.[72]

In Said Zahlan's political and social history of the Trucial States, she added that in the early twentieth century, the sheikhdoms':

> ... administrative infrastructure was so rudimentary as to be almost non-existent. The ruler had no civil service; no judges or law courts ... no army, apart from his personal guards; and no police force. He could rarely, if ever, delegate authority to an appointed person or group of persons without risking his position.[73]

A *majlis* was created in Dubai in the early 1900s to provide the ruler "advice and political assistance." It consisted of between fifteen and forty members both from the merchant class and from tribal elites in the emirate. In her analysis of the historical emergence of Dubai, al-Sayegh has documented how the merchants were "the spokesmen for popular grievances and demands" and, through their direct access to the Ruler, "wielded a great deal of influence over the economic and political decision-making process." Furthermore, the merchants occupied pre-eminent roles in public and political life in the absence of formal institutional structures in Dubai and the other Trucial States:

> the merchants, by exercising control through the Majlis, became the de facto government led by the ruler. It was they who financed internal wars between emirates, and forced the ruler to make alliances with inland tribes and neighboring sheikhdoms.[74]

Furthermore, a pearl merchant, Muhammad Ahmad bin Dalmuk, founded the first modern school in Dubai in 1903 while three other schools also were funded by the merchant elite during the early twentieth century.[75] Meanwhile, Giacomo Luciani has examined in greater detail the concept of *shura*. Writing for the (then) Dubai-based Gulf Research Centre, Luciani observed that:

> The practice of the monarchies and emirates in the Gulf is very much consensual. Very few decisions are made without extensive consultation. It is also very much inclined to forgiving and reintegrating dissenters. Opponents are frequently pardoned and offered positions in the government, even if they do not always publicly repent and ask for forgiveness ... If the required degree of consensus is not present, matters are left pending, so that the issue can ripen. This normally happens either because key people become convinced and change their minds, or, more frequently, because tradeoffs are arranged and

compromises shaped … The essential task of the ruler is to set up the system of consultation, i.e. define the circle of people whose opinion matters.[76]

To this day, the Ruler of Fujairah continues to hold an open *majlis* once a week during which any member of the community may attend and present his or her issue or case before the ruler in person. The importance of trade, pearling, customs duties, and taxes, often on maritime vessels, was essential to the maintenance of this pre-oil political economy as "the extent of a ruler's income was directly related to his power and standing in the community; this affected the rhythm of economic activity and determined whether taxes could be imposed and collected."[77]

Dubai also positioned itself, at this early stage, as a hub for transit trade between the Middle East and India, which lay five days' sail away. The final decades of the nineteenth century and opening decade of the twentieth century saw an exponential increase in demand for shipping services in the Gulf. The Ruler of Dubai, Sheikh Maktoum bin Hushur Al Maktoum, persuaded the British India Steam Navigation Company to shift its port of call in the Lower Gulf from Lingah to Dubai in 1904. This decision ensured that Dubai became the regional hub for the re-export of goods to and from India, Persia, and the interior of the Arabian Peninsula itself.[78] In 1905, thirty-four steamers with a total tonnage of 70,000 tons, many belonging also to the Bombay and Persian Steam Navigation Company, called at Dubai, a sizeable increase over the twenty-one steamers the year before.[79] Together with the aforementioned influx of Persian and Arab merchants fleeing higher taxes and greater regulation in Lingah, by 1905 Dubai emerged as the most important – and cosmopolitan – port in the Trucial States. In addition to turning Dubai into a free port, the ruler, Sheikh Maktoum, abolished or otherwise reduced import and export taxes and placed leading merchants in senior government positions as part of measures to attract further trade and boost local business.[80]

Three decades later, an additional source of income in both Dubai and neighboring Sharjah came from their hosting of new air bases and refueling stops on the imperial air route from Britain to Australasia. British officials acting on behalf of the newly created Royal Air Force (RAF) initially approached the Ruler of Ras al-Khaimah but their request to construct an airfield for civil (as well as military) aviation was turned down, and an agreement subsequently was reached with the Ruler of Sharjah instead. Imperial Airways paid the ruler of Sharjah, Sheikh Sultan bin Saqr Al Qasimi, a monthly fee of 800 rupees for landing rights and fees at the new airfield as well as a monthly subsidy of 500 rupees. For his part, the ruler constructed a rest house at the Al Mahatta Fort, which became one of the first "modern" hotels in the Gulf and the first Handley-Page biplane landed at the Sharjah airfield, en route to India with four passengers, on October 5, 1932.[81] However, the arrival of foreign visitors at Sharjah quickly created sensitivities that foreshadowed the later disquiet at the behavior of Western tourists in Dubai in the 2000s, and led the British Political Resident in the Gulf, Trenchard Fowle, to write to Imperial Airways in March 1933 to warn the company that

Passengers at Sharjah have begun going into the town, one lady passenger doing so clad in beach pyjamas ... However suitable the latter garb may be in its right place, that place is obviously not Sharjah. It must be remembered that the people of Sharjah have not up to now been accustomed to having strangers, especially ladies, wandering about their bazaars.[82]

The greater political stability and economic prosperity in Dubai was not replicated across the Trucial States as other ruling families experienced periods of factional contestation of power. This was especially apparent in Abu Dhabi in the turbulent two decades that separated the death of Zayed the Great in 1909 with the advent of Sheikh Shakhbut bin Sultan Al Nahyan in 1928. In relatively quick succession, four of Sheikh Zayed's sons became Ruler of Abu Dhabi – Sheikh Tahnoun (1909–1912), Sheikh Hamdan (1912–1922), Sheikh Sultan (1922–1926), and Sheikh Saqr (1926–1928). Of these four rulers, Sheikh Tahnoun was in poor health and died little more than three years in power, while the three subsequent rulers all died violent deaths in a period of prolonged internecine strife among the Al Nahyan. It took the third defenestration in less than six years for the family to reach agreement that the succession should pass to Sheikh Sultan's son, Sheikh Shakhbut bin Sultan Al Nahyan. Sheikh Shakhbut would go on to rule Abu Dhabi until 1966 when he was deposed (bloodlessly) in 1966 by his highly capable younger brother, Sheikh Zayed bin Sultan, who himself ruled until 2004, ushering in a period of belated political calm after such a turbulent start to the twentieth century.[83]

Instability in Abu Dhabi spilled over into regional politics as disaffected members of the ruling family made individual alliances with other tribes and, in some instances, sought protection from the governor of al-Hasa in present-day Saudi Arabia, Abdullah bin Jiluwi. A cousin once removed of the founder of Saudi Arabia, Abdul-Aziz Al Saud ("Ibn Saud"), bin Jiluwi dispatched agents to collect *zakat* (religious tax) from the tribal elements that sought his protection, "thereby establishing a basis for territorial claims at Abu Dhabi's expense."[84] This caused periodic tension to flare up around Buraimi that caused considerable friction in the 1950s when King Abdul-Aziz Al Saud sent Saudi forces in an attempt to occupy the oasis region in 1952 and was settled only in 1974. Sharjah and Ras al-Khaimah also experienced bouts of internal turbulence during the early twentieth century in stark contrast to the three Trucial States of Dubai, Ajman, and Umm al-Quwain, which all benefited from long periods of stable rule. Dubai benefited from the rule of Sheikh Saeed bin Maktoum Al Maktoum (1912–1958) and his son, Sheikh Rashid bin Saeed Al Maktoum (1958–1990) while in Ajman and Umm al-Quwain, the young rulers who came to power in 1928 and 1929 both ruled until 1981.[85]

The comparative prosperity of Dubai facilitated the emergence of a powerful merchant class that became interwoven into the sheikhdom's subsequent political and economic development. This was a process replicated across the Trucial States although the levels of economic opportunity in other sheikhdoms were far lower than in Dubai. Prior to the discovery of oil in the Trucial States, many of the merchant families were nearly as influential as the ruling families themselves due to their economic weight and their dominance of the pearl industry, which was the most important economic activity until the onset of the Great Depression and the collapse of the market for Gulf pearls in the 1930s. Major merchant families active in Dubai's pre-oil economy included the al-Futtaim, the al-Ghurair, and the al-Habtoor, all of whom retained their economic (and, to a lesser degree, political) influence into the oil and post-oil era. In Abu Dhabi, merchants from families such as the al-Fahim, al-Tayer, the al-Qubaysi, the al-'Otaiba, and the al-Suwaidi figured powerfully in the pearl industry and trade networks that dominated the emirate prior to the discovery and export of oil in the 1950s and 1960s. During this period of relative economic hardship in Abu Dhabi, the merchants not only provided the ruler and his family with loans when they needed them but also contributed the largest share of sheikhdoms' revenues through the payment of taxes and customs duties. Consequently, the economic power that the merchant elites came to wield in Abu Dhabi was comparable to Dubai even if the absolute level of economic opportunity was lower (for ruler and for merchant alike).[86]

Emirati political scientist Khalid Almezaini has noted how a select number of the most prominent families were able to "link their wide-ranging economic, political, and social interests with those of members of the ruling families, as well as with general government interests."[87] Intermarriage between members of the ruling and merchant families strengthened further the network of social relations between the two groups. Saif al-Ghurair, the founding patriarch of the Al-Ghurair conglomerate and scion of probably the most illustrious merchant family in Dubai illustrates both the continuity in pre- and post-oil social relations as he wore dark glasses at all times for decades as a result of an injury suffered while pearl diving as a young man as well as the value of proximity to the ruler, as he became a close advisor to Sheikh Zayed in the 1970s and 1980s and lifetime president of the Dubai Chamber of Commerce and Industry.[88] Another major figure in Dubai's boom years in the 2000s, Sultan bin Sulayem (the Chairman of Dubai World from 2006 until 2010) was a childhood friend of the Ruler of Dubai, Sheikh Mohammed bin Rashid Al Maktoum while bin Sulayem's father, Ahmed, had been the leading adviser to Sheikh Mohammed's father, Sheikh Rashid, who ruled Dubai between 1958 and 1990.[89]

Implicit in this "ruling bargain" between rulers and merchants (across the Gulf and not just in Dubai) was a tradeoff whereby the merchants pursued economic opportunities in return for steering clear of overtly political involvement. This quid pro quo came under great strain during the turbulent period between the collapse in the international demand for pearls from the Gulf in the 1930s and the first influx of oil revenues in the 1960s. The pearling economy was devastated by the onset of the Great Depression in 1929, which reduced the demand for luxury goods in Europe and North America, and the invention of the Japanese cultured pearl, against which natural pearls from the Gulf were no longer competitive. The damage done to local seafaring economies across the Gulf sheikhdoms was immediate and lasting, with one chronicler describing the period as "a disaster which almost overnight removed the one export on which the people of the Gulf could rely to bring in foreign earnings."[90]

Hardest hit of all the Gulf sheikhdoms was Qatar, which experienced such economic hardship in the 1930s that more than one-third of the population emigrated over the decade.[91] Qatar's economic dislocation was magnified by the relative absence of other forms of economic activity, but even more diversified entrepot economies such as Kuwait and Dubai also were heavily impacted.[92] Already by July 1929, Heard-Bey recounts how "about 60 diving ships of Dubai failed to put to sea owing to financial difficulties," while in Sharjah, conditions were exacerbated by an ongoing struggle for power between a deposed Ruler, Sheikh Khalid bin Ahmad Al Qasimi, and his young successor, Sheikh Sultan bin Saqr Al Qasimi.[93] Nor was there any respite during the 1930s as the price for pearls continued to fall while the global economic upheaval caused by World War II meant that, by 1943, pearls fetched barely 10 percent of their pre-crash 1928 price. All strata of society in the Trucial States were affected, from pearl merchants at the apex, who suffered immediate and severe financial difficulties, to the divers and other "retainers, servants, and people in lowly jobs" who experienced a sudden loss of employment and livelihood.[94]

The 1938 Reform Movement in Dubai and the Gulf

With the breakdown in the "contract" between rulers and merchants in the 1930s, it is unsurprising that incipient demands for reform were loudest in the three sheikhdoms of Kuwait, Bahrain, and Dubai, which had the strongest and most powerful merchant class, although the dynamics of each movement differed in subtle yet important ways. Kuwait was the first to experience the stirrings of what became known as the "1938 reform movement." Local dissatisfaction with the Ruler, Sheikh Ahmad al-Jabir Al Sabah was fanned, in part, by the overspill of Arab nationalist currents from neighboring Iraq that attracted the sympathy of many members of Kuwait's merchant elite who sympathized with its progressive political ideology. After a group of merchants published a political manifesto in an Iraqi newspaper, the crown prince himself, Abdullah al-Salim Al Sabah (who as Ruler between 1950 and 1965 oversaw Kuwait's independence and the formation of the National Assembly) joined the calls for reform.[95]

The intersection of merchant demands with those of senior members of the Al Sabah prompted the Ruler of Kuwait to permit an election for a Legislative Council. This took place on June 29, 1938 as the heads of 150 leading Kuwaiti families elected fourteen representatives to the council; one week later the councilors selected Sheikh Abdullah al-Salim Al Sabah as their Chairman. The new body immediately involved itself in the administrative and financial governance of Kuwait and demanded unprecedented limitations on the ruler's power. Most notably, they forced the Ruler to consent to Article 1 of the law that established the council, which stipulated that the people were the source of power as represented by elected members of the Legislative Council. Article 5 further stated that the head of the Council would exercise executive authority in Kuwait.[96]

Calls for reform spread rapidly from Kuwait to Bahrain and Dubai. In Bahrain, the first sheikhdom in the Gulf to discover oil (in 1932), demands included the greater involvement of Bahraini nationals in the emerging oil sector alongside criticism of the omnipotent role of Sir Charles Belgrave, the Ruler's British "advisor," and the establishment of a number of opposition societies.[97] However, unlike its counterparts in Kuwait and in Dubai (see below), the Bahraini reform movement did not lead to the formation of a council in 1938. Although the movement enjoyed, for a time, some degree of support from the Crown Prince of Bahrain, it ran into the implacable opposition of British officials, who were far more closely involved in the conduct of internal affairs than they were in Kuwait. A series of strikes and demonstrations by oil company workers and student leaders prompted British officials to suppress the reform movement in November 1938.[98]

The Dubai reform movement that also emerged in 1938 differed in several significant ways from its counterparts in Kuwait and Bahrain. In particular, as Herb has noted, the distinction between the merchant class and the ruling family was blurred and many of the merchants actually belonged to the broader Al bu Falasah section of the ruling Bani Yas tribe that had settled in Dubai in the 1830s.[99] Much of the merchant dissatisfaction focused on attempts by the Ruler of Dubai (under strong British pressure) to limit slavery and the firearms trade while the collapse in their economic influence upset the delicate equilibrium with the ruling family, which benefited also from an influx of revenue from the first oil concessions and airfield agreements signed in the 1930s. Faced with the decline in returns from trade and pearls, many of the "dissident" merchants "turned to the only means which seemed available to them: the arms trade, smuggling of provisions and gold, and the slave trade," and thus were directly impacted by British pressure on the ruler. In October 1938, merchant pressure on the Ruler led to the creation of a fifteen-member council selected by the notables of Dubai.[100]

Like its Kuwaiti counterpart, which immediately passed a law that established the Legislative Council as the source of power and executive authority in Kuwait, the Dubai council (*majlis*) made a significant yet ultimately short-lived and unsuccessful attempt to share in the exercise of power and redistribution of wealth. The council assumed control over state income and even, for a brief period of time, over the ruler's income from the oil concession as well.[101] Furthermore, the council attempted a series of political and economic reforms that all "served the needs of the merchant community," including expansion of the Dubai harbor, regulation of the customs service, and the channeling of the oil concession and airfield income to the state treasury.[102] These were significant powers to give away, and the contagious overspill of the reform movement from Kuwait to Bahrain and Dubai alarmed British officials as much as it did local rulers. The British Political Resident in the Gulf stated that the Kuwaiti law promulgated by the Legislative Council "reads somewhat like the declaration of the French Assembly in 1791,"[103] and attributed the council in Dubai to a "democratic wave" that was more disturbing than "one sheikh taking over from another."[104]

Like its Kuwaiti counterpart, the Dubai council proved short-lived and was suppressed by the ruler through force. In Dubai, this occurred on March 29, 1939 when the Ruler, Sheikh Said bin Maktoum Al Maktoum, "had the entire *Majlis* dissolved by ordering a contingent of Bedouin who were in town for his son's wedding to attack and disperse the members."[105] The decision to move against the council came after the *majlis* sought to impose further financial restrictions on the Ruler's purse and allow him only 10,000 rupees per month for personal expenses.[106] Two decades later, many of the same merchants, led by members of the two most powerful (non-ruling) families in Dubai, the Al Ghurair and the Al Futtaim, were again the "backbone" of the Dubai National Front, an oppositional group heavily influenced by Arab nationalism which called for a reduction of British influence and the redistribution of political power from the ruler toward the merchants.[107]

Just as in 1938, the growth of Arab nationalism in Dubai in the 1950s was part of a broader phenomenon that encompassed similar developments in Kuwait and Bahrain as the contagious overspill of ideological fervor mixed with a backlash against British policy in the Middle East. Arab nationalists both in Kuwait and in Bahrain intensified their calls for political reform and their criticism of "the privileged position of the British and the foreign oil companies."[108] In Bahrain, Bahraini academic Omar AlShehabi notes that "the early 1950s witnessed the largest public mass movement in Bahrain's modern history" as the growing Arab nationalist sentiment was buttressed by "the rise of a strong national press and the formation of the first cultural and sports centers in the Gulf Arab States."[109]

The same ingredients featured prominently in Dubai and Sharjah and illustrated the greater level of politicization in these more developed sheikhdoms (together with Kuwait and Bahrain) vis-à-vis the more isolated and inward-looking polities in Abu Dhabi, Qatar, and Oman during the same period. Iraqi teachers at the Al-Falah School in Dubai began to spread Arab nationalist sentiments in the early 1950s and, as noted in eyewitness accounts cited by Christopher Davidson, encouraged their pupils to "parade through the narrow streets of the town, carrying flags and chanting Arab nationalist slogans, applauded by their parents and citizens."[110] Moreover, a series of incidents targeted British interests in Dubai, Sharjah, and Ras al-Khaimah, particularly in the turbulent aftermath of the Suez Crisis of November 1956. Demonstrations against British policy in the Suez Crisis took place in Dubai, Sharjah, and Ras al-Khaimah while a group of students in Sharjah attempted to set fire to the British airbase in the emirate, and school sports days in Dubai and Sharjah became the setting for "nationalist occasions" as "enthusiastic speeches were made and Arab slogans on the themes of liberation and union were chanted by the students and the crowds."[111] Later, in the 1960s, British officials also expressed great unease at a decision by Sheikh Saqr bin Mohammed of Ras al-Khaimah to levy a 1 percent charge on the salaries of public officials and a 2 percent charge on all property and land deals that would go toward a fund in support of the Palestinian Al-Fatah organization.[112]

Oil and Borders

Whereas the first discoveries of oil in the Arabian Gulf took place in Bahrain (1932), Saudi Arabia and Kuwait (1938), and Qatar (1939), the first oil was

TABLE 2.1 Oil Concessions in the Trucial States

Year	Trucial State
1936	Dubai
1937	Sharjah
1939	Abu Dhabi
1945	Ras al-Khaimah
1949	Umm al-Quwain
1951	Ajman
1952	Fujairah

Source: Frauke Heard-Bey, *From Trucial States to United Arab Emirates*, pp. 296–297.

discovered in commercial quantities in Abu Dhabi in 1958 and, after several false starts, in Dubai in 1966. Geologists from the Anglo-Persian Oil Company (the forerunner of British Petroleum, today BP) first visited the Trucial States in the 1920s, while additional geological surveys took place in the mid-1930s, "with the oil company teams accompanied around the desert by a young man who later played a crucial role in the country's development," the future ruler of Abu Dhabi and founding President of the UAE, Sheikh Zayed bin Sultan Al Nahyan[113] The first oil concessions were concluded with the Ruler of Dubai in 1936 and the Ruler of Sharjah in 1937, while on January 11, 1939, Sheikh Shakhbut of Abu Dhabi signed a seventy-five-year concession for all onshore rights in Abu Dhabi to the Petroleum Development Company (Trucial Coast), a subsidiary of the Iraq Petroleum Company, a joint venture of British, American, French, and Dutch companies that included Royal Dutch Shell, the Anglo-Persian Oil Company, and the forerunners of Exxon, Mobil, and Total.[114] The offshore oil concession for Abu Dhabi was acquired initially in 1953 by the D'Arcy Oil Company and subsequently was transferred in 1955 to Abu Dhabi Marine Areas (ADMA) – itself a joint venture of British Petroleum/BP and the Compagnie Francaise des Petrole/Total.[115]

In her seminal history of the Trucial States, UAE-based historian Frauke Heard-Bey has described the political implications that the signing of the oil concessions in the 1930s and 1940s had on intra-emirate boundaries and relations, which until this point were largely undefined:

> The vagueness of political sovereignty and territorial identification suited all sides [prior to the 1930s] … The conclusion of concessionary agreements put a sudden end to this state of affairs. Now it became necessary to define precisely the boundaries of a concession area and therefore the limits of a Ruler's authority … [116]

Boundary disputes did indeed erupt between the Rulers of Abu Dhabi and Dubai which escalated into a conflict in 1945 that lasted until 1948 and was fought primarily by groups of Bedouin. While the low-level war threatened to spiral out of control into full-scale tribal retaliation in 1948 when fifty-two members of the al-Manasir tribe were killed in the Liwa region of Abu Dhabi, their deaths ultimately provided the catalyst for a peace agreement that was finalized the following year.[117]

British officials proceeded with alacrity to define both the internal boundaries of the Trucial States and their external borders with Saudi Arabia and Oman. While the inter-emirate borders necessitated the resolution of competing claims of tribal authority and allegiance, the external boundary was made more urgent by the fact that American officials working for Aramco were drawing up their own set of documents, particularly around the Buraimi area claimed by Abu Dhabi, Oman, and, more contentiously, by Saudi Arabia. The absence of any written records meant that British officials representing the Ruler of Abu Dhabi and the Sultan of Oman had to gather evidence from local tribal sheikhs to support their territorial claims against the counterclaims compiled by George Rentz, the head of the Arabian Research Division at Aramco.[118] A young British political officer, Julian Walker, spent three winters between 1953 and 1959 "touring and mapping" the internal and external boundaries of the Trucial States while Walker's nominal "boss," Christopher Pirie-Gordon, attempted in 1955 "to work on the easiest frontier, that between Ras al-Khaimah and Umm al-Quwain, about which there was said to be no dispute":

> accompanied by the Arab advisor to the Agency, he met the two rulers, each in their separate transport and accompanied by their Bedouin retainers, at a point on the coast between their two capitals. The Ras al-Khaimah representatives asserted that the frontier started further to the west. But the Umm al-Quwain team appeared more authoritative and led the cavalcade to a prominent sand dune a little further east then started southwards. Christopher followed them in his Land Rover, bouncing from one indistinguishable sand dune to the next, followed by the Ras al-Khaimah contingent which gave every indication of being in unknown territory but who complained plaintively that they were plunging deep into the Ras al-Khaimah heartlands ... The frontier over which there had been apparently no dispute had been revealed as a bone of contention by no means easy to settle.[119]

Remarkably, Walker remained engaged in settling inter-emirate boundaries (or "squiggly tribal frontiers" as he called them[120]) for forty years until 1996 when he assisted – a full quarter-century after the formation of the UAE – in finalizing the boundary between Fujairah and Ras al-Khaimah. Writing about these experiences for the UAE National Center for Documentation and Research during his retirement in 2012, Walker recalled:

> I took local guides to map the coastal frontier points ... I purloined the largest paper available on the Coast from the Oil Company accountant, took names

from any knowledgeable local tribesmen that I met, and with the help of a compass, my Land Rover milometer, and the back of my fountain pen, plotted them on the paper. I also gathered what documentation I could from the local Rulers and Sheikhs.[121]

An article in the Abu Dhabi-based English language newspaper, *The National*, in January 2012 drew attention to "the disjointed and discontiguous patchwork of different emirates that makes maps of the Hajar Mountains section of the UAE resemble a poorly stitched quilt":

> Madha, a settlement of approximately 2000 people, sits in a 75-hectare land-locked island of Oman surrounded on all sides by the emirates of Sharjah, Fujairah, and Ras al-Khaimah. But inside the Madha settlement is yet another tiny settlement, the village of Nahwa. Its 40 or so houses are entirely enclosed by Omani territory and form part of the emirate of Sharjah.[122]

The National added that Nahwa constituted "one of only a small number of examples in the world of what is known as a counter-enclave," namely "a patch of one nation contained wholly in the territory of another country that in turn is surrounded on all sides by the territory of the first nation."[123]

Several years after the creation of the UAE in 1971, tensions between the young federation and Oman briefly flared up in the form of a boundary dispute with the emirate of Ras al-Khaimah that erupted suddenly in October 1977. The incident concerned an apparent claim by Sultan Qaboos bin Said of Oman on a ten mile strip of coastline belonging to Ras al-Khaimah where oil had recently been discovered and a refinery complex was planned. The Omani claim also came at a highly sensitive time for the UAE as it was made on the day that the UAE's Minister of State for Foreign Affairs, Saif Ghobash, was assassinated at Abu Dhabi airport (see Chapter Three). Sheikh Zayed and the Ruler of Ras al-Khaimah appealed to Saudi Arabia and Kuwait to mediate and three Emirati delegations travelled to Oman in April 1978. Meanwhile, a brief armed confrontation was reported to have ended in farce as "a large number of Omanis in the UDF [the Union Defense Force set up by the UAE] refused to fight Oman's forces," before Oman finally retracted its claim in April 1979.[124]

A fractious and persistent boundary conflict with Saudi Arabia sharpened further the need to formally delineate the external boundaries of the Trucial States in general and Abu Dhabi in particular. The dispute started after Aramco geologists began exploring for oil in the southeastern portion of the *Rub' al-Khali* (Empty Quarter) and started encroaching on land claimed by Abu Dhabi and Oman. In April 1949, Aramco officials set up a camp at Khawr al-Udayd in modern-day Qatar but at the time inhabited by a section of the Bani Yas tribe loyal to Sheikh Shakhbut bin Sultan Al Nahyan of Abu Dhabi. Later in the year, in October 1949, the Saudi government produced an expansive territorial claim that would have stripped Abu Dhabi of the Liwa Oasis and much of its interior.[125] Matters escalated further in August 1952 when Turki bin Abdullah al-Otaishan, a Saudi official based at Ras Tanura, established a camp at Hamasa, one of the three villages claimed by Oman in Buraimi (with the six other villages at Buraimi being claimed by Abu Dhabi). As the governor of Abu Dhabi's Eastern Region, Sheikh Zayed worked closely with British officials to counter and contain the threat posed by Saudi encroachment on Buraimi.[126]

Together with his brother, Sheikh Hazza bin Sultan Al Nahyan, Sheikh Zayed orchestrated Abu Dhabi's case at the Buraimi Arbitration Tribunal that met in Geneva in September 1955 to adjudicate on the competing claims to the oasis region. However, the British member of the tribunal, Sir Reader Bullard, resigned in protest at what he saw as improper practices on the part of the Saudi delegation, and the tribunal never reconvened.[127] On October 26, 1955, what had developed into the "Buraimi dispute" (and threatened briefly to become a thorn in relations between the United Kingdom and the United States) was resolved decisively when two detachments of the Trucial Oman Levies moved into Buraimi and evicted the Saudis. Although the incident passed off without violence, the Levy force was supported by two RAF long-range heavy bombers from Bomber Command as well as other British aircraft based ordinarily in Aden and Bahrain. In the event, one of the heavy bombers "flew low over the Saudis to encourage their surrender, the second carried out a reconnaissance of the western approaches in case of Saudi retaliation."[128]

The display of force at Buraimi illustrated the continuing dependence of the Trucial States, together with the other pre-independent sheikhdoms in Kuwait, Bahrain, and Qatar, on external (British) protection against the far larger regional powers of Iraq, Iran, and Saudi Arabia. Small local police units were established in Dubai and Abu Dhabi in 1956 and 1957 respectively but the main defense force remained the British-led Trucial Oman Scouts. This "security dilemma" foreshadowed the later reliance on the United States as the external security guarantor from the 1980s onward. For Abu Dhabi and, after 1971, the UAE, the discovery and extraction of significant reserves of oil heightened the external threat even as the revenues from oil exports facilitated and deepened the consolidation of domestic power and control.

ADMA located the first (offshore) oil in Abu Dhabi at Umm Shaif in 1958, the same year that Petroleum Development (Trucial States) discovered the first onshore Bab oilfield. A production and processing terminal center and oil processing terminal were constructed on nearby Das Island and oil exports commenced in 1962. Also in 1962, the original onshore concession-holder, Petroleum Development (Trucial States) changed its name to the Abu Dhabi Petroleum Company (ADPC), and large new onshore deposits were discovered at Bu Hasa. Oil exports began slowly but then increased rapidly from 14,200 barrels per day (bpd) in 1962 to 186,800 in 1964 while reserves were boosted further by ADMA's discovery of the large offshore Zakum field in 1965. The Zakum Development Company (ZADCO) was established to manage the Upper Zakum portion of the field, with a minority 12 percent stake granted to the Japan Oil Development Company

(JODCO).[129] Japanese oil companies also were instrumental in the formation of the third concession-holder in Abu Dhabi, the Abu Dhabi Oil Company (ADOC), in 1968, with the Nippon Mining Company and the Daikyo Oil Company joining the Maruzen Oil Company in the joint venture. ADOC was awarded a forty-five-year offshore concession in areas relinquished by ADMA and struck oil in 1969 on the island of Mubarraz.[130]

Drilling in Dubai commenced in 1952 but oil in commercial quantities was not discovered until the early 1960s, with the "breakthrough finding" occurring in the offshore Fateh field in 1966. Exports from Fateh began in 1969 and the Continental Oil Company (today the Houston-based ConocoPhillips) made history by constructing the first underwater storage facility (with a capacity of 500,000 barrels) in the world. By 1973, oil production had started at two additional fields and during the 1970s substantial new deposits were discovered onshore at the Margham field and offshore at the Rashid field. The dynamic Ruler of Dubai, Sheikh Rashid bin Saeed Al Maktoum, who had acceded in 1958, centralized all onshore production under the Dubai Petroleum Company (DPC) and merged most offshore production into the Dubai Marine Areas Company. Dubai's oil production went on to peak in 1991 when the emirate produced about 420,000 barrels per day. Elsewhere in the UAE, oil production in Sharjah commenced in 1972 and in Ras al-Khaimah as late as in 1984.[131]

The Trucial States stood therefore on the cusp of "modernity" just as much as formal statehood as the deadline for the British withdrawal from the Gulf approached in 1971. Oil and independence proceeded hand-in-hand as the entity that came together between July 1971 and February 1972 eventually evolved into the most durable and successful example of federation in the Arab world. Such an outcome was far from preordained at the time of the creation of the UAE and required the leadership – and ability to compromise on key issues and at critical moments – of the charismatic rulers of Abu Dhabi and Dubai. The processes of state-formation and nation-building were far from smooth and required a degree of flexibility among key actors at various moments in the opening two decades of the UAE, but succeeded ultimately in grafting an "Emirati" identity that was resilient enough to survive the passing of the charismatic "founding fathers" of the federation.

Notes

1 J.E. Peterson, "Rulers, Merchants, and Shaykhs in Gulf Politics: The Function of Family Networks," in Alanoud Alsharekh (ed.), *The Gulf Family: Kinship Policies and Modernity* (London: Saqi Books, 2007), p. 30.
2 James Onley and Sulayman Khalaf, "Shaikhly Authority in the Pre-Oil Gulf: An Historical-Anthropological Study," *History and Anthropology*, 17(3), 2006, pp. 191–192.
3 Joseph Kechichian, *Power and Succession in Arab Monarchies: A Reference Guide* (Boulder, CO: Lynne Rienner, 2008), pp. 286–289.
4 Ibid.
5 George Joffe, "Concepts of Sovereignty in the Gulf Region," in Richard Schofield (ed.), *Territorial Foundations of the Gulf States* (New York: St Martin's Press, 1994), p. 85.
6 Onley and Khalaf, *Shaikhly Authority in the Pre-Oil Gulf*, pp. 202–203.

7   Cf. Lisa Anderson, "Absolutism and the Resilience of Monarchy in the Middle East," *Political Science Quarterly*, 106(1), 1991, pp. 1–15.
8   William Beeman, "Gulf Society: An Anthropological View of the Khalijis – Their Evolution and Way of Life," in Lawrence Potter (ed.), *The Persian Gulf in History* (New York: Palgrave Macmillan, 2009), p. 147.
9   D.T. Potts, "Before the Emirates: an Archaeological and Historical Account of Developments in the Region c.5000 BC to 676 AD," in Ibrahim al Abed and Peter Hellyer (eds), *United Arab Emirates: A New Perspective* (London: Trident Press, 2001), pp. 36–37.
10 D.T. Potts, "The Archaeology and Early History of the Persian Gulf," in Lawrence Potter (ed.), *The Persian Gulf in History* (New York: Palgrave Macmillan, 2009), p. 33.
11 Frauke Heard-Bey, *From Trucial States to United Arab Emirates* (Dubai: Motivate Publishing, 2007 edition), p. 22 & fn. 13, p. 427.
12 Malcolm Peck, *The United Arab Emirates: A Venture in Unity* (Boulder, CO: Westview Press, 1986), pp. 25–26.
13 Mohammad Bagher Vosoughi, "The Kings of Hormuz: From the Beginning until the Arrival of the Portuguese," in Lawrence Potter (ed.), *The Persian Gulf in History* (New York: Palgrave Macmillan, 2009), p. 97.
14 John Wilkinson, "From Liwa to Abu Dhabi," *Liwa: Journal of the National Center for Documentation and Research*, 1(1), 2009, pp. 5–8.
15 Peck, *United Arab Emirates*, p. 28.
16 Shahnaz Razieh Nadjmabadi, "The Arab Presence on the Iranian Coast of the Persian Gulf," in Lawrence Potter (ed.), *The Persian Gulf in History* (New York: Palgrave Macmillan, 2009), p. 132.
17 James Onley, "Britain's Informal Empire in the Gulf, 1820–1971," *Journal of Social Affairs*, 22(87), 2005, p. 30.
18 Kechichian, *Power and Succession*, p. 327; Michael Casey, *The History of Kuwait* (Westport, CT: Greenwood Press, 2007), p. 34.
19 Peck, *United Arab Emirates*, p. 28.
20 Sultan Souud Al Qassemi, "Tribalism in the Arabian Peninsula: It's a Family Affair," *Al Arabiya*, February 3, 2012.
21 Frauke Heard-Bey, "The Tribal Society of the UAE and its Traditional Economy," in Ibrahim al Abed and Peter Hellyer (eds), *United Arab Emirates: A New Perspective* (London: Trident Press, 2001), p. 103.
22 Christopher Davidson, *Abu Dhabi: Oil and Beyond* (London: Hurst & Co, 2009), p. 5; Christopher Davidson, *Dubai: The Vulnerability of Success* (London: Hurst & Co, 2008), p. 13.
23 Davidson, *Oil and Beyond*, p. 6.
24 "Qasr al Hosn: The Fabric of History," *The National*, February 27, 2013.
25 Michael Quentin Morton, *Buraimi: The Struggle for Power, Influence and Oil in Arabia* (London: I.B. Tauris, 2013), p. 3.
26 Heard-Bey, *Trucial States to United Arab Emirates*, pp. 50–52.
27 Jim Krane, *Dubai: The Story of the World's Largest City* (London: Atlantic Books, 2009), p. 17.
28 Davidson, *Vulnerability of Success*, p. 13.
29 Ibid., p. 15.
30 Stephen Ramos, "The Blueprint: A History of Dubai's Spatial Development through Oil Discovery," Harvard Kennedy School's Belfer Center for Science and International Affairs/Dubai Initiative Working Paper, June 2009, pp. 6–7.
31 Fatma al-Sayegh, "Merchants' Role in a Changing Society: The Case of Dubai, 1900–90," *Middle Eastern Studies*, 34(1), 1998, pp. 89–90.
32 Keith Neilson, "For Diplomatic, Economic, Strategic and Telegraphic Reasons: British Imperial Defence, the Middle East and India, 1914–1918," in Greg Kennedy and Keith Neilson (eds), *Far-flung Lines: Essays on Imperial Defence in Honour of Donald Mackenzie Schurman* (London: Frank Cass, 1997), p. 102.

33 J.E. Peterson, "Britain and the Gulf: At the Periphery of Empire," in Lawrence Potter (ed.), *The Persian Gulf in History* (New York: Palgrave Macmillan, 2009), p. 278.
34 Peck, *United Arab Emirates*, p. 31.
35 Sultan bin Mohammed Al Qasimi, *The Myth of Arab Piracy in the Gulf* (London: Croon Helm, 1986).
36 Charles Davies, *The Blood-Red Arab Flag: An Investigation into Qasimi Piracy, 1797–1820* (Exeter: Exeter University Press, 1997).
37 Ash Rossiter, "Britain and the Development of Professional Security Forces in the Gulf Arab States, 1921–71: Local Forces and Informal Empire," Ph.D. Dissertation, *University of Exeter*, 2014, p. 22.
38 John Pitney, Jr. and John-Clark Levin, *Private Anti-Piracy Navies: How Warships for Hire are Changing Maritime Security* (New York: Lexington Books, 2013), p. 13.
39 Davies, *Blood-Red Arab Flag*, pp. 300–304.
40 Donald Hawley, *The Trucial States* (London: George Allen & Unwin, 1970), pp. 129–130.
41 James Onley, "Britain and the Gulf Shaikhdoms, 1820–1971: The Politics of Protection," Georgetown School of Foreign Service in Qatar: Center for International and Regional Studies, *Occasional Paper* (2009), p. 6.
42 Rossiter, *Professional Security Forces*, p. 22.
43 Husain Albaharna, *The Legal Status of the Arabian Gulf States: A Study of Their Treaty Relations and Their International Problems* (Manchester: Manchester University Press, 1968), pp. 26–27.
44 Rossiter, *Professional Security Forces*, p. 24.
45 Onley, *Politics of Protection*, pp. 4–5.
46 Ibid., pp. 6–8.
47 Ibid., p. 5.
48 Davidson, *Oil and Beyond*, pp. 23–24.
49 Heard-Bey, *Trucial States to United Arab Emirates*, p. 293.
50 Ibid., p. 295; Bianca Sarbu, *Ownership and Control of Oil: Explaining Policy Choices across Producing Countries* (Abingdon: Routledge, 2014), p. 128.
51 Rosemarie Said Zahlan, *The Origins of the United Arab Emirates: A Political and Social History of the Trucial States* (London: Macmillan, 1978), p. xvii.
52 Mohammed Morsy Abdullah, "Changes in the Economy and Political Attitudes, and the Development of Culture on the Coast of Oman between 1900 and 1940," *Arabian Studies*, 2 (1975), p. 170.
53 Nicholas Stanley-Price, *Imperial Outpost in the Gulf: The Airfield at Sharjah (UAE) 1932–1952* (London: The Book Guild Ltd, 2012), p. 162.
54 Ibid.
55 House of Lords Debate, "Great Britain and the Persian Gulf," May 5, 1903. *Hansard*, vol. 121, column 1348.
56 David Gilmour, *Curzon* (London, John Murray, 1994), p. 203.
57 Quoted in Gary Troeller, *The Birth of Saudi Arabia: Britain and the Rise of the House of Sa'ud* (London: Frank Cass, 1976), p. 12.
58 Briton Cooper Busch, *Britain and the Persian Gulf, 1894–1914* (Berkeley, CA: University of California Press, 1967), p. 225.
59 Quoted in Troeller, *Birth of Saudi Arabia*, p. 11.
60 Helene von Bismarck, *British Policy in the Persian Gulf, 1961–1968: Conceptions of Informal Empire* (London: Palgrave Macmillan, 2013) p. 7.
61 Glencairn Balfour Paul, *The End of Empire in the Middle East: Britain's Relinquishment of Power in Her Last Three Arab Dependencies* (Cambridge: Cambridge University Press, 1991), p. 102.
62 Glencairn Balfour Paul, *Bagpipes in Babylon: A Lifetime in the Arab World and Beyond* (London: I.B. Tauris, 2006), p. 198.
63 Matthew Teller, "The Diplomat's Portable Handbook (Wheelbarrow Required)," *BBC Magazine Monitor*, December 6, 2014.
64 Heard-Bey, *Tribal Society of the UAE*, p. 100.

65 Ibid., p. 115.
66 Wanda Krause, *Women in Civil Society* (Basingstoke: Palgrave Macmillan, 2008), p. 31.
67 Al-Sayegh, *Merchants' Role in a Changing Society*, p. 90.
68 Fred Lawson and Hasan al-Naboodah, "Heritage and Cultural Nationalism in the United Arab Emirates," in Alanoud Alsharekh and Robert Springborg (eds), *Popular Culture and Political Identity in the Arab Gulf States* (London: Saqi Books, 2008), p. 18.
69 "Al Ain Inscribed on World Heritage List," *Khaleej Times*, June 29, 2011.
70 Hendrik van der Meulen, "The Role of Tribal and Kinship Ties in the Politics of the United Arab Emirates," Ph.D. thesis presented to the *Fletcher School of Law and Diplomacy*, May 1997, pp. 46–47.
71 Onley and Khalaf, *Shaikhly Authority in the Pre-Oil Gulf*, pp. 204–205.
72 Rosemarie Said Zahlan, *The Making of the Modern Gulf States: Kuwait, Bahrain, Qatar, the United Arab Emirates and Oman* (Reading: Ithaca Press, 1998 edition), pp. 28–29.
73 Rosemarie Said Zahlan, *The Origins of the United Arab Emirates: A Political and Social History of the Trucial States* (London: Macmillan, 1978), p. 57.
74 Al-Sayegh, *Merchants' Role in a Changing Society*, p. 91.
75 Ibid.
76 Giacomo Luciani, "Democracy vs. Shura in the Age of the Internet," in Abdulhadi Khalaf and Giacomo Luciani, eds., *Constitutional Reform and Political Participation in the Gulf* (Dubai: Gulf Research Centre, 2006), p. 277.
77 Said Zahlan, *Making of the Modern Gulf States*. p. 29.
78 Michael Quentin Morton, "The British India Line in the Arabian Gulf, 1862–1982," *Liwa: Journal of the National Center for Documentation and Research*, 5(10), 2013, p. 50.
79 Al-Sayegh, *Merchants' Role in a Changing Society*, p. 90.
80 Pardis Mahdavi, *Gridlock: Labor, Migration, and Human Trafficking in Dubai* (Stanford, CA: Stanford University Press, 2011), pp. 46–47.
81 Lizette van Hecke, "How Sharjah's Airport Showed the Emirate the World," *The National*, June 28, 2009.
82 Ibid.
83 Davidson, *Oil and Beyond*, pp. 28–30.
84 David Commins, *The Gulf States: A Modern History* (London: I.B. Tauris, 2012), pp. 152–153.
85 Ibid.
86 Marc Valeri, "Toward the End of the Oligarchic Pact? Business and Politics in Abu Dhabi, Bahrain, and Oman," in Kristian Coates Ulrichsen (ed.), *Changing Security Dynamics of the Persian Gulf* (London: Hurst & Co, 2017 forthcoming).
87 Khalid Almezaini, "Private Sector Actors in the UAE and their Role in the Process of Economic and Political Reform," in Steffen Hertog, Giacomo Luciani, and Marc Valeri (eds), *Business Politics in the Middle East* (London: Hurst & Co, 2013), p. 44.
88 Davidson, *Vulnerability of Success*, pp. 45–46.
89 "Bin Sulayem Exit Ends Tumultuous Era," *Financial Times*, December 13, 2010.
90 John Bullock, *The Gulf: A Portrait of Kuwait, Qatar, Bahrain and the UAE* (London: Century Publishing, 1984), p. 119.
91 Jill Crystal, *Oil and Politics in the Gulf: Rulers and Merchants in Kuwait and Qatar* (Cambridge: Cambridge University Press, 1990), pp. 5–6.
92 Kristian Coates Ulrichsen, *The Gulf States in International Political Economy* (London: Palgrave Macmillan, 2015), p. 18.
93 Heard-Bey, *Trucial States to United Arab Emirates*, pp. 219–220.
94 Ibid.
95 Mary Ann Tetreault, "Autonomy, Necessity, and the Small State: Ruling Kuwait in the Twentieth Century," *International Organization*, 45(4), 1991, p. 576.
96 Kamal Osman Salih, "The 1938 Kuwait Legislative Council," *Middle Eastern Studies*, 28(1), 1992, p. 77.
97 Said Zahlan, *Making of the Modern Gulf States*, p. 66.

98   Michael Herb, *The Wages of Oil: Parliaments and Economic Development in Kuwait and the UAE* (New York: Cornell University Press, 2014), p. 63.
99   Ibid., p. 80.
100   Al-Sayegh, *Merchants' Role in a Changing Society*, p. 95.
101   Kamal Osman Salih, "The 1938 Kuwait Legislative Council," *Middle Eastern Studies*, 28(1), p. 77.
102   Al-Sayegh, *Merchants' Role in a Changing Society*, p. 95.
103   Osman Salih, *1938 Kuwait Legislative Council*, p. 77.
104   Davidson, *Vulnerability of Success*, p. 33.
105   Heard-Bey, *Trucial States to United Arab Emirates*, p. 257.
106   Ibid., p. 256.
107   Davidson, *Vulnerability of Success*, pp. 46–49.
108   Miriam Joyce, *Kuwait 1945–1996: An Anglo-American Perspective* (London: Frank Cass, 1998), p. 32.
109   Omar AlShehabi, "Political Movements in Bahrain: Past, Present, and Future," *Jadaliyya*, February 14, 2012.
110   Christopher Davidson, "Higher Education in the Gulf: a Historical Background," in Christopher Davidson and Peter Mackenzie (eds), *Higher Education in the Gulf States: Shaping Economies, Politics and Culture* (London: Saqi Books, 2009), p. 19.
111   Mohammed Morsy Abdullah, *The United Arab Emirates: A Modern History* (London: Croon Helm, 1978), p. 144.
112   A.L.P. Burdett, *Records of the Emirates: 1966–1971, Volume 4: 1969* (Farnham: Archive Editions, 2002), p. 414.
113   Peter Hellyer, "End of a 75-Year Era of Oil-Fuelled Progress for Abu Dhabi," *The National*, January 8, 2014.
114   Gerald Butt, "Oil and Gas in the UAE," in Ibrahim al Abed and Peter Hellyer (eds), *United Arab Emirates: A New Perspective* (London: Trident Press, 2001), p. 232.
115   Ibid.
116   Heard-Bey, *Trucial States to United Arab Emirates*, p. 300.
117   Ibid., pp. 301–302.
118   J.E. Peterson, "Sovereignty and Boundaries in the Gulf States," in Mehran Kamrava (ed.), *International Politics of the Persian Gulf* (Syracuse, NY: Syracuse University Press, 2011), p. 38.
119   Julian Walker, "Practical Problems of Boundary Delimitation in Arabia: the Case of the United Arab Emirates," in Richard Schofield (ed.), *Territorial Foundations of the Gulf States* (New York: St Martin's Press, 1994), p. 110.
120   Ibid., p. 109.
121   Julian Walker, "Personal Recollections of Indigenous Sources and the Rapid Growth of Archives in the Emirates," *Liwa: Journal of the National Center for Documentation and Research*, 4(8), 2012, p. 22.
122   "Madha Village's Pledge of Allegiance Changed the Map Forever," *The National*, January 27, 2012.
123   Ibid.
124   Hassan Hamdan al-Alkim, *The Foreign Policy of the United Arab Emirates* (London: Saqi Books, 1989), pp. 49–50.
125   Quentin Morton, *Buraimi*, pp. 78–82.
126   Ibid., pp. 101–102.
127   Heard-Bey, *Trucial States to United Arab Emirates*, pp. 304–305.
128   Rossiter, *Professional Security Forces*, p. 111.
129   Butt, *Oil and Gas*, p. 232.
130   Ibid. p. 233.
131   Davidson, *Vulnerability of Success*, pp. 100–101.

3

POLITICS

The decade prior to the formation of the United Arab Emirates was one of danger for the seven Trucial States that came together between December 1971 and February 1972. The 1960s was a period of considerable political turbulence both domestically and regionally as the Trucial States were buffeted by the crosswinds of Arab nationalism and anticolonial sentiment. In Abu Dhabi, the exploitation of the major oil reserves discovered after 1958 was held back by the excessive caution of the Ruler, Sheikh Shakhbut bin Sultan Al Nahyan, who had been in power since 1928. Elsewhere, Dubai was the only other sheikhdom that located significant quantities of oil while mechanisms for sharing the newfound wealth across the seven Trucial States were still in their infancy and susceptible both to politicization and to rivalries among the sheikhdoms. Against this fractious backdrop, the January 1968 announcement of Britain's impending withdrawal from all positions east of Suez came as a bolt from the blue, and triggered a frenetic three-year search for a confederal entity that could hold its own as a viable sovereign state.

And yet, as this chapter documents, from these inauspicious beginnings the UAE gradually took root both on paper and, more slowly and in fits and starts, in practice. A major reason for the survival of the UAE as a federal entity (and for its very creation) lay in the charismatic authority wielded by its two most important protagonists in the late 1960s and 1970s. Sheikh Zayed bin Sultan Al Nahyan replaced his older brother as Ruler in a carefully planned palace takeover in August 1966 and set in motion the full development of Abu Dhabi's plentiful oil resources. The resulting revenues catalyzed the breakneck modernization of Abu Dhabi and provided the means to support the five less heavily-endowed "Northern Emirates" that joined with Abu Dhabi and Dubai in the UAE. Meanwhile, the Ruler of Dubai, Sheikh Rashid bin Saeed Al Maktoum, oversaw the creation of the infrastructure facilities that positioned Dubai to become the leading regional infrastructure hub, beginning with the dredging of the Dubai Creek in the late 1950s and the construction of the Jebel Ali port and free zone in the late 1970s.[1]

Waning of British Influence

Although the UAE only came into existence in 1971 the preceding decade witnessed the start of initiatives to bring the seven Trucial States closer together both politically and economically amid a perceptible waning of British influence and control. A Trucial States Council was formed under British auspices as early as 1952 to provide a forum for the seven rulers to meet on an annual basis. Despite the fact that executive control remained in British hands, over time the Council did "establish a framework for cooperation and consultation" among the seven Rulers while tensions between Abu Dhabi and Dubai also decreased markedly.[2] The Council remained under the chairmanship of the British Political Agent until 1965 when the responsibility was passed to the rulers on a rotating basis and the Ruler of Ras al-Khaimah, Sheikh Saqr bin Mohammed Al Qasimi, became Chair. The Trucial States Council (which evolved into the Supreme Council of Rulers in 1971) slowly increased its remit and expanded the rulers' influence in decision-making processes.[3] Three sub-committees were formed in 1958 to cover education, agriculture, and public health, and in 1964 a Deliberative Committee consisting of two representatives from each of the seven sheikhdoms was formed to facilitate the alignment and implementation of policy decisions.[4]

Most early progress was made in development planning. Beginning in 1955, the Trucial States Council adopted a series of five-year development plans that focused on the health and education sectors and aimed to construct and strengthen administrative and institutional capacity. The first five-year plan (1955–1960) was financed by the British Government to the tune of £450,000 while £500,000 was allocated to the second five-year plan (1961–1966).[5] A significant step forward occurred in 1965 with the establishment of the Trucial States Development Office, which was based in Dubai and intended to increase considerably the aid spent on the northern sheikhdoms. The Development Office constituted an important shift away from British influence and control, in part because its launch coincided with the change to a more proactive leadership in Abu Dhabi; Sheikh Zayed immediately donated £500,000 to the fund after taking power in August 1966 and by the time the fund was wound up and incorporated into the newly created federal infrastructure in 1972, contributions from Abu Dhabi accounted for 80 percent of the budget.[6]

Contributions to the Trucial States Development Fund came also from Qatar (£250,000) and Bahrain (£40,000) while Qatar and Kuwait provided educational support and resources in the form of financing for a secondary school in Sharjah and sixty teachers from Kuwait. The earliest school curricula in the Trucial States (and, after 1971, the UAE) drew heavily from Kuwait (and Jordan), with Sheikha Khulood Sagr Al Qassemi, the Director of the curriculum department at the Ministry of Education, recalling in 2011 that "We were still using the Kuwaiti curriculum in government secondary schools, and it was not until 1993 that we began designing our own."[7] Other support from Kuwait came in the form of an advisory delegation headed by the Director-General of newly independent Kuwait's Department of Social Affairs and Labor, Sayyid Abdul-Aziz al-Sarawi that visited Abu Dhabi in 1961 in response to a request from Sheikh Shakhbut for assistance. The al-Sarawi mission assisted in the creation of municipal, health, and social services as well as blueprints for customs, passports, labor affairs, and public works, modelled after Kuwait and Bahrain, then the two most advanced of the Gulf sheikhdoms.[8]

British officials expressed far greater alarm at the interest shown by the Arab League in the internal (and developmental) affairs of the Trucial States and viewed the attempted inroads by the Arab League as a direct threat to their position in the Trucial States.[9] The Secretary-General of the Arab League, Abdelkhaleq Hassouna of Egypt, toured the Gulf on a proclaimed "mission of brotherhood" in October 1964 and recommended that the League establish a development fund of its own for the Trucial States. Although British officials coached the rulers of the seven Trucial States (and Bahrain and Qatar) on how to receive Hassouna, the Rulers of Ras al-Khaimah and Sharjah openly welcomed the Arab League visit and attendant proposals of support. British officials additionally suspected the Ruler of Sharjah, Sheikh Saqr bin Sultan Al Qasimi, of orchestrating a 3,000-strong crowd that welcomed Hassouna to neighboring Dubai and of organizing a march through Dubai "during which Adeni and Yemeni laborers shouted pro-Nasser and anti-imperialist slogans."[10]

A follow-up delegation from the Arab League arrived in the Trucial States in December 1964 and shortly thereafter proposed to create a fund worth £5 million – a figure that far exceeded the amount British officials had been prepared to allocate to the first and second development plans. British concern at the apparent Arab League "encroachment" on the Trucial States increased further in May 1965 when the Assistant Secretary-General of the Arab League secured agreement from the Rulers of Sharjah and Ras al-Khaimah for the opening of Arab League offices in each sheikhdom.[11] News of the agreement rattled British officials who remained avowed opponents of the Cairo-based organization and determined to counter any perceived expansion of Nasserist interest in their sphere of influence in the Gulf. In response, Sir William Luce, the British Political Resident in the Gulf, thundered that the Ruler of:

> Sharjah has for years been flirting with the UAR [United Arab Republic] and now he has come out openly in his true colours ... our aim is to isolate Sharjah and if he does let the A.L. into his State, to isolate them too. It's a tricky game, and takes up a great deal of time and thought – but I'm determined to defeat the Egyptians if I possibly can.[12]

British concerns were reinforced by a resolution approved by the seven Rulers at the 21st meeting of the Trucial States Council on March 1, 1965 that declared that

"The Council welcomes unconditional aid from any source for the development of the Trucial States and is grateful for the interest shown by the Arab League and others in contributing to this development."[13] At this time, British officials believed that the Rulers of Ajman, Sharjah, Ras al-Khaimah, and Umm al-Quwain were "meeting daily to formulate a joint policy towards Britain and the question of the Arab League."[14] The alarm of Luce and his colleagues in the Trucial States then was amplified in comments by senior British policymakers at the Foreign Office in London. The Minister of State, George Thomson, claimed that Britain faced "a determined attempt to undermine our whole position in the Trucial States" while the Foreign Secretary, Michael Stewart, added that "This Arab League visit represents a watershed for us in our relations with the Trucial States. We can no longer exclude the forces of modern Arab nationalism from the area."[15]

In an attempt to counter the inroads of the Arab League, British officials pressured the Rulers of the five northern sheikhdoms, and particularly the "lost lambs" of Sharjah and Ras al-Khaimah, to refuse the Egyptian entreaties.[16] A cat and mouse game developed between the two Qawasim sheikhs and British political representatives in the Trucial States who closed down Sharjah's airspace to prevent any further visits from Arab League representatives and cut off the supply of electricity to the Ruler's palace.[17] Neither Sheikh Saqr bin Sultan Al Qasimi (of Sharjah) nor Sheikh Saqr bin Mohammed Al Qasimi (of Ras al-Khaimah) buckled under the pressure, and an attempt by the British Agent in Dubai (with the support of King Faisal of Saudi Arabia) to rally support among the other three Rulers of the northern sheikhdoms by pledging to contribute £1 million to the Trucial States Development Fund also failed.[18] In June 1965, British patience with Sheikh Saqr snapped and Glencairn Balfour Paul, the Political Agent in Dubai, was tasked with informing the Ruler of Sharjah of his deposition and sending him into exile in Cairo. Nearly seven years later, in January 1972, Sheikh Saqr returned to Sharjah and was implicated in the murder of his cousin and successor as Ruler in an unsuccessful attempt to regain power, whereupon the present Ruler (as of 2016), Sheikh Sultan bin Mohammed Al Qasimi, assumed power.[19]

Little more than a year after the June 1965 palace coup in Sharjah, British officials again were involved in a change of leader in Abu Dhabi that was to have momentous consequences for the future not only of Abu Dhabi but also for the yet-to-be-created UAE. In power since 1928, discontent at the rule of Sheikh Shakhbut was growing among members of his own family as well as watchful British officials, who contrasted Shakhbut's parsimonious governance with the dynamic leadership qualities of his younger brother, Zayed. Sheikh Shakhbut had come to power just prior to the Great Depression and witnessed first-hand the economic hardship caused by the collapse of the pearl trade in the 1930s. These formative experiences deeply shaped Shakhbut's subsequent rule during which he developed "a reputation for being extremely reluctant to spend more money than was absolutely essential."[20] However, the inflows of oil revenues in the 1960s highlighted Shakhbut's resistance to economic development that might lead to social or political change. While Hugh Boustead, the British Political Agent in Abu

Dhabi, acknowledged that "It is clearly no easy task for a Ruler, after a lifetime of poverty, to accustom himself to the idea that his income will henceforward be counted not in hundreds of pounds but in millions," he added condescendingly that "Shakhbut is finding the mental adjustment much more difficult than have any other Rulers of oil states and it is questionable whether he wishes to make the adjustment at all."[21] In 1965, the Political Agent's annual report for Abu Dhabi labelled Shakhbut "an autocrat who tries to run the state single-handed and whose insistence on personal control of even the minutest details of government would make Louis XIV look like a constitutional monarch."[22]

Another British official, T.F. Brenchley at the Foreign Office in London, damned Shakhbut with the faintest of condescending praise when he stated that while:

> Shakhbut is a bad ruler, he is probably not the worst in the Gulf; when he was poor, he was not as corrupt as is the Shaikh of Ras al-Khaimah; now that he is rich, he does not squander his wealth like the Shaikh of Qatar; nor does he stir up petty border troubles, like the Shaikh of Fujairah … [23]

Following a period of reflection, Sir William Luce, the powerful British Resident in the Persian Gulf, came to argue forcefully for the removal of Sheikh Shakhbut as he suggested that "The stakes appear to me to have become now so great that I have no hesitation whatever in urging with all the force at my command that H.M.G. [Her Majesty's Government] should agree to go, if necessary, to the limit."[24] Luce did acknowledge that any such removal of a sitting ruler "would be inconsistent with our public assertions that the Gulf States are independent entities with whose internal affairs we do not interfere," though he resolved this particular dilemma by meeting on several occasions with Sheikh Zayed to discuss the issue.[25] On a separate occasion, the British Foreign Secretary, Patrick Gordon Walker, reported to Prime Minister Harold Wilson that Luce believed that Shakhbut was determined to "disassociate Abu Dhabi from the rest of the Trucial States" and that "so long as Shaikh Shakhbut is the ruler, federation including Abu Dhabi, which is the only state with any substantial revenue, is out of the question."[26]

The growing sense of frustration among leaders both in Abu Dhabi and in London that Sheikh Shakhbut was not the person to lead Abu Dhabi into the oil era coalesced into a conviction that power should lie instead with his dynamic younger brother, Sheikh Zayed bin Sultan Al Nahyan. Sheikh Zayed had served as the Ruler's Representative in the Eastern Region of Abu Dhabi since 1946 and had developed a reputation as a charismatic and highly capable leader with a strong record of local development, which included the renovation of the historic *aflaj* system of irrigation canals in Buraimi and the opening of a local school – staffed with Jordanian teachers – and hospital – staffed by American and Indian doctors – that indicated a willingness to open up to the wider world and that "was far in advance of any comparable facilities available in Abu Dhabi at that time."[27] Sheikh Zayed also impressed British officials who noted the close relationship Zayed had with local tribes, beginning with the British adventurer, Wilfred Thesiger, who met with Sheikh Zayed in Buraimi (today Al-Ain) in 1948 and who recorded how:

> ... he had a great reputation among the Bedu. They liked him for his easy informal ways and his friendliness, and they respected his force of character, his shrewdness, and his physical strength. They said admiringly, "Zayid [sic] is a Bedu. He knows about camels, can ride like one of us, can shoot, and knows how to fight."[28]

In the months that preceded the deposition of Sheikh Shakhbut in August 1966, Sheikh Zayed held a series of meetings with British officials that indicated that any assumption of power by Sheikh Zayed would have the overwhelming support not only of the Al Nahyan family but also of the most important tribal leaders. The discussions allayed the concerns of British officials who worried that any perception that they were intervening in the domestic politics of Abu Dhabi would arouse further anti-British sentiment in the Arab world only a decade after the Suez Crisis of 1956.[29] Luce himself stated of Sheikh Zayed that "he would be an immense improvement on Shakhbut as a Ruler" and "is aware of the need for drastic changes in Abu Dhabi and is ready to listen to advice and to use people who can help him."[30]

In the event, after detailed plans had been drawn up, Sheikh Zayed seized power in a carefully orchestrated palace coup on August 6, 1966. Glencairn Balfour Paul, who was serving as the acting British Resident in the Gulf (based in Bahrain) following Luce's retirement, recorded one of the only openly available accounts of the day's events, as official accounts in British government files remain classified. In his memoirs, *Bagpipes to Babylon*, Balfour Paul recalled how he travelled from Bahrain to Abu Dhabi:

> ostensibly to pay a routine call on Shakhbut. Two companies of the Trucial Oman Scouts (the TOS) were privily positioned overnight on 'training manoeuvers,' sufficiently near the palace to intervene forcefully if needed ...
>
> In the small upstairs room of his mud-walled palace, Shakhbut grew white with anger when I told him that his family wanted him out. He growled inaudibly to a summoned servant, and shortly I could see his fifty palace guards carrying ammunition boxes up the stairs ...
>
> My object had been to persuade Shakhbut to step down with dignity. A TOS guard of honour would be fallen in outside the palace to present arms on his way to a special plane waiting on the airstrip. He would have none of it, and I was glad to be able to make my escape unscathed ...
>
> The TOS finally closed in all round the palace, shouting at the armed retainers to come out and lay down their muskets. Group after group nervously emerged, and eventually word came that Shakhbut would do so too. The guard of honour did its stuff, and off he was flown to Bahrain.[31]

Sheikh Shakhbut departed first for Bahrain, where he stayed in the guest-house of the Ruler, Sheikh Isa bin Salman Al Khalifa and later for Beirut. In 1970, Shakhbut was permitted to return to Abu Dhabi and he proceeded to live for the rest of his life in Buraimi. In historical perspective, Sheikh Zayed's accession as Ruler was the decisive turning point in Abu Dhabi's twentieth-century development. The sheikhdom had stagnated during the latter years of his brother's long rule and was in danger of becoming a backwater just at the moment that Dubai and the other coastal sheikhdoms entered into an era of rapid economic growth. History is replete with examples of "what-ifs" but had Shakhbut, who lived until February 1989, remained in power in Abu Dhabi until his death it is likely that Dubai, rather than Abu Dhabi, would have been the driving force behind the creation of the UAE. Indeed, Luce, the British Political Resident in the Gulf, identified Sheikh Rashid as "a leader whose interests and aims are broadly in harmony with ours" and hoped that oil revenues would allow the Ruler of Dubai to become "the dominant leader of the Northern Trucial Coast."[32]

Once in power, Sheikh Zayed set about rebuilding the relationship between Abu Dhabi and British officials as well as reaching out to the sheikhs of the five northern emirates with immediate pledges of aid and development funds. This included the aforementioned £500,000 donation to the Trucial States Development Fund as well as an immediate grant to Sheikh Saqr bin Mohammed of Ras al-Khaimah.[33] Development projects completed in 1968 alone included electricity and water schemes in Ajman, Fujairah, Ras al-Khaimah, and Umm al-Quwain as well as a geographical survey of the Trucial States, an improvement to coastal security, and the first population census.[34] Zayed also instituted a Council for Higher Planning in Abu Dhabi and formulated a five-year plan that spearheaded the long-awaited economic development and set in motion the redistribution of oil income to its inhabitants.[35] Within the space of a generation, these measures transformed Abu Dhabi from little more than a coastal village into an urban cityscape and constituted the political and economic center of gravity for the federation of emirates that slowly took shape between January 1968 and February 1972.

Formation of the United Arab Emirates

On January 16, 1968, British Prime Minister Harold Wilson announced to the House of Commons in London that Britain intended to withdraw from all positions east of Suez by the end of 1971. The Labour government Wilson had led since October 1964 was under growing economic pressure from a serious financial crisis that started in 1966 and a balance of payments crisis that resulted in the devaluation of sterling in November 1967. Beset both by economic crisis and an ideological distaste for colonialism, Wilson's government already had expressed in 1966 its intent to withdraw from Aden by the end of 1968 and, in 1967, drew up plans for its departure from Malaysia and Singapore as well.[36] The announcement of Britain's impending withdrawal from all positions "East of Suez" nevertheless took the sheikhs (and British officials) completely by surprise, particularly since the

Minister of State at the Foreign Office, Goronwy Roberts, had toured the Gulf in November 1967 and visited the rulers of the Trucial States, Bahrain, and Qatar. During his November meetings, Roberts had reaffirmed Wilson's pledge, made just seven months earlier in the House of Commons, that "the Gulf is an area of such vital importance not only to the economy of Western Europe but also to world peace that it would be totally irresponsible of us to withdraw our forces from the area."[37]

What changed in the two months between November 1967 and January 1968 was the near-bankruptcy of the UK public finances which forced both the devaluation of sterling and a humiliating request to the International Monetary Fund for an emergency loan. In the ensuing atmosphere of fiscal crisis in London, officials opted not to continue the £12 million it cost annually to maintain its military presence in the Gulf.[38] The British Government also rebuffed the offers that subsequently came in from Kuwaiti diplomats as well as the Rulers of Qatar and Abu Dhabi to meet the costs of the British garrisons themselves; an account in the Foreign Office of a meeting with Sheikh Zayed recorded how "in order to secure indefinite continuation of British military presence he was prepared to contribute financially to its cost whether publicly or secretly."[39] This proposal, together with a similar suggestion from Sheikh Ahmed bin Ali Al Thani, the Ruler of Qatar, elicited a condescending outburst from the leftwing Defense Secretary, Denis Healey, for which he later apologized, that "I don't very much like the idea of being a sort of white slaver for the Arab sheikhs ... I think it would be a very great mistake if we allowed ourselves to become mercenaries for people who would like to have a few British troops around."[40]

Just over a month later, the Rulers of Abu Dhabi and Dubai met at As-Sameeh, a location close to their border, and agreed to create a two-emirate union as the basis for a larger federal entity and to invite the other five sheikhdoms (as well as Bahrain and Qatar) to join. (The agreement reached between Sheikh Zayed bin Sultan and Sheikh Rashid bin Saeed also resolved a number of outstanding issues relating to the onshore and offshore boundary between Abu Dhabi and Dubai. This involved the cession of the territory that is today the Jebel Ali port and free zone from Abu Dhabi to Dubai.)[41] The first meeting of all nine rulers (the seven Trucial States plus Bahrain and Qatar) subsequently took place in Dubai on February 25, 1968 and two days later the Dubai Agreement provided for the creation of a Union of Arab Emirates to take effect on March 30. Sheikh Zayed of Abu Dhabi would become the President of the union while the Deputy Ruler (and Emir from 1972 to 1995) of Qatar, Sheikh Khalifa bin Hamad Al Thani, its Prime Minister. Further progress was, however, complicated by underlying tensions, particularly between the Rulers of Bahrain and Qatar and the two dominant Trucial States (Abu Dhabi and Dubai) over how such a union should be realized. Moreover, Sheikh Mohammad bin Hamad Al Sharqi, the Ruler of Fujairah, expressed his unease about the dominance of the "big four" at the Dubai meeting and suggested that the rulers of the five smaller sheikhdoms had only been given an hour to study the Dubai Agreement before signing it. A proposal by Sheikh Ahmed bin

Ali Al Thani of Qatar that the five smaller sheikhdoms be represented by just a single ruler and vote also caused tension, and Sheikh Mohammed told the British Political Agent in Dubai, D.A. Roberts, that "The so-called big four were only big because they happened to have struck oil. This did not entitle them to more votes or to a more flattering description of themselves."[42]

Although a further meeting of the Supreme Council of (nine) Rulers that took place in October 1968 resulted in an agreement on the creation of an external defense force while recognizing the right of each sheikhdom to maintain its own armed force, two subsequent gatherings in Doha in May 1969 and Abu Dhabi in October 1969 ended in failure. Strong support for the nine-member Union of Arab Emirates came from Kuwait with the Foreign Minister (and later the Emir from 2006), Sheikh Sabah al-Ahmad Al Sabah being a particularly forceful advocate for the concept. However, persistent disagreements between Qatar and Bahrain over the location of a permanent capital overshadowed the Doha meeting in May 1969 while the October meeting in Abu Dhabi saw attempts by Qatar and Dubai (which had been linked through dynastic intermarriage and, since 1966, through a currency union that created the Qatar and Dubai Riyal) to force Bahrain out of the union. Sheikh Saqr bin Mohammed of Ras al-Khaimah also walked out of the Abu Dhabi summit after demanding control of the Ministry of Defense, which had been earmarked for Abu Dhabi. While the October 1969 gathering broke up without agreement, it nevertheless revealed the closer alignment between the four other northern sheikhdoms (Ajman, Fujairah, Sharjah, and Umm al-Quwain) and Abu Dhabi as the basis for a union of the Trucial States minus Bahrain and Qatar.[43]

In the event, the dismissal of Iran's longstanding territorial claim on Bahrain by a United Nations mission which visited the archipelago in 1970 paved the way for Bahrain to go it alone and declare its independence as a sovereign state on August 15, 1971. Qatar followed suit on September 3, in spite of its Ruler, Sheikh Ahmed bin Ali Al Thani, choosing to remain in Geneva over returning to Doha for the ceremonies marking the transition to independent rule (just five months later, on February 22, 1972, Sheikh Ahmed bin Ali was deposed by his cousin and Deputy Ruler, Sheikh Khalifa bin Hamad Al Thani). Sheikh Rashid bin Saeed Al Maktoum of Dubai entertained brief thoughts of "going it alone" but ultimately reached agreement with the other Trucial leaders in July 1971.[44] Thus, a meeting of the Trucial States Council in Dubai on July 10, 1971 was followed eight days later by the announcement that the United Arab Emirates would come into effect before the end of the year. Only six of the rulers opted in at this stage with Sheikh Saqr of Ras al-Khaimah standing aside while not ruling out joining the federation at an unspecified later date.[45] Although Sheikh Saqr justified his decision not to participate in the formation of the UAE on the grounds of the inequality of representation in federal organizations, a group of Ras al-Khaimah notables formed a committee and submitted a petition to the ruler urging him to change his mind and join the federation.[46]

In contrast to the issues of representation and power-sharing that constituted the major obstacles to the realization of the nine-member Union of Arab Emirates, a series of mutual compromises between the Rulers of Abu Dhabi and Dubai made possible the creation of the UAE. One account of the formation of the UAE by Malcolm Peck referred to "Rashid's shrewd bargaining skills and Zayed's readiness to be magnanimous to ensure the success of the new union led the latter to make numerous concessions to the former." These included the granting of veto rights in the Federal Supreme Council to Dubai as well as Abu Dhabi, an agreement that all substantive issues decided at the federal level must have the support of both emirates, and equal representation in the Federal National Council.[47] However, Peck added accurately that Sheikh Rashid "would not, however, yield more autonomy than was absolutely necessary and the contention with Zayed over the nature of the union continued long after 1971."[48]

Creation of Federal Institutions

The six-strong federation that formed on December 2, 1971 faced a challenging domestic and regional environment as well as a protracted struggle over the balance of power between the federal and emirate levels. Even as a collective entity, the UAE was tiny in terms of population, if not as territorially small as Bahrain and Qatar: the first formal census taken in 1968 revealed the population of Dubai to be approximately 59,000 compared with 46,000 for Abu Dhabi and just 3,744 in Umm al-Quwain out of a total population of 180,000.[49] The fact that federal arrangements had been drawn up in haste as a series of compromises meant that in the early years of the federation a number of issues remained flashpoints of political tension among the emirates. Further, as Frauke Heard-Bey has observed, whereas in 1971 most of the individual emirates harbored hopes of striking oil and becoming as wealthy as Abu Dhabi and Dubai, it was only when this did not materialize that the centralization of the federal infrastructure could begin in earnest.[50] Another challenge in the early years of the UAE was ensuring that pre-existing historical links between individual Emirs and neighboring countries would eventually be incorporated into a new set of bilateral relationships as foreign policy developed at the federal level.

Far from being a "core–periphery" issue as in many of the postcolonial states that came into existence during the decolonization period in the 1950s and 1960s, the splits in the UAE resembled more of a tug-of-war between its two most powerful constituent emirates with associated "coalitions" of supporting emirates on either side. This was most evident in the persistent tension over constitutional arrangements and the integration of local security forces as well as the conduct of regional and foreign policy in the 1970s and 1980s, when, in all three cases, sharp divisions occurred. Moreover, the "founding fathers" of the UAE had to forge a working relationship with each other and balance individual emirate and collective federal interests in policymaking. This was not always an easy task for Rulers who had been used to wielding sole executive authority and had, in two cases, been in power since 1928 (Ajman) and 1929 (Umm al-Quwain) respectively.

The constitutional arrangements of the UAE and, in particular, the distinction between the federal and the emirate-levels of responsibility were worked out in the frenetic months leading up to the declaration of independence. Six of the seven Trucial States agreed on a provisional constitution on July 18, 1971 which the holdout emirate of Ras al-Khaimah ultimately affirmed on February 11, 1972 after its belated accession completed the formation of the UAE. Although the constitution was intended to be provisional for a five-year period pending agreement on a permanent constitution, the compromises reached in 1971 proved both too durable and too sensitive to successfully revisit. Thus, as Heard-Bey observed, the constitution – which eventually was declared permanent in 1996 – represented a "delicately balanced compromise" drawn up in 1971 and "in some cases a subject which was hotly disputed while the constitution was being prepared [subsequently] became an integral part of the political life of the country."[51]

From the beginning, the new federal institutions that came into existence were faced with the challenge of formalizing and institutionalizing the mechanisms for inter-emirate cooperation and the upward transfer of authority (and legitimacy) in specific areas to the federal level. Federal Law No.1/1972 established the structure of governance in the UAE and laid out the jurisdictional remit of the ministries and the authority vested in the ministers. The principle of power-sharing (albeit in a federation dominated by Abu Dhabi and Dubai) was enshrined in the first Cabinet unveiled by Sheikh Zayed, who had been elected President of the UAE alongside Sheikh Rashid of Dubai as Vice-President and Sheikh Rashid's eldest son, Sheikh Maktoum bin Rashid Al Maktoum (who served later as Dubai's ruler between 1990 and 2006) as Prime Minister. Six Cabinet posts were allocated to representatives of Abu Dhabi, including the key ministries of the interior, foreign affairs, and information while Dubai received the defense, finance, and economy and industry portfolios in addition to the abovementioned post of Prime Minister. Three Cabinet posts were also apportioned to Sharjah while Ajman and Umm al-Quwain received two each and Fujairah one.[52]

Ras al-Khaimah's belated accession to the UAE in February 1972 necessitated an expansion of the Cabinet and was noteworthy also for the appointment of Saif Ghobash, a leading local notable, as First Minister of State for Foreign Affairs, a position he held until he was assassinated at Abu Dhabi International Airport on October 25, 1977 as he accompanied Syrian foreign minister Abdel-Halim Khadim, the intended target of the assassin's bullet.[53]

Institutional capacity-building took time to develop and proceeded from a very low starting point in 1971. J.E. Peterson has observed that the inaugural federal civil service numbered just 4,000 in 1971 (though rising rapidly to 24,000 by 1977 and 38,000 by 1983) and that all federal ministries "had to be built entirely from scratch" and, most remarkably, the Ministry of Foreign Affairs "began with only the minister and a staff of three."[54] In addition to integrating senior members of the seven ruling families into positions of leadership, other key posts were filled by their senior technocratic advisers such as Ahmad Khalifa al-Suwaidi and the twenty-five-year-old Mani bin Said al-Otaiba who became respectively the UAE's first Foreign Minister and Minister of Petroleum, and Mehdi al-Tajir, one of the Ruler of Dubai's closest advisors who was named the UAE's first Ambassador to the United Kingdom in 1971. All three were scions of leading tribal families and among the first generation of Emiratis to acquire a formal education and professional training. Their appointments reflected in part the fact that, as Andrea Rugh observed in her study of the political culture of leadership, after the creation of the UAE:

> another way that rulers cemented their relationships was through appointments to advisory councils, federal cabinet positions, heads of organizations, and other highly visible positions. Barring other circumstances, these positions were assigned in recognition of family or tribal loyalties. The position in effect co-opted future commitment and provided access to influence for the group's members – a patronage system of sorts.[55]

Chapter One mentioned in passing the distribution of power among the seven emirates in the Federal Supreme Council (FSC – which consists of the seven rulers and acts as the source of executive and legislative authority) and the Federal National Council (FNC – which consists of forty members). In-between the FSC and the FNC is the Council of Ministers – the Cabinet – which handles the majority of the day-to-day tasks of governance and is also representative of all seven emirates, as noted above. Writing in 2009, Christopher Davidson noted that the ten ruling family members on the Council of Ministers was the highest number since the formation of the UAE in 1971 and that "the remainder are all either identifiable as members of established families or powerful technocrats with close links to the rulers of their respective emirates."[56] As of 2015, eight of the nineteen federal ministries were headed by ruling family members, including five from Abu Dhabi, two from Dubai, and one from Sharjah.[57]

The FNC also came into existence with the passage of the Provisional Constitution and convened for the first time in February 1972 as a permanent body of forty members drawn from across the seven emirates. Until 2006, the membership of the FNC was entirely appointed by the ruler of each emirate and the seats apportioned according to the emirates' relative size. Thus, Abu Dhabi and Dubai were assigned eight members while Ras al-Khaimah and Sharjah appointed six representatives and Ajman, Fujairah, and Umm al-Quwain each selected four. The FNC views all federal legislation and can vote to approve, amend, or reject draft bills, although Article 110 of the constitution gives the FSC the power to pass a bill over the objections of the FNC. Membership of the FNC, particularly when it was an all-appointed body, tended to be drawn from the business community and prominent local merchant families.[58]

Evolution of Representative Institutions

While the FNC never threatened to shift the focus of decision making away from the FSC or the Council of Ministers, there were occasions when it achieved success in raising and channeling broader concerns over sensitive issues. A prominent example occurred in 1986 when the FNC succeeded in amending a law on state security that had sparked widespread public debate.[59] Another example of a law that provoked rigorous debate was the draft penal code, as:

> a number of stormy debates accompanied the article-by-article process of approving the country's penal code, making it the most debated legal document in the history of the UAE ... objections were raised to an article providing for up to 10 years of imprisonment for membership in subversive organizations ... a related article, proposing stiff penalties for the establishment of organizations without government consent, as well as for membership in any un-approved organization even while outside the country, was roundly attacked as abridging the personal rights and liberties of UAE citizens. Although the articles eventually were passed, they had been amended by the minister of justice, who had been present throughout the debates.[60]

The FNC also played a prominent role in attempts to resolve the constitutional impasse in the late 1970s (see below) as it held a joint session with the Council of Ministers in February 1979 that resulted in a memorandum to the FSC that recommended measures to strengthen the federation.[61] Together, the creation of the FNC and the FSC in the 1970s were instrumental in the development of a hybrid system of governance aptly described by Sheikh Fahim bin Sultan Al Qasimi, the UAE Minister of Economy and Commerce in the 1990s, as one in which:

> ... we have developed without undermining the social, cultural and political fabric of our society. This has been due in large part to leadership [of Sheikh Zayed] ... Our system combines the best of the old with the best of the new. We have retained democratic Islamic traditions, foremost among which is the *majlis*, the open council in which national and local leaders meet regularly with citizens to discuss issues of concern.[62]

While the FNC remained an appointed and strictly consultative body for the first thirty-four years of its existence, a cautious and initially very limited exercise in political participation began shortly after the passing of Sheikh Zayed in November 2004. In early 2006, the formal position of Minister of State for Federal National Council Affairs was created and Anwar Mohammed Gargash, the Minister of State for Foreign Affairs, was appointed to oversee the first election in the UAE's history for half of the forty seats on the FNC (the remaining twenty council members remained appointees). A National Election Committee (NEC) was formed under Gargash and worked closely with Bahrain's Central Informatics Organization (CIO) to customize a system for electronic voting that the CIO originally had co-developed with Microsoft.[63] The first election took place in December 2006 with a small electoral college that was chosen by each of the seven emirate leaderships who nominated potential electors 100 times larger than their FNC representation. After security vetting of the electoral lists, a total of 6,595 people, including 1,162 women, eventually comprised the Electoral College that was eligible to vote for the 456 candidates (391 men and sixty-five women) – a figure that amounted to just 0.08 percent of the population. The final voting pool was composed predominantly of university graduates and people aged between 21 and 40 who were forbidden to form political parties and alliances or campaign on "national" issues.[64]

One woman, Dr. Amal al-Qubaisi, was elected in Abu Dhabi in the 2006 election and eight others were nominated subsequently for the twenty appointed FNC seats to give a total female representation of nine out of forty. However, the greater visibility of women in public and political life, while positively encouraged at the federal level, did not always unfold as smoothly in some of the more conservative emirates. In a study of the 2006 election compiled by researchers at the Dubai School of Government (renamed the Mohammed bin Rashid School of Government in 2013), one female candidate stated that "In Ras al-Khaimah, we found many obstacles since the nature of our society there is a tribal one, which prevents women from playing a leadership role."[65] Another interviewee added that "Even if the trend is generally positive in the UAE, based on what I witnessed in Umm al-Quwain, there was no female participation."[66]

Several of the twenty elected members did use the subsequent FNC term (2006–2011) to request that the UAE government submit draft laws to the FNC for debate prior to their approval, but without success. Ahead of the 2011 election, which took place in September, the electoral register was expanded twenty-fold to 129,274, but turnout fell sharply to 27.75 percent and voting largely followed tribal lines, particularly in the more conservative Northern Emirates. Once again, one woman was elected, this time in Umm al-Quwain, where Sheikha Issa bint Ghanem al-Arrai, a school principal, was successful.[67] However, some FNC members expressed their disappointment at what they considered the "slow pace" of FNC sessions and, in particular, persistent ministerial absences from the council. One member from Dubai, Hamad al-Rahoomi, summarized in 2015 the challenges he felt were undermining the performance of the FNC:

> How can we tell people, "Come and vote, the council is important, we monitor the Government?" How can we give ourselves to the people when it is no secret that we are struggling now to meet with the Government? This is unacceptable. We have a problem with low turnout during the elections and want to give the council value. One of the reasons why people are not getting involved in the elections is because no minister is available to attend the sessions. This affects the reputation of the FNC.[68]

Ahead of the October 2015 elections to the FNC the franchise was extended yet again as the size of the Electoral College rose substantially to 224,279 – a figure thirty-four times higher than the initial 2006 list and itself a 65 percent increase on the 2011 figure.[69]

The emirate-level allocations in the 2015 Electoral College were 90,408 from Abu Dhabi, 53,568 from Dubai, 31,766 from Sharjah, 27,455 from Ras al-Khaimah,

10,887 from Fujairah, 6,090 from Ajman, and 4,105 from Umm al-Quwain.[70] The 2015 figures illustrated a striking discrepancy between the number of eligible voters for the same number of FNC seats in Abu Dhabi and Dubai and may be attributable partly to differences in the citizen–expatriate ratios in each emirate. A breakdown of the voting patterns in the October 2015 elections to the FNC show also a disparity in participation as turnout varied sharply and was below 30 percent in Dubai and Sharjah compared to rates that neared 50 percent in Fujairah and exceeded 50 percent in Umm al-Quwain. Moreover, while women constituted 44.5 percent of voters in Abu Dhabi, 40.2 percent in Dubai, and 40.1 percent in Sharjah, the proportion fell to just 28.6 percent in Fujairah and 25.9 percent in the more "conservative" Ras al-Khaimah (Ajman and Umm al-Quwain were in-between with female proportions of 37.9 percent and 35.5 percent respectively.)[71] Following the October 3, vote, the UAE made regional history (and international headlines) as Amal al-Qubaisi, previously the Director General of the Abu Dhabi Education Council, who had been the first woman to be elected to the FNC back in 2006, became the female Speaker of any Arab parliamentary chamber.[72]

At the level of the individual emirates, local councils also developed in several areas, most notably in Sharjah. Initially launched in 1999, the forty-two-seat consultative council in Sharjah made headlines in January 2016 when half of the seats were opened to election for the first local vote in UAE history, held under the slogan *Take Part in Decision Making*. The Ruler of Sharjah, Sheikh Sultan bin Mohammed Al Qasimi, justified the retention of a hybrid council of elected and appointed members on the grounds that:

> Half of the council's members will be appointed in order to address any shortcomings that might result from the elections, such as if the minimum number of seven women members is not met or in case the council requires experienced members with special expertise.[73]

Unlike the FNC elections, all Emirati nationals of Sharjah origin were eligible to register to vote providing they were over 25 years of age, "of good standing in the community," had no criminal record, and were able to read and write. The 195 candidates included forty-three women and the significance of the event was captured by one female voter who told *The National* newspaper that "With this we prove our presence as Sharjah citizens, and we prove to everyone that we are with the democratic process."[74] Another female voter added specifically that "We need women to make important rules and speak on behalf of other women."[75] Turnout was noticeably higher than for the FNC elections at 57 percent for men and 42 percent for women and, while only one woman (Fatima Ali al-Muhairi) was elected, another (Khawla Abdulrahman al-Mulla) subsequently was appointed by the Ruler as the first female chair in the council's seventeen-year history.[76]

Similar to the appointment of Amal al-Qubaisi as the Speaker of the FNC, the appointment of a woman to head the Sharjah Consultative Council illustrates the broader public relations value of such "progressive" measures that appear, in the eyes of many external observers, to go against the grain of stereotyped views of regional politics. To be sure, neither the appointments, nor the carefully managed (semi-)electoral experiences, shifted in any meaningful way the structure or balance of political power either at the federal or the emirate levels. Neither has the electoral opening been anything like as robust as in Kuwait and Bahrain, where political "societies" and "clubs" have long articulated collective demands and pressured government decision-making processes. Rather, the process of political engagement in the UAE bears closer resemblance to similar outcomes in Saudi Arabia and Qatar, where the growth of representative institutions has served a technocratic purpose and widened the participatory involvement of qualified experts in policymaking.

Constitutional Gridlock

The growth and expansion of the FNC lay in the future in the 1970s and was not inevitable. At the time, three major challenges – two domestic and one regional – dominated the opening two decades of the federal experiment in the UAE between 1971 and the Gulf crisis of 1990. As such, it was by no means inevitable that the federal arrangement put in place in 1971 would thrive, or even survive, as many other such experiments in the previous decade had failed. British officials, in particular, viewed the early development of the UAE with a cautiously optimistic yet still ambivalent attitude. One such assessment was prepared in June 1973 by Anthony Harris, then a young official at the Middle East Department of the Foreign and Commonwealth Office in London who served later as the British Ambassador to the UAE between 1994 and 1998, and who cautioned that "in forming our policy towards the UAE we must bear in mind the chances of it falling apart" and added that:

> We still believe that the arrangement which we helped to establish in the Gulf in 1971 is a suitable basis for its development and stability. The UAE however is the most vulnerable of the new states. It is bedevilled by a lack of co-operation between the rulers of the constituent states, which is a continuation of their traditional distrust and tribal rivalries ... Although other rulers are not so important, they have considerable nuisance value, notably Sharjah and Ras al Khaimah.[77]

Among British officials serving "on the ground" in the UAE, the mood was more upbeat, with the Consul-General in Dubai, Albert Saunders, offering a particularly colorful assessment in December 1973:

> Tribal factions as previously identifiable are not dead ... [but] feuds, rivalries, petty jealousies and pride associated with the old system have already begun to and will in the long term completely shed their old crustacean shapes and emerge sideways in the new guise of nationalism with its crabby gamut ranging from extreme left to autocratic right wing so called progressive movements.[78]

Although the provisional constitution carefully delineated the separation of powers between the federal and emirate levels, as detailed in Chapter One, throughout the 1970s arguments raged over the balance of power between the two. Malcolm Peck has summarized succinctly the key fault-line as being:

> ... whether the union would take the form of a centralized state, with the seven emirates closely integrated under the Federal Government, or would pursue a gradualist approach towards greater federal power, with each emirate retaining its essential autonomy.[79]

Sheikh Zayed was the leading proponent of a stronger "presidential" system and during the decade he redistributed the oil wealth that accrued to Abu Dhabi in a bid to build stronger federal institutions. In February 1972, the federal government intervened in the succession process in Sharjah after the assassination of the sitting ruler, Sheikh Khalid bin Mohammed Al Qasimi by his predecessor whom the British had ousted seven years earlier (see Chapter Two) to ensure that Sheikh Sultan bin Mohammed Al Qasimi became ruler. Later in 1972, the federal government intervened again to end a brief yet violent territorial clash between Sharjah and Fujairah that killed four people, while another, more serious, incident between Fujairah and Ras al-Khaimah culminated in the accidental shooting down of a helicopter carrying one of the sons of the Ruler of Dubai over the disputed Masafi zone.[80] In his history of UAE foreign policy, Emirati scholar Hassan Hamdan al-Alkim suggests that the helicopter that was shot down was carrying the present Ruler of Dubai, Sheikh Mohammed bin Rashid Al Maktoum,[81] and that it actually related to another long-running frontier dispute involving an area of land astride the Dubai–Sharjah boundary, that was only resolved by a demarcation agreement in 1985 after an earlier attempt at international mediation had failed.[82] In his 1979 history of the UAE, revealingly subtitled "Unity in Fragmentation," Saudi academic Ali Mohammed Khalifa recorded Sheikh Zayed expressing his frustration over the persistence of inter-emirate flashpoints in 1976:

> I spent nearly a week in the northern emirates in an attempt to settle some border disputes of minor consequence ... I can say, with both bitterness and sorrow, that their disputes often involve a few tens of meters, and do you believe that we have not been able to build a hospital on a piece of real estate because two emirates claim sovereignty over it?[83]

Sheikh Rashid of Dubai led the alternative group that fiercely resisted the centralization of authority and advocated instead the preservation of strong emirate-level power. Dubai's more advanced economic development and bureaucratic and physical infrastructure meant the emirate was far less reliant upon support from the federal (or Abu Dhabi) level than the Northern Emirates. With the UAE's budget being funded almost entirely by Abu Dhabi, the leadership in Dubai was less directly vested in the federal level than its larger sister emirate, at least initially.

Moreover, the spirit of compromise between Sheikh Rashid and Sheikh Zayed that had made possible the union of 1971 was not infinite, and on several occasions during the mid- and late-1970s policy disagreements between Dubai and Abu Dhabi threatened to tear apart the fledgling federation.[84]

One example occurred in May 1976 in a stormy debate in the Federal National Council as recorded by al-Alkim:

> a disagreement arose in the FNC over the question of contributions by individual emirates to the federal budget. Abu Dhabi's representatives in the FNC urged other members not to pass the budget until the Finance Minister had made public the contribution of each emirate. Although Dubai was not mentioned in what was reported to be a "heated debate", some members demanded that all emirates should contribute in accordance with their national resources. Dubai's members responded to the "unspoken attack" by demanding information about the alleged deposits of the UAE Development Bank in foreign banks.[85]

Amid such tensions, the debates over constitutional arrangements escalated in 1976 when a twenty-eight-strong committee of ministers and FNC members was appointed to draft a permanent constitution as the provisional document agreed in 1971 indicated would happen after five years. Working with the assistance of a legal expert, the committee reflected the broader schism within the UAE as its members diverged over the degree of centralization that would (or would not) limit the powers of the individual emirates. Particular controversy centered over Article 23 of the provisional constitution, which gave the individual emirates control over all natural resources (and the resulting revenue from them). At issue was the question of whether resource revenues should be considered the property of the emirate or the nation as a whole. Supported by Sheikh Zayed, the supporters of greater federalization argued that Article 23 was impeding the redistribution of wealth across the UAE and called for the other emirates, particularly Dubai, to increase their contributions to the federal budget.[86] As a result, the constitutional committee recommended that each emirate would transfer 75 percent of its income to the federal treasury and retain just 25 percent locally while it also suggested that Abu Dhabi and Dubai would lose their veto in the Supreme Council of Rulers.[87]

The staunch opposition of the leaders of Dubai and Ras al-Khaimah to any modification of Article 23 and strengthening of the federal layer of authority pitched the UAE into a three-year constitutional impasse between 1976 and 1979. Abdullah Omran Taryam served in the Council of Ministers as Minister of Education and then Minister of Justice between 1973, when he was just twenty-five years old, and 1979, when he resigned, in part after concerted opposition to his educational reforms from Islamists and members of Muslim Brotherhood–affiliated groups in the UAE, and recounted later how Mehdi al-Tajir, the Ruler of Dubai's key adviser, "was of the opinion that the new constitution should not be adopted as a whole, but rather a step-by-step gradual process should be sought." As a result, "the committee's activity became largely ceremonial" and "reminiscent of those pre-union meetings which had been characterized by lobbying."[88] Frustration at the deadlock led Sheikh Zayed to declare that he would not accept a further term as President after his five-year mandate expired at the end of 1976. The draft constitution was presented to the Supreme Council of Rulers in July 1976 but the inability to reach consensus meant that the provisional constitution was extended for a further five-year period. This was a pragmatic outcome that reflected the deadlock between the two camps and "mindful that such a fundamental revision could jeopardize many of the compromises on which the federation was based."[89] Although the compromise meant that a crisis was averted and Sheikh Zayed continued as President, the failure to resolve the contested issues meant that it was only a matter of time before the matter resurfaced three years later.

An increase in regional volatility in early 1979 led to a renewed attempt to strengthen the federal powers of the union to better equip the UAE to confront the turbulent aftermath of the Islamic revolution in Iran. Members of the FNC and the Council of Ministers, which had developed a close working relationship, had initially held a joint meeting on June 27, 1978, just as the series of protests that ultimately ousted the Shah were gaining in momentum, and started a debate on how to strengthen the national government.[90] The FNC and the Council of Ministers met again on February 3, 1979, eighteen days after the Shah fled Iran, and submitted an eleven-point memorandum to the Supreme Council of Rulers that called for a significant increase in the powers of the federal government, including the abolition of internal borders, the unification of all armed forces, and the federal management of oil revenues. Indeed, the memorandum stated explicitly that "It is not acceptable that the state relies, in organizing its finances, on what one emirate might give it, and what another emirate does not."[91] The measures to create a stronger and more cohesive federal government were supported by the rulers of Abu Dhabi, Ajman, Fujairah, and Sharjah, and were discussed by the Supreme Council of Rulers on March 19, 1979.[92]

Simultaneously to the submission of the memorandum, a series of demonstrations in support of greater federal power were held across the UAE amid an outpouring of public support for Sheikh Zayed.[93] In his 1987 account of the formation of the UAE and its early years, Taryam described what happened on March 19, 1979 when the Supreme Council of Rulers met in Abu Dhabi to "discuss the federal issue and study the joint committee's memorandum":

> Thousands of citizens from various walks of life, students, government officials, and tribesmen, assembled in process from various emirates and marched towards the palace where the meeting was in progress. There they shouted slogans, calling upon the rulers to collaborate, demanding consolidation of the union, more powers for the federal institutions, support for the President of the state, and approval of the memorandum. They were not against their rulers, on the contrary they were supporting them, but they wanted them to come closer together for the sake of the future of the region … [94]

Taryam further describes how:

> The rulers interrupted their meeting and Sheikh Zayid came out and, deeply moved, made a speech before the crowds thanking them for their sentiments and their united stand and telling them it was his desires and that of the other rulers to try to realize what they were demanding. He then asked them to return to their work and leave their demands in his good care.[95]

The unprecedented public protests in support of the federation were not sufficient to break the deadlock as the Rulers of Dubai and Ras al-Khaimah withdrew from the meeting of the Supreme Council of Rulers and Abu Dhabi and Dubai subsequently traded verbal blows. For the second time in a decade, the Kuwaiti Foreign Minister (and future Emir from 2006), Sheikh Sabah al-Ahmad Al Sabah, was called in to mediate after an appeal by Sheikh Rashid of Dubai. As a result of Sheikh Sabah's mediation, and also that of King Khalid bin Abdulaziz Al Saud of Saudi Arabia, Dubai agreed to contribute to the federal budget and, crucially, Sheikh Rashid himself was named Prime Minister of the UAE on April 30, 1979, replacing his son (and eventual successor as Ruler of Dubai) Sheikh Maktoum bin Rashid Al Maktoum, who had become the inaugural Prime Minister of the UAE in 1971.[96] Ever since 1979, the Ruler of Dubai has continued to hold the Prime Ministership first through Sheikh Maktoum again (1990–2006) and subsequently through the current Ruler of Dubai, Sheikh Mohammed bin Rashid Al Maktoum.

In his comparative study of development trajectories in the UAE and Kuwait, Michael Herb has suggested that "From 1976 to 1979, a space opened in Emirati politics as a result of the dispute between Abu Dhabi and Dubai." Moreover, Herb has noted additionally that "Citizens used this political space to press for reforms that would create a UAE with a stronger federal government" and "a political system that would give citizens a stronger voice. In short, they wanted the UAE to be more like Kuwait" with its active and vocal parliamentary life.[97] Certainly, the eyewitness account provided by Taryam to the events of 1979 would suggest a groundswell of support not for any Western-centric notion of "democracy" but rather for a stronger and more functional federation that blended the "traditional" exercise of power and authority with modern bureaucratic forms of governance.

Slow Integration of Defense Capabilities

An issue closely intertwined with the inter-emirate disputes over the degree of federal power and authority was the question of whether, when, and how to integrate the local defense units in each emirate in a union-wide force. The defense and security forces were the last to integrate and were not fully unified until the mid-1990s, fully a quarter of a century after the formation of the UAE.[98] Four separate military forces continued to operate as individual units under local leadership – the Abu Dhabi Defense Force (ADDF), the largest and best equipped with more than 10,000 men divided into land, air, and sea branches; the Dubai Defense Force

(DDF), nearly 1,000 strong and set up by Dubai's current Ruler, Sheikh Mohammed bin Rashid Al Maktoum in the late 1960s; and the National Guard of Sharjah and a Mobile Force in Ras al-Khaimah, each with a strength of about 250 men. The autonomy of the individual units was closely guarded for much of the 1970s as it was felt that, according to Khalifa, "to transfer control over such a force to a higher authority might also mean the transfer, or, at least, the division of loyalty and allegiance of the men involved, something the rulers were reluctant to accept."[99]

The two issues intersected on November 6, 1976 when – in spite of the abovementioned constitutional deadlock – the Supreme Council of Rulers repealed Article 142 of the provisional constitution, which had allowed the individual emirates to establish their own defense forces, and stipulated instead that "only the union state had the right to establish armed land, sea, and air forces."[100] This attempt to merge the disparate emirate-level units into a unified armed force came after an Arab committee of military officers from Kuwait, Saudi Arabia, and Jordan had been invited to the UAE in 1975 to study and advise on the options for force integration.[101]

An enduring challenge was posed by the persistent and frequently overlapping arms purchases made by the individual emirates, which included orders of tanks, patrol boats, and even fighter aircraft. British officials at the Foreign and Commonwealth Office in London intervened on at least one occasion in the mid-1970s to query an attempt by Umm al-Quwain to purchase sophisticated weaponry.[102] The request by the Ruler of Umm al-Quwain for various armaments, including an advanced wire-guided anti-tank Beeswing missile, alarmed British Embassy officials in Abu Dhabi, who believed that they had a responsibility to inform the federal authorities of arms requests from the individual emirates in order to allay suspicions from Abu Dhabi that British arms sales were actively contributing to inter-state rivalry.[103] This particular request led the British Ambassador to the UAE, Donal McCarthy to question caustically whether Britain should "contemplate supplying sophisticated weaponry to a fishing village which, unlike Ras al Khaimah, we have never supplied in the past," and his Consul-General in Dubai, St John Armitage, to recommend that the UAE Foreign Minister, Ahmed al-Suwaidi, be informed "before this nonsense develops as well it might."[104]

Remarkably, and despite the fact that Sheikh Mohammed bin Rashid of Dubai was both the head of the Dubai Defense Force and the UAE Minister of Defense in the 1970s, it took a further two decades to finally unify all defense forces in the emirates into the Union Defense Force (UDF). The UDF was set up in 1978 when Sheikh Zayed merged the ADDF into what he hoped would become the umbrella military organization in the UAE and named his second-eldest son, Sheikh Sultan bin Zayed Al Nahyan, its first commander-in-chief. Although Sharjah supported the move to create a unified defense force and integrated the Sharjah National Guard into the UDF, unification was long opposed by Dubai, Ras al-Khaimah, and Umm al-Quwain. Thus, both the Dubai Defense Force and the small force maintained in Ras al-Khaimah maintained a separate existence up until the mid-1990s, when military unification belatedly was achieved in 1996 with the merger of the DDF and Ras al-Khaimah National Guard into the UDF.[105] As a result, Christopher Davidson has observed how, even as late as the 1990s:

> given that Dubai had been procuring equipment independently of Abu Dhabi for over twenty-five years, this meant that the newly reinforced and genuinely federal UAE Armed Forces was made up of largely incompatible hardware and munitions … Even more incongruous was the equipment used by the various other emirate-level defense forces which had followed Dubai's lead and had also agreed to integrate.[106]

The 1980s Consolidation

While the integration of defense forces remained a contentious issue throughout the 1980s, the decade did not witness a repeat of the constitutional crisis that had marked the period between 1976 and 1979. There were several reasons for this "rapprochement" among the emirates, one of which was the worsening regional situation, which will be analyzed below and in Chapter Five. Another was that, over time, the "founding fathers" – those rulers who had participated in the fraught negotiations to create the federation between 1968 and 1971 – gradually left the stage and a new generation of rulers came to power in a series of orderly transitions that contrasted markedly with some of the violent contestations of power that had characterized previous eras of change. The year 1981 saw the deaths of Sheikh Ahmed bin Humaid Al Nuaimi of Ajman and Sheikh Ahmed bin Rashid Al Mu'alla of Umm al-Quwain, who had been in power since 1928 and 1929 respectively, while in May Sheikh Rashid of Dubai suffered a severe stroke. Although Sheikh Rashid made a partial recovery and remained the Ruler of Dubai until his death in October 1990, progressively more power and responsibility devolved onto his sons, particularly his designated successor, Sheikh Maktoum bin Rashid, and his dynamic third son, Sheikh Mohammed bin Rashid.[107]

For Emirati historian Fatma al-Sayegh, the period between 1979 and 1986 was one of "accepting the federation." During this period, Dubai began to contribute systematically to the federal budget and by 1986 all seven emirates were doing so in accordance with their respective economic size. In December 1980, the UAE Currency Board was upgraded into a Central Bank seven years after its launch – without central bank power or regulatory authority – in May 1973, although the new entity initially struggled to gain credibility across the federation.[108] In particular, the Central Bank was unable to assist the Ras al-Khaimah National Bank when it collapsed in 1985 or prevent the collapse of Sharjah's four commercial banks after the emirate defaulted on a loan in 1989. Moreover, in 1991, the Central Bank "was relegated to being little more than a bystander" during the spectacular implosion of the Bank of Credit and Commerce International (BCCI), despite the fact that many of BCCI's "majority shareholders were resident in Abu Dhabi and included some of the greatest champions of federal integration."[109]

A report for the United States Congress into the collapse of BCCI carried out by Senators John Kerry and Hank Brown painted a highly unflattering portrait of the myriad links between the bank and senior figures in Abu Dhabi. Indeed, their report presented to the Senate Committee on Foreign Relations in December 1992 stated unequivocally that "There was no relationship more central to BCCI's existence from its inception than that between BCCI [in 1972] and Sheikh Zayed and the ruling family of Abu Dhabi ... Abu Dhabi was present at BCCI's creation as one of two providers of BCCI's capital. It was BCCI's largest depositor, and its largest borrower, and for most of BCCI's existence, its largest shareholder."[110] Damagingly, the Senate report suggested that:

> despite Abu Dhabi's withholding of essential witnesses and documents, BCCI financial records obtained to date by investigators, together with testimony and statements from BCCI insiders, outline a picture of the relationship which suggests that Abu Dhabi officials were indeed knowing participants in substantial wrongdoing pertaining to BCCI's activities in the United States and elsewhere, that members of the Abu Dhabi ruling family participated in risk-free investments in BCCI banks, and that Abu Dhabi officials engaged, as of April 1990 on some issues and on others much earlier, in a cover-up of fraudulent activity involving BCCI, which continues, in substantial part, to this day.[111]

It was not for nothing that the Kerry–Brown report stated that "In short, there is no question that the relationship between Abu Dhabi and BCCI was central to both, and that no understanding of BCCI is possible without an understanding of the Abu Dhabi relationship."[112] Following the collapse of BCCI, the UAE Central Bank instituted a creditor protection scheme for creditors of the local branches of the bank and the Government of Abu Dhabi agreed to compensate small creditors and contribute US$2.2 billion to BCCI's liquidation funds. Remarkably, while liquidators for the eight UAE branches of BCCI were appointed in 1996, their liquidation was completed only in June 2013.[113]

A December 2015 interview in *ArabianBusiness.com* with the Sharjah-born, Harvard-educated lawyer Essam al-Tamimi, illustrated the enduring challenge of updating laws originally formulated in the early years of the federation in order to meet the complex challenges of the twenty-first century. Al-Tamimi, founder in 1989 of the eponymous (Al Tamimi & Co.) law firm which subsequently grew into the largest indigenous law firm in the Middle East with more than 350 lawyers in nine countries, made the point that:

> Most of the country's laws were enacted in the late 1970s or early 1980s, barely a decade after the unification of the emirates. The legal map of the UAE has changed; particularly in the last 10 to 15 years, it has become a totally different country. The UAE has moved from being a traditional port-based Arabic state to an international hub used by companies to house goods or command regional banking and finance operations ... [114]

Central bank laws here date back to 1979. They have done a wonderful job in protecting the currency and fiscal structure but banking has changed since then, new ideas have evolved and there are areas where the law needs fixing ... the establishment of different types of investment vehicles and how they operate deserves a dedicated law, as it is a highly complex field ... [115]

Take construction. The whole process involves multiple contracts – procurement, leasing, supply – and when you increase the number of projects taking place, the probability is that a higher percentage are going to fall apart. Goods will not be delivered, goods will arrive but be defective, buildings will not be built in the way they were envisaged. And if one payment stops it has a knock-on effect on the others and you suddenly have the laborer who has not been paid, the building materials that have not arrived, a stalled property and an investor who has not got his return. That is why disputes are rising ... [116]

We've been very late to arbitration here ... It is not a popular form of dispute resolution, perhaps because it requires a certain maturity, and the large number of family businesses in the region in particular tend to [be] more emotional. There are certain laws – shipping is another – where you cannot deviate from the [global] norm. If you want to be a banking center, if you want to be an arbitration hub, you have to speak the same language and fly at the same altitude. If you fly differently, you fly alone.[117]

With domestic political issues becoming less controversial as the 1980s progressed and the federation matured (with the attempted coup in 1987 in Sharjah, discussed below, a notable exception), the primary focus of inter-emirate divergence shifted toward the Iran–Iraq War. Although the outbreak of the conflict in September 1980 was one of the triggers for the creation of the Gulf Cooperation Council the following May, the eight-year war left the UAE split down the middle as four emirates (Abu Dhabi, Ajman, Fujairah, and Ras al-Khaimah) backed Saddam Hussein's Iraq while the other three (Dubai, Sharjah, and Umm al-Quwain), leaned toward Iran, "their primary trading partner and the home of many of their merchant expatriates."[118] During this period, "Abu Dhabi, along with other Gulf Cooperation Council and Arab nations bankrolled Saddam's war against Teheran; Dubai served as a key transit point for war material destined for Iran."[119] The closer ties with the Khomeini regime favored by Dubai and Sharjah exposed the federal UAE government "to embarrassment and pressure from Saudi Arabia and other neighbors," which provided staunch political and financial support to Iraq throughout the war.[120]

An attempted takeover of power in Sharjah in June 1987 – when the Iran–Iraq War was still raging – provided an illustration that, while the constitutional disputes of the 1970s no longer posed an existential threat to the survival of the UAE, sharp inter-emirate divisions could still erupt with little warning. What was effectively a palace coup began when the ruler since 1972, Sheikh Sultan bin Mohammed Al Qasimi, made a private visit to the United Kingdom during the course of which his older brother, Sheikh Abdul Aziz bin Mohammed Al Qasimi, issued a statement that Sheikh Sultan had abdicated. Years later, the editor of Dubai's *Gulf News* newspaper recalled the hours of confusion that followed before it became clear that Sheikh Abdul Aziz's action had in fact left Abu Dhabi and Dubai on opposing sides in the factional struggle in Sharjah:

> Over the afternoon the facts on the ground became clear. The police and other security forces in Sharjah had taken control of the city and Shaikh Abdul Aziz had indeed announced himself as the new ruler in his brother's place. The take-over was not done with any consensus within the ruling family in Sharjah, and was vigorously disputed by Shaikh Sultan, so the move was not seen as a normal internal succession.
>
> Over the afternoon it emerged that the government of Abu Dhabi favored the take-over, and as a consequence of the Abu Dhabi position, the federal ministries moved to support Shaikh Abdul Aziz.
>
> However, the attitude of the rest of the UAE was not clear at all … All through the long evening, the federal government kept making it clear that the new ruler of Sharjah was Shaikh Abdul Aziz … Eventually, well after midnight, it became clear that the Government of Dubai did not support the coup, and it considered the rightful ruler of Sharjah to be Shaikh Sultan …
>
> Until the coup was resolved, Shaikh Sultan stayed in the Dubai Ruler's guest palace in Jumeirah … On June 20, the Supreme Council met in Al Ain and reinstated Shaikh Sultan as ruler, after hearing a report from a committee made up of their Highnesses the rulers of Ras al Khaimah, Ajman and Fujairah, and Shaikh Hamdan bin Rashid Al Maktoum.[121]

In spite of the abovementioned obstacles to formalizing the closer integration of the seven emirates and the temporary spikes in tension, the general direction throughout the 1980s and into the 1990s was toward gradual and incremental cooperation as the very *idea* of the UAE became more deeply embedded in everyday life. The very survival of the federation marked the UAE out as distinct from almost every other attempt to create federal entities in the Arab world between the 1950s and the 1970s. High-profile failures during this period included the short-lived political union of Egypt and Syria between 1958 and 1961 (the United Arab Republic) as well as the even-shorter Arab Federation that tied together the Hashemite kingdoms of Iraq and Jordan for five months prior to the bloody coup that toppled the Iraqi monarchy in July 1958. Moreover, a British attempt in 1962 to unify a collection of British-protected emirates and sultanates in south Yemen into the Federation of South Arabia also ended in ignominy five years later with the full withdrawal of British forces from Aden in the face of a violent anticolonial insurgency directed against them.[122]

No one factor in itself led to the widespread acceptance of the federation as fact; rather, it was a combination of the passage of time and generational change among the ruling elites and general population alike, the steady leadership and adherence to the spirit of political compromise and consensus provided by Sheikh Zayed together with the utilization of Abu Dhabi's oil reserves for the federation, and the external legacy of the 1990 invasion of Kuwait, which illustrated the dangers facing the smaller Gulf States in a volatile regional neighborhood, as well as the 1991 Gulf War, in which forces from the UAE participated as part of the multinational coalition put together by the George H.W. Bush administration in the United States.[123]

Speaking in 1996, on the twenty-fifth anniversary of the creation of the UAE, Sheikh Zayed offered his own perspective on the formation and durability of the union:

> We believe that wealth in itself is of no value unless it is dedicated to the prosperity and welfare of the people. States cannot be built upon wishes, nor can hopes be achieved by dreams. Our federation has stood firm in the face of crisis. It has prospered through hard work, perseverance and sacrifice and by placing the interests of the nation above any other.[124]

Fittingly, in 1996, in the UAE's twenty-fifth year, the long-running constitutional issue was laid to rest with the removal of the "provisional" aspect from the 1971 document while the reference to Abu Dhabi as the "temporary" capital pending the construction of the new Al Karama city also was dropped.[125] The decision to make permanent the two most visible symbols of statehood – the constitution and the capital – signified the durability of a federation that had, at times in its opening two decades, appeared to be destined for fragmentation and even failure.

Managing Political Transitions

When Sheikh Zayed died at the age of eighty-six on November 2, 2004 after a period of declining health the Presidency of the UAE and Rulership of Abu Dhabi passed smoothly to his oldest son and designated successor, Sheikh Khalifa bin Zayed Al Nahyan. While Sheikh Khalifa had been Heir Apparent for more than three decades since his appointment as Crown Prince of Abu Dhabi in 1966, his uncontested assumption of power in 2004 took some external observers by surprise. The primary reason for such uncertainty over the management of the leadership transition lay in a (mis)reading of familial dynamics among the many sons of Sheikh Zayed. In particular, the fact that Sheikh Khalifa had no full brothers was held to weaken his power in the face of powerful factions of brothers such as the six "Bani Fatima" sons of Sheikh Zayed's favored wife, Sheikha Fatima bint Mubarak al-Qitbi, in much the same way that King Abdullah of Saudi Arabia was believed to be at a significant disadvantage against his "Sudairi Seven" faction of brothers.[126] Sheikh Zayed's decision in December 2003 to bring his increasingly powerful third son (and elder Bani Fatima) Sheikh Mohammed bin Zayed formally into the line of succession (as Deputy Crown Prince of Abu Dhabi) further encouraged such speculation during the last year of his long life.[127]

The first (and, as of 2015, the only) presidential succession in the history of the UAE (as a federation) began on November 1, 2004 with the announcement of a

Cabinet reshuffle of the Council of Ministers. Said to have taken place with Sheikh Zayed's approval, the reshuffle included the appointment of the first female Cabinet member in UAE history as Sheikha Lubna bint Khalid Al Qasimi (a member of the ruling family of Sharjah) became Minister of Economics and Planning. Sheikha Lubna had largely been responsible for overseeing the automation of the federal government during her tenure as the Dubai branch manager of the General Information Agency.[128] Sheikh Zayed's death was announced the following evening, bringing to an end a period of some uncertainty that saw the UAE withdraw from hosting the annual GCC Summit scheduled for December 2004 and reportedly block internet "websites relating to pancreatic cancer."[129] A forty-day period of mourning was declared on November 4, although, as a British academic then resident in the UAE observed:

> It is worth noting how differently this period of mourning was interpreted by the different emirates ... in Fujairah, Umm al-Quwain, and Ajman ... the interpretation was very strict: in exactly the same way as Abu Dhabi, posters of Zayed were mounted everywhere ... In stark contrast, apart from a few large-scale mourning posters hung off the sides of (mainly non-governmental) buildings dotted around the city, in Dubai it was really "business as usual."[130]

Sheikh Khalifa's decades-long service as his father's deputy ruler and his chairmanship both of the Supreme Petroleum Council (SPC) and the Abu Dhabi Investment Authority (ADIA) meant that even prior to 2004 he had largely been responsible for the day-to-day running of governmental affairs, particularly in the key areas of overseeing energy and investment policy.[131] Sheikh Khalifa wielded great influence over economic policymaking in part through the work of the Research and Studies Department as well as through a sophisticated public relations unit in his Crown Prince's Court that was itself closely linked to the *Akhbar al-Arab* newspaper, and buttressed his social support by reaching out to influential tribal groups across Emirati society.[132]

However, after becoming president, power and influence – both at the federal level and in Abu Dhabi – began to ebb away from Sheikh Khalifa toward the bloc of "Bani Fatima" princes led by Crown Prince Sheikh Mohammed bin Zayed Al Nahyan (MBZ). Meanwhile, after the January 2006 accession of Sheikh Mohammed bin Rashid Al Maktoum (MBR) as Ruler of Dubai (and as Prime Minister of the UAE), the federal structure of the UAE came under growing strain as Dubai under the leadership of MBR began to follow increasingly autonomous positions on a number of key domestic and external issues. The empowerment of the Bani Fatima and the rise of Dubai converged in one of MBR's first acts as federal Prime Minister in February 2006 when he undertook a sweeping government reshuffle that reshaped the contours of the political landscape within the UAE in the new "post-Zayed" era. The two features that stood out in the reshuffle were the further empowerment of key "Bani Fatima" figures, most notably through the appointments of Sheikh Abdullah bin Zayed Al Nahyan, as UAE Foreign Minister and

Sheikh Hamdan bin Zayed Al Nahyan, as Deputy Prime Minister, and the appointment to formal Cabinet posts of several of MBR's most important Dubai-based advisors, among them Dr. Anwar Mohammad Gargash (who, as noted earlier in this chapter, became Minister of State for the Federal National Council), and the head of MBR's Executive Office in Dubai and Chief Executive of Dubai Holding, Mohammed Abdullah al-Gergawi, who was named Minister of State for Cabinet Affairs.[133]

As such, the smooth shift in presidential leadership from Sheikh Zayed to Sheikh Khalifa masked a number of other transitions that quietly gathered pace during the opening decade of Sheikh Khalifa's presidency. In addition to the two trends described above – the growth in influence of the "Bani Fatima" sheikhs in Abu Dhabi and the autonomy of Dubai under MBR's rule – the deaths of Sheikh Zayed in November 2004 and Sheikh Saqr bin Mohammed Al Qasimi of Ras al-Khaimah in October 2010 marked the definitive passing of the era of the seven leaders who came together between November 1971 and February 1972 to create the UAE. The successors to the "founding fathers," and particularly to Sheikh Zayed, all struggled to replicate their charismatic political authority and intensely personalized styles of rule in an increasingly bureaucratized world. As government became larger and more complex, rulers inevitably became separated from their people by intermediary layers of bureaucracy that weekly *majlis* meetings could, at best, only alleviate. In Sheikh Khalifa's case, the greater sense of remoteness was magnified by a series of health scares that eventually culminated in the debilitating stroke in January 2014 that marked his formal exit from public life, although for several years beforehand he had effectively ceded day-to-day control over policymaking to MBZ in Abu Dhabi and MBR at the federal level.[134]

Away from the federal political landscape, an unseemly spat that began in Ras al-Khaimah in 2003 illustrated how a badly managed or contested transition potentially could cause internal rifts and damage the carefully constructed international image of the UAE. One of the longest-serving rulers in the world since his accession in 1948, in 1999 the aging Sheikh Saqr bin Mohammed Al Qasimi devolved most of his powers to his elder son and longstanding Crown Prince, Sheikh Khalid bin Saqr Al Qasimi, only to replace Sheikh Khalid as Crown Prince with his much younger half-brother, Sheikh Saud bin Saqr Al Qasimi, in June 2003. The precise reasons for the sudden switch from Sheikh Khalid – who had been Crown Prince for more than four decades since 1961 – to Sheikh Saud are unknown, although Sheikh Khalid's well-publicized opposition to the US-led invasion of Iraq and his publicly stated support for an elected FNC in which women too could vote may have played a role. Reports at the time additionally speculated that the outspoken women's activism of Sheikh Khalid's wife represented another point of friction with his father. The new Crown Prince, Sheikh Saud, was, moreover, linked by blood and marriage to two of Dubai's most important merchant families, and may also have been seen as a more "business-friendly" leader-in-waiting than his half-brother.[135]

Sheikh Khalid and his supporters did not accept the change of Crown Prince and a sizable crowd chanting "with our souls and blood we defend you Khalid" threatened briefly to besiege the palaces belonging to Sheikh Saqr and Sheikh Saud before federal UAE forces intervened to maintain order. Sheikh Khalid himself vowed that "I will continue to oppose this decision for as long as I live" and complained that "I don't think this is my reward for 40 years of service."[136] In 2008, moreover, Sheikh Khalid set up an international lobbying network in the United States and the United Kingdom as part of a high-profile public relations campaign intended to secure his reinstatement as Crown Prince. This involved an elderly miniature steam railway enthusiast and solicitor in London's sleepy suburb of Uxbridge as well as the high-powered California Strategies public affairs group in the US.[137] In 2009 and 2010, as Sheikh Saqr weakened, Sheikh Khalid mounted a lobbying blitz in Washington, DC, which included meetings with Members of Congress, the formation of a dedicated website and early Twitter feed (rak-forthepeople.com), as well as advertisements on public buses in the US capital that thanked the American people for their support of Sheikh Khalid.[138] Rather more negatively, Sheikh Khalid initiated a media campaign designed to portray Ras al-Khaimah as the weak point in the "war on terror" and link it with international criminal and smuggling groups, Al Qaeda, and Iran. Illustrative of this was a speech given by Sheikh Khalid in Washington, DC, in February 2010, in which he alleged (without offering supporting evidence) that:

> I am troubled that the current regime has allowed RAK to devolve into a rogue state and strategic gateway for Iran … Iran has taken advantage of our free trade zones, using them as a transfer point to smuggle cargo, including arms, electronics, weapons parts, drugs and even humans to Africa, Europe and Asia.[139]

Even more damagingly to the international profile of the UAE, California Strategies commissioned a private security expert in the US to compile a report on the security of Ras al-Khaimah that highlighted putative links to global terror networks to cause maximum damage to Sheikh Saud. The report duly pressed all the red buttons for US policymakers as it suggested that Ras al-Khaimah had become "a thoroughfare for smuggling drugs weapons, explosives and personnel from Iran, Afghanistan and specific African countries" as well as "a point of entry for terrorists" and "a base of operation allowing Iranian personnel to operate within the confines of the UAE." For good measure, the report alleged additionally that "RAK's open and loosely controlled ports provide supply lines to counter any Iranian sanctions imposed by the international community," and sought to associate Sheikh Saud with the uncovering of an Al Qaeda-linked cell in 2009 that had allegedly planned to target the Burj Khalifa in Dubai.[140]

In the event, Sheikh Khalid made an abortive attempt to seize power after Sheikh Saqr died at dawn on October 27, 2010 as he entered Ras al-Khaimah and proclaimed himself ruler. However, federal security forces surrounded Sheikh Khalid's compound and placed him under "palace arrest" as the Federal Supreme Council acknowledged Sheikh Saud's accession. As in 2003, federal pressure was instrumental in determining the pathway of succession and putting an end to the attempted contestation of power – just as had occurred in Sharjah in the aftermath of the aborted coup there in 1987.[141]

The Islamist Challenge

The sheer rapidity of economic development that took place in the UAE during the opening two decades of the federation did not take place entirely within a political vacuum. The growth of Arab nationalism in Dubai already has been examined while the rise of educated urban elites in Sharjah and other emirates magnified broader awareness of political issues and ideologies. As in other Gulf States that also experienced an oil-fueled socio-economic transformation at this time, education emerged as a critical battleground between Islamists and ruling families. This was, in part, due to the influential early role of teachers and other professionals from states such as Egypt, Palestine, and Jordan who settled in the Gulf and exercised a formative role in the development of educational (and legal) institutions; this was particularly pronounced in Kuwait and in Qatar. Similarly, the introduction of the first "modern" schools in the 1950s and 1960s and the return home of the first generation of students who had ventured abroad for their studies provided a boost to local and nationalist presses and the first cultural clubs that began to appear in the years immediately prior to 1971.[142] As Mohammed Morsy Abdullah noted in his history of the early years of the UAE, "education soon became a force in accelerating cultural and political change" as:

> With grants from Kuwait and Qatar these students continued their studies at universities, mainly in Cairo, Beirut, Damascus and Baghdad. Two of the earliest students to leave in search of educational facilities, one from Ras al-Khaimah and the other from Sharjah, finally obtained scholarships in Leningrad … The progress made in education led inevitably to an awareness of the contemporary Arab nationalist movement, and the help offered by the Arab countries strengthened the ties between the Trucial Coast and their Arab brothers.[143]

In addition to Arab nationalists, many of the incoming professionals either were members of the Muslim Brotherhood fleeing the crackdown on the organization in Egypt in the 1960s or were sympathetic to the Brotherhood ideals they had been exposed to as students in major Arab capitals. This included a cadre of Emirati students and activists who had studied in Egypt and in Kuwait and who formed, in 1974, the Association for Reform and Guidance (*Jamiat al-Islah wa Taujih*) in Dubai. Inspired by the ideals of the Muslim Brotherhood but claiming to be operationally and ideologically autonomous, initially *Al-Islah* was not only tolerated but cautiously welcomed by several of the rulers in the UAE, as Mansour al-Noqaidan, the (Saudi) Chief Editor of the Dubai-based Al Mesbar Center for Studies and Research, noted in an otherwise-hostile account of the organization published in 2012, as the founding members approached the Ruler of Dubai, Sheikh Rashid bin Saeed Al Maktoum, for permission to register the Society and:

> Sheikh Mohammed bin Khalifa Al Maktoum was the first Chairman of the Board of Directors of the Society. Meanwhile, Sheikh Rashid bin Saeed Al Maktoum volunteered to build the Society's headquarters in Dubai at his own expense, which he followed by establishing two more branches of the Society in the emirates of Ras al-Khaimah and Fujairah. It was also said that the then Head of State, late Sheikh Zayed bin Sultan Al Nahyan, donated a plot of land for establishing a branch of the Society in Abu Dhabi in the late 1970s, but the decision to establish such a branch was put off later.[144]

Important assistance to *Al-Islah* during this formative period also was extended by the Kuwaiti branch of the Muslim Brotherhood, that helped both administratively and through the organization of a series of exchanges, meetings, and summer camps in Kuwait.[145] Within the UAE, an important patron was the Ruler of Ras al-Khaimah, Sheikh Saqr bin Mohammed Al Qasimi, who was said to have been a member of *Al-Islah* and whose cousin, Sheikh Sultan bin Kayed Al Qasimi, served reportedly as Chairman of the organization.[146]

The initial policy of acquiescence toward *Al-Islah* by the UAE authorities manifested itself in the appointment of two members of the organization to Cabinet positions in the 1970s. A founding member of *Al-Islah* from Ras al-Khaimah, Saeed Abdullah Salman, became Minister of Housing in the very first federal Cabinet formed after the formation of the UAE in 1971 and eight years later replaced Abdullah Omran Taryam as Minister of Education, while in 1977 Mohammed Abdulrahman al-Bakr was appointed Minister of Justice and Islamic Affairs and Endowments (*Awqaf*).[147] One prominent member of *Al-Islah* noted retrospectively that, in the early years, "the government was happy with us, they trusted us at that time."[148] As Courtney Freer has observed in her study of *Al-Islah*, by allocating members of the group positions in government, "the state allowed them a platform through which they could enact policies that remained in place for decades – particularly in the education sector."[149] Thus, by the end of the 1970s, the two ministerial portfolios of Education and Justice enabled *Al-Islah* "to establish a firm foothold in the religious and educational institutions of the UAE."[150]

In large part due to their prominence and influence within the education sector, relations between the federal government and *Al-Islah* began to cool during the 1980s in a process that accelerated in the 1990s as members of the group drifted into what the UAE authorities perceived as overt political activism.[151] The concern of the federal government at the potential extension of *Al-Islah* influence among Emirati society was well-merited as members of the group had by the start of the 1980s occupied key positions within the educational establishment in the UAE. Members of *Al-Islah* waged a campaign against Abdullah Omran Taryam during his tenure as Education Minister (1973–1979), documented by al-Noqaidan:

After Abdullah Omran took over the Ministry of Education, the group sought to thwart attempts to teach English in primary schooling … The group further fought against inclusion of music courses and urged female students not to attend music and dancing classes … Instead, the group started such kind of lectures and seminars dealing with the danger of westernization and intellectual invasion.[152]

When Saeed Abdullah Salman was appointed Minister of Education in 1979 he also became the Chancellor of the newly created UAE University, formed to be the flagship university within the UAE but which also developed into a hotbed of student activism by university members drawn from *Al-Islah*.[153] Indeed, Sheikh Sultan bin Kayed Al Qasimi, the cousin of the Ruler of Ras al-Khaimah, directed the Curriculum Division within the Ministry of Education between 1977 and 1983, the year that both *Al-Islah* Cabinet members (Salman at Education and al-Bakr at Justice) were dismissed.[154]

Al-Islah influence survived the loss of ministerial posts in 1983 and continued to percolate through Emirati society for another decade until the start of the first concerted government crackdown on the group in 1994. Control of student unions and the organization of summer camps and other organized activities, such as Scout groups, for Emirati youth was one source of unease for the authorities, as was the influence of *Al-Islah* preachers at increasingly politicized Friday prayers.[155]

Synchronously, during the 1980s, *Al-Islah* published a regular magazine of the same name which portrayed the organization as a defender of traditional social values against the perceived encroachment of "Western" values and issues such as the sale of alcohol in the UAE.[156] One example of this occurred in July 1980 when the magazine published "An Urgent Telegram to the General Manager of Dubai TV" asking whether he aimed "at spreading vice and corruption among the youth of this Muslim nation, or is there someone who is pushing him to do such a shameful thing? If you cannot stop this overwhelming flood of corruption, you should submit your resignation, as that is more honorable."[157] By the late 1980s, a number of articles that appeared in *Al-Islah* indicated that the organization was moving beyond social criticism into outright opposition to government education policy. Hence, in 1987, *Al-Islah* campaigned sharply against the acting Minister of Education, Ahmed Humaid al-Tayer, while a year later the magazine virulently opposed the introduction of a Basic Education Project, a pre-university course in Arabic, English, and Mathematics for incoming students at UAE University.[158]

The first overt clash between *Al-Islah* and the political authorities occurred in October 1988 when the magazine ceased publication for six months and subsequently adopted "a more subdued tone" when it reappeared in April 1989. Over the next five years, the magazine dropped much of its political edge and focused instead on less directly sensitive aspects such as "the risk posed by foreigners against the culture and identity of the country."[159] Also in 1988, the Ministry of Awqaf (Religious Endowments) at the emirate level in Dubai started requiring preachers to submit in advance written copies of their Friday sermons and avoid all areas of potential controversy.[160] However, *Al-Islah* influence within the education sector continued unabated through the early 1990s with an additional area of government concern emerging over the group's control over the allocation of student scholarships which were given almost exclusively to sympathizers and members.[161]

Mounting concern at *Al-Islah's* stature as a potentially powerful alternative focus of loyalty led to the start of a systematic federal government crackdown on their activities in 1994 when the group's headquarters in Dubai was closed down and transferred to Ras al-Khaimah. One reason for the shift in government attitude was a visit to the Gulf States, including the UAE, by Egyptian President Hosni Mubarak, during the course of which he warned Gulf rulers of the growing threat that he saw from Islamist groups, which were waging a low-intensity insurgency in Egypt at the time. Mubarak also stepped up Egyptian support for security agencies in GCC states, again including the UAE, with an (unnamed) member of *Al-Islah* claiming to *Gulf States Newsletter* (in 2012) that "After Mubarak's visit to the UAE, Sheikh Zayed gave the file to state security for them to investigate and because state security's survival is based on presenting threats they made the case against us."[162]

Also in 1994, the federal government replaced the hitherto-independent Board of Directors of *Al-Islah* with government appointees and began to make it progressively more difficult for *Al-Islah* to function autonomously from government control. The years after 1994 were a period of "silent tension" and "soft pressure" as *Al-Islah* retreated to its stronghold in Ras al-Khaimah, where the protection of Sheikh Saqr bin Mohammed caused periodic tension between the emirate and Abu Dhabi.[163] In the late 1990s and early 2000s, many members of *Al-Islah* who had worked, some for many years, in the Ministry of Education began to be transferred to jobs elsewhere in the public sector. Among those affected was Mohammed al-Roken, a lawyer and human rights activist (and one of the "UAE94" detained in 2012 – see Chapter Six), who was banned from writing his regular newspaper column in 2000 and removed from his position as Vice Dean of *Sharia* and Law at UAE University two years later. After 9/11, moreover, the authorities' disquiet about Islamist activities within the UAE increased further with the discovery that two of the nineteen hijackers had been Emirati citizens (see Chapter Five). As a result, more than 250 people, mainly Islamists, were arrested between 2001 and 2003 as officials, particularly in Abu Dhabi, increasingly came to view such groups as a threat to state security.[164]

In August 2003, a series of meetings took place between three senior members of *Al-Islah* and the then-Deputy Crown Prince of Abu Dhabi, Sheikh Mohammed bin Zayed Al Nahyan, during which Mohammed bin Zayed reportedly asked the delegation from *Al-Islah* "to choose between renouncing their Islamist ideology, ceasing the public propagation of their ideas, or remaining affiliated with the Brotherhood but transferring out of the education sector."[165] However, the meetings broke up without agreement from *Al-Islah* and, in the years that followed, the political authorities in the UAE continued to transfer members of *Al-Islah* out of educational positions and into less directly sensitive areas of employment. At this stage, in the mid-2000s, government policy in the UAE toward *Al-Islah* still resembled a pattern of quiet harassment rather than the full-blown attempt to suppress the organization that commenced in 2011.

During this period, *Al-Islah* was cushioned from the full force of a security crackdown by the protected space offered by the aging ruler of Ras al-Khaimah who was, after Sheikh Zayed's death in 2004, the last surviving member of the seven original founders of the UAE and thus an elder of considerable prestige. Sheikh Saqr bin Mohammed's death in October 2010 removed this influential protective layer less than three months before the Arab Spring provided state security hawks with the opportunity to systematically dismantle the group and eliminate its perceived "threat" once and for all.[166]

Emerging GCC Focus

This chapter has focused primarily on the consolidation of federal structures and the maintenance of the integrity of the UAE in the formative decades of state-building after 1971. As a small, newly independent state in a volatile regional neighborhood, the UAE also faced considerable challenges of survival during its first two decades of existence. Chapter Six will examine how Iran under the Shah ruthlessly took advantage of Britain's withdrawal from the Gulf to seize three islands belonging to Sharjah and Ras al-Khaimah on the very eve of the formation of the UAE. However, in common with Bahrain and Qatar – the other two British protected states that became independent in 1971 – and Kuwait, which had become independent a decade earlier, in 1961, policymakers in the UAE faced a difficult decade in the 1970s without their traditional external guarantor of security. This vulnerability manifested itself in the massing of Iraqi troops on the Kuwaiti border less than a week after Kuwaiti independence in June 1961 and persistent Iranian territorial claims on Bahrain in addition to the Shah's islands grab in the UAE.

The 1970s represented therefore a decade of great danger for the new states on the shore of the Arabian Peninsula, and for the only time in the past two centuries there was no "great power" presence in the Gulf as Britain was until 1971 and the United States gradually assumed after 1980. There thus was a greater onus on the Gulf States to make their own arrangements for security and survival, and just as six of the seven sheikhdoms of the Trucial States came together to create the UAE in 1971 so six of the seven states in the Arabian Peninsula (barring Yemen) announced the formation of the Gulf Cooperation Council (GCC) at a regional Summit that took place in Abu Dhabi in May 1981. Although at least three different proposals for a Gulf-wide entity had been floated by Kuwait, Saudi Arabia, and Oman in the late 1970s, the GCC was, in practice, a defensive reaction to the systemic regional shocks of the Iranian revolution and the outbreak of the Iran–Iraq War. Emirati political scientist Abdulkhaleq Abdulla has argued persuasively that the speed with which the GCC came together indicated that it was "a panic response to a situation of profound uncertainty" following the twin regional shocks of the Islamic Revolution in Iran in 1979 and the outbreak of the Iran–Iraq War in 1980. Abdulla suggested that:

... there was an immediate, ad hoc reaction to the turbulent regional events of 1979–80 ... the typically recalcitrant and normally conservative Arab Gulf States took less than three months (February–May 1981) to unanimously agree on the broad ideas and goals of the GCC, approve of its final charter, sign many intricate documents on rules and structures, and hastily announce its formal birth. Such extraordinary speed is practically unheard of in the history of regional integration and is particularly uncharacteristic of the rulers of the six Arab Gulf states whose normal tendency is to procrastinate on a decision with potential ramifications on their sovereignty.[167]

The new body was neither a political nor a military alliance, and it lacked an integrative supra-national decision-making institution for the sharing of sovereignty, akin to the European Commission. It had no explicit treaty-based foreign policymaking power as the Charter called only for a coordination of foreign policy and political cooperation. Its member governments retained responsibility for almost all aspects of political and economic policy, and resisted any putative limitations on their sovereignty.[168] Saudi Arabia apart, the other five members were still young nations in the process of state and bureaucratic consolidation, and they were also wary of the potential for Saudi dominance or hegemony within the new organization, whether in terms of population, size of armed forces, intra-regional trade flows and geostrategic importance.[169] In part to obviate this imbalance of power, the GCC presented itself from the beginning as a cautious status quo entity that intended to shield its member states and societies from the trans-national and unconventional threat of the spill-over of instability from Iran and Iraq.[170]

The UAE constitutes by some distance the second largest economy of the six GCC states with about a 20 percent share of overall GCC GDP compared with a figure of about 45 percent for much-larger Saudi Arabia, and Sheikh Fahim bin Sultan Al Qasimi, a member of the ruling family of Ras al-Khaimah, served as the GCC Secretary-General between 1993 and 1996. While the GCC has consistently been unable to agree or formulate common approaches to major foreign policy issues, such as relations with Iraq, Iran, and Yemen, and key relationships, such as with the United States, remain largely run on bilateral country-specific levels, its durability nevertheless has marked it as one of the more successful cooperative entities in the Arab world. Greater progress has been made in the economic sphere with the launch of a common market and customs union in the 2000s, although the UAE notably withdrew in May 2009 from the flagship GCC project of monetary union just days after the announcement that the planned GCC Central Bank would be based in Riyadh. The UAE had campaigned hard for the bank to be based in Abu Dhabi, in part to offset the Saudi-heavy structure of the GCC with its secretariat in Riyadh, and comments made at the time by the UAE Minister of Economy, Sultan bin Saeed al-Mansouri, reflected the level of anger at the decision:

The UAE was the most entitled to host the GCC Central Bank in Abu Dhabi as its banking sector is strong and its Central Bank is one of the world's best.

The non-selection of the UAE for hosting the GCC Central Bank did not take into consideration the state's importance and its economic development.[171]

One reason why the decision not to locate the GCC Central Bank in Abu Dhabi came as such a shock to Emirati officials is that many believed that an informal undertaking had been given in 2004 when the UAE proposed Abu Dhabi as an ideal site for a common bank.[172] Despite the strong support hitherto given to the monetary union project by the Governor of the UAE's own well-regarded Central Bank, Sultan Nasser al-Suwaidi, the sudden Emirati withdrawal left the monetary union project floundering and unable to meet its self-imposed 2010 deadline; in the words of HSBC's Dubai-based chief economist for the Gulf region, Simon Williams, "A GCC monetary union without the UAE would lack substance and relevance."[173]

And yet, the GCC has endured and has evolved considerably in the three-and-a-half decades since its creation. While agreement, still less consensus, on the "big-ticket" items that involve the pooling of sovereignty and issues of foreign policy will likely continue to remain elusive, progress on more "technocratic" issues such as the standardization of legal and regulatory frameworks and the creation of a customs union and common market – has proceeded quicker. Such practical cooperation has grafted a pronounced regionalist identity onto the GCC even if the organization continues to lack the supranational institutional "glue" that has characterized the growth of the European Union. In 2009, UAE officials played a key role in harmonizing "rules of origin" regulations ahead of the introduction of the GCC Customs Union even as they withdrew in acrimony from the currency union project.[174] The incongruous pathways – of closer technocratic integration on the one hand and sudden policy divergence on the other – illustrated the unresolved challenges at the heart of the GCC as the six member states balance, sometimes uneasily, the maintenance of national sovereignty with collective approaches to regional affairs.[175]

In 2021, the UAE will celebrate its half-century with a series of high-profile events, including the Dubai World Expo and the planned Emirates Mars Mission. Both the expo and the space mission will be designed to showcase the UAE as a dynamic, innovative, and youthful society that rises above its region and transcends negative international stereotypes of the Middle East. The appointment of a much-publicized Minister of Youth in 2015 and the series of Youth Councils inaugurated across the seven emirates in 2016, together with the development of innovative new types of electronic ("e") and mobile ("m") government, appear to constitute an attempt to carefully balance the demands of a highly networked young society for interaction among themselves and with the state in a manner that minimizes the political aspects of such interaction.[176] Moreover, the Mohammed bin Rashid Space Center in Dubai exemplified the emphasis on youth and innovation as it featured an all-Emirati seventy-five-strong team with an average age of thirty-two.[177] These themes form the backbone of the following chapters as well, which analyze how and why policymakers in the UAE acquired such international focus in the 2000s and invested so heavily in creating a sophisticated – and nuanced – global image with the aspirant "global cities" of Dubai and, later, Abu Dhabi, at its heart.

Notes

1 Donald Hawley, *The Trucial States* (London: George Allen & Unwin Ltd, 1970), p. 244.
2 Simon Smith, *Britain's Revival and Fall in the Gulf: Kuwait, Bahrain, Qatar, and the Trucial States, 1950–1971* (Abingdon: Routledge, 2004), pp. 50–51.
3 David Commins, *The Gulf States: A Modern History* (London: I.B. Tauris, 2012), p. 189.
4 Ibrahim al-Abed, "The Historical Background and Constitutional Basis to the Federation," in Ibrahim al-Abed and Peter Hellyer (eds), *United Arab Emirates: A New Perspective* (London: Trident Press, 2001), p. 127.
5 Frauke Heard-Bey, *From Trucial States to United Arab Emirates* (Dubai: Motivate Publishing, 2007), pp. 320–321.
6 Ibid., p. 323.
7 Afshan Ahmed, "The UAE's History Lesson," *The National*, November 8, 2011.
8 Abdullah Omran Taryam, *The Establishment of the United Arab Emirates 1950–1985* (London: Croon Helm, 1987), p. 47.
9 Helene von Bismarck, "'A Watershed in our Relations with the Trucial States': Great Britain's Policy to Prevent the Opening of an Arab League Office in the Persian Gulf in 1965," *Middle Eastern Studies*, 47(1), 2011, p. 3.
10 Ibid., p. 3.
11 M.W. Daly, *The Last of the Great Proconsuls: The Biography of Sir William Luce* (San Diego, CA: Nathan Berg, 2014), pp. 240–241.
12 Ibid., p. 241.
13 Heard-Bey, *From Trucial States to United Arab Emirates*, p. 322.
14 Ash Rossiter, "Britain and the Development of Professional Security Forces in the Gulf Arab States, 1921–71: Local Forces and Informal Empire," Ph.D. Dissertation, University of Exeter, 2014, p. 195.
15 Helene von Bismarck, *British Policy in the Persian Gulf, 1961–1968: Conceptions of Informal Empire* (London: Palgrave Macmillan, 2013), pp. 137–137.
16 Rosemarie Said Zahlan, *The Making of the Modern Gulf States: Kuwait, Bahrain, Qatar, the United Arab Emirates and Oman* (Reading: Ithaca Press, 1989), p. 117.
17 Von Bismarck, *British Policy*, p. 139.
18 Ibid.
19 Glencairn Balfour Paul, *Bagpipes in Babylon: A Lifetime in the Arab World and Beyond* (London: I.B. Tauris, 2006), pp. 198–199.
20 Von Bismarck, *British Policy*, p. 160.
21 Quoted in von Bismarck, *British Policy*, p. 161.
22 Archibald Lamb, "Annual Review of Events in Abu Dhabi in 1965," in Robert Jarman, *Political Diaries of the Arab World: The Persian Gulf. Volume 24: 1963–1965* (Chippenham: Archive Editions, 1998), p. 520.
23 Daly, *Last of the Great Proconsuls*, p. 235.
24 Ibid., p. 233.
25 Ibid., p. 234.
26 Simon Smith, *Britain's Revival and Fall in the Gulf: Kuwait, Bahrain, Qatar, and the Trucial States, 1950–1971* (London: Routledge, 2004), p. 63.
27 Davidson, *Oil and Beyond*, p. 46.
28 Wilfred Thesiger, *Arabian Sands* (London: Penguin, 1991 edition), pp. 268–269.
29 Davidson, *Oil and Beyond*, pp. 42–43.
30 Von Bismarck, *British Policy*, p. 169.
31 Balfour Paul, *Bagpipes in Babylon*, pp. 204–205.

32 Smith, *Britain's Revival and Fall*, p. 65.
33 Ibid., p. 66.
34 Taryam, *Establishment of the United Arab Emirates*, p. 54.
35 Christopher Davidson, *Abu Dhabi: Oil and Beyond* (London: Hurst & Co, 2009), pp. 50–51.
36 Shohei Sato, "Britain's Decision to Withdraw from the Persian Gulf, 1964–68: A Pattern and a Puzzle," *Journal of Imperial and Commonwealth History*, 37(1), 2009, pp. 103–104.
37 Quoted in W. Taylor Fain, *American Ascendance and British Retreat in the Persian Gulf Region* (Basingstoke: Palgrave Macmillan, 2008), p. 166.
38 Jeffrey Macris, *The Politics and Security of the Gulf: Anglo-American Hegemony and the Shaping of a Region* (London: Routledge, 2010), p. 156.
39 Sato, *Britain's Decision to Withdraw*, p. 108.
40 Quoted in James Onley, "Britain and the Gulf Sheikhdoms, 1820–1971: The Politics of Protection," Georgetown University School of Foreign Service in Qatar, Center for International and Regional Studies, *Occasional Paper No. 4* (2009), p. 22.
41 Al-Abed, *Historical Background and Constitutional Basis*, p. 128.
42 Smith, *Britain's Revival and Fall*, pp. 80–81.
43 Ibid., pp. 92–97.
44 Ibid., pp. 103–104.
45 Al-Abed, *Historical Background and Constitutional Basis*, p. 132.
46 Taryam, *Establishment of the United Arab Emirates*, p. 176.
47 Malcolm Peck, "Formation and Evolution of the Federation and its Institutions," in Ibrahim al-Abed and Peter Hellyer (eds), United Arab Emirates: A New Perspective (London: Trident Press, 2001), p. 151.
48 Ibid.
49 Frauke Heard-Bey, "The United Arab Emirates: Statehood and Nation-Building in a Traditional Society," *Middle East Journal*, 59(3), 2005, p. 360.
50 Ibid., p. 363.
51 Heard-Bey, *From Trucial States to United Arab Emirates*, pp. 270–271.
52 J.E. Peterson, "The Future of Federalism in the United Arab Emirates," in H. Richard Sindelar III and J.E. Peterson (eds), *Crosscurrents in the Gulf: Arab Regional and Global Interests* (London: Routledge, 1988), p. 208.
53 "Late Minister Saif Ghubash is Honoured with Road in Abu Dhabi Named after Him," *The National*, February 22, 2014.
54 Peterson, *Future of Federalism*, p. 208.
55 Andrea Rugh, *The Political Culture of Leadership in the United Arab Emirates* (New York: Palgrave Macmillan, 2007), p. 228.
56 Christopher Davidson, "The United Arab Emirates: Economy First, Politics Second," in Joshua Teitelbaum (ed.), *Political Liberalization in the Persian Gulf* (London: Hurst & Co, 2009), p. 238.
57 A full list of UAE Federal Ministries can be found at http://www.uaeinteract.com/government/ministry.asp.
58 Shahid Jamal Ansari, *Political Modernization in the Gulf* (Delhi: Northern Book Center, 1998), p.116.
59 Michael Herb, *The Wages of Oil: Parliaments and Economic Development in Kuwait and the UAE* (Ithaca, NY: Cornell University Press, 2014), p. 52.
60 Ansari, *Political Modernization*, pp. 116–117.
61 Malcolm Peck, *The United Arab Emirates: A Venture in Unity* (Boulder, CO: Westview Press, 1986), p. 131.
62 Fahim bin Sultan Al Qassemi, "A Century in Thirty Years: Sheikh Zayed and the United Arab Emirates," *Middle East Policy*, 6(4), 1999, p. 2.
63 Fadi Salem, "Enhancing Trust in e-Voting Through Knowledge Management: the Case of the UAE," *Dubai School of Government Research Paper*, June 2007, pp. 5–6.

64 May al-Dabbagh and Lana Nusseibeh, "Women in Parliament and Politics in the UAE: A Study of the First Federal National Council Elections," *Dubai School of Government/Ministry of Federal National Council Affairs paper*, February 2009, p. 22.

65 Ibid., p. 29.

66 Ibid., p. 32.

67 "FNC Women Left to Wonder Why," *The National*, October 10, 2011.

68 "Some FNC Members Unhappy with Pace of Current Term," *The National*, March 17, 2015.

69 "UAE's Electoral Base for FNC Polls gets 66% Wider," *Khaleej Times*, July 6, 2015.

70 "Electoral College Increases," *Gulf States News*, 39(997), July 16, 2015, p. 8.

71 "Small Steps Forward in Elections for UAE's 'Gradualist' Democracy," *Gulf States News*, 39(1002), October 15, 2015.

72 "UAE Elects First Female Parliamentary Speaker," *Gulf News*, November 18, 2015.

73 "Election Decision for Sharjah Consultative Council Hailed," *Gulf News*, June 10, 2015.

74 "Sharjah Voters Honoured to Take Part in UAE's First Local Election," *The National*, January 28, 2016.

75 "Historic Sharjah Election Worth the Trip for Many Voters," *The National*, January 28, 2016.

76 "First Woman Chairperson of Sharjah Consultative Council Elected," *Gulf News*, February 11, 2016.

77 Dispatch from A. D. Harris (Middle East Department) to P. R. H. Wright (Head of Middle East Department) and R. M. Hunt (Assistant Head of Middle East Department), June 19, 1973, London, *The National Archives*, file FCO 8/2142.

78 Letter from Donald J. McCarthy (British Ambassador to Abu Dhabi, 1973–77) to Patrick Richard Henry Wright (Head of Middle East Department, FCO, 1972–74), December 31, 1973, London, *The National Archives*, file FCO 8/2354.

79 Peck, *Formation and Evolution,* p. 154.

80 Taryam, *Establishment of the United Arab Emirates*, p. 228.

81 Hassan Hamdan al-Alkim, *The Foreign Policy of the United Arab Emirates* (London: Saqi Books, 1989), p. 39.

82 Taryam, *Establishment of the United Arab Emirates*, p. 232.

83 Ali Mohammed Khalifa, *The United Arab Emirates: Unity in Fragmentation* (London: Croon Helm, 1979), p. 103.

84 Heard-Bey, *Statehood and Nation-Building*, p. 364.

85 Al-Alkim, *Foreign Policy of the United Arab Emirates*, p. 42.

86 Christopher Davidson, *Dubai: The Vulnerability of Success* (London: Hurst & Co, 2008), p. 221.

87 Peck, *Statehood and Nation-Building*, p. 138.

88 Taryam, *Establishment of the United Arab Emirates*, p. 234.

89 Heard-Bey, *From Trucial States to United Arab Emirates*, p. 379.

90 Frauke Heard-Bey, "The United Arab Emirates: A Quarter Century of Federation," in Michael Hudson (ed.), *Middle East Dilemma: The Politics and Economics of Arab Integration* (New York: Columbia University Press, 1998), p. 139.

91 Herb, *Wages of Oil*, p. 126.

92 Heard-Bey, *Quarter-Century of Federation*, p. 139.

93 Heard-Bey, *From Trucial States to United Arab Emirates*, p. 407.

94 Taryam, *Establishment of the United Arab Emirates*, pp. 242–243.

95 Ibid., p. 243.

96 Ibid., p. 246.

97 Herb, *Wages of Oil*, p. 123.

98 Khalifa, *Unity in Fragmentation*, p. 80.

99 Ibid., p. 82.

100 Taryam, *Establishment of the United Arab Emirates*, p. 237.

101 Khalifa, *Unity in Fragmentation*, p. 82.

102 Davidson, *Vulnerability of Success*, p. 264.
103 Letter from Brian Pridham (Head of Chancery, British Embassy, Abu Dhabi) to Anthony D. Harris (Middle East Department, FCO), June 23, 1975, London, *The National Archive*, file FCO 8/2430.
104 Ibid.; also Letter from H. St J Armitage (Consul-General to Dubai, 1974–78) to Terry J. Clark (Assistant Head of Middle East Department, FCO), July 3, 1975, London, *The National Archive*, file FCO 8/2430.
105 Davidson, *Vulnerability of Success*, p. 264.
106 Ibid., pp. 264–265.
107 Jim Krane, *Dubai: The Story of the World's Largest City* (New York: St Martin's Press, 2009), pp. 99–100.
108 Fatma al-Sayegh, "Diversity in Unity: Political Institutions and Civil Society," *Middle East Policy*, 6(4), 1999, pp. 15–16.
109 Davidson, *Oil and Beyond*, p. 65.
110 "Abu Dhabi: BCCI's Founding and Majority Shareholders." Section 14 of "The BCCI Affair: A Report to the Committee on Foreign Relations United States Senate by Senator John Kerry and Senator Hank Brown December 1992," *102d Congress 2d Session Senate Print 102–140*. Available online at http://fas.org/irp/congress/1992_rpt/bcci.
111 Ibid.
112 Ibid.
113 "After 22 Years, UAE Branches of Defunct BCCI Finally Liquidated," *The National*, July 5, 2013.
114 Sarah Townshend, "Legal Eagle: Essam Al Tamimi," *ArabianBusiness.com*, December 11, 2015.
115 Ibid.
116 Ibid.
117 Ibid.
118 Christopher Davidson, *The United Arab Emirates: A Study in Survival* (London: Lynne Rienner, 2006), p. 206.
119 Karim Sadjadpour, "The Battle of Dubai: The United Arab Emirates and the U.S.-Iran Cold War," *Carnegie Papers Middle East*, July 2011, p. 6.
120 Malcolm Peck, *The United Arab Emirates: A Venture in Unity* (Boulder, CO: Westview Press, 1986), p. 133.
121 Francis Matthews, "A Trip Down Memory Lane," *Gulf News*, September 30, 2008.
122 Fred Halliday, *Arabia without Sultans* (London: Saqi Books, 2002 edition), p. 221.
123 Peck, *Formation and Evolution*, p. 155.
124 Quoted in Fahim bin Sultan Al Qasimi et al, "A Century in Thirty Years: Sheikh Zayed and the United Arab Emirates," Middle East Policy, 6(4), 1999, p. 2.
125 Peck, *Formulation and Evolution*, p. 155.
126 Christopher Davidson, "After Sheikh Zayed: the Politics of Succession in Abu Dhabi and the UAE," *Middle East Policy*, 13(1), 2006, pp. 47–48.
127 "With MBZ's Promotion, Sheikha Fatima Sons Take Center Stage," *Gulf States Newsletter*, 27(724), December 12, 2003, p. 1.
128 "Al-Nahayans Reshuffle the Deck, Shaping the UAE's Succession," *Gulf States Newsletter*, 28 (745), November 12, 2004, pp. 4–5.
129 Davidson, *Politics of Succession*, p. 45; "GCC Summit Moves to Manama as UAE Looks Closer to Home," *Gulf States Newsletter*, 28(742), October 1, 2004, p. 1.
130 Ibid., p. 46.
131 Ibid., p. 47.
132 "C.P. Khalifa Holds the Purse Strings as Abu Dhabi's Younger Generations Emerge," *Gulf States Newsletter*, 26(683), April 3, 2002, p. 5.
133 "Radical Cabinet Shake-up Represents a Step towards UAE Integration," *Gulf States Newsletter*, 30(776), February 24, 2006, pp. 8–9.
134 Simeon Kerr, "UAE President Stable after Suffering Stroke," *Financial Times*, January 26, 2014.

135 Simon Henderson, "Succession Politics in the Conservative Gulf Arab States: the Weekend's Events in Ras al-Khaimah," The Washington Institute, *Policywatch No. 769*, June 17, 2003.
136 "Five Years On, RAK's Sheikh Khalid is Back," *Gulf States Newsletter*, 32 (842), December 5, 2008, p. 12.
137 "How Peter Cathcart's Uxbridge Offices Became the Base for a Coup," *The Guardian*, June 6, 2010.
138 Ibid.
139 "More Press Chatter about RAK 'Plots,' while Sheikh Saqr Remains in Hospital," *Gulf States Newsletter*, 35 (879), June 18, 2010, p. 8.
140 "How Peter Cathcart's Uxbridge Offices Became the Base for a Coup," *The Guardian*, June 6, 2010.
141 Simon Henderson, "The Iran Angle of Ras al-Khaimah's Succession Struggle," The Washington Institute, *Policywatch No. 1714*, October 29, 2010.
142 Mohammed Morsy Abdullah, *The United Arab Emirates: a Modern History* (London: Croon Helm, 1978), pp. 146–148.
143 Ibid., pp. 143–144.
144 Mansour al-Noqaidan, "Muslim Brotherhood in UAE: Expansion and Decline," Dubai: Al Mesbar Center for Studies and Research, 2012, pp. 2–3.
145 Ibid.
146 "Wave of Arrests Puts Al-Islah Back in the Spotlight," *Gulf States Newsletter*, 36 (924), May 24, 2012, pp. 3–4.
147 Courtney Freer, "The Muslim Brotherhood in the United Arab Emirates: Anatomy of a Crackdown," *Middle East Eye*, December 17, 2014.
148 "Wave of Arrests Puts Al-Islah Back in the Spotlight," *Gulf States Newsletter*, 36(924), May 24, 2012, p. 3.
149 Ibid.
150 "Wave of Arrests Puts Al-Islah Back in the Spotlight," *Gulf States Newsletter*, 36 (924), May 24, 2012, pp. 3–4.
151 Sultan Sooud Al Qassemi, "The Brothers and the Gulf," *Foreign Policy*, December 14, 2012.
152 Ibid., p. 5.
153 Freer, *Anatomy of a Crackdown*.
154 Al-Noqaidan, *Muslim Brotherhood in UAE*, p. 4.
155 Freer, *Anatomy of a Crackdown*.
156 Ibid.
157 Al-Noqaidan, *Muslim Brotherhood in UAE*, p. 18.
158 Ibid., pp. 5–6.
159 Ibid., p. 7.
160 Freer, *Anatomy of a Crackdown*.
161 Al Qassemi, *The Brothers and the Gulf*.
162 "Wave of Arrests Puts Al-Islah Back in the Spotlight," *Gulf States Newsletter*, 36 (924), May 24, 2012, p. 4.
163 Al-Noqaidan, *Muslim Brotherhood in UAE*, p. 9.
164 Freer, *Anatomy of a Crackdown*.
165 Lori Plotkin Boghardt, "The Muslim Brotherhood on Trial in the UAE," The Washington Institute Policywatch No. 2064, April 12, 2013.
166 Birol Baskan, "The Police Chief and the Sheikh," The Washington Review of Middle Eastern & Eurasian Affairs, April 2012.
167 Abdulkhaleq Abdulla, "The Gulf Cooperation Council: Nature, Origin and Process," in Michael Hudson (ed.), *Middle East Dilemma: The Politics and Economics of Arab Integration* (New York: Columbia University Press, 1999), p. 154.
168 Abdulla Baabood, "Dynamics and Determinants of the GCC States' Foreign Policy, with Special Reference to the EU," in Gerd Nonneman (ed.), *Analyzing Middle Eastern Foreign Policies* (London: Routledge, 2005), p. 148.

169 Anthony Cordesman, quoted in Ibrahim Suleiman al-Duraiby, *Saudi Arabia, GCC and the EU: Limitations and Possibilities for an Unequal Triangular Relationship* (Dubai: Gulf Research Centre, 2009), p. 89.
170 Interview with Abdulla Bishara, Secretary-General of the Gulf Cooperation Council 1981–1993, Kuwait City, October 21, 2009.
171 "Withdrawal from GCC Single Currency 'Final'," *Emirates 24/7,* May 22, 2009.
172 "Abdullah Woos the UAE after Central Bank Split Highlights Lack of Trust in the GCC," *Gulf States Newsletter,* 33 (854), May 29, 2009, p. 14.
173 Ibid.
174 Fred Lawson, "Transformation of Regional Economic Governance in the Gulf Cooperation Council," Georgetown University School of Foreign Service in Qatar, *Occasional Paper,* 2012, p. 14.
175 Christian Koch, "GCC Confronted by Disunity," Dubai: *Gulf Research Center Note,* December 22, 2012.
176 "UAE-wide Youth Councils to be Established as Part of 100-Day Plan," *The National,* April 10, 2016; "Fourteen Emiratis Make Up Fujairah's First Youth Council," *The National,* June 9, 2016.
177 Jeremy Howell, "The United Arab Emirates' Mission to Mars," *BBC News,* November 13, 2015.

4

ECONOMICS

This chapter shifts the focus beyond the political realm and onto the economic factors that propelled the UAE into the global arena in the 1990s and 2000s, setting the stage for the analysis of the UAE's role in contemporary global structures of power, politics, and policymaking. As the UAE transitioned into a new era as power passed – relatively smoothly – to a younger cohort of rulers, the new leadership in Dubai took the lead in creating specialized cities and zones that marked the emirate as a pioneer in economic liberalization across the broader Gulf region. These built upon the incipient moves undertaken in the 1970s and 1980s that had positioned Dubai as the leading infrastructural hub in the Gulf. However, the measures introduced in the 1990s and 2000s differed in scope and scale from their predecessors and constituted a wide-ranging attempt to shift Dubai into a post-oil economy once production peaked in 1991. Several of the other emirates also began to develop into niche concentrations of expertise, most notably Sharjah in arts and culture, Ras al-Khaimah in cement and heavy industry, and Fujairah with oil storage and bunkering.

An opening section in this chapter picks up where Chapter Three left off and provides contextual analysis of the early moves to create and expand the federal economic infrastructure as well as an overview of individual emirates' moves into economic diversification in specialist niche sectors. This is followed by a section that examines Dubai's growth as an infrastructural and logistics hub that paved the way for the emirate's emergence as a global city and a regional hub for foreign direct investment. This is followed by two sections that examine the growth of the UAE as a financial hub and the rise of sovereign wealth funds and government-related enterprises in Abu Dhabi. The energy sector in Abu Dhabi is covered in the following sections, which explore Abu Dhabi's different pathway of economic development and the evolution (and diversification) of the atomic and renewable energy sectors and the creation of intended "national champions" in specific economic sectors. The chapter ends with sections that examine the rise of global brands and look ahead to the development strategies that are intended to transform the UAE into an innovation hub and knowledge economy over the coming decade.

Challenge of Building a Federal Economy

The UAE contains the seventh-largest proven reserves of oil in the world at 97.8 billion barrels and was the world's sixth-largest oil producer in 2014 with an average production of about 2.8 million barrels of oil. Figures provided by the International Monetary Fund show that hydrocarbon export revenues rose rapidly from US$75 billion in 2010 to US$123 billion in 2013 during a long period of high international oil prices. These made the UAE the second-largest economy in the Middle East after Saudi Arabia, with an estimated Gross Domestic Product (GDP) of US$416 billion in 2014. Such figures, however, disguise the great disparity between Abu Dhabi, which holds 94 percent of total UAE oil reserves, and the other six emirates which, other than Dubai, hold negligble amounts of oil or gas.[1] As such, there were – and are – two near-parallel economies at work in the UAE as Abu Dhabi's resource-rich energy sector coexists with the non-resource economies of Dubai and the five Northern Emirates. Thus, while Abu Dhabi–derived hydrocarbon revenues continue to underpin federal budgets, the UAE is also the most economically diversified of all six Gulf Cooperation Council (GCC) economies. Indeed, the proportion of UAE GDP accounted for by hydrocarbons has fallen from as high as 90 percent in the 1970s to about 28.2 percent in 2013 as estimated by the International Monetary Fund (IMF).[2]

The strong divergence in economic parameters between Abu Dhabi and the other emirates has impacted policymaking in the UAE in various ways, both positive and negative, over the four decades since independence, although certain economic commonalities exist throughout the federation, such as the importance of immediate- and extended family-owned enterprises in the economic and state-business landscape.[3] Writing in 1987, Abdullah Omran Taryam, who served in the first federal cabinets after the formation of the UAE, reflected on the policy challenges of building a federal economy and aligning development among the seven emirates in the absence of any form of overall development strategy in the early years of the federation:

> The absence of such a strategy during the first years of the state can be justified since the emirates were in need of practically every amenity and, therefore, things had to be done very quickly. Most areas were without education, a health service, roads, electricity and water, proper housing and communication, and unemployment was common. Provision of all these services was supposed to constitute the priority at a time when no strategic plan existed, and untried official institutions started to acquire experience only after the state came into being. After some years had elapsed, a plan or strategy should have

been made to guarantee the success of an overall development process. However, nothing of the sort was done …

… examples of overlapping projects are numerous. In each emirate a cement plant was established; four international airports were built, one each in Abu Dhabi, Dubai, Sharjah and Ras al Khaimah, and a fifth one is being built at Al-'Ayn; high-capacity seaports were established in Abu Dhabi, Dubai (two seaports), Sharjah and Ras al-Khaimah, all along one short coastline … Obviously, this reflects unplanned deployment of economic resources and a wasteful use of oil revenues.[4]

Chapter Three documented how Sheikh Zayed bin Sultan Al Nahyan began to utilize Abu Dhabi's oil wealth for the benefit of the Trucial States after he became Ruler of Abu Dhabi in 1966, and, after 1971, President of the UAE. Less than two years after the formation of the federation, the Arab oil embargo between October 1973 and March 1974 led to international oil prices quadrupling and a corresponding surge in oil revenues that accrued mostly to Abu Dhabi. Taken as a whole, Trucial State/UAE oil revenues grew by about 2475 percent between 1970 (US$233 million) and 1975 (US$6000 million) as production more than doubled from 253 million barrels per day to 619 million barrels per day during the same period.[5]

The rapid increase in government revenues facilitated the task of building up and financing the federal structures during the formative first decade of the UAE as Sheikh Zayed's redistribution of wealth across the federation underpinned the growth of the welfare state. In 1974, the Council of Ministers drew up a comprehensive blueprint for federal development that emphasized both the "expansion and exploitation of natural resources" and the creation of a comprehensive system of social services as "a basic right" for Emirati nationals.[6] As Karen Young has noted, the fact that the oil price boom of 1973 happened less than two years after the creation of the UAE meant that, from the beginning, the processes of state formation and consolidation were closely intertwined with "resource rents" from the energy sector. This heavy exposure to the oil and gas sector introduced a high degree of volatility to economic policymaking in the UAE, as in the other Gulf States, as evidenced in 1986 when a plunge in oil prices caused a 40 percent drop in oil revenues that year.[7]

Yet, the differential in economic performance and prospect among the seven emirates has proved stubbornly persistent. Data compiled in 1998 – twenty-seven years after federation – by Ali Tawfik al-Sadik found that Abu Dhabi and Dubai together accounted for more than 83 percent of the UAE's overall GDP, and that GDP per capita ranged from US$23,929 in Abu Dhabi and US$16,094 in Dubai to just US$7955 in Fujairah, US$7154 in Umm al-Quwain, and US$6047 in Ajman.[8] Since 1998, it is likely that these differentials between Abu Dhabi and Dubai and the other five emirates have widened still further as Abu Dhabi benefited from the decade-long oil-price boom after 2002 and Dubai accelerated its ambitious plans for economic diversification. Selected economic indicators for 2013 for Abu Dhabi and Dubai compiled by *Gulf States News* showed that the size of Abu Dhabi's GDP continued to be roughly twice that of Dubai's at 707,516 million dirhams and 325,687 million dirhams respectively.[9]

Federal economic structures evolved gradually and at times haphazardly due to the abovementioned divergences. The UAE joined the International Monetary Fund in 1972, shortly after independence, while another significant measure was (as detailed in Chapter Three) the creation of the UAE Currency Board in May 1973. The formation of the Currency Board occurred on the same day as the launch of the unified national currency, the UAE Dirham, ending the practice whereby Abu Dhabi had used the Bahraini Dinar while the other Trucial States had adopted the Qatar-Dubai Riyal.[10] Elsewhere, while Abu Dhabi initially was the sole contributor to the federal budget, Chapter Three noted that Dubai and other emirates began to contribute in the 1980s, and in 1981 the UAE drew up its five-year economic plan for the period 1981–1985. The plan aimed to enhance the skills and capabilities of Emirati citizens and expand the productive base of the economy by increasing the size of the non-oil sector. However, the decline in oil prices and government revenues after 1982 meant the plan was not fully implemented, contributing to "uncoordinated investments in the emirates that produced over-capacity and duplication in several activities in the economy."[11]

As the federal level of governance slowly took root, with a federal planning ministry being created in 1977, individual emirates gradually began to carve out areas of specialist expertise in niche sectors, with Abu Dhabi's focus since the early 2000s on renewable energy and clean technology only the most recent example of many. Another is Sharjah's creation of a network of educational and cultural institutions that has projected the emirate as an outpost of learning with particular emphasis on the promotion of local heritage. Although most pronounced in Sharjah, the emphasis on heritage revivalism (*ihya al-turath*) forms part of a broader focus on attempts to reclaim (and re-invent) often-romanticized aspects of the past, documented by UAE-based sociologist Sulayman Khalaf as encompassing:

> invented cultural traditions, newly built heritage institutions, such as heritage villages and museums, cultural festivals like annual camel racing and commemoration of pearl diving, renovation of old historic buildings, as well as support for expressive folk and popular culture … [12]

This strategy had considerable success as Sharjah was designated a cultural capital of the Arab world by the Arab League in the early 1990s and by UNESCO in 1998. Moreover, the restoration of historical Sharjah brought "back to life the old buildings adjacent to the sea portage" and was supported by the Ruler, Sheikh Sultan bin Mohammed Al Qasimi, as a formal development strategy.[13] In addition to the work of the Sharjah Heritage Directorate, Ras al-Khaimah and Dubai also have invested heavily in "heritage revivalism" projects, with the Documentation and Studies Center in Ras al-Khaimah focusing on local heritage and history and Dubai restoring the historic *Bastakiya* quarter of the city with its signature wind towers and establishing the Dubai Heritage Village in 1996.[14] All of these efforts were consistent with the vision of Sheikh Zayed himself, who commented on one occasion that "A nation without a past is a nation without a present or a future."[15]

More recently, Ras al-Khaimah has emerged as a global hub for the manufacture of armored vehicles with at least ten major manufacturers setting up in the emirate, including Canada's Streit Group, which set up a 1.4 million square foot facility in 2006 which tripled in size in 2012. Four of the companies opened in the Ras al-Khaimah Free Trade Zone, whose marketing director, Ahmad Numan, expressed the view that:

> ... RAK today has the highest level of industrialization in the UAE [28 percent of GDP in 2011] ... The cost of renting facilities and land for development, procuring licenses and providing housing for employees, along with other costs, can be 25 to 50 percent lower in RAK than in other emirates ... it [the free zone] is less than an hour's drive from Dubai International Airport [and] is also easily accessible from everywhere in the UAE.[16]

Numan added that the decision to concentrate on heavy manufacturing in Ras al-Khaimah made strategic sense given the emirate's abundance of (non-oil) resources, which included the easy availability of limestone, rock, and clay, all of which facilitated the initial growth and rapid expansion of local cement, ceramics, manufacturing, and construction sectors.[17] The ceramics sector proved particularly successful and within fifteen years of the opening of the first factory in 1989 had expanded to encompass eight different factories with a turnover of US$300 million and sales to 125 countries across the world.[18]

Ras al-Khaimah's lack of direct reliance on the energy sector and its relatively robust manufacturing base meant that it was one of the few emirates in the UAE that preserved its credit rating during the prolonged oil price collapse in 2015.[19] Indeed, the Ras al-Khaimah Free Trade Zone, which opened in 2000, was a notable economic success for the emirate with heavy initial investment coming from countries such as Iran, India, China, Russia, and Pakistan, and which by 2015 had expanded to more than 8,000 companies from over 100 countries and 50 economic sectors, while figures for 2013 showed that free zone revenue had accounted for 16.3 percent of the emirate's GDP. Such rapid growth led to concerns about the availability of sufficient power from local sources, which necessitated the connection of the free zone to the national grid maintained by the Federal Electricity and Water in order to make possible a new phase of expansion to overcome the other challenge of near complete occupancy.[20]

Fujairah also has developed considerable niche expertise in the oil storage and bunkering sectors and maximized its geographical location on the Gulf of Oman and beyond the strategic chokepoint of the Strait of Hormuz. As with Ras al-Khaimah, the move to build up the port of Fujairah, which was completed in 1982, stemmed from the decision of the ruling family to diversify economically in order to overcome the lack of substantive oil reserves. The port benefited almost immediately from the disruption to commercial shipping during the Iran–Iraq War as it became a bunker stop for tanker traffic awaiting safe passage through the mined waters of the Strait of Hormuz. After the war, the Fujairah Offshore Anchorage Area (FOAA) expanded subsequently into one of the three global hubs for bunkering and marine logistics alongside the ports of Rotterdam and Singapore. Fujairah's importance to the UAE oil sector increased markedly in 2006 when approval was granted for the construction of the strategic Abu Dhabi Crude Oil Pipeline linking Abu Dhabi's oil hub at Habshan to Fujairah's greatly expanded port facilities. Funded by Abu Dhabi's International Petroleum Investment Corporation (IPIC), the US$3.3 billion 370 kilometer pipeline opened, two years behind schedule, in June 2012, enabling 1.5 million of the UAE's then 2.7 million barrels of oil per day to bypass the Strait of Hormuz.[21] The opening of the pipeline occurred in the midst of a near-doubling of Fujairah port's oil storage capacity as well as the construction of a new US$3 billion 200,000 barrels per day refinery (funded by IPIC) as well as a liquefied natural gas (LNG) terminal in a joint-venture between IPIC and another Abu Dhabi-owned fund, the Mubadala Development Company.[22]

Infrastructure, Investment, and Economic Diversification in Dubai

Dubai today is the preeminent regional logistics and infrastructure hub not only in the Gulf but also for the broader Middle East region. Facilities such as the Jebel Ali port and free zone were pioneering developments in the 1970s and 1980s that changed the business landscape across the Gulf and generated a wave of similar projects in other Gulf States. These "early-movers" in economic diversification have since been augmented by more recent developments such as the massive Dubai World Central mixed-use economic, commercial, and residential area centered on what will become the largest airport in the world when it opens fully in the 2020s. Moreover, Dubai's successful bid to host the 2020 World Expo – which will take place in allocated land directly adjacent to Dubai World Central and is anticipated to draw 25 million visitors – is expected to lead to more than US$130 billion in additional spending in the infrastructure and construction sectors.[23]

The emergence of Dubai as an infrastructural hub built upon the sheikhdom's centrality in trans-national trading patterns as described in Chapter Two. It also reflected the far-sighted leadership shown by successive rulers throughout the twentieth century that first transformed Dubai into a free port in the early 1900s and, from the 1950s, created the modern infrastructure that underpinned all sub-sequent developments. By the mid-1950s, the silting up of the Dubai Creek proved the catalyst for a series of major projects that dredged the creek, expanded the customs facilities, and reclaimed land for additional wharves and an associated industrial and commercial zone. After the dominant (at the time) British Bank of the Middle East (BBME) refused Dubai's initial request for a loan, the Ruler borrowed £400,000 from the Kuwait Development Fund to finance the dredging of the Dubai Creek and the upgrading of the port facilities.[24] An additional grant of

£190,000 from Qatar, whose ruler, Sheikh Ahmed bin Ali Al Thani happened to be the son-in-law of Sheikh Rashid of Dubai, helped to finance the first bridge across the creek in 1962.[25] Dubai expanded so rapidly in subsequent decades that when Sheikh Rashid appointed the English architect John Harris to prepare a master plan for urban development in the mid-1960s, the pace of growth was so quick that Harris had to issue a second report in 1971, which itself was quickly overtaken by the post-1973 oil-price boom.[26]

Just as the entrepreneurial spirit and greater economic freedom in Dubai enabled the sheikhdom to take advantage of the eclipse of the Persian port-city of Lingah at the start of the twentieth century and become a center of informal (as well as formal) region-wide trading networks, so too did Dubai benefit greatly from the decision of India's newly independent government in the 1950s to outlaw the trade in gold and severely restrict the domestic textiles market. Dubai-based traders took full advantage of both measures introduced by Indian Prime Minister Jawaharlal Nehru to position the emirate as the regional epicenter of the lucrative re-export trade whereby Dubai became the intermediary for goods shipped into and out of the Indian subcontinent.[27] A particularly lucrative trade route was the trans-shipment in Dubai of gold from Switzerland on its way to its final destination in India, which had been Asia's primary gold market prior to Nehru's restrictive policies, while the trans-shipment of consumer electronics to the Indian market also soared in the 1970s and 1980s.[28] Among the many merchants who plied their dhows between Dubai and India laden with gold and other merchandise during the 1940s and 1950s was Saif Ahmad al-Ghurair, one of the founders of the eponymous Al Ghurair Group, which has since expanded into one of the largest family-owned conglomerates in the Gulf.[29]

Dubai's infrastructural development accelerated sharply in the 1970s. Port Rashid opened in 1972 but was superseded just seven years later by the phased completion of the enormous Jebel Ali port and industrial free zone twenty miles from the center of Dubai. Although Jebel Ali was seen by many external observers as a "white elephant" prestige project similar to many others that were launched at the time in the Gulf, business boomed after the outbreak of the Iran–Iraq War the following year when Dubai – and the UAE – became a safe haven for maritime traffic in the Gulf. While the original intention to utilize Jebel Ali as a base for US and NATO aircraft carriers did not materialize during the Iran–Iraq War, both Jebel Ali and the opening of Dubai DryDocks adjacent to Port Rashid in 1983 anticipated the soaring demand in the Gulf for modern maritime facilities and shipping services.[30] Over the subsequent three decades, Jebel Ali has grown into the largest manmade harbor in the world and the busiest port in the Middle East and has developed into one of the most frequent ports of call for the US Navy outside the United States, as well as the flagship facility in DP World's sprawling global assets.

Together with the growth of Abu Dhabi under Sheikh Zayed, the rise of Dubai under Sheikh Rashid bin Saeed Al Maktoum illustrates the centrality of the projection of charismatic authority in driving personalized decision-making processes during the formative years of emirate-building. In October 1990, a tribute to Sheikh Rashid published in the *Gulf States Newsletter* after his death described him as "more like a latter-day Doge of Venice presiding over a vigorous merchant co-operative than the ruler of a traditional Gulf Arab state." The tribute added that Sheikh Rashid was "closely concerned in practically every detail of the emirate's affairs" and "never afraid to back his own commercial judgement, even when it was against the opinion of experts and professionals."[31] A similar authority was transmitted to Sheikh Rashid's third son, Sheikh Mohammed bin Rashid Al Maktoum, who became Crown Prince in 1995 and Ruler when Sheikh Rashid's eldest son and immediate successor, Sheikh Maktoum bin Rashid Al Maktoum, died suddenly on a visit to Australia in January 2006 (their brother "in-between," Sheikh Rashid's second son, Sheikh Hamdan bin Rashid, has served since 1971 as the UAE's Minister of Finance). As Crown Prince from the mid-1990s on, Sheikh Mohammed built up an Executive Office of dynamic managers and advisors who formed the core of a "highly-active and personalized government" that transformed Dubai into a global city.[32] Moreover, in 1999, Sheikh Mohammed informed government personnel that he wanted Dubai "to grow into the world's finest global center for finance, investment, and tourism in the twenty-first century."[33]

As such, in the mid-2000s, Dubai grabbed the media headlines with its array of ostentatious and eye-catching initiatives such as the Palm Islands and The World archipelago as well as the regional trend-setting liberalization of the real estate sector. These built upon the very first "branding campaign" in the Gulf that was inaugurated in Dubai as early as July 1990 when the Dubai Commerce and Promotion Tourism Board hired a team of marketing consultants in London and launched an "aggressive drive" to promote the emirate's business and tourism potential in the United Kingdom, but unfortunate timing meant the initiative was overshadowed by the Iraqi invasion of Kuwait and the resulting military build-up and conflict in the Gulf.[34] In 1992, after the dust had settled on the Gulf War, the Government of Dubai launched a new branding exercise with the "Decide on Dubai" initiative aimed at a target audience of potential tourists and shoppers.[35] While the campaign was successful in marketing Dubai to the British market, in particular, and the inaugural Dubai Shopping Festival (modelled on the Great Singapore Sale) took place in 1996, it was dwarfed by the scale of the later visions that were unveiled during the boom years of the mid-2000s. These included the *Vision for Dubai* unveiled in 2000, whose targeted increase in GDP to US\$30 billion by 2010 was achieved by 2005, and the *Dubai Strategic Plan*, announced in February 2007, which mapped growth strategies for Dubai by concentrating economic development in sectors where the emirate already enjoyed a comparative advantage.[36]

Dubai was also among the pioneers of the creation of specific investor-friendly free zones that have since proliferated elsewhere in the Gulf and in the wider world. While the port and free trade zone of Jebel Ali was the first of these to appear, as early as 1979, it was followed two decades later by a multitude of additional sectoral developments, often with catchy titles such as Dubai Internet City and Dubai Media City, which opened in 1999 and 2000, respectively, and the

Dubai International Financial District (which opened in 2004 as a federal financial free zone and which is examined later in this chapter), and Dubai International Academic City, which launched in 2006. One of the few academic analyses of free trade zones (from a political economy perspective) defined them as:

> ... geographically demarcated areas within which certain governmental taxes and regulations are waived completely or for a short period of time. In general, free trade zones include absolute or relative shelter from corporate and income taxes, import duties and quotas, and foreign ownership restrictions. More successful zones also include bureaucratic centrality and time-saving features ("one-stop shopping") as well as advanced facilities and infrastructures for transport, communication, and storage.[37]

In 2006, a spokesperson for three related free zone areas – Dubai Internet City, Dubai Media City, and Dubai Knowledge Village – summarized thus the (self-perceived) advantages of the free zone concept then prevalent in the emirate:

> ... Dubai has probably got one of the most advanced transportational hubs in the region, in terms of land, sea, and air ... this is a tax-free environment ... within a free-zone setup ... No income tax. It has various options and advantages being located within this free zone that other companies wouldn't necessarily find in other parts of the world, one of them being the convenience with which a business can be set up here ... We have particular organizations here who work directly with all the government services so that you actually have a one-stop shop for all these services. Life is made a lot more simple and a lot more easy.[38]

One of the key elements of Dubai's economic diversification and inward investment strategies was the implementation of the series of policy decisions that had been taken during the 2000s to liberalize the real estate sector and open up categories of residential visas to non-nationals. Beginning in Dubai in the late 1990s and since spreading to most other Gulf States with the exception of Saudi Arabia and Kuwait, longstanding national laws that banned the ownership of property by non-nationals began to be superseded by large-scale property developments that targeted specifically high-end Western or expatriate buyers. One of the earliest such instances occurred in 1997 with the launch by Emaar Properties of the "Emirates Hills" residential project in which direct foreign ownership was not only marketed but encouraged.[39] Bahrain was the first GCC state to allow expatriates to buy real estate in 2001 with Dubai formalizing its own position the following year. Qatar and Oman followed in 2004 and 2006, as did four of the other six emirates in the UAE, including Abu Dhabi. These measures typically permitted foreigners to purchase properties in pre-approved, mostly gated communities. Bahraini sociologist Omar AlShehabi has calculated that, at the peak of the oil-price and real estate boom in 2008, at least 1.3 million housing units were being planned for foreign ownership in Bahrain, Oman, Qatar, and the UAE. This startling figure had "the potential to house more individuals than the total of all the citizens of these four countries," assuming an average of three inhabitants per unit and had they all subsequently been built.[40]

In 2008, an overheated real estate sector was one of the reasons for the debt crisis that rocked Dubai's "business model" and changed its relationship with Abu Dhabi. Initial hopes that the global financial crisis that had originated in the United States might bypass Dubai (and the Gulf) proved misplaced as world oil prices plunged, project financing dried up, and the real estate speculative bubble burst. The financial crisis exposed the fragility of Dubai's economic diversification based on a combination of the construction and real estate sectors, high-end tourist development, and a financial sector reliant underpinned by state-owned conglomerates such as Dubai World and Dubai Holding relying heavily on continuous foreign direct investment and access to cheap international credit.[41] As early as 2005, industry analysts had noted with scepticism how:

> Marketing brilliance, the capacity to forge a sense of excitement around apparently insignificant news … and the shrewd targeting of potential investors who want to shift a chunk of their capital abroad have characterized the development campaign mounted by the two state-owned property companies Nakheel and Emaar.[42]

Even at its formative stage in 2005, an op-ed in Gulf States Newsletter had warned of "stormy weather ahead" and predicted that a market correction was needed "to ensure that today's property boom is not a bubble, and can evolve into a resilient and long-term commercially viable property market."[43] However, officials in Dubai were slow in 2008 to acknowledge the impact of the broader financial slowdown and tightening of liquidity on the emirate, with Sheikh Mohammed describing the global downturn as "a passing cloud that will not stay longer" in September 2009 and subsequently telling critics of Dubai to "shut up and do your homework" shortly before the Dubai World debt standstill in November brought the issue into worldwide focus.[44]

The bursting of the real estate bubble in October 2008 reverberated across Dubai's economic landscape as much construction came to a halt and projects with an estimated value of more than US$300 billion were either scaled back, put on hold, or cancelled altogether. This occurred, as was noted by the *Middle East Economic Digest*, while "the Dubai government was itself solvent … government-related entities such as Nakheel [a part of the Dubai World conglomerate] had borrowed heavily to pay their projects."[45] The end of the speculative bubble has been documented by a scholar of the political economy of finance in the UAE, Karen Young, who noted how:

> After the Lehman Brothers bankruptcy [in September 2008], real estate prices in Dubai began to collapse. Developers like Nakheel had been selling units off

plan at a loss or giving them away to well-connected individuals for years. The basic revenues of the company paid for the architects, designers, marketers, and junkets for the next off-plan concept. The company had relied on speculation of future development projects, rather than the sale of completed units to grow the business.[46]

By early 2009, Dubai's debt reached an estimated US$120 billion, a figure higher than the emirate's GDP, and in February that year the Abu Dhabi–based UAE Central Bank stepped in to purchase US$10 billion of bonds from the government of Dubai. Matters came to a head in November 2009, when Dubai World surprised local and international markets by requesting a standstill on US$26 billion of its debt and Nakheel came very close to defaulting on a US$3.52 billion Islamic bond (*sukuk*). As in February 2009, so too in November Abu Dhabi came to the assistance of Dubai with a second tranche of aid, on this occasion in the form of a US$10 billion loan through two emirate-owned banks (the National Bank of Abu Dhabi and Al Hilal Bank) to Dubai – both at an interest rate of 4 percent. (In March 2014, the UAE Central Bank announced that it would extend by five years the repayment deadline and refinance the 2009 bond and loan at a rate of 1 percent, and added that both the bond and the loan could be renewed when they mature in 2019.)[47]

The Dubai World incident highlighted one of the defining characteristics of the "Dubai model" of development and the opacity in untangling the intricate ties between (and among) key stakeholders in the ruling family and local business landscape and with the emirate of Dubai itself. This characteristic had first been noted (in a very different context) in *Sand to Silicon*, a glowing account of Dubai's rapid growth published in 2003 by two authors associated with the London Business School, who observed (approvingly) that:

> … Many of the senior government officials in Dubai also run businesses and head other organizations. This has provided a direct communication channel between business and government and therefore enabled rapid and effective responsiveness.[48]

The Dubai World crisis began in late November 2009 when Dubai World sought to restructure some US$26 billion (out of a total debt of US$60 billion) and asked creditors to agree to a six-month extension of a maturing US$3.52 billion *sukuk* (Islamic bond) due to mature in mid-December. While Dubai's Supreme Fiscal Committee (SFC) announced that its Dubai Financial Support Fund (DFSF) would oversee the restructuring of Dubai World's debt, the government of Dubai made it clear that it would not guarantee Dubai World's debt, contrary to the (mistakenly) widespread assumption by many creditors that it would do so, given that Dubai World was "wholly owned by the government of Dubai and, as such, is treated as part of the government of Dubai for many purposes under Dubai law."[49]

The Dubai World repayment standstill came to symbolize the bursting of the Dubai bubble although predictions at the time that Dubai was about to default on all of its debt did not materialize. Instead, Dubai World and other GREs restructured the majority of their debts following prolonged – and, in the case of Dubai DryDocks World (DDW), sometimes acrimonious negotiations with creditors.[50] In 2012, DDW used a new insolvency law (Decree 57) to force through its debt restructuring. Decree 57 was initially created in anticipation of being used for the debt restructuring of Dubai World and Nakheel and permitted approval for a company's restructuring plan if holders of 75 percent of the company's debt gave their assent. DDW became the only entity within the Dubai World umbrella that had to resort to Decree 57 as a US-based hedge fund, Monarch Capital, filed a case against DDW claiming the company was in default, in contrast to the relatively ordered (and consensual) restructuring of Dubai World. As a result of Decree 57, DDW bypassed hostile small creditors such as Monarch and obtained formal approval for its restructuring plan in August 2012 from larger DDW creditors, which included banks such as HSBC, Singapore's DBS, Mashreq, and Standard Chartered.[51]

As with his father, Sheikh Mohammed bin Rashid has at times been described as the CEO of "Dubai Inc." as if he were administering a global corporation rather than a political entity. Together with the Executive Office, which in the mid-2000s was entrusted with the management of all new developments, mega-projects, state-owned enterprises, free zones, and ports, Sheikh Mohammed's role in developing Dubai was buttressed by a small group of hand-picked senior executives who led the major holding groups that formed the centrepiece of the "Dubai model."[52] During the boom years of Dubai's dizzying economic expansion prior to the 2009 debt crisis, three of the key "lieutenants" around Sheikh Mohammed were Mohammed al-Gergawi of Dubai Holding (and also the Minister of Cabinet Affairs) and Sultan bin Sulayem (Chairman of Dubai World), as well as Mohammed Alabbar (Chairman of property and real estate developer Emaar). All three men served on the Investment Corporation of Dubai, an investment vehicle for channelling funds into the myriad state-owned companies, and a competitive atmosphere emerged among them as each vied to pursue the most eye-catching initiative. Their activities were underpinned by the Executive Office, which provided strategic planning and gradually replaced the more traditional Ruler's Court as the epicenter of decision making in Dubai in the freewheeling years of breakneck growth in the 2000s.[53]

The strengthening of Dubai's reputation as an ideal place to do business benefited directly from the fact that all elements of the bureaucratic apparatus were overseen closely by the Ruler and his immediate circle of core advisers as described above. This facilitated the establishment and growth of the free zones, such as the Jebel Ali Free Zone (founded in 1985 by Sultan bin Sulayem), which aimed to boost foreign (and non-oil related) investment with incentives such as full foreign ownership, specialized new cities such as Internet City and Media City (both developed by al-Gergawi) to attract new economic sectors, and the creation of the

Dubai International Financial Centre (DIFC – operated by another key adviser to Sheikh Mohammed, Omar bin Suleiman) to allay investor concerns about local bureaucratic issues by drawing up its own legislative and regulatory framework based on English common law.[54] These early-mover efforts to diversify paid off as the non-oil sector accounted for 82 percent of Dubai's GDP by the mid-1990s while a decade later the emirate accounted for 54 percent of all incoming foreign direct investment in the UAE.[55]

An example of the exceptionally close relationship between Sheikh Mohammed and the leaders of Dubai's flagship entities was provided in a candid interview given in April 2015 by Alabbar, founder and chairman of Emaar Properties, one of the largest real estate developers in the world. As noted above, as a supposedly private company originally founded with state funding, Emaar exemplifies the cross-cutting nature of "private/state enterprise" in Dubai through the 29 percent stake currently held by the Government of Dubai's investment arm, the Investment Corporation of Dubai (chaired by Mohammed bin Rashid). In the interview with ArabianBusiness.com, Alabbar stated emphatically that:

> I do not do anything without me talking to HH, he is the man who gave me unimaginable opportunities, and he gave me a chance to be who I am. And to trust me. And to create my career and my personality. And when I make mistakes he comes and pulls me up again. So I don't do anything without talking to him.[56]

In a similar manner, Zayed University academic Martin Hvidt cites an interview with the CEO of Dubai DryDocks World, a subsidiary of Dubai World, in December 2006:

> If I want to spend 40 million dollars on an extension of the repair facilities here at the Dry Dock, I will pass the request to the head of Dubai World, Mr. Sulayem, who is right under Sheikh Mohammed. Usually I will get an answer within thirty minutes … Here they are much more forward thinking, dynamic, and a lot more trusty … [57]

For all of the difficulties encountered during and after the 2008 debt crisis and its turbulent aftermath, Dubai succeeded in carving for itself a reputation as an aspiring "global city" and by 2015 was ranked as the third-fastest growing metropolitan area in the world in a Brookings Institution study.[58] Indeed, the renowned Dutch-American sociologist Saskia Sassen wrote in 2015 that she considered Dubai to rank alongside Singapore and Hong Kong as one of the three most important "niche global cities" in the twenty-first century world economy. Sassen argued that "global cities, not nation-states, are now the key nodes of global operational space for both economic and cultural processes" and function as "the ultimate bridge into the global economy."[59]

Also in 2015, an editorial in *The Economist* magazine eulogized the factors that had transformed Dubai into "a major transit hub, especially for people and goods moving into or through the Middle East." In addition to the lack of exchange controls and taxes, *The Economist* identified as an enabling factor the emirate's highly developed "soft infrastructure" such as "the customs-free corridor between the port and the airport, which allows businesses to import and export raw materials without charge."[60] Somewhat more contentiously, a 2013 article by Sharjah-based commentator Sultan Sooud Al Qassemi argued that, along with Abu Dhabi and Doha, Dubai had replaced the "traditional Arab capitals" of Baghdad, Beirut, and Cairo as:

> the nerve center of the contemporary Arab world's culture, commerce, design, architecture, art and academia, attracting hundreds of thousands of Arab immigrants, including academics, businessmen, journalists, athletes, artists, entrepreneurs and medical professionals. While these Gulf cities may be unable to compete with their Arab peers in terms of political dynamism, in almost every other sense they have far outstripped their sister cities in North Africa and the Levant.[61]

Al Qassemi's bold claim attracted a fair amount of comment from critics who suggested that the Gulf cities remained consumers, rather than producers, of art and culture, and lacked the vibrant associational spaces and related freedoms of expression. Nevertheless, just two months after the article appeared in print, Dubai beat off competition from Sao Paulo in Brazil, Izmir in Turkey, and Yekaterinburg in Russia to win the hosting rights for the 2020 World's Fair (Expo 2020). Held every five years and responsible for such iconic architecture such as the Eiffel Tower (built for the 1889 World's Fair in Paris) and Seattle's Space Needle (built for the 1962 World's Fair), Dubai's expo, around the theme *Connecting Minds, Creating the Future*, will take place from October 2020 until April 2021 and form one of the centerpieces of the UAE's half-century commemoration. The successful bid for Expo 2020 was also seen by champions of Dubai as evidence of the emirate's successful re-emergence from the depths of the 2009 debt crisis, although other analysts noted that Dubai continued to bear a very large debt burden that was estimated at US$142 billion at the time of the bid in 2013.[62]

Growth of the UAE as a Regional Financial Hub

The Gulf region has been an aspiring financial hub for more than four decades. The outbreak of the Lebanese civil war forced a flight of capital and expertise from the Arab world's first financial center and the neighboring Gulf state of Bahrain actively constructed a business-friendly image designed to appeal to regional and international investors alike. In 1975, the same year the Lebanese conflict began, the Bahraini government followed the Cayman Islands and Singapore and introduced regulations that allowed the creation of offshore banking units (OBUs). Exemptions from corporate tax and low start-up fees increased further the attractiveness of Bahrain as a regional hub for financial organizations and the number of OBUs in the country rose to 48 in 1978 and peaked at 76 in 1984.[63] During the same period, the volume of assets managed by OBUs in Bahrain increased from US$23.4 billion to US$62.7 billion.[64] Among the leading international banks that relocated their regional headquarters to Bahrain were Chase Manhattan, Citibank, Credit Suisse, the Société Générale, and the Bank of Tokyo. By 2010, the "vast majority" of the 133 banks registered in Bahrain operated offshore, along with a further 270 financial institutions such as insurers and fund management companies.[65]

The abovementioned measures transformed Bahrain into the first financial hub in the Gulf in the 1980s and 1990s but since the 2000s they were surpassed in order of magnitude by regulatory and institutional developments in the UAE (Dubai and Abu Dhabi) and, to a lesser extent, Qatar and Saudi Arabia. A key component of the market liberalization and corporatization programs underway in each case was the adoption of Western formal institutions and rules. These independent regulatory agencies (IRAs) were designed to reassure and attract international investors with the promise of predictable, efficient, and fair domestic governance.[66] Another vital trigger in the adoption of new legal and regulatory regimes was the impact of the September 11, 2001 attacks and the disclosure that several of the attackers, and much of the funds, had passed through Dubai at various points in the build-up to 9/11. Policymakers in the United States had, in fact, expressed concerns about the laundering of criminal financial flows through the Dubai banking system for several years prior to 2001, with one US intelligence agency warning that "Dubai has become a significant center for financing illicit activities, in part because the preference of many businesses to deal in large amounts of cash makes it difficult for banks to distinguish between legitimate and illicit transactions."[67]

The shock of 9/11 (which will be examined in greater detail in Chapter Five) on the federal authorities paved the way for "an exceptionally close working relationship" between the UAE Central Bank and US authorities, and led to the passage of a new anti-money laundering law in January 2002 and closer surveillance of the *hawala* networks used overwhelmingly by migrant workers in the UAE to remit money to their home countries in South and Southeast Asia, as part of a general crackdown on illegal money movements that targeted in particular the "informal economies" that thrived on the margins in Dubai, Sharjah, and the Northern Emirates.[68]

At the time (2002), the *Gulf States Newsletter* noted that the international pressure on the UAE was designed to accelerate and support the transition "from a souk mentality to a market mentality" and added that:

> ... This was based on persuading Dubai and Sharjah that it made more sense to live as business hubs for the globalized and regulated formal economy, rather than risk finding themselves pushed to the margins of life as "no questions asked" second league offshore centres.[69]

One particularly important measure adopted soon after the 9/11 attacks was a significant reduction in the threshold for which formal identification was required for money transfers, from Dh. 200,000 to Dh. 2000.[70] Another significant measure was the creation of a Financial Intelligence Unit (FIU) – the first in the Gulf – within the UAE Central Bank and the appointment of mandatory financial compliance officers by all banks and money changers in order to actively monitor *hawala* and other previously lightly regulated financial flows. In April 2006, the Governor of the Central Bank, Sultan bin Nasser al-Suweidi, stated that, with regard to the *hawala* networks that provided essential and cheap financial services to the tens of thousands of low-paid foreign workers who lacked access to formal banking systems:

> It is better to control it than to prohibit it … By covering *hawala* under our regime we have covered the three dimensions of the financial transfer system – formal transfers through banks, formal transfers through exchange houses and informal movements through *hawala*. [71]

Dubai subsequently led the way in the creation of a new financial hub after a change to the federal UAE constitution in 2004 that allowed the individual emirates to establish free trade zones. That same year, the Dubai International Financial Centre (DIFC) was legally established with its own stock market, the Dubai International Financial Exchange (DIFX). Significantly, the DIFC and the DIFX operated under the regulatory auspices of the Dubai Financial Services Authority (DFSA), which was based largely on the Anglo-Saxon legal system. As a result, "almost all dealings within the DIFC were exempt from UAE civil law."[72]

The DIFC and its related entities were integral to the development and diversification of Dubai's non-oil economy by Sheikh Mohammed bin Rashid, the Crown Prince of Dubai at the time (in 2004). Over the decade since its formation, the DIFC came to dominate the regional financial scene and also moved beyond its initial status as a regulatory "island." In particular, the DIFC Judicial Authority (known as DIFC Courts) became increasingly available to the business community at large as, in 2011, the Dubai government significantly expanded the jurisdiction of the DIFC Courts to allow any parties, even those not incorporated within the DIFC free zone, to use the DIFC Courts to resolve commercial disputes. Previously, only companies based in the DIFC or those that had an issue related to the DIFC could use the DIFC Courts, although the court will only hear a dispute if both parties agree to it. Based on the common law English model and using international judges from common law jurisdictions such as England, New Zealand, and Malaysia, the DIFC Courts developed a reputation among multinationals as more predictable and transparent with English as the working language and mechanisms in place for the winning party to claim costs from the losing party. For these reasons, the DIFC Courts emerged as the jurisdiction of choice for many international contracts and a major center for dispute resolution not only in Dubai but also for the region as a whole.[73]

Elements of institutional overlap and policy diffusion demonstrate how the DIFC was both a trend-setter and a model of emulation in the Gulf. This became evident in the founding in 2005 of an outwardly similar Qatar Financial Centre (QFC) nested within a distinct Qatar Financial Centre Regulatory Authority (QFCRA) and also using a bespoke legal system based on international law. The institutional similarities between the Dubai and Qatar models are in part attributable to the fact that they were designed by the same British expert, Philip Thorne, himself a former managing director of the Financial Services Authority (FSA) in London.[74] There were, nonetheless, significant differences between the QFC and the DIFC as the QFC did not launch a separate exchange as the DIFX. In addition, officials and regulators in Doha focused on creating niche expertise in areas such as reinsurance, captive insurance, and asset management rather than competing directly with the DIFC's broad-brush approach. By 2014, however, the QFC had found it difficult to compete with the much larger DIFC and the longer established Bahraini financial market, and was forced to draw up a new strategy designed to attract more non-financial firms that would be less likely to compete directly with Dubai.[75]

The launch in October 2015 of the Abu Dhabi Global Market (ADGM) as an institutional anchor of the Al Maryah Island urban redevelopment has added further concentrations of expertise to an already crowded regional financial sector. The ADGM is planned to form the centerpiece of a new financial free zone in Abu Dhabi and focuses broadly on asset management, private banking, and wealth management with its own civil and commercial legal regime incorporating aspects of English common law. The enabling legal and regulatory environment for the ADGM has been based on the announcement of a new law by the Abu Dhabi Executive Council (ADEC) in May 2013. A *Reuters* report noted that the decision to incorporate English common law, as in the DIFC, was very likely made in order to "facilitate ties between the ADGM and the DIFC, allowing the large community of bankers and lawyers that has developed in Dubai over the past decade to engage more easily with Abu Dhabi."[76] This strong element of institutional diffusion has further been evident in the fact that the executive adviser to the ADGM, Jan Bladen, was earlier a part of the team that put together the Dubai Financial Services Authority in 2004.[77] The hiring of ADGM's top leadership demonstrated also the internationalization of Gulf finance as the chief regulatory officer of the Singapore Exchange (SGX), Richard Teng, resigned in October 2014 to become chief executive of the regulator of ADGM.[78] Two months later, ADGM engaged Sir Hector Sants, the former Chief Executive of Britain's FSA, on a consulting contract to advise ADGM's regulatory framework in the run-up to its formal launch.[79]

In June 2013, global index compiler Morgan Stanley Capital International (MSCI) upgraded the UAE (and Qatar) from "Frontier" to "Emerging Market" (EM) status after five unsuccessful reviews that dated back to 2008. The move, which took effect in June 2014, signified a new era for capital flows in the UAE and Qatar as well as greater access to global funds.[80] The upgrade meant that investors in funds that track MSCI's popular Emerging Markets Index would be allocated weighted shares in each country. This gave the UAE weighted access to the estimated US$1.4 trillion in funds linked to the Emerging Markets Index, more than a hundredfold greater than the value of funds tied to the MSCI Frontier Markets Index.[81] Later in 2014, rival index compiler S&P Dow Jones Indices also promoted the UAE and Qatar to its own S&P Emerging Market BMI index series at the same time as the compiler downgraded Greece from Developed to Emerging status.[82]

Abu Dhabi Sovereign Wealth Funds and Government-Related Enterprises

A great deal of academic and policymaking attention has focused since the mid-2000s on the rise of GCC-based sovereign wealth funds (SWFs) and government-related enterprises (GREs). The Sovereign Wealth Fund Institute defines a sovereign wealth fund as "a state-owned investment fund or entity that is commonly established from balance of payments surpluses, official foreign currency operations, the proceeds of privatisations, governmental transfer payments, fiscal surpluses, and/or receipts resulting from resource exports."[83] After the Kuwait Investment Board (the forerunner to the Kuwait Investment Authority), which was established in 1953, the Abu Dhabi Investment Authority (ADIA) is the other long-established sovereign wealth fund in the Gulf. Founded in 1976, five years after the creation of the UAE, ADIA replaced the Financial Investment Board that had been created in 1967 by the Abu Dhabi Ministry of Finance and is owned and operated by the government of Abu Dhabi through the Abu Dhabi Investment Council (ADIC), itself founded in 2006 as a successor to the Abu Dhabi Investment Company. ADIA's governance is regulated by Law No. 5 of 1981 that mandates ADIA to invest funds on behalf of the Government of Abu Dhabi "to make available the necessary financial resources and maintain the future welfare of the Emirate." The Ruler of Abu Dhabi (and President of the UAE), Sheikh Khalifa bin Zayed Al Nahyan, is Chairman of the Board of Directors of ADIA, just as his half-brothers Sheikh Mohammed bin Zayed and Sheikh Mansour bin Zayed perform identical roles at two of the leading GREs in Abu Dhabi, the Mubadala Development Corporation and the International Petroleum Investment Company (IPIC) respectively.[84]

Together with the Kuwait Investment Authority, ADIA has developed a reputation as a cautious and low-risk investor in instruments such as US Treasury securities and government bonds, in contrast to the greater flamboyance of many of the younger generation of SWFs launched during the 2000s oil price boom, although it became more risk-tolerant in the 2000s.[85] ADIA has invested primarily in developed equities in North America and Europe, although greater attention has in recent years been paid to emerging markets in Asia, and in 2010 issued its very first annual review, which stated that:

> In total, around 80% of our assets are managed externally, in areas including equities, fixed income, foreign exchange, money markets, real estate, private equities and alternative investments.[86]

In 2009, ADIA reported twenty-year and thirty-year annualized rates of return of 6.5 percent and 8 percent respectively, which compare with returns of 13 percent and 16 percent reported over the same periods by Singapore's SWF, Temasek Holdings.[87] Nevertheless, ADIA and its counterparts across the UAE did develop into what two leading regional analysts have described as "sophisticated fund management houses, employing in-house experts with rich backgrounds in finance and investment banking."[88]

Moving beyond ADIA, each of the subsidiary sovereign wealth funds and GREs that were launched subsequently in Abu Dhabi were set up to fulfil a specific, and increasingly strategic, purpose. IPIC was established in 1984 by ADIA and the Abu Dhabi National Oil Company (ADNOC) to invest globally in energy and energy-related industries. Mubadala was launched in 2002 as a wholly owned Abu Dhabi government investment vehicle to focus on investment in capital intensive industries such as healthcare, semiconductor computer chip manufacturing, aerospace, and renewable energy, including the iconic Masdar City cleantech development in Abu Dhabi. The Abu Dhabi National Energy Company (known as Taqa) was formed in 2005 as an energy holding company for the government of Abu Dhabi and subsequently made substantial international investments in the North Sea, Canada, Africa, and Asia. Sara Bazoobandi has shown how, in practice, there has been significant overlap among ranking officials and board members across ADIA and the other three sovereign wealth funds, with individuals serving on multiple and, in the case of Taqa Chairman Hamad al-Hurr al-Suwaidi, all four boards simultaneously.[89]

Table 4.1 shows the inward and outward flows of foreign direct investment for the UAE between 2005 and 2014 and illustrates the scale of the decline in both flows after the 2008 global financial crisis and the Dubai debt crisis and their recovery as oil prices recovered prior to their 2014 fall.

Four examples illustrate how Abu Dhabi is able to mobilize and interconnect the resources available in its GREs in support of strategic investments that tie into broader economic diversification initiatives and attempts to broaden the industrial base and create skilled jobs for UAE nationals. The first has been the creation and expansion of the range of products and global partnerships of the Abu Dhabi Polymers Company (known also as Borouge), a joint venture launched in 1998 by ADNOC and Borealis, itself co-owned by IPIC and the Austrian oil and gas group

TABLE 4.1 Foreign Direct Investment Flows, 2005–2014

Year	Inward FDI (US$ millions)	Outward FDI (US$ millions)
2005–2007 (avg.)	12,631	9737
2011	7679	2178
2014	10,066	3072

Source: adapted by the author from the United Nations Conference on Trade and Development (UNCTAD) Country Fact Sheet: United Arab Emirates.

OMV. Borouge started producing polyethylene in 2001 and, as of 2015, has a production capacity of 3.5 million tons of polyolefins per year with plans to increase this further to 4.5 million tons per year.[90] Moreover, the "Borouge 2" project tripled the polyolefins manufacturing capacity of the petrochemical facility at Ruwais and installed the largest ethane cracker in the world, while "Borouge 3" launched a further phase of expansion into high added-value products in partnership with South Korea's Hyundai Engineering and Construction and Samsung Engineering.[91]

The second example of Abu Dhabi's "strategic investment" in practice lies in the formation of an Emirati aerospace industry, due in part to the launch of Strata Manufacturing as a wholly owned subsidiary of Mubadala and reflective also of the UAE's pivotal role in the reshaping of global aviation markets. Launched in 2009, Strata has concluded agreements with industry giants Boeing and Airbus to manufacture various aircraft parts at its composites aerostructures manufacturing facility in Al-Ain. In April 2012, Boeing and Mubadala announced a ten-year contract whereby Strata would manufacture empennage ribs for the Boeing 777 and vertical fin ribs for Boeing's flagship 787 Dreamliner. Jim Albaugh, the President and CEO of Boeing Commercial Airplanes, was explicit in linking the Strata contract – the first such partnership with a supplier in the Arab world – within the broader context of Boeing's strategic partnership with the UAE:

> The UAE is one of Boeing's most important commercial and defense customers, and its leaders have transformed its economy with aerospace investment and development. Boeing has been committed for several years to build a partnership with Mubadala Aerospace that brings long-term, mutual benefits to both companies.[92]

In June 2015, Boeing delivered the first 787 Dreamliner with vertical fin ribs manufactured at the Nibras Al Ain Aerospace Park to Abu Dhabi's Etihad Airways, an occasion that led Strata's chief executive, Badr al-Olama, to proclaim that the aircraft had, in part, been "made in the UAE, for the UAE."[93]

A third illustration of the strategic deployment of Emirati GREs was the June 2013 announcement that, after five years of negotiations, Emirates Aluminium (Emal) and Dubai Aluminium (Dubal) were to merge to create what the *Financial Times* labelled "a United Arab Emirates industrial champion valued at US$15 billion."[94] Emal itself had been created in 2006 as a partnership between Dubal and Mubadala and the formal merger of the companies brought together their smelters hitherto operated separately at Jebel Ali and Taweelah respectively. Mubadala of Abu Dhabi and the Investment Corporation of Dubai each took a 50 percent stake in the new Emirates Global Aluminium (EGA), which became the fourth largest producer of aluminium in the world. The partnership between the two government-owned investment branches of Abu Dhabi and Dubai was both symbolic as well as a rational consolidation to avoid duplication of efforts in a strategically significant sector. More than 6,000 new jobs in the Emirati aluminium sector were expected to result from the merger, which was described by the Oxford Business Group as "part of a broader effort to use the UAE's abundant energy supplies to diversify the country's economy."[95]

A similar sectoral consolidation of support behind a new "national champion" was the merger of 16 formerly separate UAE-based defense firms – primarily subsidiaries of Mubadala, Tawazun Holding (launched in 2007 as an industrial investment arm for the Offset Program Bureau), and the Emirates Advanced Investment Group (EAIG) – into the Emirates Defense Industries Company (EDIC) in December 2014. The firms included an unmanned systems developer created by Mubadala (Abu Dhabi Autonomous Systems Investment) as well as an advanced military repair, maintenance, and overhaul center that was a joint venture between Mubadala and global defense partners Lockheed and Sikorsky. The US-based *Defense News* website described the new entity as "the region's premier integrated national defense services and manufacturing platform" and a rationalization of a sprawling defense sector that would provide economies of scale and avoid duplication of effort. Indeed, *Defense News* noted further that:

> The UAE has the highest number of defense companies covering shipbuilding, unmanned systems, aviation and land systems in the region. More than 80 registered companies are based in Abu Dhabi, Dubai and Ras al-Khaimah, and at least 15 of those are state-owned firms.[96]

Ahmed al-Attar, a defense and security analyst at the Abu Dhabi-based *Delma Institute* think tank added that "This approach is part of the UAE government's drive to bring down cost and is a push to be more lean and efficient ... this is part of making the industry more globally competitive."[97] Toward the end of EDIC's first year of operation, its Chairman, Homaid al-Shemmari (formerly the chief executive of Aerospace and Engineering Services at Mubadala), mapped out a more expansive pathway of deepening integration with international partners and moving beyond local assembly in the UAE to functioning as a major regional hub and eventually operating as a world-leading defense industry closely aligned with changing geopolitical and strategic patterns and local security requirements:

> We hope to benefit from localization, knowledge transfer and capability building, while our partners will benefit from enhanced technological resources and expertise from a centralized hub of world-class products and services ... In essence, we are a hub that can facilitate the UAE's relationship with international OEMs [original equipment manufacturers], ensuring that our businesses are strategically aligned with the needs of GHQ [the UAE armed forces' General Headquarters].[98]

Finally in this section, and distinct from the examples cited above, is a fourth case that illustrates the use of "strategic investment" not for economic diversification or industrial development within the UAE but as a tool of UAE foreign policy.

Chapter Six will examine in detail the UAE's policy responses to the political upheaval that shook parts of the Middle East and North Africa during the "Arab Spring" of 2011. In addition to high levels of state support to the restoration of military rule in Egypt following the ousting of the Muslim Brotherhood government in Egypt in July 2013, the involvement of Emirati-based companies in Egypt provides insight into the thin lines that separate ostensibly "private sector" initiatives from the state and GREs. Particular attention focused on a March 2014 announcement that Dubai-based construction giant Arabtec would construct up to one million homes in Egypt as well as a March 2015 announcement that Abu Dhabi-based Capital City Partners would lead on the construction of a new administrative capital for Cairo.[99]

The initial agreement reached between the Egyptian government and Arabtec envisaged the construction of a million new homes across thirteen sites in Egypt over five years in a contract valued at up to US$40 billion. Arabtec's then CEO, Hasan Abdullah Ismaik, who resigned during the summer of 2014 as shares in the company plunged, stated that the agreement owed much to the architect of Abu Dhabi's regionally assertive policy toward Egypt, Crown Prince Mohammed bin Zayed:

> … who has been very keen to mobilize all efforts to boost support to our brothers in Egypt through a multitude of humanitarian, economic and social initiatives.[100]

Indeed, the largest institutional shareholder in Arabtec (with a 36.1 percent stake) is Aabar Investments, a "private" joint stock Abu Dhabi–based company majority-owned by IPIC, while Khadem Abdullah al-Qubaisi was (in 2014) simultaneously the Chairman of Arabtec, Chairman of Aabar, and the Managing Director of IPIC. (Al-Qubaisi relinquished all his roles in April 2015 after being caught up in the widening scandal linked to Malaysia's 1MDB state investment fund, with whom Aabar had partnered, and substantial unexplained payments seemingly made in part through a Swiss-based private bank owned by IPIC to Malaysia's Prime Minister, Najib Razak.)[101]

With Arabtec in financial difficulty and unable to put in place sufficient financing for the scheme, reports in the Egyptian media in September 2015 indicated that the project would be scaled back to just one-tenth of its original size and that only 100,000 housing units would eventually be built.[102]

A broadly similar fate befell the planned US$45 billion Capital Cairo scheme. The initial announcement of the leadership of Capital City Partners, a private real estate fund founded by the previously mentioned Emaar chairman Mohammad Alabbar, came at a high-profile economic summit organized in part by the UAE to kick-start foreign investment into Egypt four years after the revolution that swept away the longstanding President, Hosni Mubarak. Alabbar's intensely close relationship with Sheikh Mohammed bin Rashid, the UAE Prime Minister (as well as Ruler of Dubai) has already been noted in connection with Emaar. However, as with Arabtec, difficulties arose over the financing of the project with Alabbar reportedly insisting on securing financing from external sources rather than from Egyptian banks. An Egyptian newspaper claimed in September 2015 that Egypt's Investment Minister Ashraf Salman had cancelled the Memorandum of Understanding (MOU) with Alabbar to develop the scheme, and it was later confirmed that Capital City Partners would only be one of several partners in the project as it moved forward.[103]

Evolving Energy Dynamics

Policymakers in Abu Dhabi followed a different investment strategy from their counterparts in Dubai during the 1990s and 2000s. While officials in Dubai, led proactively by the Ruler, Sheikh Mohammed bin Rashid Al Maktoum, focused on building up global brands such as Emirates Airline, Abu Dhabi concentrated instead on attracting inward investment in commercial sectors such as aviation and semi-conductors that tied directly into economic diversification efforts in the emirate.[104] Such approaches reflected also Dubai's relatively more urgent need in the 1990s to broaden the economic base away from energy and more actively pursue higher-risk strategies to attract inward foreign direct investment. Policymakers in Abu Dhabi, by contrast, concentrated on maximizing the emirate's comparative advantage in the energy sector and building up large stocks of overseas capital held in sovereign wealth funds and other investment vehicles. Perhaps most obviously, Abu Dhabi, unlike Dubai, has a substantial non-oil deficit that reflects the centrality (although not exclusivity) of oil and gas to Abu Dhabi's economy, which itself made up 61 percent of UAE GDP in 2011.[105]

Chapter Two covered the early development of the oil sector in Abu Dhabi in the 1960s. The Abu Dhabi National Oil Company (ADNOC) was formed in 1971 to manage and operate all oil and gas operations in Abu Dhabi following the formation of the UAE. ADNOC acquired a 25 percent stake in the Abu Dhabi Petroleum Company (ADPC) and the Abu Dhabi Marine Areas (ADMA) which, as Chapter Two noted, was originally set up as a joint venture between British Petroleum/BP and the Compagnie Francaise des Petrole/Total. Two years later, in 1973, ADNOC increased its stake in both ADPC and ADMA to 60 percent, giving it a controlling interest in each company but without the outright nationalization of the energy sector that happened in Kuwait and Saudi Arabia. The continuing partnership with international oil companies set Abu Dhabi apart from most other OPEC oil-producing states during the wave of energy-sector nationalizations in the 1960s and 1970s, and was based upon long-term production sharing agreements (PSAs) between ADNOC and its partners. Further reorganization of Abu Dhabi's oil sector occurred in April 1977 when ADMA became the Abu Dhabi Marine Operating Company (ADMA-OPCO) and formally took control of all offshore operations. The shareholding representation in ADMA-OPCO remained unchanged and was divided among ADNOC (60 percent), British Petroleum (14.66 percent), Total (13.33 percent), and the Japan Oil Development

Company (JODCO – 12 percent). The following year, in September 1978, saw the formalization of all onshore operations within the newly created Abu Dhabi Company for Onshore Oil Operations (ADCO), with the shareholding split among ADNOC (60 percent), British Petroleum, Total, and Royal Dutch Shell (9.5 percent each), and Exxon and Mobil (4.75 percent each).[106]

Since 1971, ADNOC has developed into one of the largest and most diversified oil companies in the world with extensive upstream and downstream holdings as well as a corporate reach that spans all aspects of the oil and gas sector. As of 2015, ADNOC operates sixteen subsidiaries while ADCO has become the largest crude oil producer in the southern part of the Gulf, although the oil price fall that began in mid-2014 inevitably had an impact and led to a significant leadership reshuffle and job losses among the 60,000 strong workforce.[107] While recent exploration efforts have failed to yield major new discoveries, investment in enhanced oil recovery (EOR) techniques has resulted in a near-doubling of proven reserves from existing fields. The average daily production of 2.7 million barrels of oil in 2014 made the UAE (Abu Dhabi) the fourth-highest crude oil producer in OPEC after Saudi Arabia, Iraq, and Iran.[108] Officials in Abu Dhabi plan a further expansion of oil production to 3.5 million barrels per day through a combination of EOR and additional development of the Upper Zakum offshore field. However, delays in the awarding of initial contracts and in the exploration and production phases have resulted in the timeline for reaching the 3.5 million mark being pushed back from 2017 to 2020.[109]

On January 10, 2014, the historic seventy-five-year ADCO concession granted originally by Sheikh Shakhbut to the Petroleum Development Company (Trucial Coast) expired. Although the terms of the concession were altered subsequently by the ADNOC purchase of 25 percent and 60 percent stakes after independence, the initial concessionaires or their successor entities remained in place until 2014. The lengthy (and, at the time of writing in late 2016, unresolved) process of negotiating a new concession – covering the fifteen major onshore fields in Abu Dhabi and more than half of the emirate's total production – cast light upon the substantial changes to both the global energy landscape and to the changing regional geopolitics of the UAE itself. The January 2015 announcement of France's Total as the first partner (with a 10 percent stake worth an estimated US$2.2 billion) in the new forty-year concession was uncontroversial as the company had held a 9.5 percent stake in the historic concession. Subsequent concessions announced in the spring of 2015 included Inpex of Japan (5 percent) and GS Energy of South Korea (3 percent). Oil giant ExxonMobil, holder of two of the historic concessions (for Exxon and for Mobil) withdrew from the bidding in 2014 but other companies that remained in competition for the remaining 22 percent stake in the concession include BP and Shell (like ExxonMobil, historic concession holders) as well as the Korea National Oil Company and PetroChina.[110]

ADNOC and its subsidiaries have also played the primary role in extracting and exporting the significant reserves of natural gas in Abu Dhabi. Estimated gas reserves of 215 trillion cubic feet constitute the seventh largest in the world although the majority is "associated gas" tied to oil extraction. Data compiled by Justin Dargin on the breakdown of gas reserves by emirate reflects the extreme concentration in Abu Dhabi, which contained 92.58 percent of total UAE gas reserves in 2009, compared with 4.99 percent in Sharjah, 1.87 percent in Dubai, 0.56 percent in Ras al-Khaimah, and no discernible reserves in Ajman, Fujairah, or Umm al-Quwain.[111] An estimated 26 percent of gross natural gas production between 2003 and 2012 was injected back into the oilfields as part of the enhanced oil recovery measures to boost production from mature fields.[112]

Onshore natural (and associated) gas is processed by the Abu Dhabi Gas Industries Limited Company (GASCO), a joint venture between ADNOC and its long-established partners from the historic oil concession, Total, Shell, and Partex.[113] In 1973, the creation of Abu Dhabi Gas Liquefaction Company (AdGas) marked the launch of the first Liquefied Natural Gas (LNG) production company in the Middle East with the exclusive right to export LNG – processed primarily from offshore fields – from Abu Dhabi. AdGas has been structured in a similar pattern to the Abu Dhabi oil companies and features a majority ADNOC shareholding (70 percent) alongside trusted international partners.[114]

Significantly, in view both of the subsequent destination of the majority of Abu Dhabi gas exports and Japan's key role in the growth of the LNG industry in neighboring Qatar, the largest international shareholding in AdGas is Mitsui & Co (15 percent), followed by BP (10 percent) and Total (5 percent). East Asian markets, particularly Japan, have taken the vast majority of LNG exports from Abu Dhabi over the past four decades. Energy demands soared as East Asian economies recovered from the devastation wrought by World War II transformed into early proponents of highly specialized, value-added "knowledge economies." Japan began to import LNG in the late 1960s and played the pivotal role not only in creating the demand for LNG from Abu Dhabi (and, later, Qatar) but also in financing and constructing the complex infrastructure needed to underpin LNG exports. In addition to Mitsui's involvement in AdGas from the very beginning, a 2012 research paper from French energy think-tank IFRI made clear the totality of Japanese involvement in the origins of Abu Dhabi's LNG sector:

> ... Mitsui's contacts with large Japanese electricity production and distribution companies allowed the first contract to be signed in 1972, whereby AdGas supplied the Tokyo Electric Power Company (TEPCO) ... this agreement, which guaranteed a market for Abu Dhabi, allowed the production of LNG to be launched ... Japan's role was also fundamental in financing the project, via the Export-Import Bank of Japan (J-Exim), guarantees by the Ministry of Trade and Industry (MITI) and the participation of Japan's private banking sector.[115]

In 1977, the first cargo of LNG left Das Island in Abu Dhabi for Japan under the abovementioned long-term supply agreement with TEPCO. The gas liquefaction trains at Das Island were themselves constructed by the Japanese Chiyoda

Corporation and TEPCO has remained the major consumer of Abu Dhabi's LNG ever since. Indeed, by 2010, Japan was the destination for no less than 86 percent of Abu Dhabi's LNG exports.[116]

Since 2008, the UAE has been in the paradoxical position of being both an LNG exporter and a net importer of natural gas. Gas consumption in the UAE outstripped production for the first time in 2006 and, by 2009, reached 59.1 billion cubic meters (bcm) per day compared with a production figure of 48.8 bcm. As Justin Dargin has noted, "one reason Emirati natural gas demand is so high is because of the disproportionate role it plays in power generation [where] it accounts for 98 percent" of the total.[117] Moreover, rapid demographic growth in the UAE and the pattern of energy-intensive industrialization in industries such as fertilizer and aluminum also contributed to the sharp rise in energy consumption across the seven emirates in the 2000s, as did a rise in the proportion of the UAE's demand for water being met from energy-intensive desalination plants from 63 percent in 1990 to 85 percent fifteen years later.[118]

The emerging gap between energy production and consumption levels led to a two-pronged policy response in the UAE. First, Abu Dhabi took the lead in forming Dolphin Energy Limited in 1999 in which the wholly Abu Dhabi–government owned Mubadala Development Corporation held a 51 percent stake alongside Total and Enron, which each held a 24.5 percent stake (with Enron's share being acquired by Occidental Petroleum after Enron's ignominious 2002 collapse). The current Crown Prince of Abu Dhabi, Sheikh Mohammed bin Zayed Al Nahyan, was one of the driving forces behind the Dolphin project in the 1990s in his capacity as the head of the UAE Offsets Group. The Dolphin project partnered with Qatar Petroleum to produce and supply natural gas from Qatar's giant North Field by undersea pipeline to a gas receiving facility at Taweelah in Abu Dhabi for onward utilization in both the UAE and Oman. However, political opposition from Saudi Arabia meant that initial plans for a broader Gulf Cooperation Council (GCC) wide gas grid never came to fruition despite an agreement on nearly all aspects of such a regional grid, except for the price of the gas, as far back as the annual GCC Summit in December 1990.[119]

Complications over pricing have also undermined the subsequent "pared down" Dolphin Project. The inaugural pipeline from Al-Ain to Fujairah was completed in January 2004 and gas production to the UAE began in 2007 and to Oman in 2008, marking a milestone as the first ever cross-border transmission in the history of the GCC. A second pipeline was completed from Taweelah to Fujairah in December 2010 and gas from the Dolphin project now supplies the eastern region of the UAE, including the relatively resource-poor Northern Emirates. Dolphin nevertheless operates well below its 33 bcm per day capacity as pricing disputes with Qatar have prevented its full utilization; in 2011, the pipeline carried 17 bcm per day to Abu Dhabi and a further 2 bcm per day to Oman. The UAE and Oman pay US$1.50 per MMBtu under a pricing formula that was negotiated at the start of the Dolphin Project and before oil and gas prices began to rise exponentially in 2002. The "political price" of the Dolphin gas stands in sharp contrast to the price of US$11–16 per MMBtu that Dubai began to pay on the open market after it started to import LNG in the late 2000s. Steven Wright and Jim Krane have observed how:

> while Qatar judged the exports politically important during the negotiations in the 1990s, subsequent disagreement over Qatar's attempts to seek higher prices for the remaining capacity – and a recalibration of Qatar's geopolitical priorities – have pushed Qatari gas marketers to seek oil-linked prices and markets outside the Gulf. The pricing conundrum is based on opposing valuation methods. Qatar's neighbors are willing to pay what they consider a reasonable mark-up on production costs below US$1 MMBtu. But Qatari officials, who value gas by the far higher netbacks from customers in Asia and Europe, view regional requests for "discounted" gas as unrealistic.[120]

Separate from the Dolphin Project, in the late 2000s the UAE became an importer of LNG. In 2008, Dubai reached fifteen-year supply agreements with Royal Dutch Shell and QatarGas and constructed a floating regasification plant that opened in Jebel Ali in 2010. Gas imports were needed to meet the surging growth in demand for power and water that exceeded 20 percent per year at the height of the pre-crisis Dubai boom.[121] The imported gas also plugged peak-demand shortages during the summer months between May and September and reflected the fact that the majority of the gas from the Dolphin Project was earmarked for Abu Dhabi rather than Dubai.[122] In 2015, a combination of falling worldwide LNG prices and continuing growth in domestic demand for electricity and water led the UAE Energy Minister, Suhail al-Mazrouei, to announce plans to further expand the capacity of the Dubai import terminal, in addition to pre-existing plans to construct a LNG import facility in Fujairah with a capacity of 9 million tons per year, three times that of the Dubai facility.[123]

Responsibility for the Fujairah LNG import facility is vested in Emirates LNG, a joint venture established in 2012 in a 50:50 partnership between two of Abu Dhabi's most prominent investment funds, Mubadala and the International Petroleum Investment Company (IPIC). Upon completion in 2018, the Fujairah terminal will increase the total LNG import capacity of the UAE to 18 million tons per year, more than double the current export capacity of 8 million tons of LNG annually.[124] The Fujairah initiative is significant both for Abu Dhabi's hands-on involvement and because it ties into the rapid growth in energy infrastructure in the emirate as UAE officials take advantage of its location outside the Strait of Hormuz chokepoint with direct access to the Gulf of Oman and the Indian Ocean beyond.

Neighboring Sharjah also looked to import gas in the 2000s in order to safeguard its role as the energy hub for the Northern Emirates as its own limited reserves of associated gas produced by BP from the Sajaa field neared depletion. Notably, Fujairah, Ras al-Khaimah, and Umm al-Quwain had all been generating electricity with gas produced in Sharjah.[125] In 2001, officials from Sharjah and Iran agreed to construct a pipeline that would transport Iranian gas to Sharjah, and

Sharjah-based Crescent Petroleum negotiated a purchase price with the National Iranian Oil Company (NIOC).[126] Under the agreement, the gas would be processed in Sharjah and transported to utility and industrial users by Dana Gas, an independent company that counted Crescent Petroleum as one of the major shareholders (with a 20.9 percent stake) alongside Gulf-wide stakeholders that also included the Sharjah government, the Bank of Sharjah, and private Kuwaiti and Saudi interests. An official from the Sharjah Electricity and Water Authority (SEWA) summed up the anticipated benefit of the deal as he told the *Oxford Business Group* that "Iranian gas will be very cheap, with power at 4 to 5 fils per MWh to produce."[127] However, while the pipeline linking the Salman gas field south of Lavan Island in Iran to the Hamriyah Free Zone in Sharjah was completed in 2008, a dispute of pricing in 2010 as well as internal political opposition within Iran to the export of gas at a time of mounting domestic energy shortages saw the deal collapse in acrimony.[128]

After the case moved to a tribunal held under the auspices of the International Court of Arbitration, which ruled in favor of Crescent Petroleum in 2014, an op-ed in Abu Dhabi's English-language *The National* in April 2015 described how the outcome of the arbitration award "is being watched closely by international oil companies eyeing the prospect that Iran's hydrocarbons sector will once again open up" following the implementation of the Joint Comprehensive Plan of Action between Iran and the international community. Nevertheless, *The National* recounted also how:

> originally an argument about price, the Crescent dispute ended up involving accusations of corruption and conspiracy in which a British-Iranian businessman, Abbas Yazdi, was roped in to testify and ended up becoming the victim of kidnap and murder in Dubai in 2013 … While a direct link was never categorically established, the chief prosecutor Khaled Al Zarouni told the Dubai Criminal Court during the case that Mr. Yazdi had given video evidence to the tribunal hearing the Crescent-Iran case in The Hague shortly before he was kidnapped.[129]

It emerged also that Yazdi was an associate of Mehdi Hahsemi Rafsanjani, son of the former Iranian President Akbar Hashemi Rafsanjani, who had been involved in the original negotiations with Crescent but had fallen out of political favor in Iran and was sentenced in March 2015 to fifteen years' imprisonment on corruption charges.[130] As of mid-2016, the Crescent dispute remains unresolved and the opening of the Iranian energy sector (and wider economy) to international investors has been complicated by overlapping US sanctions that prohibit direct financial dealings with Iran. If and when these non-nuclear and secondary sanctions are lifted, the UAE may stand to gain considerably as a launching-pad for international groups and investors seeking to re-engage with Iran but doing so from the comparatively greater "familiarity" of the UAE rather than setting up operations within Iran itself.

Renewable and Atomic Energy

The rapid, even startling growth of renewable energy in Abu Dhabi since the mid-2000s provides a case study in how a determined leadership campaign dovetailed with the ready availability of investment resources to reposition the UAE in one key facet of international energy governance. The launch in April 2006 of the Masdar Initiative – a wide-ranging blueprint for renewable energy that encompassed the Masdar City project, Masdar Power, the Masdar Institute of Science and Technology, and the Masdar Cleantech Fund was sweeping in its ambition and policy objectives. Three years later, the capturing of the right to host the International Renewable Energy Agency (IRENA) meant that, for the first time, an intergovernmental organization was headquartered in the Middle East. Both the Masdar Initiative and IRENA were impressive milestones that immediately marked Abu Dhabi as a niche leader in renewable energy even as the emirate also developed a major civil nuclear energy program.[131]

On the surface, the grandiose plans unveiled in Abu Dhabi to become a world-leading center of research and development into renewable energy stood in marked contrast to the environmentally damaging policies of economic (and fossil fuel) development in the country. By the late 2000s, the UAE ranked second globally on a list of carbon emissions per capita (behind Qatar) with a figure nearly 50 percent higher than that of the USA. Also in the late 2000s, the UAE had the world's largest ecological footprint per capita with a figure of 11.9 global hectares/person against a world average of 1.8 global hectares/person, and significantly higher than the comparable figures for GCC neighbors Kuwait (7.6 global hectares/person) and Saudi Arabia (4.6 global hectares/person).[132] Water desalination plants, made possible by cheap domestic feedstock, coupled with heavily subsidised rates for water usage, compound the problem of resource over-consumption, with Mari Luomi finding that the average resident of the UAE used more than four times more water per day (equivalent to 550 litres) than their counterpart in the United Kingdom.[133] Between 1990 and 2005 alone, the proportion of water demand met by desalination – an energy-intensive and environmentally damaging process – rose steadily from 63 percent to 85 percent.[134]

And yet, against this pattern of the unsustainable and environmentally destructive use of resources, officials in Abu Dhabi invested considerable time, effort, and capital to become a world leader in renewable and alternative energy. Investment in the UAE rose substantially after 2004, building upon the strong environmental legacy of the nation's founding father, Sheikh Zayed bin Sultan Al Nahyan, who died the same year. In April 2006, the Masdar Initiative was launched under the auspices of the Abu Dhabi Future Energy Company, itself a subsidiary of Mubadala and intended, from the beginning, as an overarching strategy for renewable energy rather than merely a project in itself.[135] The initiative encompassed not only the expansive "Masdar City" project of creating a zero-carbon city in the desert adjacent to Abu Dhabi's international airport, but also a wider technology hub and cluster for research and investment into renewable and future energies as well as technology transfer and job creation in Abu Dhabi. Other relevant entities included the Masdar Institute of Science and Technology, which opened in September 2009 in a partnership with the Massachusetts Institute of Technology (MIT), and the World Future Energy Summit, which has taken place every year since 2008. Moreover, Abu Dhabi campaigned vigorously to host IRENA at Masdar City, successfully beating out Germany and South Korea in the process. Together, these developments enabled the emirate to brand itself, somewhat improbably in light of its ecological footprint, as a global leader in the renewable energy field.[136]

Closer examination of Abu Dhabi's approach toward the Masdar Initiative and the IRENA bid illustrates some of the comparative advantages – and also the pitfalls – of attempts to create strategic niches in sector-specific areas. The plans for Masdar City unveiled with great fanfare in 2006 had to be scaled back significantly following the financial slowdown in 2009 and a slew of other difficulties in translating initial intent into capability. In her work on energy and sustainable development in the UAE, Mari Luomi has summarized the challenges that faced the developers as including "over-optimistic assumptions, hasty marketing, colossal promises, rushed implementation, and, most likely, bad recruitment choices," and has observed further that:

> one of Masdar's major mistakes has been over-reliance on technologies that were not yet ready or could not be implemented on the city site. Technical problems began emerging as early as 2008, as tests revealed that because of the high temperatures and dust, PV solar panels were operating at less than 40 percent of advertised minimum capacity … Policy obstacles were also a major hindrance: wind turbines, originally in the master plan, could not be set up on the city area because of restrictions due to the vicinity of the airport.[137]

Moreover, Dennis Kumetat, a German diplomat who conducted extensive doctoral research on renewable energy in Abu Dhabi, added that a further obstacle to Masdar's organic growth at the time of its inception was the absence of a significant:

> local industry structure to which a fledgling technology hub such as Masdar can relate, from which it can draw a trained workforce and with which it can share market expertise … in the absence of a domestic market there is only a tiny workforce that is trained in the renewables sector … Therefore, as long as the basic market structures in the UAE and in the GCC region itself are absent, any technology hub will face great difficulties in translating the expertise and know-how that it develops into a meaningful domestic economic advantage.[138]

Kumetat also recorded strong criticism from an external interviewee who asked "How could they [Masdar] talk about technology transfer and then open a PV plant in Germany and axe the one they wanted to build here. This is exactly the opposite of what should be done."[139] Following the financial crisis, the operating budget for Masdar City was cut by a quarter in 2010, the timeline for its development extended, and a number of technical features cancelled. These had the effect of transforming the original intent of creating a "zero-carbon" city first to a "carbon-neutral" city and subsequently merely to a "low-carbon" city.[140]

The above should not imply that the Masdar Initiative has failed; indeed, it may be argued that the reformulation of the plans in 2010 made the city and its associated ventures more realistic both in policy scope and implementation timetable. Key deliverables certainly have materialized. MIST opened on schedule in 2009 and graduated its first class of 82 students in 2011, while by 2014 an expanded internship and outreach program among Emirati youth meant that 162 Emiratis were among the 417-strong student cohort.[141] MIST also worked with IRENA to establish a center for energy policy and technology designed to boost research and development into energy supply infrastructure in developing countries.[142] Meanwhile, in March 2013 Masdar opened the world's largest solar power plant in operation when it inaugurated the first phase of the Shams solar power station in western Abu Dhabi, a joint initiative between Masdar Power (60 percent) and Total and Abengoa Solar (20 percent each). More than seventy local Emirati companies were involved in manufacturing equipment for the plant, whose inauguration meant that Masdar controlled no less than 12 percent of installed global capacity for concentrated solar power (CSP) technology.[143]

The opening of Shams-1 was celebrated in Abu Dhabi not only as a step toward achieving the broader strategic vision of transitioning into a knowledge economy by 2030 but also as part of the ambitious target of getting 7 percent of the UAE's energy from renewable sources by 2021 as laid out in the National Agenda 2021. The director of clean energy at Masdar, Bader al-Lamki, acknowledged in 2013 that "Hydrocarbons will diminish one day and it is important that we diversify the mix. Abu Dhabi has been a leader in this field, and we would like to continue in that role on the global stage."[144] Elsewhere in the UAE, the Dubai Supreme Council of Energy launched an annual World Green Energy Summit (WGES) in April 2014 in another initiative aimed at fostering global partnerships.[145] Notwithstanding sceptics in the energy community who doubted the feasibility of the 2021 target of securing 7 percent of UAE energy from renewable sources, the Government of Dubai in January 2015 tripled its own emirate-specific target to increase the share of renewables to 15 percent of its total energy mix by 2030 as it cited the falling cost of solar energy technology.[146] Much of Dubai's output comes from the giant Mohammed bin Rashid Al Maktoum Solar Park, which opened in 2013 as the largest single-site project to generate electricity in the world and whose phased expansion forms the cornerstone of the emirate's ambitious renewable plans.[147]

The examples of growing collaboration between local and global providers of renewable energy technology are intended to accelerate the transfer of technology and the creation of organic research clusters that will, in turn, form the cornerstone of economic diversification in the UAE. These have raised considerably the international profile of the UAE in ways that have belied stereotypical views of the country as merely an oil state. Moreover, the moves to develop nuclear and solar power are needed to meet the rapid increase in UAE energy demand, estimated to grow at 9 percent annually in a government report published in 2015, which also laid out the rationale both for greater energy diversification and efficiency. This is enshrined also in the *UAE 2021* vision, which set out an ambitious target of reducing the proportion of natural gas in the energy mix from 98 percent to 76 percent, largely through the anticipated use of nuclear and renewable energy sources.[148]

Yet, the energy case for diversification notwithstanding, it is also the case that careful leveraging of the oil-derived largesse available to policymakers in Abu Dhabi has made possible many of the breakthroughs in renewable energy that have propelled the emirate to global recognition. This is evident in the successful campaign to bring IRENA to Abu Dhabi, at the expense of competitors with far longer records of engaging with renewable energy. Luomi has outlined the package of financial incentives that made the Abu Dhabi bid for the right to host IRENA in 2009 difficult to turn down. These included a pledge by Abu Dhabi to cover "all the building and operating costs of the agency" as part of a commitment of US $135 million to the new organization. In addition to these fixed costs, the financial package included an offer of annual loans of US$50 million from the Abu Dhabi Fund for Development to fund IRENA-approved projects in developing states between 2009 and 2015. Luomi noted further that the largesse of the Abu Dhabi "bid" far exceeded that of Germany's, which included US$46 million for setting up IRENA and US$3–4 million for annual operating costs, and concluded that "Abu Dhabi's oil wealth may have been the deciding factor in its victory over Europe's leader in renewable energy, which had originally envisioned the launch of the organisation."[149]

In June 2015, IRENA moved into a new permanent headquarters in the heart of Masdar City hailed as one of the greenest and most sustainable buildings in the world for energy, water, and carbon efficiency, Five months later, the announcement that Israel – which has been a permanent member of IRENA since the start and whose participation in an IRENA conference in Abu Dhabi in January 2014 led to a Kuwaiti boycott of the event[150] – would station a diplomatic representative – named by *Haaretz* as diplomat Rami Hatan – accredited to IRENA in Abu Dhabi caused international headlines and sparked talk of a thaw in Gulf–Israel relations. Notwithstanding that Israeli trade offices had been opened in Qatar and Oman in the late 1990s and that the move would not have been the first Israeli diplomatic mission in a GCC state, the delicate nature of the issue prompted the UAE Ministry of Foreign Affairs to emphasize that representation would be confined to IRENA and not extended to the UAE as a whole. Indeed, after the participation of Israeli Minister of National Infrastructure, Energy, and Water Resources Silvan Shalom, Anwar Gargash, the Minister of State for Foreign Affairs, was at pains to clarify that:

the UAE has been able, through a delicate balance, to differentiate between Israel's membership in IRENA and the normalization of bilateral ties, which

Israel has been seeking ... [The UAE] will not rush into a free normalization with Israel, like other countries did.[151]

Gargash's comments notwithstanding, a slew of former Israeli officials have hinted at the thawing of ties between Israel and the UAE and other Gulf States, with Israel's former Ambassador to Egypt, Zvi Mazel, stating, three days after the January 2016 "Implementation Day" of the Iranian nuclear agreement, that "During the Iran nuclear talks Israel's intelligence community starting having more effective ties with Gulf countries ... The Emirates have ties with us due to our common interests against Iran and the Muslim Brotherhood."[152] Such sentiments echoed a streak of pragmatism that had been voiced several years earlier, in 2011, when Dubai's outspoken Chief of Police, Lieutenant General Dahi Khalfan Tamim, acknowledged in an interview with Germany's *Spiegel Online* that:

> we know that many Israelis come here with non-Israeli passports, and we treat them the way we treat anyone else. We protect their lives just as we protect the lives of others, and we don't concern ourselves with their religion.[153]

In addition to IRENA, policymakers in Abu Dhabi launched a civil nuclear energy program that eventually will consist of four nuclear reactors situated in the western region of Abu Dhabi. Conceived in 2007, shortly after the failure of a mooted GCC-wide nuclear energy project, construction on three of the reactors began in 2012 and the first is expected to begin operation in 2017. The policy motivation for the choice to pursue nuclear energy was laid out in a March 2007 government white paper entitled *The Policy of the UAE on the Evaluation and Potential Development of Peaceful Nuclear Energy*. One of the key determinants was a finding that domestic demand for electricity would increase by 165 percent by 2020 and natural gas would be able to supply less than half of that demand along with the above-mentioned 7 percent from renewable sources. This formed the prelude to the launch of a tender process in June 2008 for the construction of the four nuclear reactors through joint ventures with local Emirati partners.[154]

From the start of the nuclear program, policymakers in Abu Dhabi cooperated intensively with the International Atomic Energy Agency (IAEA) and international partners such as the United States to ensure that its nuclear plans met the highest standards of transparency, safeguarding, and monitoring. Such attention to meeting and even going beyond the requirements of global best-practice, was seen as vital in order to gain the support of the international community in general, and the United States in particular.[155] This was made clear during a February 2015 interview by the UAE resident representative to the IAEA, Ambassador Hamad al-Kaabi:

> Transfer of technology, nuclear material and knowledge can only be done through a robust nuclear cooperation framework. The UAE has concluded nine bilateral nuclear cooperation agreements with responsible and experienced nuclear countries ...

From the outset, all steps taken have been in line with the IAEA's Mile-stones Approach ... Additionally, the UAE has concluded and implemented all relevant international agreements under the auspices of the Agency covering all areas of safety, security, non-proliferation and nuclear liability ...

The IAEA has been supporting us in developing the nuclear reactor, its legal framework and training. An Integrated Work Plan with the Agency enabled us to establish a holistic approach of IAEA assistance towards the UAE program ... [156]

US Congressional approval for the "123" nuclear cooperation deal offered by the outgoing Bush administration in January 2009 sent a powerful signal of geopolitical support for the UAE as a stable actor implementing nuclear energy in a responsible manner that addresses proliferation concerns and forms a model for other Middle Eastern states seeking a nuclear energy capability.[157] Most notably, in order to reassure the international community regarding proliferation concerns (and to stand in direct contradistinction to Iran's highly contentious nuclear program), the UAE foreswore "proliferation-sensitive capabilities" such as uranium enrichment and spent fuel reprocessing.[158]

International Aviation and Global Branding

The startling rise of Emirates and Etihad, together with Qatar Airways, has reshaped global aviation markets around the three hubs of Dubai, Abu Dhabi, and Doha as the Gulf airlines have developed into what the *Economist* magazine has labelled "global super-connectors" capable of connecting any two points in the world with one stopover in the Gulf.[159] This culminated in the January 2015 announcement that Dubai International Airport had overtaken London's Hea-throw Airport to become the world's busiest airport for international passengers. Significantly, the 6 percent annual rise in Dubai's international passengers (to almost 70 million in 2014) contrasted with the far smaller rate of increase caused by Heathrow operating at near-peak capacity owing to space and regulatory con-straints. Both Emirates and Etihad have, moreover, benefited from the relative absence of political or legal constraints compared with European and North American "legacy carriers," much to the chagrin of those airlines.[160]

For many years after the formation of the UAE, the "national" airline was Gulf Air, which had initially been created as Gulf Aviation in 1951 with the support and involvement of the British Overseas Airways Corporation (BOAC – the forerunner of British Airways). The governments of the UAE, Bahrain, Oman, and Qatar bought out the BOAC stake in 1973 and the airline became an early symbol of pan-Gulf unity with ownership divided among the four Gulf States. Yet, it was Gulf Air's relative neglect of Dubai that prompted the ruling circle in that emirate to form their own airline, Emirates, which catapulted Dubai (and the UAE) to the pinnacle of the changing landscape of global aviation. The standoff between Gulf Air and the Ruler of Dubai began in 1984 after the company reduced the number of weekly flights from Dubai from eighty to thirty-nine. In response, Sheikh Mohamed bin Rashid Al Maktoum, the third son of the then Ruler, Sheikh Rashid bin Saeed Al Maktoum, resolved to create a new airline. In an illustration of how closely Sheikh Mohammed has been involved in the creation and operations of all of Dubai's flagship state-owned entities, Ismail Ali Albanna, one of the seven men entrusted with launching Emirates in 1985 recounted, on the airline's thirtieth anniversary, how:

> ... His Highness called for a meeting with some of us at dnata and told us that he wanted to create an airline and that it should be in the air in seven months' time. Not only that, but we were told the plans should be kept completely confidential – I wasn't even allowed to tell my wife ... To be honest, it was a lot of pressure. But I know that when this gentleman [Sheikh Mohammed] says you must do something, you do it. And he was right – we made sure we worked day and night to make sure the aircraft would be in the sky in October.[161]

With US$10 million in seed funding from the ruling family together with a US$88 million gift of two Boeing 727s from the royal fleet and an Airbus and a Boeing leased from Pakistan International Airways, Emirates' four-strong fleet commenced operations with a flight from Dubai to Karachi on October 25, 1985. Throughout its history, Emirates has benefited from the close support of Dubai's ruling family through the Chairmanship of Sheikh Ahmed bin Saeed Al Maktoum, an uncle of the present Ruler, Sheikh Mohammed, even though he is nine years younger in age. Moreover, the airline was one of the few in the Gulf that maintained a full service throughout the Gulf War (January–February 1991) and picked up additional traffic during the conflict, especially from the temporarily grounded Kuwait Airways.[162]

Emirates based much of its early growth on the mass markets used by labor migrants to the Gulf with Mumbai, Delhi, Colombo, and Dhaka quickly joining the initial route from Dubai to Karachi. This was followed by expansion into regional markets (Cairo and Amman) and subsequently, in 1987, into Europe with flights to London's Gatwick, Frankfurt, and Istanbul. The London flight was noteworthy as Emirates offered alcoholic beverages to all passengers in a move that marked out the airline as distinct from its regional competitors and able both to anticipate and cater to customer demand, which surged as a result. In response, Emirates subsequently made alcohol available in all classes of service on all routes save those to and from Saudi Arabia (and while over Saudi airspace). This was a highly innovative concept for a Middle Eastern airline to introduce at the time. Routes to East Asia (Bangkok, Singapore, and Hong Kong) followed in the late 1980s and early 1990s, and Manila, and by the time of Emirates' tenth year of operation in 1995, it was already serving thirty different countries.[163]

Two significant factors lay behind (and made possible) the great acceleration of Emirates' growth in the late 1990s. The first was the aggressive marketing of Dubai as an international shopping and mass tourism destination while the second element of Emirates' breakneck expansion was the series of massive new orders for long-range aircraft. The influx of state-of-the-art Boeing 777s in the 1990s and Airbus A340s and A380s in the 2000s gave the airline a transcontinental reach that offered passengers the option of bypassing traditional European hubs such as London, Frankfurt, Paris, and Amsterdam. The first Boeing 777s entered the fleet in 1996 but it was the arrival of the A340 in 2003 that enabled Emirates to launch direct services to the lucrative North American market. By 2014, Emirates linked Dubai with nine cities across the United States, the most of any Gulf airline, and flew as far afield as Houston, Los Angeles, San Francisco, and Seattle. Another successful approach saw the airline fly to hitherto-"secondary" airports in key European countries allowing travellers direct routings that would previously have required a stop in their capital's "hub" airport: examples in the United Kingdom include Glasgow, Manchester, and Newcastle (bypassing London Heathrow), Hamburg and Dusseldorf in Germany (bypassing Frankfurt), and Nice and Lyon in France (bypassing Paris Charles de Gaulle).[164]

Emirates predated by two decades the formation of Etihad in Abu Dhabi but together the two airlines have emerged as the "global faces" of the UAE and secured worldwide recognition for the country and for the two emirates. Established by an Emiri Decree in July 2003 and chaired by Sheikh Hamad bin Zayed Al Nahyan, a half-brother of President Khalifa bin Zayed Al Nahyan, Etihad commenced operations that November and almost immediately made a large, multi-billion dollar acquisition of new aircraft from Boeing and Airbus. Later, in 2008, the airline made international headlines when it announced the largest aircraft order in history with the planned purchase of up to 205 new planes worth more than US$20 billion. The arrivals facilitated the rapid expansion of the Etihad network, which like Qatar Airways added new destinations at often dizzying speeds. Comments by Etihad's chief executive, former Gulf Air head James Hogan, captured the bullish mood among Gulf airlines: "The size of our order also mirrors the rising prominence of the Middle East and its increasing emergence as a new focal point for global aviation. The Gulf is a natural air bridge between East and West ... "[165]

Etihad has followed its own distinct growth model that differs both from Emirates' organic expansion in tandem with Dubai's growth and the Qatar Airways' emphasis on business and transit passengers. The most notable feature of this strategy has been the formation of "equity alliances" with struggling airlines, many in Europe, that enable Etihad to "add more spokes to its Abu Dhabi hub" and differ sharply from the Qatar Airways perspective on growth.[166] These equity alliances include 49 percent stakes in Alitalia and Air Serbia, 40 percent in Air Seychelles, a 34 percent stake in Darwin, a Swiss regional airline since rebranded as Etihad Regional, 29.21 percent in Germany's Air Berlin, 24.2 percent in Virgin Australia, and 24 percent in India's Jet Airways. The stakes were intended to give Etihad a foothold in regional markets and provide feeder traffic for the long-haul flights operated by the parent airline but the Darwin acquisition, in particular, faced fierce local opposition by Swiss and its parent company, Lufthansa. Embattled European carriers also turned to the European Commission for support in their campaign to limit foreign ownership of European airlines with an investigation into the issue launched in 2014.[167]

The emergence of the Gulf airlines (the two UAE-based airlines plus Qatar Airways) shook global aviation markets to their core. An example of the speed and scale of their rise was evident in a February 2015 report by the US aviation industry that indicated that the Gulf carriers' share of bookings between the United States and the Indian subcontinent rose from 12 percent in 2008 to 40 percent by 2015. This surpassed the share of the international US carriers (American Airlines, Delta Air Lines, and United Airlines) and their alliance partners such as British Airways and Air France, which fell from 39 percent to 34 percent over the same period.[168] Such trends and shifts in market share have generated widespread concern among competitors who perceive that the state-backed carriers benefit from unfair competitive advantages. Particular resentment focused around a "home market rule" preventing European and North American airlines originating from countries where Airbus and Boeing construct aircraft from using export credit agencies to assist their carriers buy aircraft. This regulation impacted all US carriers due to Boeing and most of the larger airlines in Europe owing to the pan-European nature of Airbus but left Gulf airlines unaffected. Skepticism toward the Gulf airlines was strongest in Germany, where Lufthansa vociferously alleged that Gulf carriers utilize public subsidies to finance aircraft deals, and in Canada, where the government transport agency initially declined (in 2010) to make additional landing slots available to Emirates and Etihad.[169]

Ottawa's action triggered a damaging spat between Canada and the UAE as the Emirati government retaliated by closing a military base near Dubai that was being used to support Canadian troops in Afghanistan. An additional flexing of bilateral muscles occurred when the Emirati authorities suddenly introduced steep visa fees for Canadian citizens wishing to enter the UAE even as visas for most other European and North American visitors remained free at the port of entry. In a direct attempt to retaliate by gaining market share from Canadian airlines, Emirates and Etihad offered passengers significant discounts if they arranged their visas and their travel through the UAE carriers.[170] The new regulations remained in place for nearly three years as officials struggled to rebuild the bilateral relationship with Canada's largest export market in the Middle East. In April 2013, the announcement of a codeshare agreement between Air Canada and Etihad that would open up the Canadian market signified the end of the Ottawa government's effort to protect the national airline that increasingly came at the cost of Canadian trade relations.[171]

European and North American carriers' concerns were not without foundation. The CEO of American Airlines acknowledged in September 2014 that "I worry about our ability to compete with other countries that are much more understanding and supportive of global aviation."[172] Indeed, the three Gulf airlines fall within the nebulous state–business landscape in the Gulf where the line between public and private enterprise (as well as state and ruling family wealth) can be opaque at best. As documented above, both Emirates and Etihad are chaired by the uncle and half-brother of the respective rulers. Meanwhile, in May 2014, Qatar Airways chief executive Akbar al-Baker noted that "We became fully government owned in July last year" after the state bought out private investors who previously had a 50 percent share in the airline.[173]

For their part, the three Gulf airlines responded robustly to the criticisms and allegations levelled against them, which include that they benefit from an un-unionized and lower-wage workforce in addition to access to cheaper fuel or financing options. Many of the international airlines' accusations against Gulf airlines revolved around subtle matters of interpretation of direct and indirect government support that, at times, resembled the splitting of hairs. Thus, Qatar Airways chief executive al-Baker denied that his airline received government subsidies but added that "What the government has given us is equity into an airline which they own."[174] His counterpart at Etihad, James Hogan, was equally vague as he acknowledged – under pressure from negative publicity in the United States – that "Like any new airline, there was seed money and there was shareholder equity." Suspicion around such arrangements was magnified by the fact that neither Qatar Airways nor Etihad have allowed public scrutiny of their finances, in marked contrast to Emirates, which does disclose its financial accounts and uses international auditors.[175]

In February 2015, the three largest US carriers – American, Delta, and United – revived the subsidy issue as their chief executives claimed that the Gulf airlines received an "unfair advantage" from state support and called on the Obama administration to review the US government's air treaties with Gulf partners. This represented a major step away from the Open Skies policies that US airlines had for years advocated. In meeting with Obama administration officials, the three US airlines compiled a fifty-five-page dossier detailing alleged irregularities in Gulf airlines' financing, which they did not make public. According to a report that appeared in the *New York Times*, the dossier alleged that the three Gulf airlines had received more than US$38 billion in government subsidies. The dossier suggested that Etihad alone had benefited from US$17 billion in government subsidies in its first decade of existence, including US$6 billion in interest-free loans from the Abu Dhabi government to fund new airplane acquisitions and a further US$6.5 billion to cover operating losses. Belligerently, the dossier also claimed that:

> Etihad's argument fundamentally misunderstands the international consensus on the definition of subsidy. Given the company's dismal financial performance over the last 10 years, if not for the subsidies, Etihad would have gone out of business.[176]

Moreover, the dossier suggested that Emirates had benefited from varying levels of support from the leadership in Dubai, which allegedly included their assumption of a US$2.4 billion loss from fuel hedging, a further US$2.3 billion in savings from artificially low airport charges, and, rather intangibly, US$1.9 billion in savings from the airline's non-unionized workforce.[177] However, Emirates Chairman Sheikh Ahmed bin Saeed Al Maktoum responded bluntly to the allegations of uncompetitive advantage by calling on the US carriers to "improve their service" and stating that "Offer the best to the passengers and people will fly with you."[178]

The above notwithstanding, the Gulf airlines have taken advantage of a more benign set of domestic circumstances and have, on occasion, been robust in saying so. In a 2010 interview, chief executive James Hogan explained the benefits Etihad derives from operating within the political economy of Abu Dhabi, and as a latecomer relative to established European "legacy" carriers:

> I don't have to tackle the union issues of these other carriers and I don't have additional costs because we can outsource a lot of things. When it comes to other carriers, we are both similar service airlines, but they are bound by agreements, employment agreements, 15, 20, 30, or 40 years old that are very hard to renegotiate. They are bound by infrastructure – facilities and bases that were right for them 30 years ago or even 20 years ago, but aren't today. I am fortunate that I have a clean sheet of paper.[179]

Such comments encapsulate the commercial advantages to Gulf operators of working without the constraints imposed by organized labor on European and North American competitors, and by the less stringent social welfare requirements that impart a certain advantage over Western rivals.[180]

Gulf airlines have also been recipients of major levels of what might be construed as indirect or "soft" support by their parent emirates through the construction of some of the largest and most modern airports and associated infrastructure in the world. Both Dubai and Doha opened new airports in 2013 and 2014 respectively while Abu Dhabi is engaged in a large-scale expansion of its own international airport. In addition to Dubai International Airport, officials in Dubai have started to open in phases what will eventually become the world's largest airport, Al Maktoum International, reinforcing the emirate's role as the preeminent logistical and infrastructural hub in the region. The centerpiece of the *Dubai World Central* economic, commercial, and residential zone, the airport is expected to have a capacity of 160 million passengers a year when it becomes fully operational. Remarkably, the construction of the massive new airport will complement the existing Dubai International Airport, which already contains the largest terminal building in the world. As mentioned above, Dubai International handled almost 70 million international passengers in 2014 and work is underway to add a new concourse that would raise capacity to more than 90 million. This has induced a weary acceptance from long-established competitors such as Heathrow, as evidenced in a statement following the news that Dubai had become the busiest international airport in the world: "Britain has benefited from being home to the world's largest port or airport for the last 350 years. But lack of capacity at Heathrow means we have inevitably lost our crown to Dubai."[181]

A different form of leverage has been exercised by Abu Dhabi, which built up a close political, defence, and security relationship with the US government, focused around (but not limited to) the emirate's plans to develop civilian nuclear energy. Such ties were illustrated by the January 2014 launch of the first customs and border pre-clearance facility to open outside the United States since the 1980s. The pre-clearance facility encountered strong opposition from aviation leaders in the US, who worried it would give a further competitive advantage if passengers from Abu Dhabi could avoid potentially long lines on arrival at US airports. These concerns were offset by an agreement that Abu Dhabi would meet 80 percent of the cost of the facility, including the salaries of the Customs and Border Patrol officers needed to staff it. Fourteen members of Congress argued in a letter to the Department of Homeland Security in Washington, DC that the facility in Abu Dhabi represented a "dangerous precedent" of basing customs and border control on third-party financing rather than national security interests.[182] Ironically, the pre-clearance facility was beset by chronic overcrowding in its first year of operation, leading to persistent delays on US-bound flights and causing frustration among passengers and Etihad staff alike.[183]

Innovation and the Knowledge Economy

Looking forward, the future economic objectives of Abu Dhabi and Dubai share a number of features in common even as they diverge in sectoral scope. A central commonality is a focus on innovation and entrepreneurship and support for a loosely defined concept of the "knowledge economy" as the drivers of economic transition in the twenty-first century. In the mid-2000s, the UAE Foreign Minister, Sheikh Abdullah bin Zayed Al Nahyan, was one of the earliest leaders, both in the UAE and in the GCC more widely, to capture this mood of change when he warned that the UAE (and the other Gulf States) "must not be left behind in this global transformation of ideas and attitudes" and added that "to be e-active is no longer a matter of choice, but of necessity."[184] The UAE's *Vision 2021* – the national blueprint for development in advance of the country's fiftieth anniversary – has enshrined as its objective the transformation of the UAE into a knowledge-based economy in which growth is driven by research, development, and innovation and the creation of internationally competitive high value-added economic sectors. Key pillars of *Vision 2021* include the enhancing of the ease of doing business in the UAE and the strengthening of innovation, entrepreneurship, and research and development indicators, with specific policy goals including an increase in the non-oil real GDP growth rate from 3.5 percent to 5 percent; a rise in expenditure on research and development from 0.5 percent of GDP to 1.5 percent; and a top-twenty ranking in the Global Innovation Index.[185] Table 4.2 illustrates the UAE's rank as of 2015 set against selected regional and international comparison, with only Saudi Arabia among Arab (and Gulf) states achieving a higher ranking.

TABLE 4.2 Global Innovation Ranking, 2015 – UAE and select regional/international states

Country	Rank
Switzerland	1
United Kingdom	2
Sweden	3
Netherlands	4
United States	5
Israel	22
Saudi Arabia	43
Greece	45
Poland	46
UAE	47
Qatar	50
Bahrain	59
Oman	69
Jordan	75
Kuwait	77
Iran	106

Source: adapted by the author from the Global Innovation Index 2015: Effective Innovation Policies for Development (https://www.globalinnovationindex.org/userfiles/file/reportpdf/GII-2015-v5.pdf).

TABLE 4.3 Global Competitiveness Ranking 2015 – UAE and Select Regional/International States

Country	Rank
Switzerland	1
Singapore	2
United States	3
Germany	4
Netherlands	5
Qatar	14
UAE	17
Saudi Arabia	25
Israel	27
Kuwait	34
Bahrain	39
Oman	62

Source: adapted by the author from the Global Competitiveness Index 2015 produced by the World Economic Forum (http://reports.weforum.org/global-competitiveness-report-2015-2016/competitiveness-rankings/).

In the Global Competitiveness Ranking, the UAE also ranks second among the Gulf States (behind Qatar rather than Saudi Arabia) and was placed seventeenth in 2015, in between New Zealand and Malaysia, as Table 4.3 shows.

In support of the overarching *Vision 2021* and at a cabinet meeting held inside Fujairah's picturesque and historic old fort, the UAE Government declared 2015 to be the "Year of Innovation" and launched a National Innovation Strategy with a focus on seven sectors ranging from education, health, and technology to water, renewable energy, transport, and space. A February 2015 report by a leading Middle East law firm (Al Tamimi & Co) based in the UAE illustrated the scope of the planned strategy:

> … Thirty governmental initiatives are aimed to be taken within a three year period in the optic of fostering innovation in these sectors, including new legislation, innovation incubators, investment in specialized skills, private-sector incentives, international research partnerships and an innovation drive within government.[186]

A range of other initiatives also underpinned the focus on innovation and show-cased the ability of a "state capitalist" model of economic development to swiftly mobilize nationwide resources behind an agreed policy objective. Two new entities aimed at small businesses and start-ups that launched in late 2014 were an Innovation Hub, set within Dubai Internet City, and a Creative Community, located in the Dubai Technology and Media Free Zone.[187] Also in 2014, the Mohammed bin Rashid Center for Government Innovation opened in Dubai with a mandate to catalyze innovation in the public sector and build innovative capacity across the workforce. The center outlined a range of ambitious targets designed to turn the UAE into "the global hub for innovation and best practices," while the eponymous Ruler of Dubai also opened the Dubai Foundation of the Future, envisioned as an incubator of ideas that will underpin the UAE's emergence as a global innovation hub when it opens in 2018.[188] Speaking at the launch of the Dubai Foundation of the Future, Sheikh Mohammed stated that:

> Our vision for development is driven by a deep understanding of future needs, and built on proactive ideas because we want to be in first place globally. The future does not wait for those who hesitate and slow down. The next stage requires us to act fast and utilize the opportunities.[189]

While, at the time of writing in mid-2016, it is too early to judge results, the resources mobilized in support of government innovation in the UAE have far exceeded those in neighboring GCC states such as Kuwait, Saudi Arabia, and even Qatar. However, capital alone will not be sufficient to achieve the far-reaching economic shift toward a knowledge-based economy, particularly if the sharp decline in international oil prices that began in 2014 persists for a considerable length of time. A successful and sustainable transformation into a knowledge economy as a key component of economic diversification will involve an ongoing process of structural and also intangible change and will be intergenerational in nature. In the East Asian cases of Japan, Taiwan, and South Korea, the overhaul of economic structures that began in the early 1960s only reached fruition in the 1980s. The UAE certainly has made significant progress in creating enclaves of concentrated expertise in which research and development and sector-specific university–industry collaboration can take root and flourish. Embedding and expanding the share of these enclaves and free zones will be central to the long-term task of moving from a political economy based on a comparative advantage in hydrocarbons to a knowledge-intensive economy based on a competitive advantage in a globalized setting.[190]

Higher education and the high-profile attraction of international branch campuses illustrate the challenge of translating initial measures into lasting impact. Dozens of universities opened branches in the UAE in the mid-2000s and by 2009 the UAE hosted more international branch campuses (forty-one) than any other country in the world; moreover, the Dubai schooling system has more international schools (253) than any other country.[191] Many of the higher education campuses were located within the Dubai Knowledge Village (DKV), an educational free trade zone established in 2003, and its larger successor entity, the Dubai International Academic City (DIAC), which was launched in 2007. Such was the concentration of private (and often foreign) higher education providers that in 2010 a study conducted by a researcher at the Dubai School of Government found that only three out of the fifty-three post-secondary educational institutions licensed to award degrees or diplomas in Dubai were part of the federal public higher education system.[192] The phenomenon of branch campuses was less pronounced elsewhere in the UAE, although the opening in 2010 of NYU Abu Dhabi was a landmark move as it involved the launch of an entire research university rather than the import of a single faculty or school (as in the US university branches based in Qatar's Education City).[193]

The same Dubai School of Government study referred to above suggested additionally that only a minority of the students enrolled in the international branch campuses in Dubai were actually Emirati nationals, and, moreover, that the majority of them expected to return to their home countries following completion of their studies in the UAE.[194] Further, the rapid influx of foreign providers into the educational free zones (and exempt from federal regulation) led to questions regarding the academic standard and integrity of some of the new arrivals.[195] Nor was the establishment of international branch campuses an unqualified success, as reflected by the closure of the George Mason campus in Ras al-Khaimah in 2009 and the decision of the Michigan State campus in Dubai to terminate its undergraduate programs in 2010. Both campuses suffered from poor timing as their opening coincided with the global economic downturn and the aftermath of the financial crisis that hit Dubai, and in each case, the far lower than anticipated student uptake led to unsustainable budgetary shortfalls.[196] Their difficulties rekindled memories of the ill-fated rush by almost forty American universities to establish branch campuses in Japan in the 1980s. By 2010, just one had survived the combination of precarious financial foundations and clash of cultures that confronted this previous generation of international branch campuses.[197]

Genuine transformation of economic structures will likely require concomitant shifts in largely intangible social and behavioral mentalities that continue to be reflected in the labor and demographic imbalance within the UAE. Support of the "software" of knowledge economies is an essential complement to the investments in the "hardware" that already have manifested in the hugely impressive university campuses and related infrastructure throughout the UAE. Moreover, policymakers must acknowledge that the transition into knowledge economies cannot be a one-off "acquisition" but instead represents a series of incremental steps on a journey without a fixed start or endpoint. Lessons from countries that have undergone relatively successful transitions – such as South Korea and Taiwan but also Finland – suggest that the transition will involve a series of incremental changes that build upon each other. It is undeniable that the UAE has progressed farther than other GCC states in the construction of centers of innovation and hubs of agglomeration for knowledge-intensive goods and services; the next step of the challenge lies in enlarging the enclave-based approaches and ensuring that the existing examples of knowledge creation constitute the building blocks for deepening and widening the economic transition across all sectors of the economy.[198]

The Emirati economy has been transformed by the heavy investments in infrastructure that have positioned the country at the forefront of many of the logistical nodes in the global supply chains of the twenty-first century. The "first-mover" advantage and concentration of expertise in Dubai, in particular, offer economies of scale that provide a powerful cushion against any economic downturn or period of lower oil prices and government revenues. Often companies that establish branch offices in the Middle East do so first in Dubai then expand to other locations in the Gulf, such as Abu Dhabi or Doha. Company behavior during the oil price slump in 2015 illustrated the comparative advantage of Dubai as a number of international law firms opted to scale back their regional presence by closing other Gulf branches and retreating solely to Dubai.[199] More so than Abu Dhabi, Dubai has become an integral component of the world economy in the early twenty-first century with a powerful global brand and a reputation as a social and entertainment hub. The challenge for the advocates of the innovative and entrepreneurship-led economy is to anchor the next phase of transformation in human and social capital that can accomplish the transition to a genuinely post-oil political economy across the UAE as a whole.

Notes

1 "United Arab Emirates: International Energy Data and Analysis," *US Energy Information Administration*, May 18, 2015.
2 "IMF Executive Board Concludes 2015 Article IV Consultation with United Arab Emirates," *International Monetary Fund Press Release No. 15/370*, August 4, 2015.

3 Martin Spraggon and Virginia Bodolica, *Managing Organizations in the United Arab Emirates: Dynamic Characteristics and Key Economic Developments* (New York: Palgrave Macmillan, 2014), p. 171.
4 Abdullah Omran Taryam, *The Establishment of the United Arab Emirates 1950–85* (London: Croon Helm, 1987), pp. 254–255.
5 Ali Tawfik al-Sadik, "Evolution and Performance of the UAE Economy 1972–1998," in Ibrahim al-Abed and Peter Hellyer (eds), *United Arab Emirates: A New Perspective* (London: Trident Press, 2001), p. 208.
6 Ibid., p. 209.
7 Karen Young, *The Political Economy of Energy, Finance and Security in the United Arab Emirates: Between the Majlis and the Market* (New York: Palgrave Macmillan, 2014), p. 38.
8 Ibid., p. 203.
9 "'Dubai: Selected Economic Indicators' and 'Abu Dhabi: Selected Economic Indicators'," *Gulf States News*, 39(997), July 16, 2015, p. 17.
10 Ragaei el Mallakh, *The Economic Development of the United Arab Emirates* (New York: Palgrave Macmillan, 2001), p. 132.
11 Al-Sadik, *Evolution and Performance of the UAE Economy*, p. 217.
12 Sulayman Khalaf, "Globalization and Heritage Revival in the Gulf: an Anthropological Look at Dubai Heritage Village," *Journal of Social Affairs*, 19(75), 2002, p. 14.
13 John W. Fox, Nada Mourtada-Sabbah, and Mohammed al-Mutawa, "Heritage Revivalism in Sharjah," in John W. Fox, Nada Mourtada-Sabbah, and Mohammed al-Mutawa (eds), *Globalization and the Gulf* (Abingdon: Routledge, 2006), pp. 268–269.
14 Miriam Cooke, *Tribal Modern: Branding New Nations in the Arab Gulf* (Berkeley, CA: University of California Press, 2014), pp. 100–101.
15 Ibid., p. 77.
16 "Armor Firms Flocking to UAE," *Defense News*, September 6, 2014.
17 Ibid.
18 "Those Entrepreneurial Al-Qasimis," *Gulf States Newsletter*, 27(797), April 4, 2003, p. 12.
19 "Ras al-Khaimah: Positive Review from S&P," *Gulf States News*, 40 (1010), February 18, 2016, p. 9.
20 "Ras al Khaimah Free Trade Zone Set for Expansion," *Oxford Business Group*, June 26, 2015.
21 Gaurav Sharma, "UAE's Oil Storage Hub of Fujairah Taking on Established Ports," *Forbes.com*, October 6, 2015.
22 "Tests Begin on Abu Dhabi-Fujairah Pipeline," *Gulf States Newsletter*, 36 (927), p. 8.
23 "Dubai Plans for 25m Visitors for World Expo 2020," *Gulf News*, March 26, 2014.
24 Stephen Ramos, "The Blueprint: A History of Dubai's Spatial Development through Oil Discovery," *The Dubai Initiative – Working Paper*, June 2009, pp. 12–13.
25 Donald Hawley, *The Trucial States* (London: George Allen & Unwin, 1970), pp. 244–245.
26 Stephen Ramos, *Dubai Amplified: The Engineering of a Port Geography* (London: Ashgate, 2012), p. 86.
27 Christopher Davidson, *Dubai: The Vulnerability of Success* (London: Hurst & Co, 2008), pp. 69–71.
28 Ibid.
29 Jim Krane, *Dubai: The Story of the World's Fastest City* (London: Atlantic Books, 2009), pp. 73–74.
30 Edmund O'Sullivan, "Big Bang Beginning to a Year of Fresh Starts," *Middle East Economic Digest*, January 24, 2014, p. 3.
31 Tribute to Sheikh Rashid bin Saeed Al Maktoum, published in *Gulf States Newsletter*, 15(396), October 15, 1990.
32 "MbR's Accession Injects a New Dynamic into Dubai/Abu Dhabi Ties," *Gulf States Newsletter*, 30 (773), January 13, 2006, p. 20.
33 Pranay Gupte, *Dubai: The Making of a Megapolis* (New York: Penguin/Viking, 2011), p. 272.
34 "Oil and Energy: UAE," *Gulf States Newsletter*, 15 (391), August 6, 1990, pp. 14–15.

35 "DCTPB Unveils New Advertising Campaign," *Emirates News*, December 8, 1992.
36 *Ministry of Cabinet Affairs*, United Arab Emirates, "UAE Vision 2021," available online at http://www.moca.gov.ae/?page_id=620&lang=en.
37 Arang Keshavarzian, "Geopolitics and the Genealogy of Free Trade Zones in the Persian Gulf," *Geopolitics*, 15(2), 2010, p. 266.
38 Nick Tosches, "Dubai's the Limit," *Vanity Fair*, September 2006.
39 Christopher Davidson, "The Impact of Economic Reform on Dubai," in Anoushiravan Ehteshami and Steven Wright (eds), *Reform in the Middle East Oil Monarchies* (Reading: Ithaca Press, 2008), p. 164.
40 Omar AlShehabi, "Migration, Commodification, and the 'Right to the City'," in Abdulhadi Khalaf, Omar AlShehabi, and Adam Hanieh (eds), *Transit States: Labour, Migration & Citizenship in the Gulf* (London: Pluto Press, 2015), p. 106.
41 Christopher Davidson, "Dubai and Abu Dhabi: Implosion and Opportunity," *Open Democracy*, December 4, 2009.
42 "Dubai Prepares to Road Test Audacious Development Model," *Gulf States Newsletter*, 29(771), December 9, 2005.
43 Ibid.
44 Kristian Coates Ulrichsen, *Insecure Gulf: The End of Certainty and the Transition to the Post-Oil Era* (Oxford: Oxford University Press, 2015 edition), p. 94.
45 Edmund O'Sullivan, "Big Bang Beginning to a Year of Fresh Starts," *Middle East Economic Digest*, 58 (4), January 24, 2014, pp. 3–5.
46 Young, *Political Economy of Energy, Finance and Security*, p. 68.
47 "UAE, Abu Dhabi Roll Over $20Bln of Dubai's Debt," *Reuters*, March 16, 2016.
48 Jeffrey Sampler and Saeb Eigner, *Sand to Silicon: Achieving Rapid Growth Lessons from Dubai* (London: Profile Books, 2003), pp. 168–169.
49 Andrew Petersen and David Jones, "A Dubai World Debt and Nakheel Sukuk – Apocalypse Now?" *K&L Gates Distressed Real Estate Alert*, December 10, 2009.
50 Matthew Martin, "Dubai Drydocks Forces Debt Restructure," *Middle East Economic Digest*, 56 (14), June 4, 2012, p. 9.
51 Ibid.
52 Martin Hvidt, "The Dubai Model: An Outline of Key Development-Process Elements in Dubai," *International Journal of Middle East Studies*, 41(2), 2009, p. 402.
53 Krane, *Story of the World's Largest City*, p. 184.
54 Christopher Davidson, "The Dubai Model: Diversification and Slowdown," in Mehran Kamrava (ed.), *The Political Economy of the Persian Gulf* (London: Hurst & Co, 2012), pp. 204–206.
55 Christopher Davidson, "Diversification in Abu Dhabi and Dubai: The Impact of National Identity and the Ruling Bargain," in Alanoud Alsharekh and Robert Springborg (eds), *Popular Culture and Political Identity in the Arab Gulf States* (London: Saqi Books, 2008), p. 150.
56 Anil Bhoyrul, "Exclusive: Mohammed Alabbar – Uncensored," *ArabianBusiness.com*, April 12, 2015.
57 Interview with Geoff Taylor, CEO of Dubai Dry Dock, December 2006, cited in Hvidt, *Dubai Model*, p. 403.
58 Joseph Parilla and Jesus Leal Trujillo, "The World's 10 Fastest Growing Metropolitan Areas," *Brookings Institution blog*, February 10, 2015.
59 Saskia Sassen, "Rise of the Niche Global City," *The Straits Times*, September 7, 2015.
60 "Rise of the Gulf: Soaring Ambition," *The Economist*, January 10, 2015.
61 Sultan Sooud Al Qassemi, "Thriving Gulf Cities Emerge as New Centers of Arab World," *Al-Monitor*, October 8, 2013.
62 "Dubai Wins Expo 2020," *Gulf States Newsletter*, 37 (960), December 12, 2013, p. 4.
63 Adam Hanieh, *Capitalism and Class in the Gulf Arab States* (New York: Palgrave Macmillan, 2011), p. 44.
64 Naiem Sherbiny, "Oil and the Internationalization of Arab Banks" (Oxford: Oxford Institute of Energy Studies, 1985), p. 32.

65 Jane Kinninmont, "Bahrain," in Christopher Davidson (ed.), *Power and Politics in the Persian Gulf* (London: Hurst & Co, 2011), p. 49.
66 Mark Thatcher, "Governing Markets in Gulf States," London: *LSE Kuwait Program Working Paper No.1* (2009), p. 4.
67 Quotation taken from Christopher Davidson, "Dubai: the Security Dimensions of the Region's Premier Free Port," *Middle East Policy*, 15(2), 2008, p. 150.
68 "Emirates Come to Grips with Informal Economies," *Gulf States Newsletter*, 26 (683), April 3, 2002, p. 10.
69 Ibid.
70 "Gulf Regulators Commit to Tougher New Regimes," *Gulf States Newsletter*, 26 (680), February 20, 2002, p. 11.
71 "Abu Dhabi Wields the Hand of State, Makes Hawala Work," *Gulf States Newsletter*, 30 (779), April 14, 2006, pp. 9–10.
72 Thatcher, *Governing Markets in Gulf States*, p. 15.
73 "DIFC Courts Dealing with More Cases, 81% Rise in Claim and Counterclaim Value," *The National*, April 12, 2015.
74 Thatcher, *Governing Markets in Gulf States*, p. 17.
75 Ibid.
76 "Abu Dhabi Financial Center to Base Rules on English Common Law," *Reuters*, January 7, 2015.
77 "Bladen to Quit Advisory Role with Abu Dhabi Global Market," *The National*, February 12, 2015.
78 "SGX's Richard Teng Leaving to Join Abu Dhabi Global Market," *Business Times*, October 30, 2014.
79 "Former British Regulator Sants to Advise Abu Dhabi Financial Zone," *Reuters*, December 16, 2014.
80 "UAE/Qatar Upgraded to 'Emerging Market' Status," *Gulf States Newsletter*, 37 (949), June 20, 2013, p. 10.
81 "Qatar, UAE About to Get Major Upgrade," *CNN Money*, May 29, 2014.
82 "S&P Reclassifies Qatar, UAE to Emerging Market Status," *ETFtrends.com*, September 15, 2014.
83 "Sovereign Wealth Fund Definition," *Sovereign Wealth Fund Institute*, available online at http://www.swfinstitute.org/sovereign-wealth-fund-definition.
84 Jean-Francois Seznec, "The Gulf Sovereign Wealth Funds: Myths and Reality," *Middle East Policy*, 15(2), 2008, pp. 100–101.
85 Gawdat Bahgat, "Sovereign Wealth Funds in the Gulf: An Assessment," *LSE Kuwait Program Working Paper No. 16* (2011), p. 5.
86 "Abu Dhabi in the Spotlight as its GRE Receive Ratings Downgrades and Adia Issues First Review," *Gulf States Newsletter*, 34 (873), March 19, 2010.
87 Ibid.
88 John Sfakianakis and Eckart Woertz, "Strategic Foreign Investments of GCC Countries," in Eckart Woertz (ed.), *Gulf Geo-Economics* (Dubai: Gulf Research Center, 2007), p. 132.
89 Sara Bazoobandi, *The Political Economy of the Gulf Sovereign Wealth Funds: A Case Study of Iran, Kuwait, Saudi Arabia and the United Arab Emirates* (Abingdon: Routledge, 2013), p. 83.
90 "UAE's Borouge Says Third Phase Expansion to Reach Full Capacity by 2016," *Reuters*, May 20, 2015.
91 Giacomo Luciani, "The GCC Refining and Petrochemical Sectors in Global Perspective," in Eckart Woertz (ed.), *Gulf Geo-Economics* (Dubai: Gulf Research Center, 2007), p. 191.
92 Press Release, "Boeing Awards Direct Contract to Mubadala Aerospace's Strata Facility to Produce Composite Aerostructures for 777 and 787 Dreamliner," *Mubadala*, April 17, 2012.

93 "Etihad Receives First Dreamliner with Parts Made by Strata in the UAE," *The National,* June 10, 2015.
94 "Dubai and Abu Dhabi Create $15bn Aluminium Champion," *Financial Times,* June 3, 2013.
95 "Welcome Contribution: Manufacturing and Trans-Shipment Are Helping to Diversify the Economy," *The Report: Dubai 2014* (Oxford: Oxford Business Group, 2014), p. 266.
96 Awad Mustafa, "EDIC Acquires 5 More Companies," *Defense News,* February 21, 2015.
97 Ibid.
98 Awad Mustafa, "UAE's EDIC Looks Beyond Local Assembly Partnerships," *Defense News,* November 12, 2015.
99 "Egypt's Stalled $35bln Housing Scheme: Big Dreams to Harsh Reality," *Al Arabiya,* October 8, 2015.
100 Ibid.
101 "Malaysia's 1MDB Scandal Poses Difficult Questions for Gulf Grandees," *Gulf States News,* 39 (999), September 3, 2015, pp. 3–4.
102 "Arabtec's $40 Billion Egypt Project Cut to Just a Tenth of Original Size," *The National,* September 8, 2015.
103 "Egypt's Stalled $35bln Housing Scheme: Big Dreams to Harsh Reality," *Al Arabiya,* October 8, 2015.
104 "Abu Dhabi Takes an Even Larger Stake in Dubai Inc.", *Gulf States Newsletter,* 34 (886), October 1, 2010, p. 3.
105 Young, *Political Economy of Energy, Finance and Security,* p. 59.
106 Gerald Butt, "Oil and Gas in the UAE," in Ibrahim al Abed and Peter Hellyer (eds), *United Arab Emirates: A New Perspective* (London: Trident Press, 2001), p. 233.
107 Diane Munro, "ADNOC's CEO Institutes Seismic Shift in Corporate Strategy," *Arab Gulf States Institute in Washington blog,* June 1, 2016.
108 "United Arab Emirates – International Energy Data and Analysis," *U.S. Energy Information Administration Update,* May 18, 2015, p. 3.
109 "UAE Pushes Back 3.5m Barrel Crude Oil Target to 2020," *Gulf News,* July 1, 2013.
110 "Field of Bidders for Abu Dhabi Oil Concession Has Narrowed, Says Adnoc Head," *The National,* April 20, 2015.
111 Justin Dargin, "Addressing the UAE Natural Gas Crisis: Strategies for a Rational Energy Policy," Belfer Center for Science and International Affairs, *Harvard Kennedy School Dubai Initiative – Policy Brief,* August 2010, p. 1.
112 Roman Kilisek, "Why the UAE is Contemplating US LNG Imports," *Breaking Energy,* February 11, 2014.
113 *United Arab Emirates – International Energy Data and Analysis,* p. 7.
114 "The Evolution of AdGas," http://www.adgas.com/En/SitePages/About%20Us/Overview.aspx (accessed November 4, 2015).
115 Thierry Kellner, "The GCC States of the Persian Gulf and Asia Energy Relations," *IFRI Research Paper,* September 2012, p. 19.
116 Ibid.
117 Dargin, *Addressing the UAE Natural Gas Crisis,* pp. 1–2.
118 Mohamed Raouf, "Water Issues in the Gulf: Time for Action," *Middle East Institute Policy Brief No.22,* January 2009, p. 2.
119 Justin Dargin, "The Dolphin Project: The Development of a Gulf Gas Initiative," *Oxford Institute for Energy Studies Working Paper No. 22,* 2008, pp. 34–38.
120 Jim Krane and Steven Wright, "Qatar 'Rises Above' its Region: Geopolitics and the Rejection of the GCC Gas Market," *LSE Kuwait Program Working Paper No. 35,* 2014, p. 5.
121 "Shell, Qatar to Supply LNG to Dubai from 2010," *Reuters,* April 21, 2008.
122 "Dubai Signs Shell, QP LNG Deal, as Yet Another Gulf Market Ties to Escape Gas Crunch," *IHS Global Insight Perspective,* April 21, 2008.

123 "Dubai Considers LNG Import Terminal Expansion," *The National*, April 1, 2015.
124 "UAE's Emirates LNG to Begin Gas Imports in 2018 from Fujairah Terminal: CEO," *Platts News & Analysis*, November 12, 2014.
125 "Gas Deal with Iran is Pivotal to Sharjah's Economic Ambitions," *Gulf States Newsletter*, 30 (794), November 24, 2006, p. 1.
126 Ibid.
127 "Gassing Up: Natural Gas is Being Sourced from a Variety of Locations," *The Report: Sharjah 2008* (Oxford: Oxford Business Group, 2008), p. 67.
128 "Iran Cancels Gas Deal with Crescent Petroleum," *The National*, August 7, 2010.
129 "Iran's Gas Dispute with Sharjah's Crescent Petroleum Enmeshed in Politics," *The National*, April 13, 2015.
130 Ibid.
131 Kristian Coates Ulrichsen, "Rebalancing Global Governance: Gulf States' Perspectives on the Governance of Globalization," *Global Policy*, 2(1), 2011, p. 71.
132 Mohammed Raouf, "Climate Change Threats, Opportunities, and the GCC Countries," *Middle East Institute Policy Brief No.12* (2008), p. 15.
133 Mari Luomi, "Gulf of Interest: Why Oil Still Dominates Middle Eastern Climate Politics," *Journal of Arabian Studies*, 1(2), 2011, p. 252.
134 Raouf, "Water Issues in the Gulf," p. 2.
135 Dennis Kumetat, *Managing the Transition: Renewable Energy and Innovation Policies in the UAE and Algeria* (Abingdon: Routledge, 2015), p. 134.
136 Coates Ulrichsen, *Rebalancing Global Governance*, p. 71.
137 Mari Luomi, *The Gulf Monarchies and Climate Change: Abu Dhabi and Qatar in an Era of Natural Unsustainability* (London: Hurst & Co, 2012), pp. 125–127.
138 Kumetat, *Managing the Transition*, p. 135.
139 Ibid., p. 137.
140 Ibid.
141 *The Report: Abu Dhabi 2014* (Oxford: Oxford Business Group, 2009), p. 239.
142 Fred Moavenzadeh, "First Class Graduates from Masdar Institute," *The National*, June 5, 2011.
143 "World's Largest Solar Power Plant Shams-1 Built at Cost of $600m near Abu Dhabi," *Gulf News*, March 12, 2013.
144 Kyle Sinclair, "For Abu Dhabi 2030 Vision, Shams 1 Is about Knowing and Diversifying," *The National*, March 17, 2013.
145 "World Green Economy Summit 2014," available online at http://www.wclimate. com/wges-2014.
146 "Dubai Triples Renewable Energy Target to 15% by 2030," *Gulf News*, January 21, 2015.
147 "Costs Tumble as Dubai's Mohammed bin Rashid Al Maktoum Solar Park Sets the Mark," *The National*, May 1, 2016.
148 "UAE Energy Demand is Expected to Grow 9% Annually," *Gulf News*, April 23, 2015.
149 Luomi, *Gulf Monarchies and Climate Change*, p. 209.
150 "Israel Shrugs off Kuwaiti Boycott, Joins Arab States, Iran at Abu Dhabi Conference," *The Jerusalem Post*, January 19, 2014.
151 Mohammed Alkhereiji, "UAE Denies IRENA Representation Reflects Israel Policy Change," *The Arab Weekly*, December 11, 2015.
152 Hagar Shezaf and Rori Donaghy, "Israel Eyes Improved Ties with Gulf States after 'Foothold' Gained in UAE," *Middle East Eye*, January 18, 2016.
153 "An Eye for an Eye: the Anatomy of Mossad's Dubai Operation," *Spiegel Online*, January 17, 2011.
154 Luomi, *Gulf Monarchies and Climate Change*, pp. 132–133.
155 Ian Jackson, "Nuclear Energy and Proliferation Risks: Myths and Realities in the Persian Gulf," *International Affairs*, 85(6), 2009, p. 1157.

156 Elisabeth Dyck and Ayhan Evrensel, "From Consideration to Construction: the United Arab Emirates' Journey to Nuclear Power: a Country Case Study," *International Atomic Energy Agency*, February 3, 2015.

157 "US-UAE Nuclear Deal to Take Effect Soon – State Dept," *Reuters*, October 22, 2009

158 Christopher Blanchard, "United Arab Emirates Nuclear Program and Proposed U.S. Nuclear Cooperation," *Congressional Research Service Report for Congress* (Washington, DC: Congressional Research Service, 2010), p. 11.

159 "Aviation in the Gulf: Rulers of the New Silk Road," *The Economist*, June 3–9, 2010.

160 "Dubai Jumps Heathrow as 'World's Busiest International Airport'," *USA Today*, January 28, 2015.

161 "A Life with Emirates: Meet the Man who Played Key Roles in the Foundation of Both Dnata and Emirates," *ArabianBusiness.com*, October 25, 2015.

162 Krane, *Story of the World's Largest City*, pp. 107–108.

163 "Emirates Airline History," available online at http://www.airreview.com/Emirates/History.htm.

164 Author interviews, Dubai and London, April 2012 and January 2014.

165 "Etihad Splits Massive Order between Boeing, Airbus," *USA Today*, July 15, 2008.

166 "Qatar Airways Stake in British Airways Parent IAG Creates Intriguing Alliance," *The National*, February 3, 2015.

167 "EU Widens Etihad Probe to Include More European Carriers," *ArabianBusiness.com*, April 10, 2014.

168 "U.S. Airlines Losing Asia Market Share," *Las Vegas Review-Journal*, February 10, 2015.

169 "Lufthansa Seeks to Clip Emirates' Wings in Europe, Berlin Mayor Says," *ArabianBusiness.com*, January 16, 2011.

170 "UAE Embassy to Charge Canadians Steep Visa Fees," *The Globe and Mail*, December 28, 2010.

171 "Etihad and Air Canada Strike Codeshare Deal," *The National*, April 25, 2013.

172 Ted Reed, "Note to Abu Dhabi on Pre-Clearance: Be Careful What You Wish For," *Forbes.com*, October 14, 2014.

173 "Qatar Airways CEO Says Company Fully Govt-Owned; Interested in IndiGo Stake," *Reuters*, May 5, 2014.

174 "United States Escalates Arabian Gulf Airline Subsidies Row," *Bloomberg News*, March 5, 2015.

175 "Etihad Airways' Rapid Growth Frustrates Rivals," *New York Times*, March 2, 2015.

176 Ibid.

177 "Airline Subsidies in the Gulf: Feeling the Heat," *The Economist*, March 6, 2015.

178 "Emirates Executives Rebuff US Airlines' Claims of $40 Billion in Subsidies to Gulf Carriers," *The National*, February 11, 2015.

179 Mark Summers, "Etihad Airways: Staying the Course," *The Gulf Business News and Analysis*, May 2010, available online at www.thegulfonline.com/Articles.aspx?ArtID=3001.

180 David Held and Kristian Ulrichsen, "Introduction" in David Held and Kristian Ulrichsen (eds), *The Transformation of the Gulf: Politics, Economics and the Global Order* (Abingdon: Routledge, 2011), p. 11.

181 "Dubai Airport Claims Top Spot for Global Passenger Traffic in 2014," *Jakarta Globe*, January 27, 2015.

182 "U.S. Customs Passenger Facility Opens in Abu Dhabi," *USA Today*, January 27, 2014.

183 Ted Reed, "Note to Abu Dhabi on Pre-Clearance: Be Careful What You Wish For," *Forbes.com,* October 14, 2014.

184 Cited in Abdulkhaleq Abdulla, "The Impact of Globalization on Arab Gulf States," in John W. Fox, Nada Mourtada-Sabbah & Mohammed al-Mutawa (eds), *Globalization and the Gulf* (London: Routledge, 2006), p. 183.

185 See www.vision2021.ae/en/national-priority-areas/competitive-knowledge-economy.

186 Omar Obeidat and Ahmad Saleh, "UAE Officials Declare 2015 'Year of Innovation'," *Al Tamimi & Co*, February 2015, available at www.tamimi.com/en/magazine/law-up date/section-11/february-7/uae-officials-declare-2015-year-of-innovation.html.

187 Ibid.

188 "UAE Sets the Right Targets for the Future," *The National*, April 28, 2016.

189 Ibid.

190 Kristian Coates Ulrichsen, "Knowledge-Based Economies in the GCC," in Mehran Kamrava (ed.), *The Political Economy of the Persian Gulf* (London: Hurst & Co, 2012), p. 121.

191 "The Principal of Dubai Education: Dr. Abdullah Al Karam," *ArabianBusiness.com*, October 30, 2015.

192 Jason Lane, "International Branch Campuses, Free Zones, and Quality Assurance: Policy Issues for Dubai and the UAE," *Dubai School of Government Policy Brief No.20*, August 2010, p. 2.

193 Kristian Coates Ulrichsen, "Global Campuses Can be a Tool in Public Diplomacy," *New York Times*, January 19, 2015.

194 Ibid., p. 5.

195 "Dubai May Revoke University Licenses," *The National*, January 12, 2010.

196 "George Mason Uni to Close RAK Branch," *The National*, February 26, 2009; "University Branches in Dubai are Struggling," *New York Times*, December 27, 2009.

197 David McNeill, "Temple U Stands Tall in Japan," *Chronicle of Higher Education*, June 23, 2010.

198 Kristian Coates Ulrichsen, "Knowledge Based Economies in the GCC," in Mehran Kamrava (ed.), *The Political Economy of the Persian Gulf* (London: Hurst & Co, 2012), pp. 120–121.

199 "Slowdown Leads to Exodus of Western Law Firms from Abu Dhabi," *The National*, February 2, 2016.

5

INTERNATIONAL RELATIONS

This chapter examines the profound shifts in UAE foreign policy that have occurred since the 1990s and, in particular, the internationalization of the UAE and the emergence of Dubai and Abu Dhabi as aspirant global cities and hubs. The deaths of the UAE's founding President, Sheikh Zayed bin Sultan Al Nahyan, and Dubai's Ruler, Sheikh Maktoum bin Rashid Al Maktoum, in November 2004 and January 2006 coincided with the long upward trend in international oil prices that began in 2002. During the oil price boom, which lasted through June 2014 with a sharp yet short blip in 2008–2009, the new leadership in Abu Dhabi and Dubai leveraged the UAE's comparative advantages and capital accumulation to take full advantage of the new regional and international possibilities that opened up. Simultaneously, the UAE, led by Abu Dhabi, became far more hawkish in the politics of the Middle East and began to transform into a more muscular posture both regionally and internationally.

The analysis in this chapter examines how, since the 1990s, the UAE moved gradually away from the focus on Arab and Islamic issues and engaged proactively with key developments in the global economy and international governance to accumulate substantial reserves of "soft" and "hard" power and carve out niches in selected economic sectors such as aviation and international finance mentioned in Chapter Four. Relations with the United States deepened, particularly after the shock of the September 11, 2001 attacks, and remain a cornerstone of UAE foreign policy, but have also been complemented by the internationalization of UAE's ties with global partners and a more proactive approach to issues of global governance. Emirati policymakers additionally have accrued considerable reserves of cultural influence through the careful projection of soft and smart power; however, with increasing global visibility came growing international scrutiny of such issues as migrant labor conditions in the UAE and related labor-sending states.

Foreign Policy under Sheikh Zayed

For most of the period between the formation of the UAE in December 1971 and the death of Sheikh Zayed in November 2004, the country followed a foreign policy that was predicated heavily on close relationships with Gulf and other states in the Arab and Islamic world. Indeed, in June 1972, Sheikh Zayed stated, in an interview with *Al-Amal* newspaper, that "the Union is eager to have the same attitude, to be headed in the same direction, and to use the same road as Saudi Arabia," and abandoned plans the following year to establish diplomatic relations with the Soviet Union so as to avoid incurring Saudi displeasure.[1] Emirati political scientist Abdulkhaleq Abdulla has described the foreign policy of the UAE in this era as "mostly idealistic and humanist" and "essentially Arab-centered."[2] While this approach certainly did not preclude close strategic links with Western partners, it was punctuated by periods of friction such as the fallout from the Iranian seizure of three islands in the Strait of Hormuz belonging to Sharjah and Ras al-Khaimah in November 1971, the day before Britain's formal withdrawal from the Gulf and the creation of the UAE itself.[3]

In his study of UAE foreign policy, Khalid Almezaini has observed that Iran's occupation of Abu Musa and the Greater and Lesser Tunbs meant that "the UAE was put on test from the first day of its formation."[4] The Shah's move, together with Iraq's threatened invasion of Kuwait one week after Kuwaiti independence in June 1961 (which was prevented by the rushing back of British troops and later the deployment of Arab League forces to Kuwait) and Iran's territorial claim to Bahrain (resolved by a fact-finding mission organized by the United Nations in 1970), highlighted the dangers facing the small, newly independent Gulf States as they sought to adapt to a volatile regional environment dominated by large and periodically expansionary powers.[5] Securing strategies of survival as a small state represented a critical – indeed existential – component of foreign policy during the years of state-building and institutional consolidation. Sheikh Zayed emphasized in the early years of the UAE the construction of close friendly relations with the other member states of the Arab League and made a series of visits to key capitals to strengthen his personal relationships with other leaders. One such trip in 1974 took Sheikh Zayed to Morocco, Algeria, and Tunisia on a successful visit that was marred only by the Algerians' error in flying the Bahraini flag in his honor by mistake.[6]

Another prominent feature of UAE foreign policy during the formative years of the federation was the commitment to "Arabness" and, in particular, to Palestine. This was a constant and guiding feature of foreign policy during Sheikh Zayed's long life and was expressed repeatedly and volubly in regular interviews with Arab and Western journalists. Thus, in April 1971, Sheikh Zayed told *Akhbar al-Youm* that:

> Israel's policy of expansion and racist plans of Zionism are directed against all Arab countries, and in particular those which are rich in natural resources. No

Arab country is safe from the perils of the battle with Zionism unless it plays its role and bears its responsibilities, in confronting the Israeli enemy.[7]

Two years later, Sheikh Zayed reiterated, this time to Bahrain's *al-Adwa* newspaper, the importance of coordinating Arab action against Israel:

> What is important is that we agree among ourselves on a plan of action, co-ordinate our efforts and allocate duties at the level of the entire Arab nation. What is required is that the Arabs agree and reach a consensus. We in the UAE will never hesitate to bolster Arab strength to confront the enemy.[8]

Support for Palestine took both political and financial forms. The UAE participated in the Arab oil embargo between October 1973 and March 1974 (although Dubai only joined the embargo three days after Abu Dhabi), cut exports to the United States and Netherlands in retaliation for their support of Israel during the Yom Kippur War, and provided the "front-line states" in the Arab–Israeli conflict with wide-ranging support that included medical supplies and funding for European journalists to visit "the Arab side of the conflict."[9] In an interview with West German television, Sheikh Zayed described the oil embargo as a "token measure intended to persuade those countries to change their activities in support of the Zionist enemy and his designs."[10] Sheikh Zayed also stated, in October 1973, that "if Arab land continues to be occupied and subject to aggression we will use every weapon we possess, and first of all oil, to liberate our land," and added that:

> We do not want to confront any state, big or small, because we seek friendship in our dealings with states to benefit the economy. We co-operate with all states without conflict or dispute. We regard all the states of the world as friends. However, when wrong-doing goes too far we will return the offence ... [11]
>
> We can take other steps which would result in increased blows to United States interests, but we leave this a secret and will announce it in due course if the United States escalates its aggression against the Arab states ... [12]

UAE-based donors also made very considerable charitable donations and pledges of aid and development to Palestine, with Abdul-Monem al-Mashat estimating that more than US$20 billion was provided in the 1970s and 1980s.[13] Once again, UAE actions were consistent with broader regional trends as other Gulf States during the same period also channeled the majority of their foreign aid donations to the "front-line states." More than half of all development assistance from the Gulf States during the 1970s went to the confrontation states of Egypt, Jordan, Lebanon, and Syria, including much of the support ultimately destined for Palestine itself.[14] Sheikh Zayed stated that "Any aid we supply to any Arab country is in fact aid for the Emirates and our Arab motherland" and, on a different occasion, that "We, in the United Arab Emirates, are prepared to work night and day to put all our human and material resources at the disposal of the force of our Arab brother."[15] Sheikh Rashid bin Saeed Al Maktoum of Dubai also contributed generously to the Palestine cause with donations of US$5.4 million in October 1979 for Palestinians in south Lebanon and US$2.7 million in May 1980 for the families of Palestinian martyrs. In addition, as Almezaini notes, in 1992, the Sheikh Zayed Charitable Foundation was established "to manage the enormous amount of money donated by Sheikh Zayed."[16]

As the foregoing indicates, aid and development formed a third pillar of UAE foreign policy during the Zayed era. Similar to Kuwait, which launched the Kuwait Fund for Arab Economic Development (KFAED) upon independence in 1961, the Abu Dhabi Fund for Arab Economic Development was created in July 1971, five months before the UAE itself. The Abu Dhabi Fund for Development (ADFD as it was renamed in 1993) was launched and financed by the Government of Abu Dhabi and remains to this day an emirate-level institution led by Sheikh Mansour bin Zayed Al Nahyan, rather than a federal UAE one. Aid and development assistance was rooted in religious principles of charitable giving and humanitarian concerns, as well as a practical attempt to prevent conflicts from escalating and posing a threat to the regional status quo.[17]

Both Abu Dhabi/UAE and Kuwait used foreign aid derived from the wealth generated from oil income as an instrument of regional and foreign policy and as a means of strengthening and diversifying international relationships. This heavy emphasis on humanitarian support as a key element of international engagement also constitutes a point of continuity with the post-Zayed era following the death of the president in 2004. Five years later, in 2009, the inaugural report of the newly established UAE Office for the Coordination of Foreign Aid estimated that the ADFD accounted for more than 70 percent of all UAE aid. Supplementing this, the UAE has witnessed a considerable proliferation of state-based and private philanthropic initiatives and foundations, the majority founded by, or linked to, members of ruling families and major merchant families.[18] All of these entities were subsequently deployed in 2011 during the Emirati participation in the NATO-led intervention in Libya, when the deployment of twelve fighter jets in "hard" military operations was complemented by a comprehensive humanitarian component that included key "private" charities such as the Zayed bin Sultan Al Nahyan Charitable and Humanitarian Foundation, the Khalifa bin Zayed Al Nahyan Charity Foundation, and the Mohammed bin Rashid Al Maktoum Charity and Humanitarian Establishment, in addition to the state-directed UAE Red Crescent.[19]

A fourth component of Sheikh Zayed's approach to foreign affairs was an emphasis on diplomatic mediation. Four high-profile instances of this in action took place during the Iran–Iraq War in the mid-1980s, during the Gulf crisis caused by the Iraqi invasion of Kuwait in 1990, in an intra-GCC dispute in the mid-1990s, and toward the very end of Sheikh Zayed's life in the run-up to the US-led invasion of Iraq in 2003. Doubtless mindful of the lack of unity among the seven constituent emirates, which at times backed both sides during the

Iran–Iraq War, Sheikh Zayed sought pragmatically to steer a neutral course throughout the eight-year conflict. Particularly during 1986 and 1987, Sheikh Zayed was at the forefront of attempts to prevent the further escalation of the war and to keep open diplomatic channels that could bring about a negotiated end to the military stalemate. In August 1987, the UAE (along with Oman) made a forceful case at a meeting of Arab League foreign ministers to avoid breaking all diplomatic relations between Arab states and Iran.[20] Sheikh Zayed subsequently was delegated by the GCC Summit in December 1987 to explore the possibilities of a dialogue between the GCC states and Iran and push for a ceasefire as laid down in UN Security Council Resolution 598 of July 1987.[21]

In August 1990, as the Gulf crisis intensified in the immediate aftermath of the Iraqi invasion of Kuwait, Sheikh Zayed led attempts to coordinate an Arab and international response to Saddam Hussein's aggression. Sheikh Zayed worked with King Fahd of Saudi Arabia and President Hosni Mubarak of Egypt to organize an emergency Arab League meeting in Cairo on August 12, 1990, ten days after the invasion. When that meeting failed to provide the hoped-for Arab unity, the UAE threw its support behind the build-up of multinational forces that assembled in Saudi Arabia and provided both logistical and financial support to the US-led coalition. Air and ground forces from the UAE fought as part of the coalition during the Gulf War and were among the first to enter Kuwait upon its liberation in February 1991.[22] The UAE, along with Saudi Arabia and the Kuwaiti government-in-exile further contributed some US$12 billion to the cost of Operation Desert Shield (August 1990–January 1991) and Operation Desert Storm (January–February 1991).[23]

Later in the 1990s, Sheikh Zayed also acted as interlocutor in a longstanding territorial dispute between Bahrain and Qatar over the Hawar Islands, and paved the way toward a final settlement of the issue at the International Court of Justice in 2001.[24] Finally, in 2003, Sheikh Zayed made a last-ditch and ultimately unsuccessful effort to prevent the George W. Bush administration from invading Iraq. At the Arab League Summit that March, the UAE put forward a plan whereby Saddam Hussein would resign and move into exile in the UAE and Iraq would undergo a gradual transfer of power under the supervision of the Arab League and the United Nations. However, the plan never gained traction in Baghdad and the flawed US-led invasion and occupation of Iraq went ahead with the launch of combat operations on March 19, 2003.[25]

Deepening Relations with the United States

Officials in Abu Dhabi and Dubai forged what J.E. Peterson, writing in the context of Qatar, has labelled "strategies of survival" for small states based on enlisting a powerful external protector (the United States) as a security guarantor while developing strategic niches that facilitated and underpinned the rise to global prominence.[26] While the UAE first established an Embassy in Washington, DC, in 1974, the military relationship with the US has its roots in the legacy of the 1990

Iraqi occupation of Kuwait, which underscored not only the vulnerability of small states in a volatile regional neighborhood but also the utility of having powerful and diversified defense and security partnerships with a range of external partners. It is important to recall that Saddam Hussein threatened the UAE, as well as Kuwait, at the Arab League in mid-July 1990, and accused the two countries of driving down the price of oil which, he claimed, had deprived Iraq of US$89 billion in lost revenues. While Saddam further accused Kuwait of slant-drilling into the Rumaila oilfield, which subsequently proved a pretext for the August 2 invasion, his initial threat was taken rather more seriously at the outset by UAE officials than by their Kuwaiti counterparts.[27]

As a result, on July 22, 1990, six days after Saddam's threat but eleven days prior to the invasion of Kuwait, the UAE requested military assistance from the US in order to deter any potential Iraqi attack. The Near Eastern Bureau at the State Department expressed initial reservation but was overruled by Secretary of State James Baker, who felt that a show of force would demonstrate US intent to protect its vital interests in the Gulf, and President George H.W. Bush.[28] Two days later, the US launched *Operation Ivory Justice* and deployed three tanker aircraft capable of refuelling UAE fighter jets in flight and thereby allowing the UAE air force to maintain a continuous airborne presence in order to intercept any incoming assault. The tankers were based at Al-Dhafra airbase although the UAE leadership was reportedly "so sensitive to the deployment that [the] U.S. aircraft were hidden away at the center of the airbase lest their tails be visible to the public over its walls."[29] Interestingly, one account of *Operation Ivory Justice* has linked the limited deployment to the UAE in July 1990 to one of the most contentious incidents in US–Iraq relations in the immediate run-up to the August 2 invasion of Kuwait, as:

> word of the increased U.S. military presence led to some Arab government protests, but the UAE claimed that the US military presence was nothing more than routine training. Iraqi leaders complained to U.S. Ambassador to Iraq April Glaspie, who reassured them that the United States sought improved relations with their country. During one meeting with Hussein, Glaspie sought to strike a conciliatory tone, in line with official policy.[30]

UAE forces participated in both the air and ground phases of *Operation Desert Storm* and were among the first to enter Kuwait following its liberation in late February 1991. The UAE also sent troops to Kuwait in October 1994 after Saddam Hussein again threatened Kuwait and redeployed Iraqi troops to the UN-demarcated boundary between the two countries.[31] Both the October 1994 threat to Kuwait and renewed Iraqi troop movements in August 1995 led US policymakers to rapidly build up their onshore and offshore military assets in Kuwait and throughout the Gulf.[32] UAE–US security ties were formalized in a Defense Cooperation Agreement signed between the two countries on July 25, 1994. This bilateral pact contained a status of force agreement that covered the stationing of US troops at the Al-Dhafra base in Abu Dhabi and allowed the US to preposition equipment at bases in the UAE and utilize Jebel Ali for naval visits by American warships patrolling Gulf waters.[33] Over time, the number of US forces stationed at Al-Dhafra increased steadily from about 800 prior to the invasion of Iraq in 2003 to about 1,800 by the mid-2000s and an estimated 3,500 in 2014, by which time Al-Dhafra also was the only US overseas base permitted to station the highly advanced F-22 fighter.[34]

As with any bilateral relationship, UAE–US ties have fluctuated over the years although the general tenor of the relationship has been considerably closer over the past decade than in the pre-2004 era. Thus, the UAE has been "the only Arab nation to participate with the US in six coalition actions over the last 20 years: Afghanistan, Libya, Somalia, Bosnia-Kosovo, the 1990 [sic] Gulf War and the fight against ISIS."[35] This list notwithstanding, a significant source of friction in UAE–US relations in the final decade of Sheikh Zayed's life was his gradual yet mounting opposition to US sanctions on Iraq during the 1990s. In January 1995, the then Crown Prince of Dubai, Sheikh Mohammed bin Rashid Al Maktoum, became the first Gulf leader to call on Kuwait to drop its opposition toward the normalization of relations with Iraq while in October 1995 Sheikh Zayed stated that "the suffering of the Iraqi people should be brought to an end."[36] By 1997, Almezaini had observed that "UAE citizens, with Sheikh Zayed's support, began to take direct action to help the Iraqi people" through the provision of direct humanitarian support.[37] Such concerns formed a part of a wider questioning among many Gulf leaders and policymakers of the efficacy (and desirability) of the policy of Dual Containment in the 1990s and wariness at what one Gulf academic labelled the "smothering embrace" of US policy in the Gulf.[38]

The events of September 11, 2001 provided a hard illustration of the existence of at least a wellspring of discontent among pockets of the population at US policy in the Middle East with the disclosure that two of the hijackers were UAE nationals.[39] This meant that UAE nationals constituted the second largest group of hijackers after the fifteen Saudis, while one of the Emiratis involved, twenty-three-year-old Marwan Yousef al-Shehhi, was the pilot who flew the hijacked United Airways Flight 175 that slammed into the South Tower of the World Trade Center in New York.[40] In addition, at least nine of the 9/11 hijackers passed through Dubai on their way to the United States in the months prior to the attacks, as two local facilitators provided "assistance in purchasing plane tickets and traveller's checks." The official report of the 9/11 Commission found that "six of the muscle hijackers who arrived in this period purchased traveller's checks totalling $43,980 in the UAE and used them in the United States."[41] In addition, the 9/11 Commission emphasized the central role played in the financing of the attacks by Ali Abdul Aziz Ali, a nephew of the overall plot ringleader, Khalid Sheikh Mohammed (KSM), who:

> … lived in the UAE for several years before the September 11 attacks, working for a computer wholesaler in a free trade zone in Dubai. According to Ali, KSM gave him the assignment and provided him with some of the

necessary funds at a meeting in Pakistan in early 2000. KSM provided the bulk of the money later in 2000 via a courier ... [42]

... Ali wire transferred a total of $119,500 to the hijackers in the United States in six transactions between April 16, 2000 and September 17, 2000 ... In each case, Ali brought cash in UAE dirhams, which were then changed into dollars ... All of the bank-to-bank transactions flowed through the UAE Exchange's correspondent account at Citibank ... [43]

The Commission went on to state that Ali "relied on the anonymity provided by [the] bustling financial center of Dubai and the vast international monetary system." Moreover, it concluded that:

> ... Ali said he sent the final $70,000 in one large transfer because Shehhi had called and asked him to "send him everything." According to Ali, KSM was displeased when he later learned of the transfer because he thought the size of the transaction would alert the security services. The amount did not worry Ali, however, because he knew that Dubai computer companies frequently transferred such amounts of money. Ali said he experienced no problem with this transfer, or any transfer in aid of the hijackers. [44]

The shock provided by 9/11 led to rapid and concerted efforts in the UAE to address the issues highlighted by the radicalization of the two Emirati hijackers and the money trails that flowed through Dubai. Significantly, in light of his later rise to prominence, it was Sheikh Mohammed bin Zayed Al Nahyan who organized the policy response to 9/11 in ways that exceeded his position, at the time, as Chief of Staff of the UAE Armed Forces. Specific countermeasures included the "discrete expulsion" of suspected extremists, an intensification of educational reforms intended to promote moderate images of Islam, and vigorous cooperation with the US government and the Financial Action Task Force (FATF) to counter money laundering and illicit transfers of funds. [45] Greater attention also was paid to the *hawala* system of money transfers that had been especially prevalent among informal and small traders in Dubai and Sharjah, and a close working relationship developed between the Governor of the UAE Central Bank, Sultan bin Nasser al-Suwaidi, and US Treasury authorities. A particularly significant outcome of the post-9/11 countermeasures was a strengthening of the powers of the Central Bank and the federal government to monitor financial and business controls and regulations across the seven emirates. [46]

The third of Sheikh Zayed's nineteen sons and the oldest of a powerful bloc of six full brothers known as the "Bani Fatima" after their mother, the UAE's First Lady, Sheikha Fatima bint Mubarak Al Ketbi, Mohammed bin Zayed (known popularly as "MBZ") developed early on a reputation as an arch modernizer and highly capable administrator. Born in 1961, MBZ entered public life in January 1993 when his father appointed him the Chief of Staff of the UAE Armed Forces at the age of thirty-one. In this position, MBZ developed a close personal and working relationship with the UAE Defense Minister and (at the time) the Crown Prince in Dubai, Sheikh Mohammed bin Rashid Al Maktoum ("MBR") and also forged enduring contacts with key international partners in Washington, DC, London, and Paris. As head of the UAE Offsets Group in the 1990s and early 2000s, MBZ also played a leading role in Abu Dhabi's early internationalization and large-scale infrastructure and industrial developments.[47]

During the final years of Sheikh Zayed's long rule, MBZ in Abu Dhabi and MBR in Dubai emerged as the two most dynamic figures in the reshaping of political and economic power in the UAE. MBZ formally entered the line of succession in Abu Dhabi in December 2003 when his appointment as Deputy Crown Prince meant he leapfrogged over Sheikh Zayed's second son, the Deputy Prime Minister Sheikh Sultan bin Zayed Al Nahyan, six years MBZ's senior. Like his older brother, the longstanding Crown Prince, Sheikh Khalifa bin Zayed Al Nahyan, Sheikh Sultan was seen as more of a traditionalist with "strong connections among the tribal networks that play such an important role in Abu Dhabi politics."[48] MBZ, by contrast, was seen more as a modernizer, similar to MBR in Dubai; indeed, a US diplomatic cable written in late September 2004, a little over a month before Sheikh Zayed died on November 2, noted the close ties between MBZ and MBR and added that "the two have the ability to see the bigger picture and have compatible visions for the country's development."[49]

As Chapter Three noted, the succession to Sheikh Zayed passed smoothly in November 2004 as Sheikh Khalifa became President of the UAE and Ruler of Abu Dhabi as long planned. The Cabinet reshuffle undertaken the day before Sheikh Zayed's passing, which was notable for the inclusion of the first female Cabinet minister in UAE history as the formidable Sheikha Lubna bint Khalid Al Qasimi, a member of the Sharjah ruling family, became Minister of Economics and Planning, also confirmed the central role of the Bani Fatima both in Abu Dhabi and in federal UAE politics, focused around MBZ and three of his full brothers, Sheikh Hazza bin Zayed Al Nahyan (Security), Sheikh Mansour bin Zayed Al Nahyan (Presidential Affairs), and Sheikh Abdullah bin Zayed Al Nahyan (Information). The defense and security relationship between the UAE and the US continued to grow closer during the 2000s as both MBZ and MBR continued in their portfolios as Chief of Staff of the UAE Armed Forces and Minister of Defense and assumed pivotal roles in the economic development of Abu Dhabi and Dubai respectively. A case in point was the growth of DP World's hub in Fujairah into the major transhipment point for the US Army's operations in Afghanistan, through which all issues related to battalion rotation and rolling stock movement passed.[50]

While the UAE did not participate directly in the US-led invasion of Iraq in 2003 (although it did permit Germany to train Iraqi police forces at a base in Al-Ain), and isolated incidents, such as anti-American and pro-Saddam Hussein statements by the (soon-to-be-replaced) Crown Prince of Ras al-Khaimah, Sheikh Khalid bin Saqr Al Qasimi, before and during the invasion suggested that support for the Iraq war was not widely forthcoming,[51] other developments quickly illustrated how the UAE developed into the foremost US military partner in the Arab world. In addition to Fujairah's abovementioned transhipment role, the UAE became the primary air reconnaissance hub for the US in the Middle East particularly for high-altitude aircraft engaged on long-range reconnaissance missions in Afghanistan. A major new defense procurement program began in the early 2000s and was predicated on a comprehensive alignment with the US in terms of military doctrine, force composition, and joint development of new weapons systems. Especially notable was a US$3 billion investment from the UAE into US research programs associated with the design and production of the Lockheed Martin F-16. This made the UAE "the first major Arab partner nation to play a decisive role in the design of next-generation US defense technologies ... with the aim of making them practically exempt from defense export restrictions."[52] The Block 60 version of the F-16 subsequently made its aerial debut at the Dubai Air Show in 2005 and the UAE was the first and, for a time, the only air force in the world to operate the fighter. By the following year, *Gulf States Newsletter* reported that "the US Air Force's next generation of electronic warfare and avionics has been largely designed with UAE money and will be in service with the Emirates long before it is incorporated into US aircraft."[53]

The value of the UAE security and defense relationship with the US became very clear in early 2006 when the UAE became the subject of a Congressional backlash against the proposed acquisition of a ports management contract in the US by Dubai's DP World. While politicians such as the Senators for New York, Chuck Schumer and Hillary Rodham Clinton, led the charge against DP World and, by extension, Dubai and the UAE at large, they were rebutted in the most forceful terms by a phalanx of serving and retired senior commanders. These included both the serving commander of US Central Command (Centcom), John Abizaid, who stated that "the UAE is absolutely vital to our interests," and the Chairman of the US Joint Chiefs of Staff, General Peter Pace, who added that:

> ... the military-to-military relationship with the United Arab Emirates is superb ... They've got a world-class air-to-air training facility that they let us use and cooperate with them in the training of our pilots. In everything that we have asked and work with them on, they have proven to be very, very solid partners.[54]

General Tommy Franks, who served as Centcom commander during 9/11 and the start of the Afghanistan and Iraq wars, was even more effusive as he claimed that "I personally believe that we have had no greater ally in seeking a resolution of problems in the Middle East, the Palestinian issue, the Israeli issue, than we have found in the United Arab Emirates."[55]

The above testimonies could not disguise the damage that the DP World affair did to Dubai's (and the UAE's) reputational image, however unfairly, and demonstrated the volatility of operating in a post-9/11 environment in the US where issues could rapidly, and unpredictably, become politicized and (mis)represented as toxic threats to national security. An interview given in February 2006 by Senator Schumer to *NPR* encapsulated this toxicity as he restated his opposition to "a country [sic] with a nexus of terrorism like Dubai owning this company" and added vaguely that "Dubai has had a very strong nexus with terrorism, not necessarily the head, or the emir of Dubai, but rather so many people involved."[56] During the DP World crisis, Mark Townshend, a reporter for the UAE-based *Khaleej Times* newspaper, recounted thus his appearance on a live debate on Voice of America:

> I'm used to the rough and tumble of live debates, but the vehemence of the opposition surprised me ... I was effectively cross-examined. Did I know that Dubai could be used to smuggle radioactive materials or terrorist weapons. I was being asked to clarify earlier UAE support for Hamas. It seemed to me the debate was running away from itself and rapidly becoming polarized ... [57]

The wide-ranging military partnership between the UAE and the US ensured that the relationship survived the DP World furor intact and continued to grow both in breadth and depth after 2006. A lengthy and rather gushing article about the UAE's military prowess that appeared in the *Washington Post* in November 2014 expanded upon the closer defense and security relationship with the US and drew attention to the fact that "In the UAE, the United States has a quiet, potent ally nicknamed Little Sparta." In the article, which was written shortly after the UAE joined the US-led campaign of airstrikes against the so-called Islamic State of Iraq and al-Shams (ISIS), the author, Rajiv Chandrasekaran, explained that Emirati authorities relaxed reporting restrictions on UAE military activity "because of growing concern at senior levels of the Emirati government that keeping mum has led to an underappreciation of the country's contributions beyond what is known in a handful of offices in the Pentagon and at the State Department."[58]

Indeed, the UAE has participated in every US-led military campaign in the broader region (Somalia, Kosovo, Afghanistan, and Libya) since the 1991 Gulf War with the sole exception of the 2003 invasion of Iraq. Jebel Ali in Dubai has grown into the most frequent port of call for the US Navy outside of the United States while nearly 4,000 American troops are permanently stationed at Al-Dhafra airbase in Abu Dhabi.[59] Moreover, since 2014, the US Marine Corps has been involved in a US$150 million training contract for the UAE Presidential Guard, an elite military unit formed in 2010 (and commanded by a former Australian commander of that country's Special Forces and later its Middle East area of operations, Major-General Mike Hindmarsh). At the time of the Marine Corps contract award, in January 2014, *Defense News* noted that "the UAE Presidential Guard is a military unit that operates outside of the conventional framework of traditional armed forces such as ground, marine, and air forces" and added that it was currently engaged alongside US troops, particularly in Afghanistan.[60]

The UAE in Afghanistan, 2001–2014

UAE involvement in Afghanistan since 2001 illustrates the evolution in the country's approach toward international affairs and, in particular, in the combination of elements of "hard" and "soft" power projection along with a strong public relations component. Along with Saudi Arabia and Pakistan, the UAE was one of only three countries that recognized the Taliban regime after it took power in Afghanistan in 1996. Rather explosively, the investigative journalist Steve Coll recounted how, shortly after the African embassy bombings in August 1998, a US retaliatory strike against a hunting camp in western Afghanistan where Al Qaeda's leader, Osama bin Laden, was believed to be taking refuge, had to be aborted after surveillance imagery indicated that high-level UAE officials, possibly including ruling family members, might be present.[61] After the 9/11 attacks on the United States, a US Treasury investigation led also to speculation that Dubai had been a conduit for Taliban gold smuggling.[62]

The above notwithstanding, the UAE quickly threw its support behind the government of Hamid Karzai that came to power in December 2001. Members of the UAE Armed Forces were stationed in Afghanistan from 2001. As the only military force in Afghanistan from an Arab country, the troops engaged heavily in humanitarian work, such as providing aid and medical services, in addition to combat support for US and NATO forces. The UAE later deployed six F-16s to Kandahar between 2012 and 2014 to further support the NATO mission at a critical moment when several European members of the alliance began to withdraw from Afghanistan. The *Washington Post* noted that "the UAE pilots were deemed by NATO officials to be so skilled that they were permitted to fly hundreds of close air-support missions to protect coalition ground forces," and that the UAE and Australia were the only non-NATO members permitted to fly such missions.[63]

UAE military operations in Afghanistan operated in parallel with a humanitarian approach that meant that by 2009 fully 14 percent of the UAE's foreign aid budget was earmarked for Afghanistan. Among the recipients of US$22 million in UAE funding were six medical clinics, eleven schools, thirty-eight mosques, a hospital, and facilities for displaced persons.[64] The UAE government packaged its military and humanitarian contribution under the slogan "Winds of Goodness" and emphasized how safety and stability were essential prerequisites for the successful provision of aid and development. A slick public relations campaign was developed around the Afghan mission in partnership with the twofour54 entertainment and media free zone in Abu Dhabi and, significantly, with the Office of the Brand of Abu Dhabi (OBAD), a government entity set up in 2007 by the Executive Council with responsibility for:

> … delivering a compelling and consistent brand for Abu Dhabi, which embraces the Emirate's vision for the future and embraces the culture, heritage, and traditions of its past. OBAD acts as the guardian and patron of the brand, providing guidance to the public and private sectors on its application

in all activities that may have an impact on the reputation of the Emirate of
Abu Dhabi ... [65]

UAE involvement in Afghanistan thus featured a mixture of hard (military), soft
(humanitarian) and also smart power, the latter in the form of assistance with a
range of investment and security initiatives. Dubai hosted the inaugural Afghanistan
International Investors Conference in November 2010 and created an international
group to advise the Afghan government on laws and policies to better attract foreign investment.[66] In addition, Dubai also organized regular *Afghanistan Spotlight*
conferences on behalf of the US Commerce Department that were designed to
match US and other international investors with Afghan partners in a program that
ended in December 2014. The theme of one such Spotlight event, held in September 2014, was "Mining Your Own Business," and took place in Dubai alongside a US Department of Commerce event entitled "Emerging Afghan Extractives
and Energy Sectors."[67] At a state-to-state level, a bilateral agreement on security
cooperation was signed in July 2013 while in January 2015 a comprehensive
Enduring Strategic Partnership Agreement was signed by Afghan President Ashraf
Ghani and UAE Prime Minister (and Ruler of Dubai) Sheikh Mohammed bin
Rashid Al Maktoum. The strategic partnership provided for cooperation in security
matters and law enforcement and included an Emirati training component for the
Afghan National Police.[68]

Commercial ties between the UAE and Afghanistan also proliferated during the
2000s and early 2010s. Abu Dhabi–based Etisalat became one of the largest UAE
investors in Afghanistan in 2006 when the telecommunications provider was
awarded a GSM license to operate in the country. Afghan government officials
sought subsequently to encourage further UAE investment in the energy and
construction sectors although a combination of the global financial crisis and worsening security situation in Afghanistan contributed to a lull in investment after
2008. Meanwhile, the flow of capital from Afghanistan to the UAE intensified
ahead of the anticipated withdrawal of NATO troops from Afghanistan in 2014 as
Afghan investors sought financial safe havens in Dubai's relatively relaxed business
and real estate environment. Much of the US$3 billion that flowed out of Afgha-
nistan in the late 2000s is believed to have ended up in Dubai either in property
investment or to benefit from the UAE's tight banking secrecy laws.[69]

Many of the property investments made by Afghans turned sour during the
bursting of the Dubai real estate bubble in 2008 and contributed in large part to
the failure of the Da Kabul bank two years later amid allegations of corruption at
the heart of the government of then President Hamid Karzai. In a separate incident, in October 2009, Karzai's Vice-President, Ahmad Zia Massoud, was found to
have entered the UAE carrying US$52 million in cash. A classified US cable
released by WikiLeaks reported that such incidents supported "suspicions [that]
large amounts of physical cash transit from Kabul to Dubai on a weekly, monthly,
and annual basis." Up to US$190 million was believed to have been flown from
Kabul International Airport to Dubai between July and September 2009 alone.[70]

This occurred as the UAE, and Dubai in particular, emerged as a destination of choice for nervous Afghan investors as the 2014 deadline for the withdrawal of international troops from Afghanistan approached. After Karzai's term in office ended, his successor as President, Ashraf Ghani, ordered the Afghan Attorney General in October 2014 to investigate the disappearance of US$1 billion from Da Kabul Bank in 2010 with particular focus on the purchase of eight luxury villas on Dubai's Palm Jumeirah.[71]

The example of UAE policy toward Afghanistan therefore illustrates the nuanced use of a range of instruments of soft, hard, and smart power over an extended period of time. While a key ally of the US- and NATO-led coalition in the long struggle against the Taliban, the UAE was better positioned than its "Western" allies to understand local (and religious) sensitivities and package its military contribution as part of a broader humanitarian approach consistent with its long record of aid and development to Arab and (in this case) Islamic recipients in need. UAE involvement in Afghanistan also was highlighted and even celebrated in a much more "upfront" manner that acknowledged fully the role of public relations management in regional and international policy. Nevertheless, the growing assertiveness in UAE foreign policy also became evident in a visceral editorial published in the Dubai-based newspaper, *Gulf News*, shortly after Dubai was awarded the hosting rights to the 2020 World Expo. Entitled "UAE deserves answers from Pakistan and Afghanistan," the editorial claimed that both countries had failed to vote for Dubai's bid and suggested that Islamabad and Kabul "chose to disregard all that binds us and turned their back on us at a critical moment," a stance that *Gulf News* labelled incomprehensible "because we consider those two countries to be close friends in whom the UAE has invested so much politically and economically." Turning to Afghanistan, *Gulf News* could barely disguise feelings that bordered on betrayal:

> Our boys are still deployed in that country risking their lives to provide essential humanitarian, medical and security aid. The UAE is a major donor in rebuilding the country that has seen more than its share of wars and occupations since the Soviet invasion in the late 1970s. The UAE has put in so much effort to set up modern schools, hospitals, and road networks.[72]

The important point, which will be expanded upon in greater detail in Chapter Six, is that over the past decade the UAE increasingly has become a contributor to, rather than merely a consumer of, regional security structures not only in the Gulf but also in the broader Middle East region. Indeed, seen in retrospect, the scope and scale of the UAE's military contribution to the Afghanistan operations anticipated its involvement alongside another NATO-led venture – *Operation Unified Protector* – in Libya between March and October 2011, and, on a regional level, its contribution to the GCC Peninsula Shield Force intervention in Bahrain in March 2011 and, on a far greater scale, to the Saudi-led Arab coalition that commenced military operations in Yemen on March 26, 2015 as part of *Operation Decisive Storm*.

The Internationalization of UAE Foreign Policy

In *Sand to Silicon*, their account of the early years of Dubai's dizzying economic growth, authors Jeffrey Sampler and Saeb Eigner interviewed Sultan bin Sulayem of Dubai World on the use of Singapore both as a model of emulation and a yardstick for Dubai. Sulayem told the authors that:

> Whatever you see in Singapore you see here. Sometimes we are more advanced than them, sometimes they are more advanced than us. We invest in different things. For example, Singapore invested in a single crane that carries two containers. We decided to get a faster, more advanced crane that worked better and was less expensive. Later, they came to see ours and decided to change.[73]

A significant feature of the UAE's growing global profile has been the expansion and thickening of diplomacy and trade with "new" partners both in Asia and around the world that increasingly has combined greater economic engagement with increasingly political relationships. In recent years, policymakers in the UAE have, in many areas, developed a "nodal" foreign policy in which countries are grouped into areas of key regional geostrategic interest. Such a policy has more closely aligned UAE political, economic, and, in many areas, humanitarian interests, with an example being Emirati policy toward East Africa, which UAE officials have identified as a source both of potential (and actual) instability as well as a market for foreign investment and economic opportunity.[74] However, none of the "new" Emirati partners come close to replicating the defense relationship and security umbrella with Western states that remains intact and untouched.

This "state capitalist" approach has multiple, interlinked components that enable the rapid mobilization of political and diplomatic assets in support of a comprehensive foreign policy approach. Emirati interest in East Africa increased markedly after 2010 through a substantial increase both in foreign aid and in trading relationships as well as growing acknowledgment of the threat to regional stability posed by Islamist terrorist groups such as al-Shabaab. UAE aid to East Africa grew nearly twentyfold between 2011 and 2013 from 958 million Dirhams to 18.1 billion Dirhams (US$260.84 million to US$.4.93 billion), by which time African states, as a whole, accounted for a remarkable 84 percent of the foreign aid budget for 2013.[75]

Beyond aid, Emirati officials also identified major opportunities for UAE investors in Uganda, Kenya, and Somalia as Foreign Minister Sheikh Abdullah bin Zayed Al Nahyan visited all three countries in June 2015 and announced plans to significantly expand UAE diplomatic missions throughout the continent.[76] Key Emirati enterprises have established regional hubs in East Africa designed to take advantage of favorable demographic indicators and unlock the economic potential in sectors ranging from energy and finance to logistics and infrastructure. Bilateral trade between the UAE and Ethiopia thus increased by 100 percent in the twelve months after the Dubai Chamber of Commerce and Industry opened a trade office in Ethiopia in 2012 while in Uganda, Emirati companies were involved in projects to develop tourism around Lake Victoria, construct airports in rural areas, and construct an oil pipeline to Mombasa in Kenya.[77] Meanwhile, Emirati assistance in Somalia was channeled primarily into stabilization efforts as the UAE funded an army training center in Mogadishu with the objective of developing a Somali brigade strong enough to resist militant groups like al-Shabaab and provided practical support to Somali state institutions through the provision of armored vehicles to protect government officials and equipment to the Somali police force.[78]

To a lesser extent, owing to the greater geographical distance and lack of historical connection, UAE relations with Latin America, particularly Brazil, blossomed in the 2000s and early 2010s. Formal meetings between political and economic leaders slowly gathered pace during the 2000s beginning with a visit by then-Brazilian President Luis Inacio da Silva ("Lula") to the UAE (as well as to Egypt, Libya, and Syria) in 2003 and the signing of a bilateral aviation agreement the following year. Although the UAE then sat back as Qatar took the lead with Brazil in organizing inter-regional summits between the Gulf and Latin American states, Emirati investors expressed interest in Latin American foodstuffs, real estate, and energy markets as well as infrastructural projects such as mass transit and LNG terminals.[79] A large-scale Brazilian trade mission that visited the UAE in 2012 captured the sense of possibility as the trip resulted in the signing of a range of commercial agreements worth US$65.3 million in total.[80]

One of the first high-profile examples of UAE investment in Latin America was a US$2 billion investment by Abu Dhabi's Mubadala in Brazilian mining and energy magnate Eike Batista's EBX Group in 2012. This was part of an expansive "Strategic Framework" that covered the cement, fertilizer, entertainment, and technology sectors and formed part of "Mubadala's development of strategic opportunities in Brazil and Latin America."[81] The agreement soured the following year following the collapse of the EBX Group and Batista's losses in the precious metals mining industry. Mubadala later acquired a string of assets across Brazil in the subsequent restructuring of EBX debt, including a 10.52 percent stake in the MMX Mineracao & Metalicos SA mining company and a 10.44 percent stake in Prumo Logistica SA. Furthermore, Mubadala partnered with commodities trader Trafigura Beheer BV to purchase a US$400 million controlling stake in the Sudeste port in Rio state as a foothold for the export of iron ore.[82] Also in the same sector, DP World partnered with Brazilian operator Odebrecht to acquire a stake in Brazil's largest container port in Santos, gateway to 90 percent of the cargo traffic to the mega-city of Sao Paulo.[83]

UAE ties with Brazil mirrored the growth of relationships with the BRICS (Brazil, Russia, India, China, and South Africa) grouping of emerging economies and in particular, with trade partners in South and East Asia. Relations with Russia have drawn closer as the Russia Direct Investment Fund (RDIF) has sought inward investment from the UAE (and from other GCC states) and Russian and Emirati views on the threat from Islamist extremism gradually have converged, while the UAE has long been a major purchaser of arms from Russia.[84] Abu Dhabi's

Mubadala made the first sovereign wealth investment from the Gulf into Russia in November 2010 when it announced a US$100 million investment in a Russian hedge fund, Verno Capital.[85] During a visit to Moscow in September 2013 by Abu Dhabi Crown Prince Mohammed bin Zayed, the emirate's Department of Finance signed a letter of intent with the RDIF to commit US$5 billion to a joint investment fund. Also in 2013, Mubadala's managing director, Khaldoun al-Mubarak, joined the RDIF's international advisory board and the RDIF and Mubadala set up a US$2 billion joint investment fund of their own.[86]

On a person-to-person level, Russian tourists began to travel to Dubai in large numbers in search of a geopolitically stable, warm weather winter destination, and constitute by some margin the highest spenders at the annual Dubai Shopping Festival, even though their numbers fell sharply as the oil price downturn began to bite in 2015.[87] Similarly, the Russian Business Council in Dubai estimated that up to 100,000 Russians were resident in the emirate in 2016.[88] However, the most powerful advocate of closer UAE–Russia relations has been the UAE Ambassador to Russia, Omar bin Saif Ghobash, son of Saif Ghobash, the UAE's first Minister of State for Foreign Affairs whose assassination in 1977 was mentioned in Chapter One, and his Russian wife. Fluent in Russian, Ghobash was appointed Ambassador to Russia in 2009 and since has developed an exceptionally close relationship with the senior Russian leadership.[89]

Ties with India have historical depth but underwent a period of sustained frostiness in the decades that followed India's independence in 1947 and only belatedly began to recover in the 2000s. During this long period, the majority of India's diplomatic activity in the Gulf was focused on Iraq and Iran both for political and energy security reasons, although in the 1990s the UAE did emerge as India's main regional non-oil trade partner and accounted for two-thirds of Indian exports to the GCC by 2000. Trade flows between the UAE and India continued to far overshadow those of all other GCC states and, at US$67 billion in 2011, constituted 56 percent of the GCC–India total.[90]

Remarkably, however, no Indian Prime Minister set foot in the UAE while in office between a visit by Indira Gandhi in 1981 and August 2015, when Narendra Modi made a historic visit, during the course of which he was feted by more than 40,000 Indian expatriates at the Dubai Cricket Stadium.[91] This was in spite of the Gulf's centrality to India's energy security as collectively the GCC states came to supply some 45 percent of India's oil needs by 2015, and by the importance of remittances sent back to India by the several million migrant workers living in GCC states.[92]

The abovementioned growth in trade between the UAE and India was matched, albeit at a far lesser level, by the rise of bilateral investment linkages. By 2012, the UAE was the tenth largest international investor in India with some US$1.8 billion of investment concentrated primarily in the five sectors of energy, services, computer programing, construction, and tourism and hotels.[93] And yet, despite significant investments made by prominent Emirati entities such as DP World and Emaar Properties, concerns with the relatively poor business climate in India held back the full development of UAE interests in India. Etisalat found itself drawn into a corruption scandal in 2012 that resulted in the loss of its mobile phone license in India and prompted the company to withdraw from the Indian market altogether.[94] DP World also ran into difficulty and frustration over its underperforming International Container Transshipment Terminal at Vallarpadam, which the company blamed on the slow completion of highway links to the port and the lack of adequate deep berth facilities capable of accommodating large oceangoing vessels.[95]

The substantive yet belated growth of the relationship between the UAE and India is still some way behind the breadth and depth of Emirati ties with Southeast and Pacific Asian partners, which diversified considerably in the twenty-first century. Consistent with the move in what Danny Quah of the London School of Economics has identified as the "world economic center of gravity," flows of hydrocarbons and non-oil trade shifted east in response to the Asian economic boom in the 2000s, just as Dubai and, later, Abu Dhabi emerged onto the world stage.[96] This led to the rapid expansion of bilateral connections between the UAE and East and Pacific Asian states that simultaneously reflected and reinforced the changing macro-patterns of global trade. By 2012, the two largest export partners for the UAE were Japan (14.6 percent of total exports) and India (11.4 percent) while China was the largest import partner with 14.7 percent followed closely by India (14 percent). These figures were consistent with the geographical redistribution of trade flows as trade among developing countries ("South–South trade") rose rapidly from only 8 percent of world trade in 1990 to 16 percent in 2005 and 24 percent in 2011 while the global share of "North–North trade" declined from 56 percent to 36 percent during the same period.[97]

Chapter Four noted the instrumental role of Japanese companies in the early development of the natural gas sector in Abu Dhabi. Oil and gas ties illustrate the growing interdependencies between the UAE and Asia as joint ventures have proliferated since the mid-2000s and moved far beyond simple transactions between buyers and sellers of energy to encompass developments across the upstream and downstream sectors. Abu Dhabi government–owned Mubadala has been particularly active in the upstream sector across Southeast Asia through a joint venture in gas exploration with the Malaysian National Petroleum Company (PETRONAS) in the offshore Sarawak field in addition to participation in oilfield development in Vietnam, Thailand, and Indonesia.[98] The UAE also, in 2013, signed a US$6.75 billion agreement to establish a petroleum storage facility with a capacity of 60 million barrels of crude oil at Tanjung Piai in the Malaysian state of Johor.[99] The same year, another Abu Dhabi investment vehicle, Aabar Investments, announced the formation of a US$3 billion joint venture with 1MDB, a strategic development company owned by the Malaysian government, to invest in energy projects in the two countries, although the investment subsequently became mired in scandal and led to a dramatic fall from grace of Aabar chairman Khadem Abdullah al-Qubaisi, a member of Mohammed bin Zayed's inner circle, who was removed from all his leadership positions in the UAE in April 2015, including as Managing Director of the International Petroleum Investment Company (IPIC).[100]

Economic and political ties nevertheless expanded far beyond the energy sector, particularly since the start of the 2000s. Dubai, in particular, benefited considerably from the legacy of the decisions in the 1970s and 1980s to invest heavily in infrastructure that have turned the emirate into the preeminent regional trade and re-export hub. Estimates in 2014 showed that roughly 70 percent of all manufactured goods that left China by sea arrived initially in Dubai, where they either were unloaded for regional markets in the UAE and the Middle East or shipped onward to markets in Europe and Africa.[101] Much of this "maritime Silk Route" is visible in the enormous DragonMart emporium launched in Dubai in 2004 as a joint venture between Nakheel (a part of the Dubai World group) and the Chinese state–owned Chinamex Corporation. A 2014 feature in *Middle East Report* on DragonMart captured both its scale and its reasons for its rapid growth within the framework of a comprehensive approach that characterized the "Dubai model" of economic development:

> ... Over three-quarters of a mile in length, with nearly 4000 vendors, DragonMart attracts both retail and wholesale customers with a dizzying array of goods ... It is estimated that over a million different types of goods are sold at DragonMart, and that every year close to 2 million customers visit, spending billions of dollars.[102]
>
> One of the reasons that sales are so high is that many of the customers are wholesale buyers throughout the region, as well as Africa, who now travel to Dubai, rather than all the way to China, to place orders ... Not only is Dubai easier to get to and to navigate than the manufacturing centers in Chinese cities such as Guangzhou and Yiwu, but both warehousing and shipping services are located in DragonMart, greatly facilitating the storage and transport of trade.[103]

In large part due to the success of DragonMart, the number of Chinese residents soared from about 10,000 in Dubai in 2004 to an estimated 300,000 just a decade later, by which time more than 4,200 Chinese companies were registered in the UAE.[104] While China and the UAE only established diplomatic relations in 1984 and the first head of state visits occurred in 1989 and 1990, the bilateral relationship grew quickly as China became one of the first countries to sign a Bilateral Investment Treaty (BIT) with the UAE in 1993, the same year that China became a crude oil importer for the first time.[105] During the 1990s and 2000s the UAE became the second largest GCC exporter of oil to China, behind Saudi Arabia, as China overtook Japan to become the second largest oil consumer in the world behind the United States.[106] UAE logistical facilities such as those at Jebel Ali also came to play an increasingly important role in China's major two geopolitical initiatives, the "Silk Road Economic Belt" and the "Silk Maritime Road," known in Chinese government circles as the "Belt and Road."[107]

In similar vein to the other examples cited in this section, relations between the UAE and China simultaneously thickened and expanded in the 2010s. Abu Dhabi

Crown Prince Mohammed bin Zayed made three visits to China, in 2009, 2012, and 2015, and ties thickened beyond the purely bilateral level to encompass multilateral institutions such as the (China-proposed) Asian Infrastructure Investment Bank (AIIB), of which the UAE not only was a founding member but also host to its regional headquarters.[108] Indeed, Sultan Ahmed al-Jaber, the UAE Minister of State for Foreign Affairs in 2015 (and Chairman of Masdar) explicitly cast the UAE's decision to join the AIIB – against an appeal from the United States to its allies not to do so:

> In the light of joint strategic ties between the UAE and China, and their mutual interests in fueling growth and infrastructure development in developing countries, both countries have partnered to set up a strong international platform to actively drive development efforts ... Being a founding member of AIIB will boost the prime economic role played by the UAE regionally and internationally, by focusing efforts on development projects with great socio-economic benefits.[109]

The further diversification of bilateral relations in the 2010s expanded beyond the hydrocarbons and logistical sectors and was especially pronounced in the three areas of joint investment, green energy, and currency cooperation.[110] Crown Prince Mohammed bin Zayed and Chinese President Xi Jinping announced the launch of the UAE–China Joint Investment Cooperation Fund in December 2015 with initial capital injections of US$5 billion each from Abu Dhabi's Mubadala and two Chinese partners – the State Administration of Foreign Exchange and China Development Bank Capital.[111] The joint fund is intended to undertake "strategic investments" in the UAE and China with the latter expressing particular interest in investment in high-end manufacturing and clean energy technology. Solar energy, especially, has repeatedly been mentioned by Chinese and Emirati officials as an avenue of future cooperation in Dubai, Sharjah, and Abu Dhabi, with Masdar City and Tsinghua University signing an agreement on research cooperation, and Changzhou Almaden commencing construction of a solar panel factory in Dubai in December 2015.[112]

Closer currency cooperation – in the context of China's move to internationalize the renminbi – is illustrative of the attempts by Emirati officials to rebalance and make more competitive their global trading outlook while simultaneously maintaining established policies such as the UAE dirham's traditional peg to the US dollar. The UAE and China first signed a bilateral currency swap agreement in January 2012 for up to 35 billion renminbi – an amount that was relatively small compared to similar Chinese agreements with South Korea, Singapore, and Hong Kong, but which represented nonetheless the first such agreement with a GCC state (Qatar followed suit in 2014). In December 2015, the renminbi swap agreement was renewed, shortly after the yuan (as the renminbi is also called) secured long-sought membership of the "A-list of currencies" eligible for Special Drawing Rights (SDR) at the International Monetary Fund (IMF).[113] A *China*

Brief issued shortly thereafter by the Jamestown Foundation emphasized more the geopolitical rather than immediately practical significance of the currency swap:

> … the agreement primarily helps Chinese firms conducting business in the UAE but over the long-term should foster the UAE's ability to act as regional trade hub regardless of the currency used by firms … Efforts to bolster Abu Dhabi and Dubai as export and trading hubs are not new, but the ability to conduct business in both dollars and renminbi fosters the UAE's central financial role in the Gulf. All four Chinese banks have branches in the UAE and the currency bargain eases cross-border trade and investment for Chinese firms thus bolstering China's global financial image.[114]

Proactive Engagement with Global Processes

Although the more muscular approach of the UAE to international affairs would become most apparent during the Arab Spring upheaval in 2011 and after, it had its genesis in developments during the 2000s that opened up new opportunities for small states in world politics. This was the changing nature of the concept of power itself in an intensely interconnected world. During the 1990s and 2000s, the acceleration of globalizing forces integrated states and societies in worldwide systems and networks of interaction. Opportunities for small states abounded as the erosion of the link between size and power meant that power and influence could instead be projected through multiple channels and in various ways, taking advantage of the leverage and opportunities accorded by rising oil revenues. Policymakers in the UAE reacted pragmatically to the changing nature of world politics by pursuing a "nodal" foreign policy through which countries were grouped together into regions of geostrategic interest to the UAE.[115] Moreover, as Christian Henderson has observed, the UAE increasingly has evolved into a "nexus state" in the international system through sustained and heavy investment in logistics and infrastructure that links together countries and regions, particularly in Africa, the Middle East, and Asia.[116]

New forms of power projection available to the UAE occurred against the backdrop of two significant developments in global politics and international relations. First, the emergence of the multiple poles of geo-economic gravity and centres of influence in the international system in the 2000s opened up new possibilities for new coalitions of states and intra- and inter-regional realignments.[117] Second, geographical territory became less important to the projection of power as the latter became more variegated in the 2000s, while the evolution of information and communications technologies (ICT) created opportunities for new actors to stake an international role disproportionate to their geographical or population size. This was a significant new development that eroded many of the constraints hitherto imposed on "small states" in the international system and made it possible to overcome the "international cliency" that hitherto formed the dominant framework structuring the relationships between "strong" states and "weak" states.[118]

From about the middle of the 1990s, the UAE started to develop a more proactive approach toward issues of global governance. The UAE only became a member of the General Agreement on Tariffs and Trade (GATT) on March 8, 1994, little more than a month prior to the conclusion of the Uruguay Round of multilateral trade negotiations that led to the formation of the World Trade Organization (WTO), which the UAE promptly joined on April 10, 1996.[119] At around the same time, the UAE complemented its membership of the World Intellectual Property Organization (WIPO), which it had joined in 1974, by signing the Paris Convention for the Protection of Industrial Property and coming under heavy US pressure to formulate a new patent law and take tougher measures to combat software piracy. Even so, a research note prepared in 1999 and published in the *Arab Law Quarterly* in 2001 by a Dubai-based legal consultancy (Meyer-Reumann) observed that UAE laws still contained considerable obstacles for foreign investors, particularly with regard to sponsorship, agency, and distribution outside of the Free Zones.[120]

Chapter Four made reference to the liberalization of real estate in Dubai and the policy decision to accelerate the creation of additional Free Zones in the late 1990s and early 2000s, as well as the more recent creation of financial free zones both in Dubai and in Abu Dhabi. These new entities, as well as the related amendments to existing regulations and the introduction of new enabling legislation, allowed Dubai, in particular, to rapidly expand its international banking and insurance sectors in the 2000s.[121] Significantly, they also contributed to the growing regional appeal of the UAE as an arbitrage hub as the initial sector-specific free zones expanded their scope of activities. In November 2014, the DIFC Court ruled that it had jurisdiction to hear a claim for a foreign arbitral award "where the successful party was incorporated outside the UAE and the unsuccessful party was incorporated in Dubai but had no connection with the DIFC." Nevertheless, and after two initial test cases involving claims by Standard Chartered and Norway's DNB Bank against IGPL and Dubai's Gulf Navigation respectively, *The National* noted that obstacles still remained with regard to the enforcement of arbitral awards in the local court systems at both the emirate and the national level.[122]

The maritime sector is another that has announced a planned move into regional and international arbitration through the creation of an Emirates Maritime Arbitration Center (EMAC). Drawn up under the auspices of the Dubai Maritime City Authority, EMAC is set to become the first maritime arbitration center with international standards in the Middle East. As with the financial sector, an intention behind the launch of EMAC is that it will fill the geographic and time-zone gap between London and the Far East. Early indications additionally suggested that the default seat of EMAC would be the DIFC, which would add a regional cog to the international arbitration system long dominated by London, New York, Singapore, and Hong Kong.[123] Mark Beer, the chief executive and registrar at the DIFC Courts, noted that maritime analysts predicted that Dubai would be the world's seventh largest maritime center by 2020 and added that "the specialization of the shipping industry made arbitration a necessity":

... The courts do an excellent job of dealing with maritime disputes, just as you'd expect. Courts focus on law. But so often, maritime disputes are about more than law. The ability to have arbitration outside of the law will allow for better, faster and cheaper resolution of disputes.[124]

In addition to the industry-specific measures outlined above, UAE policymakers adopted a more robust approach to the rebalancing of power and influence within international institutions during the late 2000s. Senior Emirati officials, together with their counterparts from Saudi Arabia and Qatar, seized the opportunity to make their voice heard in debates over the restructuring of the global financial architecture in the aftermath of the global financial crash of 2008. Policymakers in GCC capitals expressed initial surprise that they were being asked to "bail out" a crisis that appeared to them to have originated in the United States, and interpreted in this context UK Prime Minister Gordon Brown's visit to the Gulf ahead of the G20 meeting in November 2008.[125] While Saudi Arabia's Finance Minister, Ibrahim Abdulaziz al-Assaf, stated that "we have been playing our role responsibly and we will continue to play our role, but we are not going to finance the institutions just because we have large reserves,"[126] the Governor of the UAE Central Bank, Sultan bin Nasser al-Suwaidi, was more blunt and more direct when he stated, in November 2008, that "If they [GCC states] are given more voice then they will provide money maybe ... They will not be providing funds without extra voice and extra recognition."[127]

As the financial crisis unfolded, the importance of sovereign wealth funds from the UAE (and other GCC states) became fully apparent as European governments, led by the United Kingdom, actively sought Gulf support for the injection of short-term liquidity into European markets, while the outgoing Bush administration reportedly sought US$300 billion from the UAE, Saudi Arabia, Kuwait, and Qatar to bail out the US automobile industry during the autumn of 2008.[128] Gulf sovereign wealth funds accounted for approximately one-third of the emergency funding that European governments made available to financial institutions in 2007–2008.[129] A prominent example was a US$7.5 billion investment by the Abu Dhabi Investment Authority (ADIA) in Citigroup in November 2007, less than a year before Citigroup required three federal bailouts. In the view of *Reuters*, the ADIA investment "was designed to shore up Citigroup as it struggled with mounting losses linked to subprime mortgages, and gave the fund a 4.9 percent stake in what was at the time the largest US bank by assets."[130] ADIA later, in December 2009, filed a complaint with the International Center for Dispute Resolution in an ultimately unsuccessful claim that their decision to invest had been "induced" by "fraudulent misrepresentations" made by Citigroup to ADIA.[131]

As Emirati investments in Europe and North America rose sharply, officials from the country took the lead in opening a dialogue between investors and recipient states over a new approach to handling sovereign wealth investment. Stung by the DP World experience of 2006, officials from ADIA and Singapore's Temasek fund reached agreement with US Treasury officials in March 2008 on a set of policy principles for sovereign wealth funds.[132] Shortly thereafter, an International Working Group of sovereign wealth funds was convened in April 2008 with the support of the Organization for Economic Cooperation and Development (OECD) and the International Monetary Fund (IMF).[133] The three meetings of the International Working Group resulted in the publication in October 2008 of a non-binding set of Generally Accepted Principles and Practices, better known as the Santiago Principles after the location of the meetings. The Santiago Principles represented an attempt "to set out common standards regarding transparency, independence, and governance." Reflecting the proactive role of ADIA in framing the Santiago Principles, the document was presented by Hamad al-Hurr al-Suwaidi, a board member of ADIA (and Chairman of Taqa as well as the Undersecretary of the Abu Dhabi Department of Finance), who noted that:

> ... this document will in both home and host countries improve the understanding of the objectives, structure, and governance of SWFs; enhance the understanding of SWFs as economically and financially oriented entities; and help maintain and open and stable investment climate.[134]

In 2014, two of the trends analyzed in this section – UAE investment and the maritime sector – came together when the Sharjah-based port operator Gulftainer secured a thirty-five-year concession to manage the container and cargo terminal at Port Canaveral in Florida. In stark contrast to the political and public relations mauling endured by DP World in 2006, barely a murmur was raised eight years later. While the concession was subject to mandatory review by the Committee on Foreign Investment in the United States (CFIUS) for security reasons, no objection was found to the transfer of exclusive operating rights to the new US$42 million container terminal to Gulftainer. While the reasoning behind the CFIUS positioning was that the concession represented a lease rather than an asset sale, and there were no aggrieved parties (as in the DP World case), the outcome reflected also the significant shift in global perceptions of the UAE over the intervening decade.[135]

Whereas in 2006, the UAE was still susceptible to association with 9/11 by significant elements of a US political landscape in the grip of the so-called "Global War on Terror," by 2014 the maturation of the UAE "brand" ensured that the country was seen in a very different light around the world. To some extent this was through the powerful global imprint of Emirati brands such as Emirates and Etihad in addition to DP World itself, as well as a generally deeper awareness of global interdependencies and greater openness to foreign investment in the wake of the 2008–2009 financial crisis. Indeed, with both Gulftainer and DP World building up truly global portfolios, often against the backdrop of struggling host economies hit hard by post-crash austerity measures, the more welcoming environment for Emirati investment was illustrated by the favorable media coverage in late 2015 of DP World London Gateway, a mega-port and logistics zone under construction in the Thames Estuary that is one of the largest privately funded construction projects ever undertaken in the United Kingdom.[136] An article in Britain's *Guardian* newspaper described the site breathlessly as:

> ... built by Dubai, is twice the size of the City of London, is run by robots, has the world's largest cranes – and it's where everything you buy will soon come from ... Running almost 3km along the Thames estuary is a £1.5 bn new megaport that has literally redrawn the coastline of Essex, and wants to make equally radical shifts to the UK's consumer supply chain.[137]

With two of the projected six berths already open, the *Guardian* report added that while the initial operating performance had been relatively disappointing, citing a failure to secure a contract from Asia, the project nevertheless had created history with the largest migration of animals in Europe "with 320,000 newts, water voles and adders relocated to a new nature reserve nearby."[138]

Soft Power and Cultural Influence

The Gulftainer and London Gateway examples cited above illustrate the extent to which global perceptions of the UAE have shifted greatly over the decade since the DP World controversy in the United States in 2006. Much of this is attributable to a combination of the new forms of power and influence available to traditionally small states in the international system, as well as the opportunities that opened up to Gulf policymakers as they took decisions to utilize the capital accumulation that accrued during the long oil-price boom that lasted from 2003 until 2014. As noted elsewhere in this book, the new generation of younger new leaders that came to prominence both in Abu Dhabi and Dubai during the 2000s recognized and adapted very quickly to the new policy landscape that opened up, and quite effectively harnessed the economic benefits from globalizing processes. This has been most visibly evident in the build-up and projection of significant reserves of "soft power" and international goodwill in the form of heavy investment in global educational, healthcare, sporting, and cultural sectors.

In his pioneering work into the concept, Joseph Nye described "soft power" as the ability to appeal to and persuade others using the attractiveness of a country's culture, political ideals, and policies. Although Nye first introduced the concept as early as 1990,[139] he explored in detail the phenomenon of co-optation rather than coercion as a means of persuasion in international politics in his 2004 book *Soft Power: The Means to Success in World Politics*. He described how states or other actors in world politics (such as non-governmental organizations) seeking to accrue soft power should:

> set the agenda and attract others in world politics, and not only to force them to change by threatening military force or economic sanctions. This is soft power – getting others to want the outcomes that you want co-opts people rather than coerces them.[140]

Nye added that soft power resources consist of the assets that induce co-optation, and that it is a complex tool that governments must build up over time as they develop a reputation for credibility in a particular field.[141] In parallel, scholars such as Peter van Ham have also focused on the notion of "state-branding" as a tool for creating a sense of national identity, loyalty, and social cohesion, in addition to defining a clear and coherent message about national purpose. In a 2001 article in *Foreign Affairs* that introduced the concept, van Ham suggested that a "brand state" "comprises the outside world's ideas about a particular country"[142] and added that:

> ... Smart states are building their brands around reputations and attitudes in the same way smart companies do ... To stand out in the crowd, assertive branding is essential ... most states still see branding as a long-term cumulative effort that will influence foreign investment decisions and the state's market capitalization.[143]
>
> The traditional diplomacy of yesteryear is disappearing. To do their jobs well in the future, politicians will have to train themselves in brand asset management. Their tasks will include finding a brand niche for their state, engaging in competitive marketing, assuring customer satisfaction, and most of all, creating brand loyalty.[144]

Writing more than a decade later, Christopher Browning made the additional point that state-branding "is not just about questions of image but also of identity, status, and recognition in a context where a lack of visibility is seen as inherently problematic," and which reflects the changing perceptions of international order, "with geopolitical frames of reference increasingly replaced by frames emphasizing the inevitability of globalization and neoliberal forms of governance ... "[145]

Dubai led the way in creating a powerful brand with a series of initiatives in the 1990s that aggressively marketed the emirate as an international shopping and mass tourism destination. The launch of Emirates Holidays in 1992 marked an early attempt to raise brand awareness of Dubai as a destination and later events included the annual Dubai Shopping Festival (first held in 1996) in the winter months and the Dubai Summer Surprises Festival to overcome the traditional lull in summer visitors. Christopher Davidson has observed that commerce and tourism represented the two planks of Dubai's early efforts in economic diversification and "transformed it into a city of shopping malls."[146] Integral components of this strategy encompassed the construction of the largest mall in the world (Dubai Mall), the launch of an artificial Ski Dubai slope in another signature mall (Mall of the Emirates), and such iconic hotels and buildings as the sail-shaped Burj al-Arab and the 2,722 feet high Burj Khalifa, the tallest manmade structure in the world when it opened in a lavish ceremony in 2009.[147]

The success of Dubai's approach was illustrated by the exponential increase in the number of visitors to Dubai, which soared from just 400,000 in 1985 to over three million in the mid-2000s and 5.8 million in the first six months of 2014

alone.[148] In May 2014, Dubai's Ruler, Sheikh Mohammed bin Rashid Al Maktoum, unveiled a new corporate branding identity and logo designed to catapult
Dubai from the ranks of a "must-see" city to a "must-experience" destination.[149]
Abu Dhabi also invested heavily on branding the emirate in the late 2000s and the
2010s while at a federal level the UAE emerged as one of the largest spenders on
lobbying and public relations in Washington, DC. Public relations expenditure rose
(understandably) in the aftermath of the DP World debacle in 2006 as the incident
"highlighted the fact that there was very little understanding in the US about the
UAE."[150] For the President of the US–UAE Business Council, lobbying and
public relations spending was "spent on providing accurate information and informing
Americans on what kind of country the UAE is today as a friend and ally of the
United States and trying to dispel the myths about what kind of a country it's
not."[151] As such, in 2014, the UAE spent a record sum of US$12.7 million in US
lobbying, primarily in defence of its Open Skies Agreement against US airlines
critical of Emirates and Etihad as well as the UAE's assertive campaign against the
Muslim Brotherhood both domestically and across the Middle East.[152]

Spending on lobbying and public relations companies – which, in Washington,
DC, included The Harbour Group, Akin Gump, and DLA Piper – was only a part
of a far broader strategy to project the soft power appeal of the UAE. The role of
philanthropic initiatives from the UAE in the US and specifically in and around
Washington, DC is illustrative of the broader "hearts and minds" strategy at work.
Thus, in 2009, the Government of Abu Dhabi donated US$150 million to con-
struct the Sheikh Zayed Campus for Advanced Pediatric Medicine at the Children's
National Medical Center while in Baltimore, the US$1.1 billion Sheikh Zayed
Cardiovascular and Critical Care Tower at Johns Hopkins Medicine grew out of
longstanding ties between Johns Hopkins and the UAE, where it operates three medical
centers and is involved in healthcare reform. Such initiatives not only provide a
platform to showcase the UAE as a hub for healthcare innovation but also constitute
a powerful example of institutional partnership-building and soft diplomacy.[153]

UAE donors also featured prominently in other high-profile philanthropic
campaigns in the US, including a US$1.6 million fundraising campaign to help the
Fight for Children nonprofit organization launch an early education program for
at-risk children in Washington, DC, and a series of initiatives to assist the town of
Joplin, Missouri, after it was ravaged by a tornado in 2011. The latter included a
US$5 million grant from the UAE to build a pediatric wing and neonatal intensive
care unit at Joplin's Mercy Hospital as well as a US$1 million grant from Abu
Dhabi to purchase personal laptops for every student at Joplin High School to
create virtual classrooms until the school facilities could be rebuilt after the disaster,
which claimed 161 people.[154] In the UAE itself, the country developed a close
working relationship with Bill Gates and the Bill and Melinda Gates Foundation.
Starting in 2012, the Government of Abu Dhabi collaborated with the Gates
Foundation on the Global Alliance for Vaccines and Immunization (GAVI) to fund
an immunization program against polio that succeeded in virtually eradicating the
disease in Nigeria.[155]

Educational initiatives were another prominent feature of the spread of "soft" power around the world. As universities in Europe and North America struggled with cuts to block government grants in the 1990s and 2000s they increasingly began to look to external fundraising streams. By virtue of the significant capital accumulation in Gulf economies after the post-2003 rise in oil prices, Gulf-based foundations and other philanthropic initiatives emerged as major sources of donations. By the mid-2000s, two of the leading British universities where Gulf and Middle Eastern studies were taught[156] had academic buildings named in honor of Sheikh Dr. Sultan bin Mohammed Al Qasimi, the doctorate-holding (from Exeter) Ruler of Sharjah. The London School of Economics and Political Science (LSE) also named its flagship new lecture theater after Sheikh Zayed in 2008 and established a Middle East Center two years later with a £9.2 million grant from the Emirates Foundation for Philanthropy based in Abu Dhabi and The Aman Trust, a philanthropic organization headed by Arif Naqvi, CEO and Founder of the Dubai-based Abraaj Capital, a private equity firm.[157]

The willingness of British universities to open up to UAE funding in the 2000s contrasted sharply with a chastening experience at Harvard University between 2000 and 2004 over a US$2.5 million gift from Sheikh Zayed to fund an endowed chair in Islamic Studies at the Divinity School. In 2003, the university put the donation on hold after a group of Harvard students challenged the gift on the grounds of Sheikh Zayed's alleged association with the Zayed Center for Coordination and Follow-Up. Specifically, the students argued that "the center promulgated anti-American and anti-Semitic views" and "had hosted speakers claiming that the Holocaust was perpetrated by Zionists, not Nazis, and that Israel plotted the September 11 terrorist attacks."[158] Negative publicity mounted as an investigation by the *Boston Globe* newspaper reported that the Zayed Center had hosted a Saudi speaker who had claimed that "Jews celebrate the holiday of Purim by killing innocent victims and eating pastries baked with their blood" and that the Center's director, no less, had declared that "Jews claim to be God's most preferred people, but the truth is they are the enemies of all nations." In August 2003, UAE officials shut down the Zayed Center citing activities that "starkly contradicted the principles of interfaith tolerance" and in 2004 the Government of Abu Dhabi requested that the Harvard gift be returned to them.[159]

Similar to the DP World scandal in 2006 that was detailed earlier in this chapter, subsequent events illustrated how the UAE's reputation improved markedly with time and distance from the events of 9/11 and its turbulent aftermath. Harvard itself forged a new partnership with the UAE shortly after the denouement of the Sheikh Zayed gift when the John F. Kennedy School of Government created the Dubai Initiative in partnership with the Dubai School of Government. The Dubai Initiative arose out of the passion of Dubai ruler Sheikh Mohammed bin Rashid, who related to Indian journalist Pranay Gupte how:

> I've always told my team that we need to start at the highest point others have attained. There's no sense reinventing the wheel. That's why we teamed with

Harvard. Our partnership wasn't a business deal. I liken it to a shared vision. Officials at Harvard were as excited as we are about improving governance in the region and they, like us, want to build a center of excellence in the Middle East.[160]

Financial difficulties in the aftermath of the bursting of the Dubai bubble in 2009 meant that the Dubai Initiative link with Harvard was quietly discontinued in 2011 and the Dubai School of Government was renamed the Mohammed bin Rashid School of Government in 2013.[161] More enduring was the Harvard Medical School Dubai Center (HMSDC) launched in 2004 as a collaboration between Harvard Medical School and the Dubai Healthcare City. HMSDC has emerged as "both an educational institution and a hub for research for health problems endemic to the area, as well as health care strategies that could be applied worldwide."[162] In 2015, a new collaboration between the same two partners created the Harvard Medical School Center for Global Health Delivery – Dubai, with a renewed focus on "how to increase research capacity in Dubai and the region and to strengthen the health care delivery infrastructure." The director of the new Harvard Medical center, Salmaan Keshavjee, waxed lyrical about the locational benefits of operating in Dubai:

> Dubai has become a vital hub for the Middle East and for parts of Africa and for a significant part of South Asia … Our reach is broad. Of course, we are thinking of the Middle East and North Africa, but we are also open to projects in India, Pakistan, Indonesia, and other places that have large populations of people working in the UAE.[163]

The educational initiative that has done more than anything else to put the UAE on the global map has been the creation of NYU Abu Dhabi (NYUAD) as a full-fledged portal campus of the New York-based liberal arts university. Launched in 2010 in temporary facilities while a permanent campus was under construction on Abu Dhabi's Saadiyat Island, NYUAD was by far the highest profile educational institution to set up in the UAE, which by 2010 was host to more than one-quarter of all university branch campuses in the world. However, data collected in Dubai for a study conducted by the then-Dubai School of Government indicated that only a minority of the students enrolled in the international branch campuses in the UAE were actually Emirati nationals.[164] This has been true of NYUAD as well, as the Class of 2016 contained seventeen Emirati students out of 151 incoming students, itself a figure nearly double the nine local students in the Class of 2015 intake.[165]

Indeed, in many ways the enduring value of the NYU partnership to the UAE is the prestige that flows from such an association with a world-leading institution. An example of the intangible associational value is the former US President Bill Clinton's speech at the inaugural commencement ceremony marking the first graduating class of New York University's Abu Dhabi campus in May 2014 at a time of considerable media interest in suggestions of ill-treatment of the migrant labor workforce that constructed the campus.[166] Specifically, a front-page investigation in the *New York Times* published days before Clinton's commencement speech drew attention to apparent endemic abuse of migrant workers on the campus worksite that appeared to diverge from a pledge made by NYU in 2009 that it would guarantee fair treatment of workers. The *New York Times* article carried words of caution with regard to the operational challenges it predicted would face NYUAD:

> By laying out its standards for labor in a country with no tradition of workers' rights, NYU took on a more considerable challenge – one that many companies in the region are content to ignore. Sustaining the academic freedom that is a core value of its New York campus will pose a similar challenge. In both cases, the challenge is made more complex by the fact that the university is in effect a guest of the ruling family, which has not only paid for the 21-building campus and for generous tuition subsidies, but also has contributed the first of what are expected to be several $50 million donations to NYU as a whole.[167]

Such concern for NYUAD's autonomy and academic freedom proved to be prescient as less than a year later, Andrew Ross, a tenured NYU Professor who had written critically about labor conditions in the UAE, was barred on security grounds from boarding an Etihad flight at New York's Kennedy International Airport bound for Abu Dhabi, where he had planned to spend his spring break conducting research at NYUAD.[168] In addition, Sean O'Driscoll, one of the two journalists who wrote the abovementioned May 2014 *New York Times* investigative report into labor conditions on the NYUAD campus, was followed by security personnel for five months before being deported in October 2014 after declining a proposition by the Chief of Security Media in the Abu Dhabi Police to spy on foreign journalists entering the UAE.[169]

Perhaps the most globally visible form of the softer forms of power and influence emanating from the Gulf in general, and the UAE in particular, has taken place in the mass culture and sporting arenas. Both Dubai and Abu Dhabi have formed the backdrop for blockbuster movies in recent years with parts of *Mission: Impossible – Ghost Protocol* (2011) and the keenly awaited new *Star Wars: The Force Awakens* (2015) being filmed in the two emirates. Both films provided ample opportunity to showcase each emirate and embed their association not only with the blockbusters but also with iconic global film stars, often through breathtaking sequences such as one in *Mission: Impossible* that featured Tom Cruise scaling the side of Dubai's signature Burj Khalifa, the tallest building in the world.[170] Meanwhile, a *CNN Money* report into the financial inducements offered by Abu Dhabi to attract major film and television productions, which included *Fast and Furious 7* and *The Bourne Legacy* in addition to *Star Wars*, observed that:

Governments around the world are touting tax breaks and other inducements to Hollywood. The idea is that big productions will pump money into the local economy, and draw tourists to the location.

Abu Dhabi offers some of the most generous incentives: 30% cash back on everything the production companies spend in the city. The Abu Dhabi Film Commission also offers free location scouting services, along with help securing permits.

The incentives are designed to turn Abu Dhabi into a production hub that rivals other attractive places in the Middle East and North Africa. The competition is stiff – Morocco and Qatar both have a strong record of attracting investment, while Jerusalem offers large international productions a cash rebate of up to 60%.[171]

Abu Dhabi and Dubai (along with Doha) also established film festivals in the late 2000s that sought to provide an opportunity for local and regional filmmakers to share a platform with Hollywood stars. However, budgetary and other pressures led to the scaling back of the Dubai festival and the decision to end the Abu Dhabi festival (as well as the Doha Tribeca festival in Qatar) in 2015. In announcing the end of the Abu Dhabi Film Festival after eight successful years, the Abu Dhabi Media Zone Authority suggested that it would refocus on investing more resources in attracting major film productions – such as Star Wars – to Abu Dhabi instead.[172]

Along with providing the backdrop to Hollywood blockbusters, the other most visible aspect of UAE "branding" since the late 2000s has been the organization of high-profile sporting tournaments and events and the sponsorship and outright acquisition of teams and franchises. These include the Mubadala World Tennis Championship held at the start of each calendar year since 2009 and regularly featuring the highest ranked male players in the world, the Dubai Tennis Championships for men and women held each year in February which again attract leading stars such as Roger Federer and Novak Djokovic, the Dubai Desert Classic professional golf tournament which began in 1989 and celebrated its quarter-century in 2014, and, also in golf, the DP World Tour Championship which forms the climax of the European Tour's "Race to Dubai" season. Meanwhile, in motor racing, Abu Dhabi's glitzy Yas Marina Circuit has since 2009 provided a spectacular day-night backdrop for the season-ending Abu Dhabi Grand Prix.

Such events not only showcase the UAE to the millions of sports fans around the world who watch coverage of the events on television but also tap into the considerable passion that sports fans bring to their favorite players, teams, and events. An example of this became visibly evident to the estimated one billion viewers of the 2014 FIFA World Cup final between Germany and Argentina who witnessed the surreal sight of a row of Emirates flight attendants handing the victorious German team their medals. Emirates had spent more than US$100 million over the 2010–2014 World Cup cycle on becoming one of FIFA's Official Worldwide Partners, alongside Visa, Sony, Adidas, Coca-Cola, Hyundai Motor, and Kia Motor, before terminating its partnership with FIFA in November 2014 amid the growing fallout from the corruption scandal enveloping the world football association.[173]

In addition to the abovementioned sponsorship of the FIFA World Cup, Emirates and other UAE (and Gulf) corporations also sponsored and, in some cases, actually purchased prominent European football clubs. Examples of teams featuring the Emirates logo on their shirts include the 2014 European Champions Real Madrid, and Arsenal, Paris Saint-Germain, and AC Milan in England, France, and Italy respectively. Arsenal also play their home games in the Emirates Stadium under the terms of a fifteen-year naming rights agreement signed in 2004 when the team still played at the fabled Highbury Stadium. Indeed, "the Emirates" has entered the European football lexicon just as "the Etihad" has and, most spectacularly, the mooted renaming of Real Madrid's iconic Santiago Bernabeu stadium (named in memory of the eponymous former Real Madrid president) to the Abu Dhabi Santiago Bernabeu.[174] Even without the renaming (as of the time of writing) renovation work at the Bernabeu has been funded through the Emirates sponsorship of Real Madrid and the strategic partnership announced in October 2014 with the Abu Dhabi–government owned International Petroleum Investment Company (IPIC).[175]

A Case Study of Soft Power: Manchester City and the Abu Dhabi United Group

More ambitious and pertinent to the state-branding of the UAE (and, particularly, Abu Dhabi) was the 2008 takeover of Manchester City by the Abu Dhabi United Group for Development and Investment (ADUG), a private equity vehicle owned by Sheikh Mansour bin Zayed Al Nahyan, a younger half-brother of the Ruler of Abu Dhabi (and President of the UAE), Sheikh Khalifa. The Abu Dhabi takeover had both a sporting and an urban transformation and catapulted a middling and historically underachieving team into the richest club in Europe and led to Premier League triumphs in 2012 and 2014. Manchester City also renamed their new stadium – built for the 2002 Commonwealth Games through lottery and local council funding – the Etihad Stadium after Abu Dhabi's airline, and during each game, pitch perimeter boards advertised a constant stream of UAE messages and entities, such as telecommunications provider Etisalat, investment group Aabar, and the Abu Dhabi Tourism Authority. Moreover, in June 2014, ADUG partnered with Manchester city council in a ten-year £1 billion agreement to regenerate the deprived post-industrial and recession-hit suburbs of Manchester and construct up to 6,000 new homes through a new joint venture, the Manchester Life Development Company, alongside the Etihad Campus, an Abu Dhabi–funded state-of-the-art training center and community hub.[176]

The public relations and branding component of such a comprehensive intermixing of sporting success and urban infrastructure marks the Manchester City initiative out as distinct from almost every other major sports takeover. This became clear in a wide-ranging interview given to Britain's *The Guardian* newspaper by Manchester City's Chairman, Khaldoun al-Mubarak, in September 2009, a year after the takeover and before the team had evolved into a championship-winning powerhouse. Also the Chief Executive Officer of Mubadala and a member both of the Abu Dhabi Executive Council and the Abu Dhabi Council for Economic Development, al-Mubarak made a series of points that underlined the "soft" benefits sought for Abu Dhabi:

> There is an appreciation of the association the club have with Abu Dhabi that we hold very dearly. There is almost a personification of the club with the values we hold as Abu Dhabi, as Sheikh Mansour. These are loyalty, commitment, discipline, long-term thinking, respect, and history ...
>
> We are acknowledging that how we are handling this project is telling a lot to the world about how we are. The UAE is different from other Arab countries. People think the Arab world is one, but it is not. This is showing the world the true essence of who Abu Dhabi is and what Abu Dhabi is about ... [177]

Tellingly, in view of the later 2014 creation of the City Football Group, a holding company set up to manage the interlocking ownership of Manchester City in England, the newly formed New York City FC in the US, and Melbourne City FC in Australia, Khaldoun al-Mubarak added in 2009 that:

> There is a pure, football, emotional side to it, and a big business side, too. I think what attracted Sheikh Mansour was the great football journey, but there is also a business sense, that we can create a franchise, a business, over years, which will create value and reap a long term return. [178]

Speaking in 2014 in more technocratic tones following the announcement of the Manchester Life development plan, the leader of Manchester city council described the planned transformation of the eastern suburbs as "the single biggest residential development Manchester has seen for a generation" and "a world-class exemplar of regeneration."[179] Meanwhile, a representative of ADUG demonstrated acute awareness of the broader value of wrapping commercial and investment decisions within the broader vision of large-scale redevelopment:

> ADUG, through Manchester City Football Club, has come to know Manchester City Council's vision for regeneration ... Given Abu Dhabi United Group's existing long-term commitment to Manchester and the Council's economic growth plan, it was a logical decision to look at ways to create a commercial partnership with the city to deliver its wider residential strategy. We are effectively investing in the opportunities and positive circumstances created by our joint investments to date. [180]

Beyond the self-congratulatory press releases and statements, grassroots organizations in Manchester remained less than fully convinced of the social utility of the partnership and noted, in particular, the apparent lack of social housing in the initial proposals. In addition, one local stakeholder expressed concern that the city was vulnerable to image "whitewashing" by what it called "the federation of small absolute monarchies on the Arabian Peninsular [sic]."[181] As it happened, similar concerns had been raised nearly a year before the Manchester Life initiative by the international non-governmental organization *Human Rights Watch* (HRW). In July 2013, following a mass trial of opposition and human rights activists in the UAE (see Chapter Six), HRW issued a critical report on the UAE and noted specifically how ownership of Manchester City enabled Abu Dhabi to "construct a public relations image of a progressive, dynamic Gulf state, which deflects attention from what is really going on in the country."[182]

Migrant Labor Conditions and Reputational Risk

The emergence of the UAE and other GCC states onto the global stage in the 2000s was accompanied by a rising chorus of international criticism over the alleged abuse of migrant laborers. Many of the concerns raised by academics, intergovernmental organizations, and international human rights and civil society groups were linked to the maintenance of the *kafala* system then in force in the UAE as in other Gulf States (it has since been modified in several states). In 2006, just as the development of Dubai into a regional hub was accelerating, *Human Rights Watch* (HRW) set the tone with a deeply critical report entitled *Building Towers, Cheating Workers: Exploitation of Migrant Construction Workers in the United Arab Emirates*. The report laid bare a pattern of exploitative conditions endemic in the construction industry as the cityscapes of Dubai and Abu Dhabi took shape. These included "wage exploitation, indebtedness to unscrupulous recruiters, and working conditions that are hazardous to the point of being deadly."[183] HRW noted that local media coverage of migrant workers' grievances had increased dramatically in the years up to 2006 in part as strikes of laborers on construction sites became more common and visible; thousands of construction workers rioted in Dubai in March 2006 and demanded an improvement to their pay and conditions. Nevertheless, HRW added that:

> Beyond the press, however, a general lack of civil society actors (particularly nongovernmental organizations) in the UAE mean that there are no private actors to fill the void of absent government protection and union championing of migrant workers' rights in the country ... There are no independent organizations to monitor the construction sector – or any other sector – to report and document abuses systematically, and to advocate for migrant workers' rights.[184]

While the UAE is a member of the International Labor Organization (ILO), the HRW report observed dryly that the country had ratified only six of the eight core ILO conventions, leaving unratified those conventions relating to Freedom of Association and Protection of the Right to Organize (No. 87) and the Right to

Organize and Collective Bargaining (No.98).[185] In addition, *Human Rights Watch* suggested that the government was failing "adequately to address these issues," and urged the authorities in the UAE to become a signatory to international conventions such as the International Convention on the Protection of the Rights of All Migrant Workers and Members of their Families.[186]

In 2007, Ahmed Kanna, a US academic, visited a series of labor camps on the outskirts of Dubai and described how:

> Squat buildings mark the spot where we turned off the main, paved road and drove along unpaved roads crowded with men in the uniforms of different companies, returning from or going to their shifts. Large buses emptied their human contents and were refilled. We passed a couple of camps. "That one is al-Habtour," said my guide, naming a Dubai construction firm. "That one is al-'Abbar." These are both large companies, with uncooperative security personnel and, presumably, stricter surveillance of workers. They are too dangerous to attempt entry ... .[187]

Even at this comparatively early stage in their rise onto the global stage, officials remained intensely wary of the prospect that international media (and academic) focus on the condition of migrant workers could cast Dubai and the UAE in a negative light. This became clear in the response to a year-long Fulbright-funded research project undertaken by Syed Ali into second-generation non-nationals in the UAE, primarily white-collar expatriates working in Dubai, where many of them had been born and raised. Ali recounted, in a newspaper article in *The Guardian*, how his fieldwork was brought to an abrupt end in 2006 when he was taken by members of the State Security Directorate, subjected to a thirteen-hour interrogation about his purpose of being in Dubai and his funding, and ordered to leave the UAE, with an officer telling him that "The research you have been doing is creating divisions in our society and we will not allow it."[188]

The potential for international scrutiny of migrant worker conditions to cause damage to the broader reputation of the UAE was illustrated again in 2009 in another critical *Human Rights Watch* report on the UAE, this time on the development of the new Saadiyat Island in Abu Dhabi. Home to the abovementioned new NYUAD campus and the planned Abu Dhabi branches of the Louvre and Guggenheim museums and spearheaded by the Abu Dhabi government–owned Tourism Development and Investment Company (TDIC), the development of Saadiyat Island into an international tourism and cultural hub was another aspect of Abu Dhabi's globalizing profile. An extensive report into Saadiyat Island by *The Guardian* newspaper in 2015 suggested that Abu Dhabi had paid more than £663 million in 2007 "to buy the use of the Louvre's name, to construct the Jean Nouvel-designed building that will house the art, and to facilitate special exhibitions and cultural loans from French institutions." Similarly, *The Guardian* noted that the planned Guggenheim Abu Dhabi which, like the Louvre, has been beset by delays and is unlikely to open before 2017, will cost £530 million to build and "be twelve times as large as the Guggenheim in Manhattan." Both museums, as well as NYUAD, were integral to the positioning of Abu Dhabi as a global cultural hub built around prestige international linkages with iconic global institutions.[189]

However, *Human Rights Watch* painted a broadly similar picture in Abu Dhabi in 2009 as it had done in Dubai in 2006 as it documented what it labelled "the severe exploitation and abuse of South Asian migrant workers on the island, and the lack of legal and institutional protections necessary to curb the abuse."[190] A subsequent *HRW* report was issued in 2012 that covered the changes instituted in Abu Dhabi and the Saadiyat development since 2009. This new report observed a pattern of partial progress:

> … in spite of commitments by both the developers and their foreign partners to take steps to avoid abuse of migrant workers on Saadiyat Island, and in spite of some improvements in the working conditions of migrant workers, abuses are continuing …
>
> Our research found notable improvements in some areas, particularly in the regular payment of wages, rest breaks and days off, and employer-paid medical insurance. However, workers continue to report indebtedness for recruitment fees paid to obtain their jobs in the UAE …
>
> Workers also reported a lack of information, or misleading information, about their terms of employment before arriving in the UAE … Contrary to commitments of the developers, only one worker of the 47 we interviewed reported that he retained custody of his passport, while the rest said that their employers retained their passports.[191]

Although TDIC, Abu Dhabi's Executive Affairs Authority (EAA), and the international educational and cultural institutions based on Saadiyat Island all pledged an immediate tightening up of labor regulations in 2009, the abovementioned *New York Times* investigation in 2014 into the apparent continuation of endemic abuses on the NYU campus construction site indicated that the new measures were only partially successful. Following the *New York Times* report, NYU commissioned an independent investigation by Nardello & Co. into the allegations of labor abuse and compliance issues during the campus construction period. In April 2015, Nardello uncovered deep flaws in the pattern of compliance and monitoring that meant that up to 10,000 laborers – one-third of the workforce – had been excluded from NYUAD's fourteen-point *Statement of Labor Values* drawn up in 2010 and intended to protect them from exploitation and abuse.[192]

Further pressure on the UAE's international image has come from sporadic incidents such as the direct action taken by the Gulf Labor Artist Coalition (GLAC) when it closed down the Guggenheim Museum in New York in May 2015 in protest at the apparent failure to protect workers at the Guggenheim construction site on Saadiyat Island. The GLAC website additionally has catalogued dozens of negative news stories and articles that have focused on the perceived inequities facing migrant workers at Saadiyat in an attempt to "shame" the cultural institutions such as the Guggenheim and the Louvre into placing pressure on the Abu Dhabi authorities to act.[193]

Set against this negativity is the more nuanced picture painted in the US State Department's annual Trafficking in Persons report, which acknowledges that several (relatively minor) reforms are underway, particularly in anti-trafficking law enforcement, where significant effort has been made, and noted that:

> ... The government continues to respond to and investigate workers' complaints of unpaid wages through a dispute resolution process and the Wages Protection System (WPS), which is intended to ensure the payment of wages to workers and punish employers with administrative and financial penalties for failing to comply ... The government continued to train judicial, law enforcement, and labor officials on human trafficking in 2014.[194]

In addition, a four-day strike in May 2013 by thousands of construction workers employed by Dubai-based Arabtec achieved partial "success" when the company agreed that September to a 20 percent pay increase for its 36,000 strong UAE workforce. The fact that the four-day strike encompassed synchronous actions at multiple worksites both in Abu Dhabi and Dubai was noteworthy for the coordination among workers that distinguished the strike from most others in the UAE.[195] More substantial progress in labor reform also was made in a series of policy changes that were announced in September 2015, which were designed to address the worst abuses in the kafala system, in part by placing workers' contracts with the Ministry of Labor rather than the employer themselves, and by allowing foreign workers to terminate their contract and change employer. Notably, the reforms were praised by Human Rights Watch as "a huge improvement and something we would fully support and applaud."[196]

On the international stage, in the late 2000s and early 2010s the UAE engaged actively in two evolving inter-state dialogues with other labor-receiving and labor-sending states on migrant worker issues. Together with Qatar, the UAE has joined and sits on the Steering Committee of the Global Forum on Migration and Development (GFMD). A United Nations-supported initiative launched in 2006, the GFMD is intended to provide an international platform for policymakers and practitioners to discuss migration and development issues, develop best practice guidelines, and establish practical partnerships and cooperation among countries and stakeholders. After the second meeting of the GFMD in Manila in 2008, the UAE funded a feasibility study to examine measures to lower the recruitment and transaction costs of Bangladeshis who sought to work in the Gulf, and subsequently co-chaired roundtables at the following annual meetings in Athens (2009) and Mexico City (2010) that addressed issues of migrant integration and human development, respectively. In 2011, moreover, the UAE hosted a meeting in Dubai that examined how to engage better with recruitment agencies to provide greater protection to overseas contract workers, and committed to working with Bangladesh, India, and the Philippines "on a generic architecture of protection and empowerment."[197]

The UAE's deepening involvement with the GFMD occurred in parallel with the emergence of the Abu Dhabi Dialogue established in 2008 by the International Organization of Migration as another framework of inter-regional dialogue. From its inception, the UAE provided a support structure for the eighteen-country group of labor-sending and receiving countries, which (as of 2014) was under the rotating leadership of Kuwait. All six GCC states joined the dialogue in tandem with eleven of the main states of origin for migrant workers (Afghanistan, Bangladesh, China, India, Indonesia, Nepal, Pakistan, the Philippines, Sri Lanka, Thailand, and Vietnam). These eleven states had earlier come together to form the "Colombo Process" of regional dialogue in 2003. Five years later, the UAE government hosted and funded the deepening of the collaborative initiative by bringing the major destination states of the Gulf (including Yemen) into a process of sustained dialogue and consultation. The meeting culminated in the Abu Dhabi Declaration that announced the launch of "a new collaborative approach to address temporary labor mobility and maximize its benefits for development … based on the mutual interests of labor origin and destination countries."[198] Under the auspices of the Abu Dhabi Dialogue, the UAE partnered with India and the Philippines in a pilot project that sought to "improve the outcomes of migration through the entire migration cycle" in the construction, healthcare, and hospitality sectors in order to "inform subsequent actions that the UAE takes with a view to better manage temporary labor migration flows."[199]

Participation in both the Global Forum on Migration and Development and the Abu Dhabi Dialogue indicates that the Government of the UAE acknowledges the significance of migrant labor issues and the multilateral initiatives that address them. Association by name with the Abu Dhabi Dialogue reinforces the UAE's role in evolving layers of regional and international engagement and governance. The internationalization of policy debates over migration is nevertheless a sign that Emirati officials remain sensitive to the damage that international concern over the issue can do to the national image and international branding efforts.

Countering negative international publicity concerning labor migrants is not only good politics on the part of UAE officials but also a delicate element of a domestic equilibrium whereby ruling elites have sought to balance the "benefits" to the UAE of a cheap imported workforce against rising concerns among Emirati nationals over the perceived erosion of identity and values. The late journalist Anthony Shadid interviewed a number of Emiratis in April 2006 for a lengthy *Washington Post* report on the dizzying pace of development in Dubai. While few were prepared to go on record, one who did was civil society activist and human rights lawyer Mohammed al-Roken, whom Shadid quoted as stating that:

> The people of Dubai are on a first-class train, a speedy one, seeing nice views but there is one drawback to this train, and many people are not aware of it. It has no brakes … The brakes are accountability, sharing in the decision-making. These things will work as brakes on the train's speed. If citizens had a say, I don't think the city would have turned into this.[200]

Shadid added that "Government surveys reflect the unease among native Emiratis, even though officials are unsure how to respond" (and, as detailed in Chapter 6, in July 2012 al-Roken was one of dozens of Emiratis arrested and later sentenced to lengthy terms of imprisonment for alleged sedition against the Rulers of the UAE).[201] Two years after the *Washington Post* article, Christopher Davidson noted, in his monograph of Dubai, how "An increasing number of nationals are beginning to voice their concerns, believing that in some cases the ruling family and the government have gone too far in their efforts to accommodate foreigners" and that national identity was under threat.[202]

Also that year, UAE President Sheikh Khalifa bin Zayed proclaimed 2008 the "year of national identity" but reportedly then "forbade the Emirates' quasi-elected, quasi-legislative body, the Federal National Council, from discussing the issue, likely out of concern that it would exacerbate bad feelings among citizens regarding the demographic imbalance."[203] An article that appeared in May 2008 in Dubai's *Gulf News* captured several of the underlying points of unease among UAE nationals as one, a cultural adviser at the Sheikh Mohammed bin Rashid Foundation in Dubai, noted that "We are not afraid of others but we are concerned about losing our identity, heritage and language," while another Emirati citizen, an Associate Professor of mass media at UAE University in Al Ain, suggested that "Nationals are concerned about their identity because they are a minority in their homeland."[204] Dr. Maha Gobash, a sociologist and president of the Ousha bint Hussain Cultural Center in Dubai, reflected further on the connection between national identity and the "unique" demographic profile of the UAE:

> ... The UAE's identity is subject to the danger of extermination by other identities because of the diversity of nationalities in the country. This drives us to stand together to face this challenge, as the Emirati identity has to be dominantly present through laws and regulations so that others accommodate living in its presence. The UAE does not need to merge expatriates' cultures into its own, as cultural dominance is negative. Instead, the UAE society needs to stand as a cultural or dominant culture.[205]

The apparent popularity among young Emiratis in Abu Dhabi of T-shirts bearing the slogan "The UAE is full. Go home!" in the early 2010s indicated the existence of a groundswell of opinion over the issue as a long-time Western resident anthropologist observed in 2012 that "Emiratis express intense feelings about the fact that English and Urdu are more commonly spoken on the streets of Abu Dhabi than Arabic."[206] Meanwhile, in October 2013, an op-ed written by Emirati political commentator Sultan Sooud Al Qasimi suggested that a pathway to UAE citizenship be opened to long-time residents who had contributed greatly to society triggered a rancorous debate and an angry Twitter campaign using the hashtag (in Arabic) "this writer doesn't represent me."[207]

The growing international visibility of the UAE carried therefore risks as well as opportunities for the global ambitions of the new generation of leadership that assumed power in the 2000s. Policymakers in the UAE consistently exhibited a more nuanced awareness of the concepts of "soft" and "smart" power than their counterparts in other GCC states, including Qatar, and proved rather more effective at public diplomacy as a result. The projection of Emirati influence on the international stage bore fruit after 2011 when the UAE evolved security responses to the Arab Spring that combined the use of "hard" military force with the aspects of "soft" and "smart" power. An examination of the policies adopted in Arab Spring transition states, to which Chapter Six turns, illustrates how far UAE foreign (and security) policy has travelled since the first three decades of the federation, aptly summarized in 2001 as "a policy of promoting conciliation, cooperation and consensus, seeking, wherever possible, to defuse confrontation and conflict."[208]

Notes

1   Vania Carvalho Pinto, "From 'Follower' to 'Role Model': the Transformation to the UAE's International Self-Image," *Journal of Arabian Studies*, 4(2), 2014, p. 234.
2   Abdulkhaleq Abdulla, "New Assertiveness in UAE Foreign Policy," *Gulf News*, October 9, 2012.
3   Wm. Roger Louis, "The Withdrawal from the Gulf," in Wm. Roger Louis, *Ends of British Imperialism: The Scramble for Empire, Suez and Decolonization* (London: I.B. Tauris, 2006), p. 902.
4   Khalid Almezaini, *The UAE and Foreign Policy: Foreign Aid, Identities and Interests* (Abingdon: Routledge, 2012), p. 38.
5   Kristian Coates Ulrichsen, "The Gulf States and the Iran-Iraq War: Cooperation and Confusion," in Nigel Ashton and Bryan Gibson (eds), *The Iran-Iraq War: New International Perspectives* (Abingdon: Routledge, 2013), p. 112.
6   Letter from Brian R. Pridham (First Secretary, Head of Chancery and Consul, British Embassy, Abu Dhabi, UAE) to Anthony D. Harris (Middle East Department, FCO). August 28, 1974, London, *The National Archives*, file FCO 8/2360.
7   Hassan Hamdan al-Alkim, *The Foreign Policy of the United Arab Emirates* (London: Saqi Books, 1989), p. 175.
8   Ibid., p. 177.
9   Fadhil Chalabi, *Oil Policies, Oil Myths: Observations of an OPEC Insider* (London: I.B. Tauris, 2010), p. 108.
10   Al-Alkim, *Foreign Policy of the United Arab Emirates*, p. 184.
11   Ibid.
12   Ibid.
13   Abdul-Monem al-Mashat, "Politics of Constructive Engagement: The Foreign Policy of the United Arab Emirates," in Bahgat Korany and Ali Hillal Dessouki (eds), *The Foreign Policies of Arab States: The Challenge of Globalization* (Cairo: American University of Cairo Press, 2008), p. 472.
14   Sultan Barakat and Steve Zyck, 'Gulf State Assistance to Conflict-Affected Environments,' *LSE Kuwait Program Working Paper No.10* (July 2010), p. 13.
15   Quoted in Almezaini, *UAE and Foreign Policy*, p. 107 and p. 123.
16   Ibid., p. 127.
17   Ibid., p. 49.
18   Ibid., p. 61.
19   Jean-Marc Rickli, "The Political Rationale and Implications of the United Arab Emirates' Military Involvement in Libya," in Dag Henriksen and Ann Karin Larsen (eds), *Political Rationale and International Consequences of the War in Libya* (Oxford: Oxford University Press, 2016), p. 143.

20   Gerd Nonneman, "The Gulf States and the Iran-Iraq War: Pattern Shifts and Continuities," in Lawrence Potter and Gary Sick (eds), *Iran, Iraq, and the Legacies of War* (New York: Palgrave Macmillan, 2004), p. 183.
21   Abdul-Reda Assiri, *Kuwait's Foreign Policy: City-State in World Politics* (Boulder, CO: Westview Press, 1990), p. 120.
22   Frauke Heard-Bey, *From Trucial States to United Arab Emirates* (Dubai: Motivate Publishing, 2004 edition), pp. 389–390.
23   "Diplomatic Lull Before the Storm?" *Gulf States Newsletter*, 15(394), September 17, 1990, p. 9.
24   Frauke Heard-Bey, "Conflict Resolution and Regional Co-operation: The Role of the Gulf Cooperation Council, 1970–2002," *Middle Eastern Studies*, 42(2), 2006, p. 210.
25   Abdul-Monem al-Mashat, "The Foreign Policy of the United Arab Emirates," in Bahgat Korany and Ali E. Hillal Dessouki (eds), *The Foreign Policy of Arab States: The Challenge of Globalization* (Cairo: The American University in Cairo Press, 2008), p. 473.
26   J.E. Peterson, "Qatar and the World: Branding for a Micro-State," *Middle East Journal*, 60(4), 2006, p. 741.
27   Spencer Tucker, *Persian Gulf War Encyclopedia: A Political, Social, and Military History* (Santa Barbara, CA: ABC-CLIO, 2014), pp. 230–231.
28   James A. Baker III, *The Politics of Diplomacy: Revolution, War & Peace, 1989–1992* (New York: Putnam, 1995), p. 271.
29   "U-2 Crash Highlighted US/UAE Intelligence Ties," *Gulf States Newsletter*, 29 (761), July 15, 2005.
30   Tucker, *Persian Gulf War Encyclopedia*, p. 231.
31   Peter Hellyer, "Evolution of UAE Foreign Policy," in Peter Hellyer and Ibrahim Al-Abed (eds), *United Arab Emirates: a New Perspective* (London: Trident Press, 2001), p. 169.
32   Anthony Cordesman, *Kuwait: Recovery and Security after the Gulf War* (Boulder, CO: Westview Press, 1997), pp. 127–128.
33   Kenneth Katzman, "The United Arab Emirates (UAE): Issues for U.S. Policy," Washington, DC: *Congressional Research Service Report for Congress*, December 8, 2008, p. 4.
34   Rajiv Chandrasekaran, "In the UAE, the United States has a Quiet, Potent Ally Nicknamed 'Little Sparta'," *Washington Post*, November 9, 2014.
35   "UAE-US Security Relationship," available online at http://www.uae-embassy.org/uae-us-relations/security_2012.
36   Abdullah al-Shayeji, "Dangerous Perceptions: Gulf Views of U.S. Policy in the Region," *Middle East Policy*, 5(3), 1997, p. 3.
37   Almezaini, *UAE and Foreign Policy*, pp. 41–42.
38   Al-Shayeji, Dangerous Perceptions, p. 6. The academic in question was Dr. Ali al-Tarrah of Kuwait University.
39   Marwan Yousef Muhammed Rashid Lekrab al-Shehhi and Fayez Rashid Ahmad Banihammad.
40   "Leadership Looks beyond 11 September Crisis Management," *Gulf States Newsletter*, 26(683), April 3, 2002, pp. 11–12.
41   *The National Commission Report: Final Report of the National Commission on Terrorist Attacks upon the United States* (New York: W.W. Norton & Company, 2004), Appendix A: The Financing of the 9/11 Plot, p. 136.
42   Ibid., p. 134.
43   Ibid.
44   Ibid., p. 135.
45   "Leadership Looks beyond 11 September Crisis Management," *Gulf States Newsletter*, 26 (683), April 3, 2002, pp. 11–12.
46   "Emirates Come to Grips with Informal Economies," *Gulf States Newsletter*, 26 (683), April 3, 2002, pp. 10–11.
47   "C.P. Khalifa Holds the Purse Strings as Abu Dhabi's Younger Generations Emerge," *Gulf States Newsletter*, 26 (683), April 3, 2002, p. 5.

48 "With MBZ's Promotion, Sheikha Fatima's Sons Take Center Stage," *Gulf States Newsletter*, 27 (724), December 12, 2003, p. 1.

49 U.S. Diplomatic Cable 04ABUDHABI3410_a, "UAE Succession Update: the Post-Zayed Scenario," September 28, 2004. Available online at the "Public Library of US Diplomacy," https://wikileaks.org/plusd/cables/04ABUDHABI3410_a.html.

50 "Ironically, DP World Debate Cements UAE's Military Bond with USA," *Gulf States Newsletter*, 30 (778), March 24, 2006, p. 16.

51 Andrea Rugh, *The Political Culture of Leadership in the United Arab Emirates* (New York: Palgrave Macmillan, 2007), p. 230.

52 "UAE Moves to Stay on Top of Future Military Challenges," *Gulf States Newsletter*, 28 (728), February 20, 2004.

53 "Ironically, DP World Debate Cements UAE's Military Bond with USA," *Gulf States Newsletter*, 30 (778), March 24, 2006, p. 16.

54 "US/UAE Military Ties after the DP World Debate," *Gulf States Newsletter*, 30(778), March 24, 2006.

55 Ibid.

56 "New York Senator Wants to Halt Ports Deal," *NPR*, February 22, 2006.

57 Quoted in Ben Simpfendorfer, *The New Silk Road: How a Rising Arab World is Turning Away from the West and Rediscovering China* (New York: Palgrave Macmillan, 2009), p. 58.

58 Rajiv Chandrasekaran, "In the UAE, the United States has a Quiet, Potent Ally Nicknamed 'Little Sparta'," *Washington Post*, November, 9, 2014.

59 "A Positive Agenda for the Middle East – Remarks by Ambassador Yousef Al Otaiba," *United Arab Emirates Embassy in the United States*, January 29, 2016, available online at www.uae-embassy.org/news-media/positive-agenda-middle-east–remarks-ambassador-yousef-al-otaiba.

60 Awad Mustafa, "US Congress Notified to Approve $150 Million UAE Training," *Defense News*, January 9, 2014.

61 Steve Coll, *Ghost Wars: The Secret History of the CIA, Afghanistan, and Bin Laden, from the Soviet Invasion to September 10, 2001* (New York: Penguin, 2004), pp. 447–449.

62 Christopher Davidson, "Dubai: the Security Dimensions of the Region's Premier Free Port," *Middle East Policy*, 15(2), 2008, p. 145.

63 Rajiv Chandrasekaran, "In the UAE, the United States has a Quiet, Potent Ally Nicknamed 'Little Sparta'," *Washington Post*, November 9, 2014.

64 "UAE Has Done Exemplary Work in Afghanistan," *Gulf News*, August 25, 2011.

65 *Mission: Winds of Goodness*, "Our Partners who Helped and Supported the Project," available online at http://www.uaeafghanistan.ae/en/Brand-of-Abu-Dhabi.php.

66 "Dubai Hosts First Afghanistan International Investors Conference under Co-Chairmanship of Governments of Afghanistan and UAE," *Middle East Economic Digest*, December 1, 2010.

67 See http://www.trade.gov/afghanistan for full details of the *Afghanistan Spotlight* events prior to the closure of the program on December 31, 2014.

68 "Afghanistan and UAE Sign Strategic Partnership Agreement and Pledge to Expand Bilateral Ties," *Afghan Zariza*, January 15, 2015.

69 "UAE Policy will Focus on Stabilisation in Afghanistan," *Oxford Analytica*, August 6, 2015.

70 "US Embassy Cables: Money Smuggling Out of Afghanistan," *The Guardian*, December 2, 2010.

71 "New Afghan President Opens Probe into Kabul Bank Scheme," *The National*, October 2, 2014.

72 "Expo 2020 Vote: UAE Deserves Answers from Pakistan and Afghanistan," *Gulf News*, December 14, 2013.

73 Jeffrey Sampler and Saeb Eigner, *Sand to Silicon: Achieving Rapid Growth Lessons from Dubai* (London: Profile Books, 2003), p. 145.

74 Theodore Karasik, "Policy in Africa is All about Stability and Cooperation," *The National*, June 18, 2015.

75 "UAE Scales Up Foreign Policy Role in East Africa," *Oxford Analytica*, July 7, 2015.
76 Ibid.
77 Theodore Karasik, "Policy in Africa is All about Stability and Cooperation," *The National*, June 18, 2015.
78 "UAE-Funded Somali Military Center Opens," *The National*, May 13, 2015.
79 Erick Viramontes, "The Role of Latin America in the Foreign Policies of the GCC States," Paper Presented at the 3rd *Gulf Research Meeting*, University of Cambridge, July 2012, pp. 10–11.
80 "UAE Wants to Build with the BRICS," *Gulf News*, April 23, 2012.
81 "Mubadala to Invest $2 Billion in Eike Batista's EBX Group as Part of Strategic Partnership," *Mubadala Press Release*, March 26, 2012.
82 "Abu Dhabi's Mubadala to Get Stake in Batista Mines, Port," *Bloomberg*, August 5, 2014.
83 "UAE Wants to Build with the BRICS," *Gulf News*, April 23, 2012.
84 Mark Katz, "Convergent Hopes, Divergent Politics: Russia and the Gulf in a Time of Troubles," The Arab Gulf States Institute in Washington, *Policy Paper #7*, 2015, p. 4.
85 "Abu Dhabi to Invest $100m," *Bloomberg*, December 1, 2010.
86 "Abu Dhabi to Invest $5bn in Russia," *Gulf States Newsletter*, 37 (954), September 19, 2013, p. 14.
87 "Russians Expected to Top Spending Charts at Dubai Shopping Festival," *The National*, February 11, 2014.
88 "A Common Wealth: Building Gulf-CIS Ties," *Economist Intelligence Unit Report*, February 2016, pp. 13–14.
89 Author Interviews, Washington, DC, February 2016.
90 Thierry Kellner, "The GCC States of the Persian Gulf and Asia Energy Relations," *IFRI Research Paper*, 2012, pp. 40–42.
91 "When Modi Rocked Dubai," *Khaleej Times*, August 18, 2015.
92 Harsh Pant, "Narendra Modi's UAE Trip Highlights India's Shifting Middle East Approach," *The Diplomat*, August 13, 2015.
93 Kellner, *Asia Energy Relations*, p. 43.
94 "Etisalat Has No Intention of Return to India Market," *The National*, February 27, 2013.
95 "DP World Says No to Audit in India," *World Maritime News*, May 21, 2015.
96 Danny Quah, "The Global Economy's Shifting Centre of Gravity," *Global Policy*, 2(1), 2011, pp. 3–5.
97 Kristian Coates Ulrichsen, *The Gulf States in International Political Economy* (New York: Palgrave Macmillan, 2015), p. 138.
98 Ibid.
99 "Abu Dhabi in Nearly $7bln Oil Investment in Malaysia," *Reuters*, March 12, 2013.
100 "Malaysia's 1MDB Scandal Poses Difficult Questions for Gulf Grandees," *Gulf States News*, 39(999), September 3, 2015, p. 5.
101 Jacqueline Armijo, "DragonMart: The Mega-Souk of Today's Silk Road," *Middle East Report 270*, Spring 2014, p. 30.
102 Ibid., p. 29.
103 Ibid., p. 30.
104 Ibid.
105 April Herlevi, "China and the United Arab Emirates: Sustainable Silk Road Partnership?" *China Brief*, 16(2), Jamestown Foundation, January 25, 2016, available online at www.jamestown.org/regions/middleeast/single/?tx_ttnews%5Btt_news%5D=45019&tx_ttnews%5BbackPid%5D=49&cHash=0230e275dd986e73fe5eb2f98d6d4f72#.VrQTHVgrLIV.
106 Christopher Davidson, *The Persian Gulf and Pacific Asia: from Indifference to Interdependence* (London: Hurst & Co, 2010), p. 24 and p. 29.
107 "Vision and Actions on Jointly Building Silk Road Economic Belt and 21st-Century Maritime Silk Road," issued by the *National Development and Reform Commission*, Ministry of Foreign Affairs, and Ministry of Commerce of the People's Republic of

China, with State Council authorization, March 2015, available online at http://en.
ndrc.gov.cn/newsrelease/201503/t20150330_669367.html.

108 "Mohamed's Visit to Bring Paradigm Shift in UAE-China Relations: Sultan al Jaber," *Emirates 24/7*, December 9, 2015.

109 "UAE Signs Up as Founding Member of Asian Infrastructure Investment Bank," *The National*, April 5, 2015.

110 Herlevi, *Sustainable Silk Road Partnership*.

111 "China, UAE Pledge to Boost Belt and Road Cooperation," *Xinhua*, December 14, 2015.

112 Herlevi, *Sustainable Silk Road Partnership*.

113 "Yuan's Ascendance is Good for Investment," *The National*, December 20, 2015.

114 Herlevi, *Sustainable Silk Road Partnership*.

115 Theodore Karasik, "Policy in Africa is all About Stability and Cooperation," *The National*, June 18, 2015.

116 Christian Henderson, "The UAE's Nexus State: Logistics, Transport and Foreign Policy," *LSE Middle East Center workshop*, October 7, 2015, available online at http://blogs.lse.ac.uk/mec/2015/11/26/the-uaes-nexus-state-logistics-transport-and-foreign-policy.

117 Kristian Coates Ulrichsen, "The GCC States and the Shifting Balance of Global Power," Georgetown University School of Foreign Service in Qatar: Center for International and Regional Studies, *Occasional Paper No. 6*, Doha, 2010, p. 17.

118 Mary Ann Tetrealt, "Autonomy, Necessity, and the Small State: Ruling Kuwait in the Twentieth Century," *International Organization*, 45(4), 1991, p. 567.

119 'United Arab Emirates and the WTO,' available at https://www.wto.org/english/thewto_e/countries_e/united_arab_emirates_e.htm (accessed December 25, 2015).

120 Meyer-Reumann, "The Endeavours of Gulf Countries to Reach WTO Requirements," *Arab Law Quarterly*, 16(1), 2001, p. 50.

121 Christopher Davidson, "The Impact of Economic Reform on Dubai," in Anoushiravan Ehteshami and Steven Wright (eds), *Reform in the Middle East Oil Monarchies* (Reading: Ithaca Press, 2008), pp. 160–162.

122 John Everington, "DIFC Courts: Question of Judgement and Jurisdiction a Key Concern," *The National*, November 16, 2015.

123 "Emirates Maritime Arbitration Center," *Clyde & Co Insight/Updates*, September 17, 2015.

124 Peter Shaw-Smith, "Emirates Maritime Arbitration Center Inches Closer to Reality," *SeaTrade*, November 15, 2015.

125 "Gordon Brown in the Gulf to Seek World Bailout Support," *Khaleej Times*, October 30, 2008.

126 "Saudi Arabia Not Mulling More Cash for IMF: Minister," *Reuters*, November 16, 2008.

127 "Gulf Central Bankers Wary of Oil, Property Declines," *Gulf Times*, November 22, 2008.

128 "US Seeks $300bn from Gulf States to Tackle Turmoil," *Agence France-Presse*, November 21, 2008.

129 Richard Youngs, "Impasse in Euro-Gulf Relations," Madrid: *FRIDE Working Paper No. 80*, 2008, p. 2.

130 "Court Upholds Citigroup Arbitration Win over Abu Dhabi Fund," *Reuters*, February 19, 2014.

131 William Cohan, "Citigroup's Amazing Abu Dhabi Adventure," *Bloomberg View*, December 10, 2012.

132 Mark Gordon and Sabastian Niles, "Sovereign Wealth Funds: an Overview," in Karl Sauvant, Lisa Sachs, and Wouter Schmit Jongbloed (eds), *Sovereign Investment: Concerns and Policy Challenges* (Oxford: Oxford University Press, 2012), p. 41.

133 Sven Behrendt, "Beyond Santiago: Status and Prospects," *Central Banking*, 19(4), 2008, p. 76.

134 Gordon and Niles, *Sovereign Wealth Funds*, p. 40.

135 Eric Kulisch, "Port Canaveral-Gulftainer Deal gets Government Ok," *American Shipper*, September 26, 2014.
136 "Inside the London Megaport You Never Knew Existed," *The Guardian*, September 15, 2015.
137 Ibid.
138 Ibid.
139 Joseph Nye, *Bound to Lead: The Changing Nature of American Power* (New York: Basic Books, 1990).
140 cf. Joseph Nye, *Soft Power: The Means to Success in World Politics* (New York: PublicAffairs, 2004).
141 Ibid.
142 Peter van Ham, "The Rise of the Brand State: the Postmodern Politics of Image and Reputation," *Foreign Affairs*, 80(5), September/October 2001, p. 2.
143 Ibid., p. 4.
144 Ibid., p. 6.
145 Christopher Browning, "Nation Branding, National Self-Esteem, and the Constitution of Subjectivity in Late Modernity," *Foreign Policy Analysis*, 11(2), 2015, p. 196.
146 Christopher Davidson, "The Impact of Economic Reform on Dubai," in Anoushiravan Ehteshami and Steven Wright (eds), *Reform in the Middle East Oil Monarchies* (Reading: Ithaca Press, 2008), pp. 157–158.
147 Christopher Davidson, *Dubai: The Vulnerability of Success* (London: Hurst & Co, 2008), p. 111.
148 "Dubai Hotels Enjoy Busiest Half-Year Visitor Numbers," *Khaleej Times*, August 25, 2014.
149 "Revealed: How New Dubai Brand Will Transform Emirate to 'Must Experience' Destination," *Emirates 24/7*, May 7, 2014.
150 Julian Pecquet, "UAE Spend Big to Avoid Another Ports World Debacle," *Al-Monitor*, August 17, 2014.
151 Ibid.
152 Julian Pecquet, "UAE Asserts Itself with Record-Smashing Lobbying Blitz," *Al-Monitor*, August 3, 2015.
153 Gail Sullivan, "For UAE, It's Better to Give than to Receive," *The Washington Diplomat*, November 28, 2012.
154 Ibid.
155 Frank Kane, "Applying Business Sense to Philanthropy in the Gulf," *The National*, November 10, 2015.
156 These being the University of Exeter and Durham University.
157 "LSE Focuses New Centre on Collaboration with the People and Institutions of the Middle East," *LSE Press Office*, May 24, 2010.
158 Stephen Marks, "Harvard Returns Gift to Arab President," *The Harvard Crimson*, July 30, 2004.
159 Ibid.
160 Pranay Gupte, *Dubai: The Making of a Megalopolis* (New York: Penguin/Viking, 2011), p. 268.
161 "Dubai School of Government Renamed after Mohammed," *Khaleej Times*, July 1, 2013.
162 Sanghyeon Park, "From Dubai, With Love," *The Harvard Crimson*, April 21, 2009.
163 Melanie Fu and Jiwon Joung, "Med School Establishes Research Center in Dubai," *The Harvard Crimson*, January 22, 2015.
164 Jason Lane, "International Branch Campuses, Free Zones, and Quality Assurance: Policy Issues for Dubai and the UAE," *Dubai School of Government Policy Brief*, No. 20 (August 2010), p. 5.
165 "NYU Abu Dhabi Welcomes Class of 2016 Comprising 151 Students from 65 Countries," *NYUAD Press Release*, September 10, 2012.

166 "Former US President Praises New York University Abu Dhabi for Tackling Labour Welfare Allegations," *The National*, May 25, 2014.

167 Ariel Kaminer and Sean O'Driscoll, "Workers at N.Y.U.'s Abu Dhabi Site Faced Harsh Criticism," *New York Times*, May 18, 2014.

168 Stephanie Saul, "N.Y.U. Professor is Barred by United Arab Emirates," *New York Times*, March 16, 2015.

169 Zoe Schlanger, "A Reporter's Saga of Being Followed, Bribed, and Recruited as a Spy," *Newsweek*, March 30, 2015.

170 "Sitting on Top of the World! Is that Tom Cruise Performing a Death-Defying Stunt on the Planet's Highest Skyscraper?" *Daily Mail*, November 24, 2010.

171 Charles Riley, "Star Wars Puts Abu Dhabi on Hollywood's Map," *CNN Money*, December 15, 2015.

172 Nick Vivarelli, "Abu Dhabi Film Festival Scrapped after Eight Editions," *Variety*, May 7, 2015.

173 "Emirates Said to Spend $100m on FIFA Sponsorship in Four Years," *ArabianBusiness.com*, July 18, 2014.

174 "Real Madrid to Rename Stadium Abu Dhabi Santiago Bernabeu," *BBC Sport*, January 29, 2015.

175 "Real Madrid Agree 'Strategic Partnership' with Abu Dhabi's IPIC," *The Guardian*, October 28, 2014.

176 "New Homes Plan Near Manchester City FC's Etihad Stadium," *BBC News*, June 24, 2014.

177 David Conn, "From Desert Skyscrapers to Manchester City's Sky Blue Land of Riches," *The Guardian*, September 18, 2009.

178 Ibid.

179 Adam Jupp, "City Owner and Council to Build 6000 New Homes in £1bn Deal," *Manchester Evening News*, June 24, 2014.

180 Ibid.

181 "Manchester's New Housing Deal: More Questions than Answers," *Steady State Manchester*, June 27, 2014.

182 David Conn, "Abu Dhabi Accused of 'Using Manchester City to Launder Image'," *The Guardian*, July 30, 2013.

183 "Building Towers, Cheating Workers: Exploitation of Migrant Construction Workers in the United Arab Emirates," *Human Rights Watch*, Volume 18 No.8E (2006), p. 2.

184 Ibid., p. 24.

185 Ibid., p. 59.

186 Ibid., p. 2.

187 Ahmed Kanna, "Dubai in a Jagged World," *Middle East Research and Information Project Report No. 243*, 2007, available online at http://www.merip.org/mer/mer243/dubai-jagged-world.

188 Syed Ali, "You Must Come with Us," *The Guardian*, November 12, 2007.

189 Kanishk Tharoor, "The Louvre Comes to Abu Dhabi," *The Guardian*, December 2, 2015.

190 "The Island of Happiness": Exploitation of Migrant Workers on Saadiyat Island, Abu Dhabi," *Human Rights Watch*, May 19, 2009, report available online at www.hrw.org/report/2009/05/19/island-happiness/exploitation-migrant-workers-saadiyat-island-abu-dhabi.

191 "The Island of Happiness Revisited: a Progress Report on Institutional Commitments to Address Abuses of Migrant Workers on Abu Dhabi's Saadiyat Island," *Human Rights Watch*, March 21, 2012, report available online at https://www.hrw.org/report/2012/03/21/island-happiness-revisited/progress-report-institutional-commitments-address.

192 "Report of the Independent Investigator into Allegations of Labor and Compliance Issues during the Construction of the NYU Abu Dhabi Campus on Saadiyat Island, United Arab Emirates," *Nardello & Co*, April 16, 2015, pp. 12–13.

193 See "Gulf Labor Artist Coalition" website available at http://gulflabor.org/press.

194 *U.S. Department of State*, "Trafficking in Persons Report 2015," available online at http://www.state.gov/j/tip/rls/tiprpt/2015, p. 348

195 Adam Hanieh, "Migrant Rights in the Gulf: the Way Forward," in Abdulhadi Khalaf, Omar AlShehabi, and Adam Hanieh (eds), *Transit States: Labour, Migration & Citizenship in the Gulf* (London: Pluto Press, 2015), p. 227.

196 "UAE Announces Labor Reforms to Protect Foreign Workers," *Al Jazeera*, September 29, 2015.

197 Susan Martin, "Protecting Migrants' Rights in the Gulf Cooperation Council," in Mehran Kamrava and Zahra Babar (eds), *Migrant Labor in the Persian Gulf* (London: Hurst & Co., 2012), pp. 226–229.

198 "Abu Dhabi Declaration of Asian Countries of Origin and Destination," *Ministerial Consultation on Overseas Employment and Contractual Labour for Countries of Origin and Destination in Asia*, Abu Dhabi, January 21–22, 2008, available online at www.iom.int/jahia/webdav/shared/shared/mainsite/microsites/rcps/abudhabi/abu_dhabi_declaration_english.pdf.

199 Karoline Popp, "Regional Processes, Law and Institutional Developments on Migration," in Brian Opeskin, Richard Perruchoud, and Jillyanne Redpath-Cross (eds), *Foundations of International Migration Law* (Cambridge: Cambridge University Press, 2012), p. 377.

200 Anthony Shadid, "The Towering Dream of Dubai," *Washington Post*, April 30, 2006.

201 Ibid.

202 Davidson, *Vulnerability of Success*, pp. 193–194.

203 David Mednicoff, "The Legal Regulation of Migrant Workers, Politics and Identity in Qatar and the United Arab Emirates," in Mehran Kamrava and Zahra Babar (eds), *Migrant Labor in the Persian Gulf* (London: Hurst & Co., 2012), p. 214.

204 "The Debate on UAE National Identity," *Gulf News*, May 26, 2008.

205 "UAE Society Needs to Stand as a Central Culture," *Gulf News*, May 26, 2008.

206 Jane Bristol-Rhys, "Socio-Spatial Boundaries in Abu Dhabi," in Mehran Kamrava and Zahra Babar (eds), *Migrant Labor in the Persian Gulf* (London: Hurst & Co., 2012), pp. 82–83.

207 "Call to Naturalize Some Expats Stirs Anxiety in the UAE," *Reuters*, October 10, 2013.

208 Hellyer, *Evolution of UAE Foreign Policy*, p. 164.

6

SECURITY

The contagious outbreak and regional overspill of the "Arab Spring" political upheaval in early 2011 ought not to have had any direct impact on the UAE. However, the unrest revealed a sense of unease among officials in Abu Dhabi at the rise of the Muslim Brotherhood to power in Egypt and Tunisia and triggered a security crackdown that targeted the Emirati offshoot of the movement. The UAE subsequently developed a hawkish and assertive approach to foreign and security policy that combined sophisticated local security capabilities with far more expansive policy intent and which sought overtly to influence the pace and direction of change in states undergoing political transition after 2011. This approach paid dividends as the rolling back of Arab Spring "gains" in Egypt and Libya was followed by immediate and high-level Emirati political and financial support to Egypt's reinstated military-led government in 2013, and strong security support to "secular" groups battling Islamist militias in Libya in 2014 and 2015.

This chapter begins by examining how and why Emirati officials, particularly in Abu Dhabi, came to view the Muslim Brotherhood as such a dangerous threat both domestically and regionally. The opening section analyzes why a far more assertive set of regional and foreign security policies emerged and is followed by a section that argues that a range of tangible and intangible factors account for the decision to nip any potential Islamist mobilization firmly in the bud and not allow any agitation to take root after 2011. This leads into the third section, which explores the different nature of the Emirati interventions in the post-regime change maelstrom in Libya and Egypt respectively, before the fourth section explores the deployment of hard and soft power in the military campaigns against ISIS since 2014 and in Yemen in 2015. The final sections in this chapter examine the troubled relationship with Iran and the tacit security links with Israel that have proliferated since the late 2000s and that together have positioned the UAE at the forefront of the realignment in regional policies as the dominating twentieth-century fissure (the

Arab–Israeli dispute) has given way to deep splits within the Middle East between Islamists and non-Islamists and between Arab and Iranian regional perspectives.

Hawkish Approach to Regional Security

The genesis of the assertive approach to regional security did not start with the Arab Spring but rather grew out of developments during the 2000s, as described in previous chapters. These included the rise to influence of Sheikh Mohammed bin Zayed Al Nahyan ("MBZ") as Crown Prince of Abu Dhabi and Sheikh Moham-med bin Rashid Al Maktoum as Ruler of Dubai, as well as the new possibilities that opened up for small states to project different forms of power and influence that far exceeded the limitations of territorial size. Synchronous changes to the regional context also spurred the UAE and Qatar (and, belatedly, after 2011, Saudi Arabia) to adopt more proactive approaches that began belatedly to shift the GCC states to being producers of, rather than merely consumers of, regional security. Specifically, the fallout from the flawed invasion and occupation of Iraq by the George W. Bush presidency in 2003 – from which UAE forces notably abstained – and the gradual rebalancing of US focus toward Pacific Asia after 2009 under President Barack Obama both injected elements of doubt into the strategic relationship with the US in Gulf capitals, including Abu Dhabi.[1]

Closely intertwined with the developments listed above was the geopolitical "fallout" from the aftermath of the 9/11 terrorist attacks on the United States and the Bush administration's controversial "War on Terror" that lasted for most of the remainder of the 2000s. Chapter Five recounted how two of the 9/11 hijackers held Emirati citizenship and an element of the planning and logistical process passed through Dubai. In addition to providing a shock to the US–UAE relation-ship, the Al Qaeda challenge manifested itself also in terms of the perceived threat posed by international terrorism to the highly multicultural nature of the UAE just as Dubai and Abu Dhabi accelerated their transformation into aspiring global cities. A spate of failed terrorist plots to target the UAE between 2005 and 2007 under-scored the continuing threat to the federation from Al Qaeda militancy. Specific plots that were foiled included three in 2005 alone: an attempt by a Somali terrorist to target the US Embassy in Abu Dhabi with a rucksack bomb that failed to explode, the discovery of a car bomb "assembled inside the UAE for planned use against a target in Dubai Internet City or Dubai Media City," and the uncovering of a cell in Fujairah that allegedly planned a triple car-bombing attack against a five-star hotel. Two years later, in 2007, authorities in Ajman disrupted a terrorist cell that reportedly was "experimenting in explosives" while, in June 2008, the Foreign and Commonwealth Office (FCO) in the United Kingdom raised its threat perception in the UAE from "General" to "High" – the uppermost of the four-scale sliding threat perception scale – amid rumors of an impending "credible attack plot" that ultimately never materialized.[2]

In the late 2000s, UAE policymakers took a series of steps that broadened and diversified the set of external security relationships beyond the critical core of the

Defense Cooperation Agreement in place with the United States since 1994. These occurred both on a bilateral and multilateral level with France and Australia and with multinational partners in the Indian Ocean and with NATO respectively. The UAE armed forces had a long record of defense procurement from France, stretching back to the earliest years of the federation in the 1970s, through the acquisition of Mirage fighter jets and Leclerc tanks.[3] Longstanding negotiations with France for a formal defense agreement commenced in 1995 during the Presidency of Jacques Chirac while in 2004 the UAE and France agreed to participate in war games. However, the war games did not immediately take place, and it took the election to the presidency of Chirac's successor, Nicholas Sarkozy, to accelerate the pace of bilateral defense and security cooperation.[4] As part of an intensification of French commercial and strategic interest in the GCC states, the delayed war games took place in January 2008, the same month that France announced it would open its first permanent military base in the Gulf in Abu Dhabi.[5] What became known as *Camp de la Paix* (Peace Camp) was opened formally by President Sarkozy in May 2009 and consisted of three naval and logistical, air force, and land facilities at Port Zayed, Al-Dhafra, and a desert training camp outside Abu Dhabi.[6]

Ties with the Australian Defence Force (ADF) proliferated over the 2000s as Australian military units participated in multinational coalition operations in Iraq and Afghanistan while from 2009 Australian warships and aircraft took part in counter-piracy operations off the Horn of Africa. Whereas in 1982 a Joint Committee on Foreign Affairs and Defence report of the Australian Parliament had concluded that Australia had no direct strategic interest in the Gulf, by the 2000s the UAE was emerging as the strategic linchpin in Australia's regional approach. Australia signed its first Defence Cooperation Agreement with a Middle Eastern partner in 2007 as military planners came to appreciate the strategic value of the UAE to a remote "middle power" that "has neither the capability nor the need to consider the permanent basing of forces within the region."[7]

This was followed in 2008 by the decision to consolidate Australian forces in the Middle East at the Al-Minhad airbase outside Dubai following the withdrawal of Australian forces from Iraq and the signing of a Status of Forces Agreement that permitted the Australians to operate from the UAE.[8] Al-Minhad subsequently became Australia's logistics and transport hub as a logistics base in Kuwait and C-130 facility in Qatar closed down. Defense and security relations continued to deepen and an inaugural GCC–Australia Strategic Dialogue took place in 2011, the same year that a report by the influential Sydney-based Lowy Institute for International Policy argued that:

> Without the permission of the UAE to operate out of one of its military bases, Australia's ability to prosecute its missions in the Gulf and Afghanistan would have been seriously compromised. Cooperation on defence issues has helped to round out an already strong economic relationship.[9]

On a more "informal" level, Australians also assumed positions of leadership in the UAE Presidential Guard after its formation in 2010. The inaugural commander of the Presidential Guard, Major-General Michael Hindmarsh, took up his post after a thirty-three-year career in the Australian armed forces, during which he headed Australia's Special Operations Command from 2004 to 2008 and commanded all Australian forces in the Middle East from 2008 until 2009. The Melbourne-based *Herald Sun* newspaper observed how Hindmarsh's appointment contributed to the broader strengthening and deepening of the defense relationship between Australia and the UAE:

> He [Hindmarsh] was a key player in the transfer of the Australian headquarters from Iraq to the UAE and had dealings at the highest security levels with senior officials and the UAE military … Dozens of ex-Australian soldiers work for the UAE military in leadership, training and mentoring roles, developing links between the two armed forces.[10]

The previously mentioned Lowy Institute report into Australian strategic alignment with the UAE noted also that the two countries increasingly shared a growing interest in regional cooperation in the Indian Ocean. From the UAE side, this has largely taken place through the deepening of defense and security cooperation with India with the formation of the Indian Ocean Naval Symposium (IONS) in 2008. Conceived by the Indian Navy as a biennial forum for naval delegations to explore common threats from challenges to maritime trade, energy, and economic security as well as explore collective approaches to humanitarian aid and natural disaster responses, the symposium has thirty-five members and the UAE hosted its second meeting in Abu Dhabi in May 2010 before the Commander of the UAE Navy assumed the rotating leadership for 2010–2012.[11] Naval cooperation between the UAE and India also strengthened around both countries' participation in the anti-piracy operations off Somalia after 2008 and in a series of maritime exercises and fleet visits that began with inaugural Navy-to-Navy Staff Talks in 2007.[12] Bilateral security cooperation was stepped up further after Prime Minister Narendra Modi's visit to the UAE in August 2015 with the establishment of a strategic dialogue between the two countries' National Security Councils,[13] and with the signing of agreements on cyber-security, counter-terrorism, and civil nuclear cooperation during a reciprocal visit to India by Abu Dhabi Crown Prince Mohammed bin Zayed in February 2016.[14]

The UAE also became the first Gulf (and Arab) state to establish a formal relationship with the North Atlantic Treaty Organization (NATO) when it appointed an Ambassador to NATO in May 2011 and opened a diplomatic mission at NATO Headquarters in Brussels in April 2013. The formalization of relations with NATO represented a logical outcome of years of steadily closer cooperation between the UAE and the alliance. In 2004, the UAE was among the four Gulf States (alongside Bahrain, Kuwait, and Qatar) that joined the Istanbul Cooperation Initiative (ICI) launched by NATO at its Istanbul Summit in June of that year.

Modelled after the Partnership for Peace initiative directed at the former members of the Warsaw Pact, through the ICI NATO aimed to "offer a rich menu of options for training and collaboration ranging from counterterrorism to greater transparency in defense budgeting and decision making" as well as greater interoperability and institutional cooperation through joint exercises, training, and intelligence sharing.[15] However, the impact of the ICI was blunted by numerous factors, including the fact that Oman and Saudi Arabia never joined the initiative, which in any case lacked a coherent strategic vision, and struggled against competing bilateral agendas and agreements at play both among NATO and Gulf member states.[16]

Unlike its fellow Gulf members of the ICI, what set the UAE apart was that its military forces already were engaged in practical cooperation with NATO forces in a range of conflict and post-conflict stabilization operations. In 1999, the UAE was one of the first non-NATO states to support the NATO air campaign in Kosovo and, subsequently, sent more than 1,000 troops to participate in the post-conflict stabilization Kosovo Force (KFOR), which marked also the first time that UAE forces deployed on operations outside of the Middle East.[17] A 1,200-strong UAE force took part in peacekeeping operations in the French-controlled sector of Kosovo while another 250 Emirati troops, who included Special Forces with Apache helicopters, were stationed in the American sector. Speaking in 2000, the Chief of Staff of the UAE Armed Forces, the future Crown Prince of Abu Dhabi, Sheikh Mohammed bin Zayed, expanded upon the broader operational benefits of the UAE deployment in Kosovo:

> This mission also offers our troops real-life operational experience and the chance to operate closely and integrate with the best militaries in the world. You can't choose better than NATO. We are also operating in a different weather and terrain ... Compared to what we are learning and the experience we are receiving, this campaign is not costing too much.[18]

The military component of the UAE contribution to KFOR was augmented by a substantial humanitarian mission labelled *White Hands* that established camps in Albania that provided temporary refuge for more than 20,000 displaced Kosovans. The very first baby born in any Kosovar refugee camp was delivered by a female Emirati doctor and promptly named Fatema in honor of Sheikh Zayed's wife, the "Mother of the Nation," Sheikha Fatema bint Mubarak Al Ketbi.[19] This integration of "hard" and "soft" aspects of military and humanitarian support prefigured the deployment of similarly integrated forms of power in Afghanistan after 2001 and Libya in 2011, again alongside and as part of NATO-led operations.

UAE involvement in Afghanistan was analyzed in Chapter Five. During the final phase of the long deployment, from 2012 until 2014, six Emirati F-16s were stationed in Kandahar in support of the NATO-led security mission in Afghanistan, and the skill and professionalization of the Emirati pilots meant that the UAE was, along with Australia, the only non-NATO partner permitted to fly close air-support missions to protect NATO ground forces in Afghanistan. The fact that the Emirati F-16s deployed at a time when many of the actual NATO member states were in the process of withdrawing their own contingents from Afghanistan constituted an additional source of alliance goodwill toward the UAE.[20]

An Islamist Crackdown

Chapter Five examined in detail the growth of the Association for Reform and Guidance (*Jamiat al-Islah wa Tawjih*), an Emirati group inspired by the ideals of the Muslim Brotherhood but which claimed operational and ideological autonomy. Although *Al-Islah* was cautiously welcomed in the 1970s both in Dubai and (less visibly) in Abu Dhabi, its rising influence in the educational and judicial sectors led to the marginalization of members from key posts in the 1980s and the start of an organized security crackdown in 1994. Following the inconclusive meetings between *Al-Islah* leaders and the powerful soon-to-be Crown Prince of Abu Dhabi, Sheikh Mohammed bin Zayed, in August 2003, an uneasy stasis descended on the tense relationship between the organization and federal officials based in Abu Dhabi. This broke down decisively in 2010 as two developments – the death of *Al-Islah's* most influential patron and the evidence that members of the group were attempting to expand beyond the confines of Ras al-Khaimah and organize campaigns nationwide – occurred in the months immediately prior to the start of the Arab Spring unrest in North Africa in January 2011.

The death of the ruler of Ras al-Khaimah, Sheikh Saqr bin Mohammed Al Qasimi, on October 27, 2010 removed the protected space hitherto granted *Al-Islah* by the Ruler, who had granted his personal patronage to the group, chaired by his nephew, Sheikh Sultan bin Kayed Al Qasimi. Earlier chapters in this book have recounted how Sheikh Saqr's singular personality had, on numerous occasions dating back to the 1950s and 1960s, placed him at odds with his peers among the Supreme Council of Rulers. However, his age and seniority, and the fact that for the last six years of his life he was the last surviving Ruler from the founding of the federation, meant that Sheikh Saqr was accorded great respect while he was still alive, which gave *Al-Islah* breathing space. It was thus not for nothing that Ras al-Khaimah emerged as the hotbed of Islamist sympathy in the UAE, as one estimate put the membership of *Al-Islah* in the emirate as high as 20,000.[21]

Although the significance of Sheikh Saqr's death only became clear in retrospect, the fact that it took place less than three months before the onset of the Arab Spring removed a significant obstacle to the State Security's subsequent decision to dismantle the organization across the UAE.

Evidence also began to accumulate during 2010 that members of *Al-Islah* were attempting to break out of their long-held stronghold in Ras al-Khaimah and lay the foundations for a national campaign that would focus on social and political issues in the UAE. One member of *Al-Islah* made clear in May 2012 the moralizing nature of the group's activities:

We try to run events and projects, the focus is charity, family projects, edu-
cating children about life, trying to enhance the morality in them, any way we
can deliver our way of thinking to society.[22]

In addition to the abovementioned activities, a Public Relations Committee based
in Ras al-Khaimah attempted to coordinate the actions of members and sympathizers across the seven emirates and reach out to the broader Emirati community. At around the same time, moreover, members of *Al-Islah* began to get
involved in calls for political reform and agitate increasingly openly for a widening
of the democratic opening initiated in 2006. Thus, several members of the Public
Relations Committee were heavily involved in the preparation of a petition submitted to the UAE President, Sheikh Khalifa bin Zayed Al Nahyan, on March 3,
2011.[23] Signed by 133 Emirati individuals, including many members of *Al-Islah*,
the two articles in the petition called for the election of all members of the Federal
National Council (FNC) and for constitutional amendments to grant the FNC full
regulatory and supervisory powers. In addition, four professional associations –
representing Emirati jurists, teachers, university faculty, and national heritage professionals – known for their Islamist leanings were institutional signatories to the
petition.[24]

The UAE petition may have appeared moderate compared with the political
upheaval that toppled Presidents Ben Ali of Tunisia and Mubarak of Egypt and set
in motion the chain of events that led to the downfall and death of Colonel
Gaddafi in Libya and the ousting of President Saleh in Yemen. One of the signatories, a female Professor of Sociology at UAE University, explained to *Agence
France-Presse* that:

Alluding to the changes in the region is not meant as a threat. But there is an
aspiration to widen the margins of freedoms, as we have seen in some Arab
countries ... Every person wants to be part of the decision-making process.
This is a just demand. The world is moving forward. The FNC should reflect
people's aspirations.[25]

However, the content appeared to strike a raw nerve among the political and
security establishment in Abu Dhabi over concern that the petition "marked the first
time that liberal and Islamist opposition had come together in such a public political
undertaking."[26] The federal authorities responded by arresting five high-profile
advocates for reform, for "breaking laws and perpetrating acts that pose a threat to
state security, undermining the public order, opposing the government system, and
insulting the President." The detainees included Ahmed Mansour, a human rights
activist, and Nasser bin Ghaith, an economist associated with the Abu Dhabi
branch of the Sorbonne. Mansour had founded the www.uaehewar.net website in
August 2009 as a platform for the discussion of politics, development, and society
in the UAE and, in 2010, had stated that "It's because I care for my country that I
feel these issues need to be discussed."[27] Bin Ghaith, for his part, had criticized the

economic handouts being promised by Arab Rulers at the time as a tool for pre-empting calls for reform and claimed, just a week before his arrest, that such handouts "only delays change and reform, which will still come sooner or later.'[28]

After eight months of detention, the "UAE5," as the detainees became known as, were convicted of insulting the Rulers of the UAE before receiving a presidential pardon from Sheikh Khalifa the following day, which happened to be UAE national day.[29] Almost immediately, state security struck again, stripping six members of *Al-Islah* of their citizenship and arresting more than ninety people during 2012. The "UAE94" included men and women from all seven emirates (twenty-eight from Sharjah, twenty-four from Abu Dhabi, fourteen from Ras al-Khaimah, eleven from Dubai, eight from Ajman, five from Fujairah, three from Umm al-Quwain, and one of unknown background) and from some of the largest and most influential tribes in the UAE, including the al-Nuaimi, the al-Shamsi, and the al-Suweidi, in addition to Sultan bin Kayed Al Qasimi himself. One of the highest-profile of those arrested was Mohammed al-Roken, who had served as co-defense counsel for two of the "UAE5" in 2011. When another lawyer (Salim al-Shehhi) went to the State Security Prosecution office to represent al-Roken, he himself was detained in July 2012.[30] The authorities also disbanded the independent boards of the Jurist Association and the Teachers' Association, which had both been institutional signatories to the March 2011 petition, and replaced them with government appointees.[31]

In the intervening period between the majority of the arrests of suspected *Al-Islah* members in July 2012 and the start of their trial in March 2013, Emirati officials portrayed the UAE as standing on the frontline of a defensive campaign against the Muslim Brotherhood across the region. The charge against *Al-Islah* and other groups perceived to be linked to the Muslim Brotherhood was led by the outspoken Director-General of the Dubai Police Force, General Dhahi Khalfan Tamim. In March 2012 Tamim claimed (without providing supporting evidence) that the Brotherhood was planning to "take over" the Gulf monarchies: "My sources say the next step is to make Gulf governments figurehead bodies only without actual ruling. The start will be in Kuwait in 2013 and in other Gulf states in 2016."[32] Remarkably, Tamim also suggested, "they [the Muslim Brotherhood] are also secret soldiers for America and they are executing plans to create tension."[33] Later in 2012, after a rapid escalation of political demonstrations in Kuwait in October, the UAE foreign minister, Sheikh Abdullah bin Zayed Al Nahyan denounced the Brotherhood as "an organization which encroaches upon the sovereignty and integrity of nations" and called upon fellow ruling families in the Gulf to join a coordinated crackdown on the group.[34] In yet another interview in 2012, Tamim warned that "if the Muslim Brotherhood threatens the Gulf's security, the blood that will flow will drown them."[35] Tamim subsequently returned to the anti-Brotherhood theme in April 2013 when he labelled them "dictators" and added that "they want to change regimes that have been ruling for a long time, but they also want to rule forever ... We have evidence this group was planning to overthrow rulers in the Gulf region."[36]

As the trial of the UAE94 got underway in March 2013, an unnamed Abu Dhabi government official told the *Gulf States Newsletter* that "It's not that we don't like them, we are against them."[37] The trial itself lasted until July 2013 and resulted in the conviction of 69 of the 94 defendants after they were found guilty of attempting to overthrow the government, and were given jail sentences that ranged from seven to fifteen years without the right to appeal as the trial took place at the State Security Chamber of the Federal Supreme Court.[38] Later in 2013, a hard-hitting report on the trial produced by the International Commission of Jurists (ICJ) indicated a number of shortcomings in due process that led the ICJ to conclude that the proceedings "fell well below international fair trial standards." Compiled by a former Judge of the Supreme Court of Norway, Ketil Lund, the report added that:

> The ICJ is deeply concerned that the proceedings against all these individuals failed to meet internationally recognized standards of fairness. In particular, the ICJ considers that the rights of the accused were violated as a result of and following their arrest, and leading up to the trial … The ICJ believes that the sweeping charges against the accused were unlawful, in particular because they were brought to criminalise the legitimate exercise of fundamental human rights, including the rights to freedom of expression, association, and assembly, all of which are recognized and protected by the UAE Constitution and international human rights law.[39]

With the majority of the membership of *Al-Islah* either behind bars or forced into hiding abroad, many in Turkey or the United Kingdom, the question remains why the authorities, particularly in Abu Dhabi, reacted so strongly when there was virtually no prospect of any mass protest in the UAE. It would appear that the primary threat from *Al-Islah in* 2011 lay less in its political demands and more in its potential to draw upon narratives of economic distress and lack of opportunity that had proven such a potent tool of mass mobilization in Egypt, Tunisia, and elsewhere in the Arab Spring. This, in turn, reflected the differential in development between Abu Dhabi and Dubai, the two richest emirates which accounted for about 90 percent of the GDP of the UAE, and the five relatively "poorer" Northern Emirates; notably, GDP per capita was estimated to be about US $110,000 in Abu Dhabi and US$41,670 in Dubai in 2011, compared with figures of US$22,100 for Sharjah and US$21,897 for Ras al-Khaimah.[40] Infrastructure also lagged behind in several of the Northern Emirates, with a Federal National Council study in 2010 reportedly finding that 900 buildings and houses were lacking access to electricity and running water, and Sharjah and Fujairah were experiencing rolling blackouts and petrol shortages in the late 2000s. Unemployment, too, was perceived to be higher in several of the Northern Emirates, with rates of up to 20.6 percent in Fujairah and 16.2 percent in Ras al-Khaimah estimated by *Gulf States Newsletter* in 2011.[41] The *Gulf States Newsletter* went as far as to refer to the Northern Emirates as a "ticking time bomb" in 2011 as it editorialized that:

It is those in the north that have the least to lose by rocking the boat. Aside from the gap in living standards, there is a perceived discrimination against those from the Northern Emirates when it comes to federal government jobs or positions in the more prestigious government companies. It is difficult to ascertain whether such overt discrimination exists, or it is simply a fact that graduates from Abu Dhabi and Dubai are more qualified for these positions. But it does not help that the standard of education in the north lags behind.[42]

Such socio-economic differentials between several of the Northern Emirates and Abu Dhabi and Dubai therefore contained the potential for grievances that might quickly acquire political dimensions as they had done elsewhere in states and societies affected by the Arab Spring, particularly should they occur in regions far from the glitz, glamor, and aspiring "global city" status of Dubai and Abu Dhabi and among more conservative communities of Emirati nationals. It was in this vein that Lori Plotkin Boghardt, a researcher at the Washington Institute who has written extensively on *Al-Islah* in the UAE and the Muslim Brotherhood in the Gulf more widely, suggested, after the end of the trial in 2013, that official nervousness stemmed from "Disparities between the northern and southern emirates [which] provide a socio-economical background in which the religious-inspired message of *Al-Islah* for a more just society resonates as it relates to a sense of injustice felt in the north."[43]

In parallel, the crackdown on *Al-Islah* formed part of a broader squeezing of freedom of association and expression that led to the government takeover of local civil society groups and the closure of a number of regional branches of international organizations that had set up in the UAE. In 2011, the hitherto elected boards of the Jurist Association and the Teachers' Association were replaced by government appointees; both organizations had been institutional signatories to the aforementioned petition in support of limited political reforms in March.[44] Meanwhile, in March 2012, the Dubai office of the National Democratic Institute was closed down by the authorities while the Abu Dhabi branches of the Konrad Adenauer Foundation and the Gallup polling center were shut down the following day, while in December 2012, the Abu Dhabi authorities asked the RAND Corporation to close its office in the emirate.[45] Speaking at the time, the Assistant Foreign Minister for Legal Affairs, Abdul Rahim al-Awadhi, attributed the spate of closures to the fact that:

> some foreign institutions that had been operating in the UAE have violated the terms of the license; some have been operating without a license. This obliged the legal authorities to issue instructions that they should cease their work in the UAE.[46]

Representatives of the institutions affected countered the claim that they had been operating without the proper licensing and a spokesperson for the Konrad Adenauer Foundation stated robustly that "We react with utter disbelief to the unexpected and completely sudden developments in Abu Dhabi" while Hans-Gert Poettering, the head of the Adenauer Foundation, lamented the closure as "an alarming signal if nongovernmental organizations and political foundations are not welcome in the Arab world."[47] Other casualties of the growing limitations on open inquiry included the Gulf Research Center, a region-leading think tank that had been based in Dubai since 2001 until it failed to secure a renewal of its operating license in 2012, the Regional Office of the US State Department's Middle East Partnership Initiative (MEPI), which was closed upon the request of the UAE government, and many Western academics based at Emirati universities who found it increasingly difficult to conduct independent research in the years after 2012 and moved on as a result.[48]

Influencing Transitions in North Africa

The previous section noted how the political upheaval of the Arab Spring resonated sharply within the UAE itself as the political and security authorities reacted firmly to contain and defeat any potential Islamist mobilization within the federation. Just as domestic security policy became more expansive in scope and less tolerant of any form of dissent lest it escalate, so too did policy toward the unfolding political transitions in states affected by the Arab Spring in North Africa in 2011. In a speech (given with the benefit of three years' hindsight "after the fact") in March 2014, Anwar Gargash, the Minister of State for Foreign Affairs, laid out the thinking at the heart of the UAE's hawkish approach to regional affairs. Beginning with the notion that "Arab affairs should be settled within the framework of the Arab world," Gargash suggested that:

> There is a very rapidly changing status quo in the region characterized by political instability and violent extremism, and we have seen it since the Arab Spring started in 2011. This added more risks in an already risky environment … There are many regional challenges so we should have the potential to face these threats … we have to start with our own self-power and potential.[49]

A regional "rivalry" between the UAE and Qatar also took root as officials in Doha and Abu Dhabi competed for influence and supported very different groups in the post-transition political reordering. This was most immediately apparent in Libya, where both the UAE and Qatar provided critical Arab support to the NATO-led military intervention that culminated in the toppling of the mercurial forty-two-year dictatorship of Colonel Gaddafi in August 2011. In Egypt, the turbulent period of post-Mubarak politics presented policymakers in the UAE with an initial challenge in the form of a Muslim Brotherhood government in Cairo backed heavily by Qatar. Once, however, the presidency of Mohammed Morsi was ousted by a military coup led by General Abdel-Fatah al-Sisi in July 2013, the UAE responded quickly to mobilize large amounts of political and financial support that far exceeded Qatar's support to the Morsi government.

The maelstrom of post-transition politics in Libya and Egypt therefore provides case studies of the Gulf States' emergence as assertive regional powers. Their growth as visible participants in regional and even international politics predated the Arab Spring but accelerated and acquired a potent new dimension once the initial shock of the 2011 upheaval had subsided. Led by the UAE and Qatar, GCC states took the lead in responding to the initially wide-ranging political and economic challenges triggered by the Arab Spring. The scope and scale of Emirati and Qatari assistance to Egypt provides a clear example of the practical and policy implications of this process in action, but highlights also how Gulf actors were far from impartial actors in picking sides and choosing how and to whom to provide aid. Gulf support differed significantly from more conventional forms of international aid by being linked indelibly to particular political *currents* rather than being tied to institutional *outcomes* such as reforms to governance or improvements in transparency. The years after the Arab Spring thus saw the Gulf States align their *growing capabilities* (in the political, economic, and security arenas) with a far more expansive *policy intent*.

Libya's uprising began in Benghazi on February 15, 2011 just four days after the fall of President Hosni Mubarak sent shockwaves throughout the Middle East and North Africa. Libya's second city and a large swathe of eastern Libya quickly fell into the hands of opposition fighters and a number of military units defected to the rebel movement. In the febrile atmosphere of the early days of the Arab upheaval, the rapid spread of the uprising across Libya seemed to confirm the contagious nature of the regional outpouring of rage against authoritarian misrule. However, by late February 2011, the ragtag groups of rebels were meeting fierce resistance from government security forces. Global condemnation of the regime's attempts to put down the rebellion escalated sharply as Gaddafi became the international pariah he had been prior to his renouncing of weapons of mass destruction in 2003. By mid-March, reports that the regime was on the verge of retaking Benghazi led to urgent calls by sections of the international community for intervention to forestall a possible massacre of the city's civilian population.[50]

Along with their counterparts in Qatar, officials in the UAE were instrumental in rallying the international community to action against Gaddafi and in securing Arab support for what otherwise might have seemed another example of a Western intervention in the region. Swiss academic Jean-Marc Rickli observed the Emirati intervention in Libya from the vantage point of a post at the Institute for International and Civil Security at Khalifa University in Abu Dhabi, and argued that "the UAE's contribution to NATO's *Operation Unified Protector* and its wider role in Libya should be seen as an attempt to maintain the regional stability of the Gulf while at the same time shaping perceptions as a reliable partner with NATO."[51] In addition, Rickli observed, persuasively, that:

> the fall of Mubarak in Egypt was a wake-up call for the Gulf monarchies that traditional Western support could no longer be taken for granted and that more efforts would have to be invested in managing their strategic alliances

while at the same time taking care of their own security. Thus, when the Western states needed help to gather an international coalition to oust Gaddafi … participating in the operation to show solidarity was a unique opportunity that the UAE was a reliable partner.[52]

Furthermore, Rickli – who moved from the UAE to a post based at Qatar's Joint Command Staff College in Doha in 2013 – suggested that the budding rivalry between the UAE and Qatar – which grew exponentially between 2011 and 2013 – added another dimension to the UAE's decision to join *Operation Unified Protector*:

> The fact that Qatar decided to contribute half of its twelve military aircraft to the operation very likely put pressure on the UAE to reciprocate. Indeed, the UAE, with more than 130 F-16s and Mirage 2000 jets had to surpass, at least in absolute terms, Qatar's contribution.[53]

Participation in the NATO-led operations also gave the UAE increased leverage over the (re)shaping of Western policy toward the Arab Spring once the initial shock of the Arab Spring wore off. Along with their Qatari counterparts, officials in the UAE were all too aware of the value of their support for the Libya intervention in terms of mobilizing the support of Arab partners for what otherwise might appear as another Western military intervention in the region. Aside from ensuring a seat at the table alongside NATO partners, Emirati policymakers reportedly leveraged their involvement in the coalition to influence the US position toward the uprising in Bahrain. Thus, after US Secretary of State Hillary Rodham Clinton delivered a speech in Paris in March 2011 that criticized the decision of the GCC to dispatch the Peninsula Shield Force to Bahrain, the *New York Times* reported that "The Emiratis promptly threatened to withdraw from the coalition then being assembled to support a NATO-led strike" in Libya and "quickly named their price for staying on board … Mrs. Clinton must issue a statement that would pull back from any criticism of the Bahrain operation."[54]

Both the UAE and Qatar therefore found themselves in the unusual positions of having intervened, within the space of five days in March 2011, in support of a government attempting to restore order (in Bahrain) and on the side of an opposition movement to an authoritarian regime (in Libya). The two cases of Bahrain (on March 14) and Libya (on March 19) illustrated how an ostensibly overarching concept of "intervention" could take on very different meanings in diverging contexts. The UAE contributed about 500 police to the Peninsula Shield Force, which consisted also of 1,000 soldiers from the Saudi Arabian National Guard (SANG), a small detachment of Qatari troops, and a naval contingent from Kuwait. Foreign Minister Sheikh Abdullah bin Zayed confirmed, at the time, that the UAE was acting at the behest of the Bahraini government, which "asked us to look at ways to help them to defuse tension in Bahrain," while Gargash, the Minister of State for Foreign Affairs, added that "The security and stability in the region requires all of us to stand united in one rank so as to safeguard our national gains and prevent any strife for a better future."[55]

In the subsequent seven-month campaign of airstrikes over Libya that ended with the ousting of Colonel Gaddafi from Tripoli in August 2011 and his grizzly death in October, the twelve fighter jets provided by the UAE constituted the largest Arab contribution to the NATO-led airstrikes. UAE participation reinforced the sense of partnership with NATO that had developed in Kosovo and Afghanistan and coincided with the naming of the abovementioned UAE Ambassador to NATO in May 2011. The deployment of UAE fighter jets provided an opportunity for Emirati pilots to gain additional operational and combat experience and reinforced the already close security and defense relationship between the UAE and the United States, with General Martin Dempsey, the Chairman of the Joint Chiefs of Staff between 2011 and 2015, commenting that "the United Arab Emirates is amongst our most credible and capable allies, especially in the Gulf region."[56]

In addition to direct military involvement in the NATO-led coalition, Abu Dhabi (in particular) extended significant logistical and material support to the Libyan rebels that coalesced around the National Transitional Council (NTC) during the spring of 2011. The emirate hosted meetings of Libyan provincial and tribal representatives in May and the third meeting of the International Contact Group in June. UAE Foreign Minister Sheikh Abdullah bin Zayed quickly announced plans to visit Benghazi to see how his country could assist the reconstruction effort while UAE charities provided humanitarian relief and essential food and medical supplies to thousands of displaced Libyans along the country's border with Tunisia.[57] Meanwhile, the Interim Prime Minister of post-revolutionary Libya, Abdurrahim El-Keib, appointed in early November 2011, days after Gaddafi's death, had been resident in the UAE since 1999, initially as a Professor at the American University of Sharjah and subsequently, since 2006, as Departmental Chair in the Petroleum Institute in Abu Dhabi. El-Keib's appointment as Prime Minister (until November 2012) cemented further the links between the UAE and the emerging contours of the post-Gaddafi transition.[58]

Like Qatar, the UAE differed from NATO and other non-NATO members of the coalition (such as Norway and Sweden) in that they not only took part in the campaign of airstrikes but also actively backed groups of militias on the ground in Libya. Moreover, the seeds of the discord that would divide post-Gaddafi Libya between Islamist and "nationalist" anti-Islamist militias (with hundreds of often-competing militias complicating this broad split) were laid from the very beginning as Qatar and the UAE channeled support to different groups of Libyan fighters in 2011. Thus, Qatar developed close links with key Islamist militia commanders such as Abdelhakim Belhadj, once the head of the Libyan Islamic Fighting Group and, in 2011, the commander of the Tripoli Brigade, and Ismael al-Salabi, the leader of one of the best-supplied rebel militias, the Rafallah al-Sahati Companies. Qatar was widely suspected of arming and funding al-Salabi's group, whose sudden munificence of resources in 2011 earned it the nickname of the "Ferrari 17 Brigade."[59]

In contrast to Qatar, the UAE chose to support an array of "more tribal-oriented and regional militias, particularly those from the conservative western mountain town of Zintan."[60] Both the UAE and Qatar assisted their local proxies through the deployment of several dozen Special Forces each and the transfer of equipment, with the UAE concentrating on Zawiya in northwestern Libya and the Qataris operating in and around Benghazi in the east.[61] The UAE also constructed an air-strip to support humanitarian missions in Libya and, beginning in the summer of 2011, "allowed the NTC to use the airstrip to operate their own air service in order to sustain the economy."[62] Special forces from the UAE (and Qatar) both assisted in the rebel advance on Tripoli in August 2011 although it was the Qatari flag that flew subsequently over Gaddafi's captured Bab al-Azizia compound and which came to symbolize the high watermark of Qatari influence in Libya.[63] This notwithstanding, a report on the NATO-led campaign issued by the Royal United Services Institute (RUSI) in London in September 2011 applauded the role of the UAE Special Forces in Libya and noted that they had benefited from the years of operational experience in working alongside NATO forces in Afghanistan.[64]

Whereas Qatar's influence in Libya peaked in late 2011 and declined rapidly thereafter (to the point where the political party established by Belhadj to contest the July 2012 constituent assembly won only one seat), the UAE continued to play a powerful, if shadowy, behind-the-scenes role in the fractured and difficult reor-dering of the post-Gaddafi political and security landscape. Several of the key figures in the Libyan uprising and the initial formation of the NTC relocated to the UAE and remained in close contact with Emirati policymakers as militia infighting tore Libya apart. Among them was Mahmoud Jibril, the leader of the NTC during the critical months of the uprising from March to October 2011 before being suc-ceeded by the aforementioned UAE-based El-Keib. Close ties also developed with Abdel Majid Mlegta, a senior figure in Jibril's National Forces Alliance (NFA) and the brother of Othman Mlegta, the leader of one of the Zintani militias (the Qaaqaa Brigade) that was said to have "paraded hardware, including armored per-sonnel carriers manufactured in the UAE, on the streets of Tripoli."[65] However, the most consequential – and controversial – link that emerged in the aftermath of the 2011 revolution in Libya was with Khalifa Haftar, a General (often referred to as a "renegade general" in international media) in the Libyan Armed Forces who had taken part in the 1969 coup that bought Gaddafi to power but who subse-quently had fallen out with the regime and resettled in the United States in the early 1990s. Although Haftar returned to Libya during the 2011 uprising he did not initially hold a top-ranking position in the armed forces and remained in rela-tive obscurity until he re-emerged in February 2014 as the leader of a powerful anti-Islamist faction pitted against the Islamist-dominated General National Con-gress (GNC). Described in a *New Yorker* profile as having "fought with and against nearly every significant faction in the country's conflicts, leading to a reputation for unrivalled military experience and for a highly flexible sense of personal alle-giance," Haftar built up a network of political and military support and launched

Operation Dignity in May 2014 with attacks on Islamist militias in Benghazi and the occupation of the parliament building in Tripoli.[66]

Operation Dignity was the prelude to the de facto division of Libya into western and eastern spheres of influence based loosely around the GNC in Tripoli and the non-Islamist House of Representatives (HoR) in the eastern city of Tobruk, near the border with Egypt. During the summer of 2014, battles raged as the Islamist factions in Libya launched rival militia operations, named *Libya Dawn*, and took control of Tripoli in August. In its specific targeting of local Islamist groups, *Operation Dignity* resembled the UAE's aforementioned crackdown on domestic Islamists in 2012; Haftar's own chief of staff in Libya described the Muslim Brotherhood as "snakes in smooth skin" and stated that "We had no intention of fighting our brother revolutionaries, but they joined these terrorists, so we had no choice."[67] Parallel power structures also emerged that amplified and solidified Libya's division into competing spheres of influence. Whereas the Libyan Supreme Court ruled that the GNC was the national legislature, the HoR secured United Nations and international recognition as the legitimate government of Libya while a third group, a constituent assembly based in the town of Beyda, worked to bring the factions together and draft a new constitution. In 2015, a series of fraught political negotiations began as the United Nations appointed a Spanish mediator, Bernardino Léon, to search for an acceptable form of power-sharing and government of national unity.[68]

UAE interests were projected at several key points in the military and political tracks described above. Two airstrikes in August 2014 that targeted Islamist militias in and around Tripoli were traced by US policymakers to Emirati jets operating from bases in Egypt and created friction with elements of the Obama administration who had neither been consulted beforehand nor approved of such unilateral military action in Libya.[69] Leaked email correspondence in 2015 then appeared to suggest that the UAE was violating an international arms embargo imposed by the United Nations on supplying arms to militia groups in Libya (in addition to violating international missile control agreements by allegedly supplying unmanned aerial vehicles manufactured by Abu Dhabi-based Adcom to Egypt).[70] Also controversial was the revelation, again in 2015, that the UN-appointed mediator, Bernardino Léon, had in fact been in undisclosed negotiations to become the inaugural Director-General of the newly formed Emirates Diplomatic Academy and had on several occasions coordinated his supposedly impartial mediation with senior foreign ministry officials in Abu Dhabi.[71]

Speaking in November 2014, more than three years after the NATO-led intervention, the Foreign Minister, Sheikh Abdullah bin Zayed, provided an illustrative insight into the UAE perspective on the difficult trajectory of post-intervention policy in Libya in an interview with *Fox News*:

> We believe especially the countries who played a role in getting rid of Gaddafi, first of all, should have played a far bigger role the day after. They haven't … I don't want to mention one country or the other, but the entire coalition had a bigger responsibility, which it unfortunately didn't live up to.[72]

Such assertiveness in regional policymaking also characterized Emirati approaches toward the tumultuous changes in Egyptian politics in the years after the toppling of President Hosni Mubarak in February 2011. Along with Saudi Arabia, UAE officials opted for regime-type continuity and backed the Egyptian military leadership – initially in the form of the Supreme Council of the Armed Forces (SCAF) and subsequently in the person of General (later President) Abdel Fattah El-Sisi – in a bid to limit the impact of rapid and unexpected political change. Just as in Libya, this stance contrasted with the nearly diametrically opposite position taken by Qatar, which threw its backing behind the Muslim Brotherhood in Egypt as it won first the parliamentary elections at the end of 2011 and then secured a narrow victory in the presidential election in June 2012. Indeed, Mohammed Morsi's slim triumph over Mubarak's final Prime Minister, Ahmed Shafiq, symbolized the clash not only between the Brotherhood and the old regime but also between the Qatar- and UAE-backed sides as Shafiq promptly moved to Dubai after his defeat.[73]

Soon after the ousting of Mubarak, the UAE pledged US$3.3 billion in aid for Egypt, although it is unclear whether any or how much of that was actually delivered before it was put on hold after the Muslim Brotherhood won the presidency in 2012. Saudi Arabia similarly had offered financial assistance to the military-led interim between February 2011 and June 2012 in the shape of a US$750 million line of credit to import oil products and US$430 million in project aid from the Saudi Fund for Development.[74] As relations between Abu Dhabi and Riyadh and the new Muslim Brotherhood government in Cairo cooled rapidly it was perhaps inevitable that Qatar emerged as the largest and most important external supporter of President Morsi. Qatar is believed to have transferred more than US$7 billion in emergency loans and direct financial aid to Egypt during the year-long Morsi presidency and provided further support through the supply of five cargoes of Liquefied Natural Gas (LNG) to plug shortfalls in domestic power generation.[75] Qatar's "influence" in Egypt arguably peaked in September 2012 when Qatari Prime Minister Sheikh Hamad bin Jassim Al Thani visited Cairo and pledged that Qatar would invest US$18 billion in Egypt over the next five years. Commenting that there would be "no limits" to Qatar's support for the Muslim Brotherhood government struggling to find conventional funds to balance Egypt's budget, "HBJ" (who was also Qatar's Foreign Minister and head of the country's sovereign wealth fund, the Qatar Investment Authority) stated that $8 billion would be invested in an integrated power plant, natural gas, and iron steel project in Port Said, while the remaining $10 billion would finance the construction of a tourism marina complex on the Mediterranean coastline. However, the announcement was noticeably lacking in details of how the funds would be disbursed and the funds ultimately never materialized.[76]

Relations between the UAE and Egypt under the Muslim Brotherhood inevitably were impacted by the domestic crackdown in 2012 on Islamists in the UAE who were perceived by security officials in Abu Dhabi to be linked to the broader Muslim Brotherhood movement. Mention also has been made of UAE Foreign

Minister Abdullah bin Zayed's October 2012 description of the Brotherhood as "an organization which encroaches upon the sovereignty and integrity of nations."[77] Emirati officials then arrested eleven Egyptians on January 1, 2013 suspected of being members of a Muslim Brotherhood cell and conspiring with counterparts in Egypt to destabilize the UAE. *Al Khaleej*, the Emirati newspaper which reported the arrests, claimed that the cell had been in "continuous coordination" with the Egyptian Muslim Brotherhood, prompting a diplomatic spat after a Brotherhood spokesperson in Cairo accused key policymakers in Abu Dhabi and Dubai of a "conspiracy" against the organization.[78] A document prepared in Saudi Arabia and released by WikiLeaks added that Emirati officials believed that the Muslim Brotherhood additionally "founded companies to illegally transfer funds to the mother organization in Egypt and were trained by local Islamists on how to overthrow the government."[79]

The sudden removal of President Morsi and the return of military-led rule to Egypt in July 2013 brought the Arab Spring full circle. Just as Mubarak's ousting in 2011 had sent shockwaves through embattled regimes throughout the Middle East and North Africa, so the re-imposition of military rule reflected a trend of greater political authoritarianism across the region. While Egypt again found itself under temporary military rule, just as it had done in February 2011, the regional context in July 2013 was very different. With no consensual political order emerging and instability worsening in the transition states of Tunisia, Egypt, Libya, and Yemen (to say nothing of Syria), the contagious revolutionary fervor that swept the Arab world in 2011 had all but disappeared by 2013. It was replaced by the reassertion of authoritarianism and the eclipse of political Islamism, and underpinned by substantial political and financial support from Qatar's Gulf neighbors, particularly the UAE and Saudi Arabia, to Egypt's new "strongman."

The speed with which Qatar's GCC neighbors backed the restoration of military rule in Egypt with direct budgetary support, shipments of fuel products, and large amounts of bilateral aid spoke volumes. With the toppling of the Muslim Brotherhood government in Cairo effectively signaling the end of the Arab Spring, at least in its initial post-2011 phase, the UAE, along with Saudi Arabia and, to a lesser extent, Kuwait rapidly stepped in to seize the regional initiative away from Qatar and offer immediate and large-scale pledges of assistance to Egypt. Over US $12 billion was promised in the week after the coup alone, and was quickly disbursed, unlike many pledges of GCC aid in other circumstances. By late October 2013, the UAE, in particular, had assembled a comprehensive economic package totaling US$4.9 billion, consisting of a US$1 billion grant transferred to the Egyptian government in July, US$1 billion in petroleum products to help meet Egypt's fuel and hydrocarbon needs, and US$2.9 billion in aid for development and infrastructure projects designed to revive Egypt's ailing economy.[80]

By the time that Emirati policymakers took the lead in early 2015 with a major international investment conference (the Egypt Economic Development Conference), the UAE had provided more than US$14 billion in aid to Egypt, which constituted by far the largest share of the more than US$20 billion in financial support from the three Gulf States of the UAE, Saudi Arabia, and Kuwait.[81] Officials from the UAE reportedly played an important role in assisting their Egyptian counterparts in devising and implementing economic reforms and in putting together packages of investment from major Emirati public and state-owned enterprises.[82] Initiatives announced in 2014 and 2015 included a massive housing project worth up to US$40 billion agreed between Dubai-based construction firm Arabtec and the Egyptian army in March 2014,[83] as well as lead UAE participation in the expansive "Capital Cairo" project to build a new administrative capital for Egypt that was unveiled a year later in March 2015. Launched after a meeting between the Ruler of Dubai (and Prime Minister of the UAE), Sheikh Mohammed bin Rashid Al Maktoum, and President Sisi, the initiative aimed to generate up to 1.5 million new jobs.[84] Construction of the city was entrusted to Capital City Partners, a private real estate investment fund led by Mohamed Alabbar, the influential chairman of the Emaar Group in Dubai whose proximity to the Ruler of Dubai was noted in Chapter Four. Other significant UAE-based entities that also made large-scale pledges of investment in Egypt included Sharjah-based Dana Gas and Dubai retail conglomerate Majid al-Futtaim.[85]

Although the UAE became the closest geostrategic supporter of Egypt under the Sisi regime, which also cracked down heavily on the Muslim Brotherhood following the 2013 toppling of Morsi, the relationship was not entirely free of tension. Senior Emirati policymakers began in 2016 to express frustration at the slow pace of economic reform under President Sisi while the two largest UAE-financed projects listed above both ran into difficulties which became more acute as oil prices fell sharply. In September 2015, Egypt's Housing Minister indicated that the US$40 billion housing project involving Arabtec had been scaled back to just 10 percent of its original size, as Arabtec itself struggled with heavy losses and "legacy issues" that arose after a sudden change of leadership.[86] The Capital Cairo project also struggled to raise financing and encountered significant complications that resulted in bureaucratic delays to the project within months of its unveiling and a lack of any meaningful progress at the time of this writing in mid-2016.[87]

The examples of Libya and Egypt highlighted and arguably magnified the sharp distinction between Emirati and Qatari approaches toward the Arab Spring. The transitions unleashed in states that experienced regime change in 2011 amplified and widened the differences between the two countries and projected them onto the regional stage. Previous chapters in this book have illustrated how a form of 'rivalry' arose as Doha competed increasingly with Dubai and Abu Dhabi in a number of economic sectors in the 2000s and early 2010s. This manifested itself in the plethora of attempts to become the regional "hub" in areas such as finance, infrastructure, and aviation, and home to a bigger and more connected financial center, port, or airport and airline, but the competition remained primarily commercial in nature and was mitigated by the different business strategies that meant that each of the three "hubs" did not compete directly for the same slice of market share. However, tensions between the UAE and Qatar spiraled and became more visceral in tone after 2011 once the scale of Qatar's apparent sympathy, even support, for the Muslim Brotherhood in Egypt and elsewhere in North Africa (and Syria) became clear.[88]

An increasingly acrimonious "war of words" between the UAE and Qatar began in April 2012 when the Qatar-based Egyptian spiritual figurehead of the Muslim Brotherhood, Yusuf al-Qaradawi, criticized the UAE on his weekly Sharia and Life program on Al Jazeera, saying that "the Emiratis are humans like us, if they think they are superior, they are wrong … They do not have rule over people more powerful than the others."[89] These comments enraged Dubai's Chief of Police, Dhahi Khalfan Tamim, and prompted a diplomatic rift between the UAE and his Qatari hosts. Khalfan Tamim responded by issuing an arrest warrant for Qaradawi, whereupon the spokesperson for the Muslim Brotherhood in Egypt warned the UAE that the whole Muslim world would rise in Qaradawi's defense if the warrant was ever carried out. Tempers flared to the point where both the Secretary-General of the GCC and the head of the Arab League had to issue statements calling upon all sides to exercise prudence and avoid making irresponsible and rash statements. As the argument threatened to escalate into an inter-state dispute between Egypt and the UAE with Qatar caught in the middle, Al Jazeera made an editorial intervention, removing Qaradawi's inflammatory remarks from repeat screenings of the show.[90]

Emirati–Qatari tensions nonetheless continued to escalate in the first half of 2013 as it emerged that several Emirati members of *Al-Islah* who escaped the domestic crackdown on the group in 2012 sought refuge and even, in some cases, employment in Qatar. By May 2013, relations had deteriorated to the point that *Gulf States Newsletter* reported how "Qataris close to the tight ruling circle have even been talking about UAE spy cells supposedly busted this year (implying the possibility of UAE attempts to engineer a coup) and the UAE and Qatar have detained each other's nationals."[91] The following month, the two architects of Qatar's controversial Arab Spring policies – Emir Hamad bin Khalifa Al Thani and Prime Minister/Foreign Minister Sheikh Hamad bin Jassim Al Thani – both stepped down, with Emir Hamad handing over power to his thirty-three-year-old son, Sheikh Tamim bin Hamad Al Thani. In his early statements on foreign policy, Emir Tamim sought to rebuild bridges and reassure skeptical Gulf allies that Qatar intended to replace the confrontational unilateralism of its 2011–2013 foreign policy with a more cooperative and multilateral and far less ideological approach.[92]

Early hopes that Emir Tamim's accession would signal an immediate change in Qatar's approach to regional and foreign policy proved misplaced. The new Qatari government found that it could not sweep away all the vestiges and supporters of its former leadership overnight. Emirati (and Saudi) policymakers kept up the pressure on Doha as evidence mounted that individuals in Qatar were continuing to extend assistance to members of the Muslim Brotherhood who had managed to escape Egypt following the toppling of Morsi and the government crackdowns that followed. Typical of such concerns was a report in the *Washington Post* in early November 2013 that "an exile leadership is starting to take shape here among the shimmering high-rises of Doha." The *Post* alleged that several of the Brotherhood exiles were being accommodated at Al Jazeera's expenses in Doha hotels, and added that "it is in those suites and hotel lobbies that the future of Egypt's Muslim Brotherhood and, more broadly, the strategy and ideology of political Islam in the country may well be charted."[93]

With Saudi Arabia during the final years of King Abdullah's reign adopting a harsher approach toward the Muslim Brotherhood, which resembled that of the UAE and which led to both countries designating the group a terrorist organization in 2014, it was unsurprising that King Abdullah "summoned" Emir Tamim to a hastily arranged meeting in Riyadh later that month, along with the Emir of Kuwait, Sheikh Sabah al-Ahmad Al Sabah, who sought to mediate between the two. During the meeting, the Dubai-based *Gulf News* newspaper indicated that Emir Tamim was "told to change Qatar's ways and bring the country in line with the rest of the GCC with regards to regional issues." Moreover, *Gulf News* suggested that Emir Tamim had signed a GCC security agreement that stipulated "non-interference" in the "internal affairs of any of the other GCC countries" as well as a pledge of compliance, and had requested six months in which to do so, citing the need to clear away "obstacles from remnants of the previous regime."[94]

The worsening relations between the UAE and Qatar came to a head in March 2014 when the UAE joined Saudi Arabia and Bahrain in withdrawing their Ambassadors from Doha. Although Saudi Arabia previously had withdrawn its Ambassador from Doha in 2002 (for five years) and Bahrain had taken twenty-six years to establish full diplomatic ties with Qatar after both countries' independence in 1971, the collective move by three GCC states against a fellow member was unprecedented. The withdrawal of the three Ambassadors was taken in the name of "security and stability" as Emirati and Saudi leaders judged that Emir Tamim was not in full compliance with the security agreement reached at the November meeting in Riyadh. The withdrawal of the Ambassadors formed the prelude to months of negotiation (again mediated by Kuwait) and a number of concessions by Qatar, among which were the enforcement of the GCC Internal Security Pact (a separate agreement made by GCC Interior Ministers in November 2012 and endorsed by GCC rulers at their annual Summit in Bahrain in December 2012) and far greater cooperation with other GCC states on matters of intelligence and policing, which included the removal from Qatar of the Emirati members of *Al-Islah* who had sought refuge in Doha in 2012–2013.[95]

Emirati officials continued to pressure their Qatari counterparts throughout the eight months until the restoration of full diplomatic relations in November 2014. A media campaign targeting international print and broadcast media and portraying Qatar as the "weak point" in the new "war on terror" against the so-called Islamic State of Iraq and al-Shams (ISIS) was traced to public relations firms in London and Washington, DC acting on behalf of UAE interests. Thirty-four articles appeared in one publication (the London-based *Daily Telegraph*) alone during a two-month period in the autumn of 2014, while in Washington, DC, public disclosure filings by a lobbying firm retained by an Abu Dhabi–based entity "showed a pattern of conversations with journalists who subsequently wrote articles critical of Qatar's role in terrorist funding."[96] Along with Bahrain, the UAE also withdrew its national men's handball team from participation in the World Championship that was set to take place in Doha in January 2015.[97]

The bitter Gulf dispute was only resolved in November 2014 at a meeting of Gulf leaders in Riyadh – which included both the Crown Prince of Abu Dhabi, Sheikh Mohammed bin Zayed Al Nahyan and the Ruler of Dubai and Prime Minister of the UAE, Sheikh Mohammed bin Rashid Al Maktoum – after Qatar relocated Muslim Brotherhood figures to Turkey and closed down the controversial pro-Brotherhood Egyptian television affiliate of Al Jazeera, Al Jazeera Mubasher Misr.[98] The "rapprochement" with Qatar was followed immediately by requests from the Emirati and Bahraini Handball Federations to rescind their withdrawals from the Handball World Championship in Doha.[99] However, the International Handball Federation ruled that the original withdrawals could not be reversed, replaced the UAE and Bahrain with Saudi Arabia and Iceland, and fined each federation 100,000 Swiss Francs.[100]

Interventionism in Practice: ISIS and Yemen

Two significant new threats to regional security and stability emerged in 2014 and prompted the UAE into the direct and – in the case of Yemen – unprecedented application of the use of military force. The challenges posed by the Islamic State of Iraq and al-Shams (ISIS) and the advance of Houthi "rebels" in Yemen took place against the backdrop of a greater questioning of US motivations and policy objectives in the Middle East and the Gulf. This began in 2011 with the withdrawal of US support for Egyptian President Mubarak at the start of the Arab Spring and continued with (muted) American criticism over the security response to the uprising in Bahrain as the Al Khalifa ruling family restored order with GCC support. Senior officials in each of the six Gulf States, including the UAE, questioned, in the words of Abdulaziz Sager, the Saudi head of the longtime Dubai-based Gulf Research Center:

> whether, after such a long period of close relations, the US still perceives a vital interest in the stability of the Gulf region as in the past … even if there are statements from Washington underscoring its continued commitment, it is not clear whether the GCC states can continue to rely on US policy to not only protect the region but to also move it toward a more stable future. Instead, the prevailing mood appears to be that the terms are beginning to change to such a degree that the GCC states have no choice but to act on their own and without consideration of US interests and concerns.[101]

Many officials in the Gulf also took the so-called "pivot to Asia" said to be favored by the Obama administration to imply tacit US abandonment of their interests even as the US outreach to Iran that began in 2013 and led to the landmark nuclear agreement of July 2015 merely reinforced such perceptions. Furthermore, an in-depth March 2016 profile of the "Obama Doctrine" in *The Atlantic* magazine elicited a furious response among Gulf leaders at the President's disparaging reference to "free-riders," which many in the Gulf felt was aimed primarily at them.[102]

In March 2014, an article in *Foreign Policy* by the well-connected UAE Ambassador to the United States, Yousef al-Otaiba, summarized the tenets of the Emirati perspective on the changing geopolitical priorities of the Obama administration. Al-Otaiba noted that "a strong partnership is essential" and pledged that "in meeting shared threats, we will share the burden" as "the United States should know that we are eager and willing to contribute to our collective security interests," which al-Otaiba listed as encompassing:

> cooperating on an economic stabilization plan for Egypt, shutting down money flows to the extremist opposition in Syria, building governance capacity in Libya, and joint planning for the "day after" the Iran talks conclude – deal or no deal.[103]

Tellingly, however, al-Otaiba gently admonished the aloof style of the Obama administration's stance toward the Gulf – which fell arguably on deaf ears – as he called for better and more regular communication and reminded the *Foreign Policy* readership that "relationships in the Middle East are built on personal contact, and maintaining a candid and vibrant dialogue with regular leader-to-leader contact is essential."[104] However, a visit to Abu Dhabi in early April 2016 – during the fallout from Obama's "free-rider" comments – by Hussein Ibish of the (UAE-funded) Arab Gulf States Institute in Washington (AGSIW) indicated how the mood among officials and policymakers in the UAE had continued to deteriorate since al-Otaiba's 2014 call:

> My visit to the UAE last week strongly reinforced for me that negative misperceptions about Gulf relations with the United States, which in fact remain very strong, are deeply felt and widespread. The sources and context of friction in the relationship are no mystery, especially persistent questions about the Obama administration's intentions behind the nuclear agreement with Iran. More surprising was the extent to which these anxieties have become so entrenched they actually resist reassurances and evidence to the contrary.[105]

The irruption of ISIS onto the regional security landscape in 2014 posed a number of critical new threats to the UAE and other GCC states, particularly Saudi Arabia but also Bahrain and Kuwait, as policymakers confronted a virulent new non-state threat, nearly a decade after Al Qaeda in the Arabian Peninsula (AQAP) was defeated and banished to Yemen. Whereas AQAP had operated almost exclusively in Saudi Arabia and targeted specifically Western interests in the Kingdom, ISIS focused instead on ruthless territorial consolidation in, and resource extraction from, the areas under its control in Iraq and Syria. Amid evidence of flows of recruits and networks of financing for ISIS from within Gulf societies, a series of opportunistic "lone wolf" attacks and organized mass-casualty bombings in 2014 and 2015 indicated that ISIS cells possessed both the capability and the intent to undertake terrorist attacks and self-radicalize followers inside GCC states.[106]

A series of "copycat" attacks in Saudi Arabia and one in Abu Dhabi in late 2014 suggested initially that the ISIS threat arose primarily from "lone wolf" operations and "copycat" attacks. Two shootings involving American employees of defense contractor Vinnell left one dead and another wounded in Riyadh in November 2014 while two more employees were wounded in the oil-rich Eastern Province in January 2015.[107] Also in November 2014, supporters of ISIS claimed responsibility for the shooting of a Danish national in the Eastern Province, while a Canadian was stabbed in a random attack at a shopping mall the same month.[108] In the UAE, an American teacher was brutally murdered in an upscale shopping mall in Abu Dhabi in December 2014, weeks after the US Embassy in the country warned of jihadi threats to attack Americans in the country. Although there was no evidence that the separate attacks were linked either to each other or to broader networks of ISIS cells, they constituted an emerging pattern that rattled expatriates and security services in the Gulf alike.[109]

Beginning with an assault that killed eight Shia worshippers in the Eastern Province in November 2014 by a cell that had pledged loyalty to the ISIS leader, al-Baghdadi, and was in frequent communication with ISIS in Iraq, a series of mass-casualty attacks throughout 2015 highlighted further the risk to internal security from radicalized militants operating within Gulf societies. Just as three Saudis were behind the November attack, so four Saudis carried out an audacious suicide bombing that killed the commander of Saudi Arabia's border operations in January 2015 after re-entering the Kingdom from Iraq's volatile Anbar province.[110] In May 2014, an ISIS affiliate that called itself the *Wilayat Najd* (Najd Province) carried out suicide bombings at Shia mosques in the Eastern Province cities Qatif and Dammam over two consecutive Friday prayers that left twenty-two and four dead, respectively.[111] The same affiliate also claimed responsibility for the suicide bombing of the Imam al-Sadiq mosque in Kuwait City in June 2015. Carried out by a Saudi citizen who transited through Bahrain on his way to Kuwait, the attack was designed to cause maximum damage to intercommunal relations and sectarian tensions in Kuwait, as it targeted the center of the *Hasawi* community of Kuwaiti Shia. Also known as *Shaykhis*, the *Hasawi* originally emigrated from the al-Hasa region of Saudi Arabia's Eastern Province in the late nineteenth and early twentieth centuries, in part to escape endemic marginalization and discrimination.[112]

The UAE figured prominently in regional and international policy responses to confront ISIS that came together in the summer and autumn of 2014. Most visibly, and building on the long record of UAE–US military cooperation, the UAE contributed a squadron of fighter jets to the anti-ISIS coalition in September 2014 and conducted air strikes against ISIS positions in Iraq and Syria. The strikes made global headlines as they were commanded by the first Emirati female fighter pilot, Major Mariam al-Mansouri, who had been among the first cohort of four women to graduate from the Khalifa bin Zayed Aviation College in Al Ain in 2008.[113]

Australia's previously noted base at Al-Minhad facilitated the deployment of 600 Australian forces to the coalition in 2014, while the UAE also created and hosted the Global Center for Excellence in Countering Violent Extremism, also known as *Hedayah* ("guidance"). Initially launched in 2012 by the Global Counterterrorism Forum of twenty-nine states co-chaired by the US and Turkey, *Hedayah* has won praise from US civil and military officials in and beyond the Department of Homeland Security as a key element of anti-radicalization initiatives aimed at tackling the root causes of violent extremism in all its forms.[114]

In November 2015, a report in the *New York Times* indicated that many of the Arab partners in the anti-ISIS coalition had scaled back their participation in the airstrikes over Syria and Iraq in large part as they become heavily involved in military operations in Yemen. Coalition officials claimed that Bahrain had not undertaken anti-ISIS airstrikes since February 2015, the UAE since March, and Saudi Arabia since September, as the US commander of the air campaign, Lieutenant-General Charles Brown, Jr. noted laconically that "They've all been busy doing other things, Yemen being the primary draw."[115] Policymakers in the UAE and other GCC capitals reacted to the rapid takeover of large parts of Yemen by Houthi militants in 2014 by accusing Iran of overtly and materially assisting the tribal movement hitherto confined to Yemen's northwestern provinces. Tensions surged following the Houthi capture of the capital, Sana'a, in September 2014 and the subsequent ousting of embattled Yemeni President Abd Rabbuh Mansur Hadi on the same day in January 2015 that King Abdullah of Saudi Arabia died and King Salman came to power. After Hadi escaped to the southern port city of Aden and re-established a base of control in the city, a further Houthi advance in March 2015 threatened to overrun the city and entrench Houthi – and, in GCC eyes, Iranian – power in Yemen. This led Saudi Arabia and nine other Arab states – including every Gulf State bar Oman – to launch air strikes on Houthi strongholds in Yemen under *Operation Decisive Storm*, as the proxy struggle for influence with Iran escalated into outright regional conflict.[116]

As the military operations in Yemen unfolded, with the initial *Operation Decisive Storm* phase giving way to a secondary phase entitled *Operation Restoring Hope* in April 2015, the UAE assumed a leading role in the ground war and in combat and humanitarian operations in southern Yemen in particular. Emirati and UAE-trained local forces constituted the most accomplished element of *Operation Golden Arrow*, the land offensive launched in July 2015 to retake Aden and southern Yemen from Houthi control, with more than 3,000 troops supported by Apache attack helicopters and dozens of tanks and armored personnel carriers as well as an amphibious assault whose tactical sophistication stunned international observers.[117] The UAE focused heavily on Southern Yemen and was more careful than Saudi Arabia to cast its actions within the framework of a broader humanitarian concern with an emphasis on post-conflict reconstruction and recovery. Significant amounts of Emirati aid arrived in Southern Yemen within months of the UAE deployment and dozens of rebuilding projects were started, including the restoration of the power grid in Aden and the reconstruction of 154 schools, as well as other initiatives that covered the training of local police and the partial restoration of health services in the city.[118]

Such a heavy policy emphasis on southern Yemen reflected in large part the many historical tribal and ancestral links between the Yemeni south and Abu Dhabi, including the Al Nahyan family itself, who trace their lineage to Wadi Nahyan, near the famous ancient dam at Marib. Sheikh Zayed visited the Marib Dam in 1977 and pledged to construct a new dam on the famous site, meaning that the area's liberation by Emirati forces in 2015 carried particular historical resonance.[119] More recently, many south Yemenis migrated to Abu Dhabi in the 1970s and assumed positions in the police and security services while southern tribal leaders who left Yemen after the Houthi takeover of much of the country in 2014 also moved to the emirate in search of refuge. It was thus almost natural that the UAE took the lead in a train-and-equip program in Aden and Hadramaut and worked closely with Yemeni counterparts to create a significant fighting force that eventually encompassed 12,000 men in order to re-seize Yemen's fifth largest city of Mukalla and the oilfields at Masila from the control of Al-Qaeda in the Arabian Peninsula.[120] The veteran defense correspondent Michael Knights summarized in detail the humanitarian operations set in motion by the UAE in Yemen during the opening year of the conflict (in 2015):

> UAE special operators and civilians have been used to covertly survey gaps in stocks of food and medicine in local warehouses and hospitals. This has allowed the coalition to immediately begin meeting local needs in terms of food security, medical and teaching support, and replacements for damaged infrastructure.
>
> In Aden, this allowed the coalition to support the reopening of numerous schools in time for the autumn 2015 term, with school furniture and uniforms sourced locally from Yemeni manufacturers to maximize the local economic impact of aid provision. Civil-military teams quickly got to work on installing diesel generators and maintaining water pumps and sewage facilities. In Mukalla, the coalition prepositioned humanitarian support onshore and aboard the UAE naval flotilla off the coast, and new supplies are now being flown in. Food, medicines and water purification materials were surged onshore. The Emirates also followed up the liberation of Mukalla by deploying military bridges into the city. If they follow patterns set in other conflict areas, road-building will likely follow, using local contractors. UAE telecommunications operators may throw up new cellphone towers as they did in Afghanistan.[121]

Military operations in Yemen nevertheless exposed the UAE to its first real experience of battle casualties. Remarkably, given the UAE's long involvement in Afghanistan and other zones of conflict since 1991, not a single Emirati serviceman died in foreign operations until First Lieutenant Tariq al-Shehhi, from Ras al-Khaimah, was killed in a bomb attack in Bahrain in March 2014.[122] Al-Shehhi became the first serviceman to die on operation since Salim Suhail bin Khamis – a police officer also from Ras al-Khaimah who headed the six-strong police force on the island of Greater Tunb – who died while defending the island against Iranian occupation on November 30, 1971 – two days before the creation of the UAE itself.[123]

Within the first six months of the campaign in Yemen in 2015, the number of UAE battle fatalities soared to seventy-six in September, with a reported 80 percent hailing from the relatively poorer Northern Emirates in a socio-economic pattern of military service common with that of many other armed forces, and up to 157 by December.[124] Many of the soldiers died in a missile attack on a coalition base at Safer in the eastern Marib province on September 4, 2015 that hit an ammunitions depot and the ensuing explosion killed fifty-two Emirati soldiers, some of whom may inadvertently have revealed their whereabouts and the layout of their camp on social media.[125]

The Safer mass-casualty attack had a cathartic impact on the UAE as the dead soldiers were referred to as "martyrs" and the idea of a "blood sacrifice" rapidly gained common currency. Official responses sought to commemorate the fallen soldiers and link their deaths to a more assertive discourse on national identity that drew parallels to the role of war and state making in European societies during the nineteenth and twentieth centuries.[126] In this regard, Al-Badr al-Shateri, an official at the UAE National Defence College, argued that the UAE "has now grown up and joined other older countries that have been commemorating their fallen soldiers" and added that "It is the natural progression of any country that, as it grows stronger and develops, sacrifices become bigger."[127] Ayesha Almazroui, an Emirati journalist at *The National* newspaper in Abu Dhabi, captured the prevailing mood in a widely-read op-ed that suggested that "National consciousness is often forged in the toughest times" and observed that:

> Losing such a large number of martyrs in one day is a new scenario that could possibly define the future of this young country. For the first time, the concept of martyrdom has been discussed in the UAE, among both intellectuals and other members of the community ... Politically, the concept of martyrdom plays an important role in the construction of national identity. The UAE identity has been discussed widely in the last few years. For example, there were questions on what draws the people of the UAE together and what it means to be an Emirati.[128]

At an institutional level, a raft of commemorative measures were also announced, ranging from the first-ever annual Commemoration Day held on November 30, 2015 to the creation of a Martyrs Family Affairs Office at the Crown Prince's Court in Abu Dhabi and the naming of public spaces (streets, squares, and mosques) in honor of the fallen in Ajman, Fujairah, and Dubai as well as the announcement of a planned martyrs' museum and archive in Abu Dhabi.[129]

And yet, even as the very terminology of "martyrdom" to describe military deaths departed significantly from more "standard" references to battlefield deaths, subsequent incidents indicated that the casualty rate in Yemen was causing some alarm among sections of the political and security leadership in the UAE. Thus, the authorities issued an arrest warrant for a person who spread a document that purported to list the fifty-two UAE soldiers killed at Safer on September 4, 2015 as the Abu Dhabi Attorney General warned against any attempt to start rumors or spread false information that aimed "to weaken the moral spirit of the people."[130] No "official" casualty list was made public although local and national media gave wide coverage to visits of Emirati leaders to wounded forces and casualties' families.[131] Concern among the authorities, particularly in Abu Dhabi, that the casualty lists might ignite political and socio-economic strain among sections of tribes or communities in parts of the Northern Emirates may constitute one reason for such reticence, which was also believed to have resulted in very senior figures in the ruling family of Ras al-Khaimah with close links to local tribes being "summoned" to Abu Dhabi in March 2016 to iron out any displays of public dissent over Yemen-related casualties.[132]

The conflict in Yemen thus showcased the new assertiveness in UAE and GCC policies as Emirati and Saudi officials worked closely together in a bid to project and protect their regional interests, and represented a potentially volatile evolution in regional security structures, as the locus of decision making lay in (Arab) Gulf capitals rather than external partners in Washington, DC. Although the campaign – which was ongoing at the time of this writing – was not without tensions, particularly in the choice of local political support networks in Yemen itself – the operations represented another example of the capability – and intent – of officials to "go it alone" in a bid to secure their interests in regional states undergoing post–Arab Spring transitions, however uncertain. And whereas the cases of Libya and Egypt described in the previous section of this chapter pitted the UAE and Qatar against each other in the volatile period between 2011 and 2014, Yemen provided an opportunity for the GCC to re-cohere and repair fractured relationships. This was symbolized by the Qatari decision to contribute ground forces to the Gulf coalition in Yemen in September 2015 and by the raft of high-level meetings between Qatari and Emirati leaders in the months that followed.[133] After one such meeting between the Emir of Qatar, Tamim bin Hamad Al Thani, and Abu Dhabi Crown Prince Mohammed bin Zayed, in March 2016, an editorial in Abu Dhabi's *Al Ittihad* newspaper waxed lyrical that:

> It was not a regular meeting but a meeting of identical visions and joint action. The UAE and Qatar work for the good of the region. They work for its security and stability, and for those who try fishing in troubled waters, we say you lose your bet every time.[134]

Relations with Iran

Ties between the UAE and Iran have, more than most bilateral relationships, fluctuated significantly since the 1970s as political and economic relations shifted more with regional developments than with domestic dynamics in either country. As such, the relationship between the UAE and Iran has been multidimensional and even cross-purpose at times. Thus, the longstanding commercial and trading relationships that existed between Dubai and Sharjah with their counterparts on the Persian shore of the Gulf have been counterbalanced by Iran's seizure in 1971 and subsequent occupation of three islands claimed by Sharjah and Ras al-Khaimah. Moreover, over the past decade Abu Dhabi has emerged as a strategic hawk on the Iranian nuclear issue even as Dubai functioned as a loophole in the international sanctions on Iran.

The primary security threat posed by Iran to the UAE during the early years of the federation lay in the grandiose ambitions entertained by the Shah of Iran, Mohammad Reza Pahlavi, of attaining Iranian hegemony in the Gulf by means of an interventionist policy in the Gulf region.[135] Examples of Iranian intervention in the Gulf in the 1960s and 1970s included the Shah's longstanding territorial claim on Bahrain, which was settled in 1970 by a United Nations mission that conducted a fact-finding mission that showed an overwhelming preference among Bahrainis to become an independent Arab state, the provision of extensive Iranian military assistance to Oman in 1973 to help Sultan Qaboos defeat a persistent insurgency in Dhofar, and the seizure of three islands belonging to Sharjah and Ras al-Khaimah – Abu Musa and the Greater and Lesser Tunbs – located strategically astride the narrow entranceway to the Strait of Hormuz. Iran seized the islands on November 30, 1971, just one day before the formal end of the British protected-status and two days prior to the creation of the UAE out of the seven Trucial States.[136] The Shah's action underscored the dangers facing the newly independent rulers of the UAE, Bahrain, and Qatar (which also gained statehood in 1971) as they navigated a volatile decade in which – uniquely in the modern history of the Gulf – there was no overarching external security guarantee for the smaller states.[137]

The revolutionary upheaval in Iran in 1978 and 1979 carried for the Gulf States ominous overtones of the Iraqi monarchy's own violent demise in Baghdad two decades earlier, in 1958. The downfall of a second regional monarchical system ensured that the needs of regime survival and self-preservation rose to the forefront of policymakers in this volatile period. Thus, all six Gulf States reacted to the outbreak of the Iran–Iraq War in September 1980 with varying degrees of support for Iraq. This was rooted in the conviction among rulers that there was no effective alternative approach to dealing with the revolutionary threat to Arab Gulf polities.[138] Threats that were seen to operate at the trans-national and the inter-cultural as well as at the traditional inter-state levels thus influenced the Gulf States' subsequent careful balancing of internal and external policy during the eight years of war that followed.[139]

In the case of the UAE, this process of cautious engagement began – as noted in Chapter Four – with the hosting of the meeting in Abu Dhabi on May 25–26, 1981 that created the Gulf Cooperation Council (GCC) as a status quo entity intended to shield its member states and societies from trans-national or unconventional spill-over from the warring parties. The concept of a cooperative union had gone through several different stages that extended back to a meeting of the foreign ministers of all *eight* Gulf States (including Iran and Iraq) in Muscat in 1976. However, both Iraq and Iran were excluded from the regional organization that was launched at the InterContinental Hotel in Abu Dhabi five years later.[140]

While the first Secretary-General of the GCC, Abdullah Bishara, quickly identified Iran's quest for regional hegemony as constituting the major threat to Gulf stability, two camps nevertheless emerged, with the individual emirates of the UAE falling – inconveniently for the architects of the federation – into both. Their geographical position in the northern Gulf and greater intermixing of Sunni and Shiite communities exposed Kuwait, Bahrain, and Saudi Arabia to a range of material and ideological threats to their security. Attacks (from both sides, Iraq and Iran) on oil infrastructure and commercial shipping passing through the Gulf demonstrated the vulnerability of the northern Gulf States arising from their proximity to the battlefield. Kuwait and Saudi Arabia therefore led the way in providing generous loans, financial assistance, and oil- and non-oil support to Iraq throughout the war, amounting to an estimated US$25 billion from Saudi Arabia alone and an additional US$13.2 billion in non-collectible "war relief" loans from Kuwait.[141]

Conditions in the southern Gulf lacked the immediate threat to security found in the northern states, both externally and internally, leaving policymakers freer to balance their limited extension of financial and declaratory (through GCC communiques) support for Iraq with their continuing commercial relations with Iran. Nowhere was this delicate balancing act more in evidence than within the UAE as the leaderships in the seven emirates pursued largely individual approaches to the conflict. While the UAE as a country remained officially neutral, Abu Dhabi, Ras al-Khaimah, Ajman, and Fujairah all sided with Iraq, with Abu Dhabi joining the Saudis and Kuwaitis in contributing financial support to Iraq and Ras al-Khaimah also offering Baghdad the opportunity to establish air bases on its territory. By contrast, Dubai, Sharjah, and Umm al-Quwain all gravitated more toward Teheran as they continued trading with Iran throughout the war with Dubai emerging as a key transit hub for war materials destined for Iran, and Sharjah seeking to maintain cordial ties and the agreement to share the oil revenues from Abu Musa. Dubai additionally derived significant benefit from damaged ships calling at the extensive dry-dock repair facilities and associated international shipping services at its major new port of Jebel Ali, which had opened, as noted in Chapter Four, with fortuitous timing, in 1979, a year before the conflict broke out.[142]

Together with Oman, the UAE took the lead in calling for diplomatic mediation between Iran and Iraq and in exploring the basis for a settlement to the conflict, particularly after the internationalization of the war following the US reflagging of the Kuwaiti tanker fleet in 1987. The UAE hosted a number of Iranian delegations in 1984 and 1985 which provided an opportunity not only to discuss the war situation but also for Iranian officials to engage in direct dialogue on sensitive matters. Thus, a delegation headed by Ali Shams Ardakani, the Head of the International Section in the Foreign Ministry in Teheran, visited Abu Dhabi on the first leg of a tour of GCC states in June 1985 to assure them that Iran had not been involved in the assassination attempt against Emir Jabir al-Ahmad Al Sabah of Kuwait. The following month, Iran's Deputy Foreign Minister, Ali Mohammad Besharati, used a visit to Dubai to express Iran's willingness to respond to any credible mediation initiative that might be forthcoming. In November 1987, Iran's Foreign Minister, Ali Akbar Velayati, travelled to Abu Dhabi to discuss with Sheikh Zayed how United Nations Security Council Resolution 598 (calling for an end to the fighting between Iran and Iraq) could be implemented. At the annual GCC Summit in December 1987, the GCC agreed to negotiate with Iran and delegated the UAE as the mediator, in large part due to its constructive ties with Teheran. This led to the dispatch to Teheran of a UAE representative, Saif Said, contributing one piece to the eventual cessation of hostilities in August 1988.[143] Emirati mediation may not have been the sole (or even the most important) contributing factor in bringing the Iran–Iraq War to a close, but it did reflect the UAE's regional positioning under Sheikh Zayed (see Chapter Five).

The death of Ayatollah Khomeini on June 3, 1989 was followed by a reorientation of Iran's domestic and regional politics under the dual leadership of his successor as Supreme Leader, Ali Khamenei, and Khamenei's replacement as President of Iran, Ali Akbar Hashemi Rafsanjani. During Rafsanjani's presidency, which lasted from 1989 to 1997, Iranian policy shed much of its earlier revolutionary fervor and refocused around a pragmatic approach to regional affairs as the domestic reconstruction of a war-ravaged economy took priority in Teheran.[144] Although the gap between the competing Emirati and Iranian security and strategic visions for the Gulf continued throughout the Rafsanjani presidency (symbolized by Iran's militarization and subsequent declaration of full sovereignty over the three disputed islands in the early 1990s), political and economic relations improved as the UAE responded to the greater caution and rationality of post-Khomeini Iran. The absence of meaningful irritants such as concerns for ethnic or sectarian identity meant there were fewer obstacles to closer political ties than in neighbors such as Saudi Arabia and Bahrain. Moreover, the presence of a substantial and thriving Iranian business community in Dubai provided a powerful incentive to closer relations, at the individual if not always at the inter-state level (this became apparent in 2003, during the presidency of Rafsanjani's successor, Mohammad Khatami, when Iranians invested heavily in Dubai following the liberalization of the emirate's hitherto-restricted real estate market, including Rafsanjani Investments LLC set up in Dubai the following year by the former president).[145]

Political relations between Iran and the UAE improved further under Mohammad Khatami's reforming presidency between 1997 and 2005. Khatami's initial efforts to reach out to GCC leaders and cultivate relationships and confidence-boosting measures continued to dispel lingering mistrust from the revolutionary era. Energy cooperation intensified in 2001 with the signing of an agreement to supply Iranian gas to resource-poor Sharjah through a pipeline that opened eventually in 2008, although, as noted previously, the gas never materialized owing to a subsequent dispute about pricing. Moreover, Dubai's expansion into a "global city" in the late 1990s and 2000s reinforced manifold its economic importance to Teheran as a re-export hub and an outlet to the global economy. Trade ties rose steadily and by the mid-2000s (before the onset of sanctions which increased its economic significance to Iran still further) Dubai alone was home to more than 400,000 Iranians and some 3,000 Iranian-owned businesses.[146] Thus, the UAE became an indispensable connection that, to some extent at least, plugged the Iranian economy into the great acceleration of globalizing processes that characterized the decade. The value of the Emirates' exports to Iran exceeded many times that of her Gulf neighbors and by 2008 amounted to US$13.2 billion against US$1.58 billion for the aggregate figure of the other five GCC states.[147]

Such close economic ties became a source of vulnerability for the UAE in the mid-2000s after the maverick hardliner Mahmoud Ahmedinejad unexpectedly won the presidential election of June 2005 and international concern at the apparent scope and scale of Iran's nuclear program escalated. The UAE had a seat on the front-line as the George W. Bush administration in the US led a tightening campaign of international sanctions on Iran designed to contain and roll back the country's supposed nuclear ambitions. This was largely a result of the close economic ties that had developed between the UAE, particularly Dubai, and Iran, as noted above. Paradoxically, the initial impact of sanctions in the mid-2000s had the effect of increasing the economic significance of the UAE to Iran owing to the comparative ease of travel to (and doing business in) Dubai when Iranian trade with European partners, particularly German, began to be impacted. Nader Habibi has observed that a similar trajectory occurred with Iran–Oman trade and that, with specific regard to the UAE, "Iranian firms that faced difficulties and long regulatory delays in direct dealings with Europe were able to avoid these difficulties by setting up UAE based firms that were not identified as Iranian entities."[148]

Nevertheless, the rapid growth of the re-export trade from the UAE to Iran did not go unnoticed in Washington, DC as a potential "loophole" in the impact of sanctions on the Iranian economy. By 2011, Iran accounted for about a quarter of total re-exports from the UAE with the figures showing a significant year-on-year rise from 14.3 billion dirhams in the first six months of 2010 to 19.5 billion dirhams a year later. In the face of the evidence that UAE–Iran trade was, in fact, thriving despite (and because of) sanctions, the US increased its pressure on UAE-based firms, especially in the financial sector, to cut back on their trade financing services for Iranian businesses and warned that violators risked losing access to the far more lucrative US market.[149] The implied threat of being excluded from the US market succeeded in dissuading UAE-based banks from opening new accounts for Iranian traders or obtaining letters of credit to finance trade, while in 2011, the UAE Central Bank informed financial institutions operating in the country to freeze Iran-linked accounts belonging to firms targeted by United Nations (UN) sanctions.[150] In this way, the UAE severed ties with no fewer than seventeen Iranian banks. In July 2013, ironically just weeks after the surprise victory of the moderate candidate Hassan Rouhani in the election to succeed Ahmedinejad, tough new international sanctions raised still further the bar on doing business with

Iranian entities that specifically targeted non-US companies still dealing with Iran. This was effective as data from the Iranian Customs Administration suggest that the value of Iran's imports from the UAE fell sharply by 21 percent in the nine months between March and December 2013 as companies were hit by the tightening of sanctions.[151]

As each round of sanctions increased Iran's isolation from the international community and the global economy, a new policy gap opened up between Abu Dhabi and Dubai over whether and how to engage with Iran. Two interconnected incidents captured the complexity of the situation and the inter-emirate dynamics at play. The first was the unfortunate Dubai Ports World incident in the United States in 2006 that was described earlier in this book. As noted, the acquisition of a port management contract from P&O to manage cargo operations in six US ports came under heavy political attack from both Republicans and Democrats who opposed the move on national security grounds and made a series of unfounded allegations identifying Dubai (and by extension the UAE) as a weak-point in the "war on terror" then into its fifth year.[152] In parallel to the fallout from the DP World issue, Abu Dhabi was engaged simultaneously in negotiations with the US for a comprehensive nuclear agreement that would permit the UAE to construct and operate a series of nuclear reactors. Abu Dhabi's push for the nuclear agreement with the United States heightened therefore the sensitivity of Dubai's commercial relations with Iran, especially given the possibility that illicit trading in dual-use material could bypass and erode the international sanctions.[153]

UAE–Iran ties reached a nadir in 2011 when senior Emirati officials ascribed the uprising in Bahrain to Iranian meddling and joined Saudi Arabia and other GCC states in sending forces (military police) to assist the Bahraini government in restoring order. Moreover, the outbreak of unrest occurred barely six months after the UAE Ambassador to the US, Yousef al-Otaiba, publicly endorsed the use of military force to halt Iran's nuclear program, stating in an interview with the *Atlantic* magazine that the long-term benefits of destroying the program through force outweighed the short-term regional backlash from any such strike.[154] The periodic tensions over the islands of Abu Musa and the Greater and Lesser Tunbs also flared in April 2012 after Ahmedinejad made a surprise (and provocative) visit to Abu Musa.[155] However, Emirati leaders responded with guarded optimism both to the election of Hassan Rouhani as President of Iran in June 2013 and to the subsequent interim nuclear agreement reached between Iranian and international negotiators in Geneva in November 2013 as well as the final Joint Comprehensive Plan of Action (JCPOA) that was signed in Vienna on July 14, 2015.[156]

Officials in the UAE had been taken by surprise at the sudden revelations in October 2013 that secret back-channel talks between US and Iranian policymakers had for months been hosted by Oman, but subsequent responses were broadly positive. Just days after the Geneva deal, UAE Foreign Minister Sheikh Abdullah bin Zayed Al Nahyan visited Iran for the first time in years, while in April 2014, Iranian Foreign Minister Mohammad Javad Zarif travelled to Abu Dhabi and Dubai. During this visit, Sheikh Abdullah went as far to describe Iran as a "strategic partner" as the two countries began the process of rebuilding trust and mutual contact after the frostiness of the Ahmedinejad years. Additionally, Sheikh Abdullah praised President Rouhani's "general approach" to the GCC states since taking office, and added that "this is an opportunity to strengthen the historic opportunity between us and do away with the problems and differences that have marred it."[157] Comments such as this built upon the sentiments expressed by the Ruler of Dubai (and Prime Minister of the UAE), Sheikh Mohammed bin Rashid Al Maktoum, in January 2014, when he called for an easing of pressure on Iran, telling the BBC that "we need to give Iran space, Iran is our neighbor and we don't want any problem."[158]

The UAE and Israel

Chapter Four noted, in the context of the opening of an Israeli mission at the Abu Dhabi–based International Renewable Energy Agency (IRENA), the gradual warming of (unofficial) ties between the UAE and Israel. While direct political ties likely remain a non-starter (and Israeli officials will recall how earlier trade offices in Oman and Qatar fell victim to the periodic flare-ups in Arab–Israeli tensions), the opening of the Israeli mission at IRENA spotlighted the indirect and discrete connections between Israel and the UAE. An alignment of interests (if not of values) on a range of defense and security issues and concern over the perceived threat from Islamism and Iran has added to a low-level trading relationship that predated the Arab Spring. The Israel–UAE relationship thus is deeper rooted than those earlier Israeli trade missions in Muscat and Oman while the regional landscape also has shifted markedly since the 2000s.

Diplomatic contacts between Israel and GCC states began tentatively after the 1991 Madrid Conference on Arab–Israeli peace. Israel opened trade offices in Muscat and Doha in 1996 but these shut in 2000 as tensions flared after the outbreak of the second Palestinian intifada. Israel subsequently maintained a token presence at its Doha mission until the Qatari government closed it permanently in January 2009 in protest against the Israeli offensive in Gaza. During this period, the most durable example of Israeli–Gulf cooperation lay in the Middle East Desalination Research Center (MEDRC) in Oman – the only surviving organization set up as a result of the 1993 Oslo Accords that became a model of cooperation in shared research and capacity-building that IRENA in Abu Dhabi appears well-placed to emulate.[159]

As Chapter Five made clear, the UAE followed a hardline position on Israel during Sheikh Zayed's lifetime that contrasted sharply with the softening of Israeli relations with Qatar and Oman in the 1990s. UAE foreign policy under Sheikh Zayed emphasized pan-Arab solidarity and was vocal in condemning Israel's occupation of Palestinian territory. Ties improved only after Sheikh Zayed's death in November 2004 and the rise to influence of the Ruler of Dubai, Sheikh Mohammed bin Rashid, and the Crown Prince of Abu Dhabi, Sheikh Mohammed bin Zayed. However, the thawing of UAE–Israel ties was not without its problems and was in fact interrupted brusquely in January 2010 when a team of twenty-seven operatives linked to the Israeli Mossad intelligence agency carried out the audacious assassination of Mahmoud al-Mabhouh, a chief weapons negotiator for the Palestinian resistance group, Hamas, in the Al Bustan Rotana hotel in Dubai. An in-depth investigation conducted by *Spiegel Online* in Germany that reconstructed the events around al-Mabhouh's killing suggested that they took the Dubai authorities by surprise and that a purpose of al-Mabhouh's visit to Dubai was to meet:

> with a banker who had already helped him with a number of international arms deals in the past, as well as with his usual contact with the Iranian Revolutionary Guards, who had flown to Dubai to coordinate two major shipments of weapons for Hamas in the coming months.[160]

In addition to noting that al-Mabhouh's purported Iranian contact portrayed Dubai as a weak link in the tightening regime of international sanctions then being imposed on Iran, the same investigative report neatly summarized the manifold security challenges facing Dubai as the emirate (and the city) evolved into an aspiring twenty-first-century global hub:

> Dubai is in a central location, roughly equidistant from Iraq, Iran, Yemen, and Afghanistan. There are more Iranians and Pakistanis living there than natives of Dubai; the city has attracted hundreds of thousands of migrants from some of the world's most explosive regions. People are constantly coming and going, large amounts of money are at stake, and the Islamic banking system is a nightmare for any police detective.[161]

The fallout from the al-Mabhouh assassination complicated but did not end the discrete and under-the-radar connections with Israeli entities and individuals. While they in no way constitute a formal rapprochement or any form of alliance, Emirati and Israeli interests nevertheless converged around a number of strategic fault-lines in the volatile aftermath of the Arab Spring. Policymakers in both countries shared in common a hawkish approach on Iran and viewed the election of the Muslim Brotherhood in Egypt with deep suspicion, and acted rapidly to cement ties with the Sisi regime after its takeover of power in Cairo in July 2013. Moreover, Israel is believed to have maintained security links with Fatah's Palestinian strongman Mohammed Dahlan, who is based in exile in Abu Dhabi where he reportedly is close to Crown Prince Mohammed bin Zayed.[162]

In January 2016, Israel's former Ambassador to Egypt, Zvi Mazel alluded to the strategic convergence of Israeli–Gulf interests, if not values:

> During the Iran nuclear talks, Israel's intelligence community started having more effective ties with Gulf countries … The Emirates have ties with us due to our common security interests against Iran and the Muslim

Brotherhood … You can definitely sense that in certain fields the Gulf countries and Israel are becoming closer.[163]

It is thus unsurprising that the post-2011 conditions of regional insecurity have meant that the defense and security sectors have grown into a microcosm of the evolving dynamic of UAE–Israel ties. Connections that developed initially in the mid-2000s have expanded since the outbreak of the Arab Spring in 2011 and look set to form the bedrock of the discreet relationship in the foreseeable future. One of the earliest such connections dates to 2008 when Abu Dhabi's Critical National Infrastructure Authority (CNIA) signed a US$816 million contract with AGT International, a Geneva-based company owned by Israeli businessman Mati Kochavi, for surveillance equipment for critical infrastructure in the UAE, including oil and gas fields.[164] In 2011, the CNIA then agreed to purchase unmanned aerial vehicles from Israel's Aeronautics Defense Systems (ADS) although the deal foundered acrimoniously after the military sales division of the Israeli Ministry of Defence failed to approve the export of the vehicles to an Arab state.[165] Most recently, AGT International has been linked through a Swiss intermediary with a joint venture with two UAE firms, Advanced Integrated Systems and Advanced Technical Solutions, in a comprehensive emirate-wide surveillance initiative in Abu Dhabi named Falcon Eye. A report on Falcon Eye on *Middle East Eye*, a UK-based website with links to Qatar, described the civil surveillance network as one that ensured that "every person is monitored from the moment they leave their doorstep to the moment they return to it."[166]

It is likely that the nascent ties between Israel and the UAE in the defense and security sectors will continue but may expand to incorporate greater dialogue on energy issues, particularly at (and through) IRENA, which may itself evolve into a staging-point for expanded contacts with Emirati policymakers, particularly as the Israel–Palestinian issue becomes ever more peripheral to regional politics. Homeland security products, agricultural and medical technology, and aerial control and communication systems headed the US$5.3 million in Israeli exports (through private and intermediary companies) to the UAE in 2013, according to Israel's Central Bureau of Statistics.[167] In addition, the heavy emphasis, as documented in Chapter Four, on innovation and entrepreneurship, particularly in Dubai, is likely to provide another area of cooperation with Israel's successful start-up culture and technology clusters widely admired in the emirate. Further opportunities exist in joint ventures overseas, such as the partnership between Israel's largest shipping company, Zim Integrated Shipping, and DP World, in the acquisition of Spanish port operator Contarsa in 2008 and assumption of joint control of the Container Terminal at Tarragona. Speaking at the time of the Contarsa venture, the CEO of DP World's shipping group, Jamal Majid bin Thaniah, caught the mood of pragmatism as he said of his Israeli counterparts that:

these people don't mix business with politics. When you're operating in a global marketplace, you can't pick and choose. You're bound by international business practices to deal with companies like Zim. We'll continue to conduct business on an unbiased basis.[168]

Technocratic and informal cooperation over issues of shared concern will not necessarily lead to the establishment of overt or formal bilateral ties between the UAE and Israel but they can represent significant confidence-boosting measures. The experience of the MEDRC in Oman suggests that the presence of such institutions can advance multi-track diplomacy between Arab states and Israel by providing opportunities for professional and diplomatic interaction. Speaking in 2011, the Dutch director of the MEDRC, Ronald Mollinger, stated that Israel "takes the MEDRC and its regional role very seriously as the center also gives them an opportunity to interact with states that they do not yet have formal diplomatic relations with."[169] IRENA provides the UAE with an opportunity to further expand such technocratic cooperation that may, over time, enhance the level of familiarity and trust among policymakers and even, at some point, the public at large.

Notes

1 Emile Hokayem and Becca Wasser, "The Gulf States in an Era of American Retrenchment," in Toby Dodge and Emile Hokayem (eds), *Middle Eastern Security, the US Pivot, and the Rise of ISIS* (London: Routledge, 2014), pp. 144–147.
2 "Cause of UK's UAE Terror Alert Buried Deep in Whitehall," *Gulf States Newsletter*, 32 (832), June 30, 2008, p. 3.
3 "Flirting with Rafale," *Gulf States Newsletter*, 32 (831), June 13, 2008, p. 12.
4 Michelle Smith and Charles Ferguson, "France's Nuclear Diplomacy," *International Herald Tribune*, March 11, 2008.
5 "UAE Agrees to French Base by 2009," *Al Arabiya*, January 16, 2008.
6 "French Base Opened, Rafale Talks," *Gulf States Newsletter*, 33 (854), May 29, 2009, p. 7.
7 Rodger Shanahan, "Why the Gulf Matters: Crafting an Australian Security Policy for the Arabian Gulf," Lowy Institute for International Policy, *Policy Brief*, May 2008, pp. 4–8.
8 "Al Minhad Air Base: a Closer Look at Australia's Base for Operations in the Middle East," *ABC News Australia*, September 15, 2014.
9 Rodger Shanahan, "Enduring Ties and Enduring Interests? Australia's Post-Afghanistan Strategic Choices in the Gulf," Lowy Institute for International Policy, *Policy Brief*, August 2011, p. 4.
10 "United Arab Emirates Poaches Former Major-General Mike Hindmarsh as Security Adviser," *Herald Sun*, December 3, 2009.
11 Lee Cordner, "Progressing Maritime Security Cooperation in the Indian Ocean," *Naval War College Review*, 64(4), 2012, pp. 71–73.
12 "Indian Ships Arrive in UAE to Enhance Defense Ties," *Business Standard*, September 16, 2013.
13 "Modi in Dubai: India, UAE to Establish 'Strategic Security Dialogue,' Boost Defence, Security Ties," *First Post India*, August 17, 2015.
14 "India, UAE Set to Ink Civil Nuclear & 15 Other Pacts during Crown Prince's Visit," *The Economic Times*, February 9, 2016.
15 Matteo Legrenzi, "NATO in the Gulf: Who is Doing Whom a Favor?", *Middle East Policy*, 14(1), 2007, p. 69.

16   Pierre Razoux, "What Future for NATO's Istanbul Cooperation Initiative?", NATO Research Division, *Research Paper No. 55*, January 2010, p. 5.

17   Peter Hellyer, "Evolution of UAE Foreign Policy," in Ibrahim al-Abed and Peter Hellyer (eds), *United Arab Emirates: A New Perspective* (London: Trident Press, 2001), p. 177.

18   "UAE to Keep Troops in Kosovo," *Reuters*, March 14, 2000.

19   "Inside Mission Kosovo: How UAE Offered Glimmer of Hope amid War," *The National*, October 24, 2013.

20   Rajiv Chandrasekaran, "In the UAE, the United States has a Quiet, Potent Ally Nicknamed 'Little Sparta'," *Washington Post*, November 9, 2014.

21   Lori Plotkin Boghardt, "The Muslim Brotherhood on Trial in the UAE," The Washington Institute, *PolicyWatch No. 2064*, April 12, 2013.

22   "Wave of Arrests Puts Al-Islah Back in the Spotlight," *Gulf States Newsletter*, 36 (924), May 24, 2012, p. 4.

23   Author Interviews, December 2015.

24   Courtney Freer, "The Muslim Brotherhood in the Emirates: Anatomy of a Crackdown," *Middle East Eye*, December 17, 2015.

25   "UAE Activists Demand Fresh Elections," *Agence France-Presse*, March 9, 2011, cached version available online at http://www.hurriyetdailynews.com/default.aspx?pageid= 438&n=uae-activists-demand-direct-elections-2011-03-09 (accessed March 23, 2016).

26   Ibid.

27   "UAE Cracks Down on Dissent Amid Calls for Reform," *Gulf States Newsletter*, 35 (899), April 29, 2011, p. 1.

28   Kristian Coates Ulrichsen, "Gulf States: Studious Silence Falls on Arab Spring," *Open Democracy*, April 25, 2011.

29   Sara Yassin, "UAE5 Still Face Restrictions after Pardon," *Index on Censorship*, January 11, 2012, available online at https://www.indexoncensorship.org/2012/01/uae5-ma nsoor-still-face-restrictions-after-pardon-emirates.

30   "UAE: US, UK Should Criticize Dissident Arrests," *Human Rights Watch*, August 1, 2012.

31   Freer, *Anatomy of a Crackdown*.

32   "Islamists Plot against Gulf, says Dubai Police Chief," *AFP*, March 25, 2012.

33   "Muslim Brotherhood Plans to Take Over Kuwait by 2013: Khalfan," *Kuwait Times*, April 18, 2012.

34   "Emirati Nerves Rattled by Islamists' Rise," *The Guardian*, October 12, 2013.

35   Alain Gresh, "Dubai's Police Chief Speaks Out," *Le Monde Diplomatique*, May 19, 2015.

36   "Brotherhood Sowing Subversion in Gulf States," *Reuters*, April 3, 2013.

37   "Limits of UAE Tolerance Tested as Tight Security Marks Start of Al-Islah Trial," *Gulf States Newsletter*, 37 (942), March 7, 2013, p. 1.

38   "UAE Sentences 69 in Al-Islah Trial," *Gulf States Newsletter*, 37 (950), July 4, 2013, pp. 7–8.

39   'Mass Convictions Following an Unfair Trial: the UAE 94 Case,' *International Commission of Jurists*, 2013, pp. 4–6. Report available online at http://www.icj.org/wp -content/uploads/2013/10/UAE-report-4-Oct-2013smallpdf.com_.pdf.

40   "Economic Divide Fosters Discontent in Northern Emirates," *Gulf States Newsletter*, 37 (950), July 4, 2003, p .8.

41   "Abu Dhabi Turns Attention to Potential Ticking Time Bomb in Northern Emirates," *Gulf States Newsletter*, 35 (906), August 5, 2011, p. 3.

42   Ibid.

43   "Economic Divide Fosters Discontent in Northern Emirates," *Gulf States Newsletter*, 37 (950), July 4, 2003, p. 8.

44   Author correspondence, March 2016.

45   "UAE Shuts Down Office of U.S. Research Institute RAND," *Reuters*, December 20, 2012.

46   Mohammed Jamjoom, "Details Emerge in UAE Closing of Pro-Democracy Groups," *CNN*, April 6, 2012.
47   Ibid.
48   Author interviews and correspondence, April 2012, June 2013, May 2016.
49   "Anwar Gargash: Six Pillars that Support Security in the UAE," *The National*, March 31, 2014.
50   Adeed Dawisha, *The Second Arab Awakening: Revolution, Democracy, and the Islamist Challenge from Tunis to Damascus* (New York: W.W. Norton & Company, 2013), p. 26.
51   Jean-Marc Rickli, "The Political Rationale and Implications of the United Arab Emirates' Military Involvement in Libya," in Dag Henriksen and Ann Karin Larsen (eds), *Political Rationale and International Consequences of the War in Libya* (Oxford: Oxford University Press, 2016), pp. 146–147.
52   Ibid., p. 147.
53   Ibid., pp. 147–148.
54   Helene Cooper and Robert Worth, "In Arab Spring, Obama Finds a Sharp Test," *New York Times*, September 24, 2012.
55   "GCC Troops Dispatched to Bahrain to Maintain Order," *Al Arabiya*, March 15, 2011.
56   "UAE-US Security Relationship," *Embassy of the United Arab Emirates in Washington, DC*, http://www.uae-embassy.org/uae-us-relations/key-areas-bilateral-cooperation/uae-us-security-relationship.
57   Rickli, *Political Rationale and Implications*, p. 144.
58   "The Long Road from Sharjah to Tripoli," *The National*, November 3, 2011.
59   "Qatar and Libya Open a New Geopolitical Axis in North Africa," *Gulf States Newsletter*, 35 (907), September 2, 2011, p. 3.
60   Mary Fitzgerald, "Libya's New Power Brokers?" *Foreign Policy*, August 27, 2014.
61   "Accidental Heroes: Britain, France and the Libya Operation: an Interim RUSI Campaign Report," *Royal United Services Institute*, London, September 2011, p. 11.
62   Rickli, *Political Rationale and Implications*, p. 146.
63   Kristian Coates Ulrichsen, *Qatar and the Arab Spring* (Oxford: Oxford University Press, 2014), p. 158.
64   RUSI, *Accidental Heroes*, p. 12.
65   Fitzgerald, *Libya's New Power Brokers*.
66   Jon Lee Anderson, "The Unravelling," *The New Yorker*, February 23, 2015.
67   Ibid.
68   Ibid.
69   David Kirkpatrick and Eric Schmitt, "Arab Nations Strike in Libya, Surprising U.S.," *New York Times*, August 25, 2014.
70   David Kirkpatrick, "Leaked Emirati Emails Could Threaten Peace Talks in Libya," *New York Times*, November 12, 2015.
71   "UN Libya Envoy Accepts £1,000-a-day Job from Backer of One Side in Civil War," *The Guardian*, November 4, 2015.
72   "Abdullah bin Zayed Gives Interview to Bret Baier of US TV Channel Fox News," *Emirates News Agency* (WAM), November 22, 2014.
73   "Ahmed Shafiq to Remain in UAE for 'Security Reasons'," *Ahram Online*, July 24, 2012.
74   "Difficult Geopolitical Context," *Gulf States Newsletter*, 36 (926), June 21, 2012, p. 3.
75   "Qatar Sends Second Shipment of LNG to Egypt," *Reuters*, August 20, 2013.
76   "Qatar Seeks to Invest – and Secure its Footing – in the New Egypt," *Gulf States Newsletter*, 36 (932), September 27, 2012, pp. 9–10.
77   "Emirati Nerves Rattled by Islamists' Rise," *The Guardian*, October 12, 2013.
78   Karim Faheem and Mayy el-Sheikh, "Growing Strains for Muslim Brotherhood and Emirates," *New York Times*, January 3, 2013.
79   Mostafa Mohie and Hossam Bahgat, "Exclusive WikiLeaks Cables Trace Ebb and Flow of Egypt-UAE Relations," *Mada Masr*, July 26, 2015.

80 "UAE Signs $4.9 Billion Aid Package to Egypt," *Reuters*, October 26, 2013.
81 "Dubai's Emaar Says Not Part of Egypt's Capital City Project," *Reuters*, March 16, 2015.
82 Author interview, March 2016.
83 "UAE's Arabtec Agrees $40 Billion Housing Project with Egypt Army," *Reuters*, March 9, 2014.
84 "UAE to Build Egypt's 'New Cairo'," *The National*, March 14, 2015.
85 "UAE to Build Egypt's New Capital City," *Gulf Business*, March 15, 2015.
86 "Arabtec's US$40 Billion Egypt Project Cut to Just a Tenth of Original Size," *The National*, September 8, 2015.
87 See, for instance, "Egypt's Capital City Project Come to Standstill," *Arabian Industry*, June 10, 2015; "Dispute with UAE Puts Brakes on Egyptian New Capital Project," *Middle East* Monitor, June 24, 2015.
88 Coates Ulrichsen, *Qatar and the Arab Spring*, pp. 154–156.
89 Birol Baskan, "The Police Chief and the Sheikh," *The Washington Review of Turkish and Eurasian Affairs*, April 2012, available online at http://www.thewashingtonreview.org/articles/the-police-chief-and-the-sheikh.html (accessed April 13, 2013).
90 "Qaradawi's Comments Spark Spat Between UAE and Egypt," *Gulf States Newsletter*, 36 (920), March 22, 2013, p. 4.
91 "Qatar Steadfast in its Support for Islamist Groups," *Gulf States Newsletter*, 37 (946), May 5, 2013, p. 3.
92 Kristian Coates Ulrichsen, "Foreign Policy Implications of the New Emir's Succession in Qatar," *Norwegian Peacebuilding Resource Center Policy Brief*, 2013, p. 3.
93 "Egypt's Muslim Brotherhood Finds Havens Abroad," *Washington Post*, November 6, 2013.
94 "UAE, Saudi Arabia and Bahrain Recall Their Ambassadors from Qatar," *Gulf News*, March 5, 2014.
95 Luciano Zaccara, "The Role of the Gulf Countries in the Mediterranean and the Middle East Following the Arab Spring," in European Institute of the Mediterranean (IEMed), *Mediterranean Yearbook 2015*, p. 72.
96 David Kirkpatrick, "Qatar's Support of Islamists Alienates Allies Near and Far," *New York Times*, September 7, 2014. The lobbying firm in question is the Camstoll Group.
97 "Bahrain and United Arab Emirates Withdraw from 2015 Men's World Handball Championship in Qatar," *Inside the Game,* November 10, 2014.
98 Simon Henderson, "Qatar Makes Peace with its Gulf Neighbors," *The Washington Institute Policy Alert*, November 17, 2014.
99 "Bahrain and UAE Want to Compete at Qatar 2015 Men's World Handball Championships After All," *Inside the Game*, November 19, 2014.
100 "IHF Council Decision on Withdrawal of Bahrain and United Arab Emirates from 2015 Men's WCh," *International Handball Federation*, November 21, 2014.
101 Abdulaziz Sager, "Whither GCC-US Relations?" *Gulf Research Center*, March 29, 2013.
102 Jeffrey Goldberg, "The Obama Doctrine," *The Atlantic*, April 2016, available online at www.theatlantic.com/magazine/archive/2016/04/the-obama-doctrine/471525.
103 Yousef Al Otaiba, "The Asia Pivot Needs a Firm Footing in the Middle East," *Foreign Policy*, March 26, 2014.
104 Ibid.
105 Hussein Ibish, "US-Gulf Ties Have Frayed but are Not Beyond Repair," *The National*, April 9, 2016.
106 "Jihadist Expansion in Iraq Puts Persian Gulf States in a Tight Spot," *Washington Post*, June 13, 2014.
107 "American is Fatally Shot in Saudi Arabia," *New York Times*, October 14, 2014.
108 "Saudi Probes Motive behind Attack on Canadian," *Al Arabiya*, November 30, 2014.
109 "US Teacher Killed as Americans Targeted in Separate Abu Dhabi Attacks," *The Guardian*, December 4, 2014.

110 Jack Moore, "ISIS 'Attack Saudi Border Post and Infiltrate Town'," *Newsweek*, January 28, 2015.

111 Rori Donaghy, "Islamic State Claims Deadly Suicide Attack on Mosque in Saudi Arabia's Qatif," *Middle East Eye*, May 22, 2015.

112 Toby Matthiesen, "Mysticism, Migration and Clerical Networks: Ahmad al-Ahsa'i and the Shaykis of al-Ahsa, Kuwait and Basra," *Journal of Muslim Minority Affairs*, 2014, pp. 12–13.

113 "Gulf Warplanes Bomb ISIL Targets in Syria," *Gulf States News*, 38 (978), October 2, 2014, p. 1.

114 Author Interviews, Washington, DC, August 2015.

115 Eric Schmitt and Michael Gordon, "As U.S. Escalates Air War on ISIS, Allies Slip Away," *New York Times*, November 7, 2015.

116 Kristian Coates Ulrichsen, "Why Have the Gulf States Intervened Militarily in Yemen?" *Houston Chronicle*, March 27, 2016.

117 Michael Knights and Alexandre Mello, "The Saudi-UAE War Effort in Yemen (Part 1): Operation Golden Arrow in Aden," The Washington Institute, *Policywatch No. 2464*, August 10, 2015.

118 "Aden the Focus of Dh500m UAE Aid Effort," *The National*, October 7, 2015.

119 Peter Hellyer, "A 2,000 Year Bond between the UAE and Yemen That Will Never Break," *The National*, October 13, 2015.

120 Michael Knights, "The UAE Approach to Counterinsurgency in Yemen," *War on the Rocks*, May 23, 2016.

121 Ibid.

122 "Emirati Hero Killed in the Line of Duty in Bahrain Laid to Rest," *The National*, March 4, 2014.

123 "UAE's First Martyr Remembered," *The National*, December 6, 2012.

124 "Regional Conflicts Stimulate Culture of 'Martyrdom' in the UAE," *Gulf States News*, 39(1001), October 1, 2015, p. 7. On November 30, 2015, *The National* ran a photographic gallery in honor of the fallen on the occasion of the UAE's first "Commemoration Day," which included 157 people.

125 Author Interviews, Washington, DC, March 2016.

126 Kristin Smith Diwan, "Soldiers and the Nation," *Arab Gulf States Institute in Washington*, September 18, 2015.

127 "Regional Conflicts Stimulate Culture of 'Martyrdom' in the UAE," *Gulf States News*, 39(1001), October 1, 2015, p. 7.

128 Ayesha Almazroui, "National Identity is Often Forged in Tough Times," *The National*, September 8, 2015.

129 "Museum to be Built to Commemorate UAE's Fallen Heroes," *The National*, September 7, 2015.

130 "Arrest Ordered after False List of UAE's Fallen Soldiers Circulated Online," *The National*, September 6, 2016.

131 Smith Diwan, *Soldiers and the Nation*.

132 "Signs of Strain in UAE Reflected in Abu Dhabi-RAK Tensions," *Gulf States News*, 40(1012), March 31, 2016, p. 13.

133 "UAE Newspapers Hail Emir of Qatar's Visit to the UAE," Emirates News Agency, March 18, 2016; "Deep Freeze between Qatar and the UAE is Over," *Doha News*, May 3, 2016.

134 Ibid.

135 Fred Halliday, *The Middle East in International Relations: Power, Politics and Ideology* (Cambridge: Cambridge University Press, 2005), p. 103.

136 Wm. Roger Louis, "The Withdrawal from the Gulf," in Wm. Roger Louis, *Ends of British Imperialism: The Scramble for Empire, Suez and Decolonization* (London: I.B. Tauris, 2006), p. 902.

137 This began to change, albeit gradually and in ways that were not necessarily discernible at the time, with the Carter Declaration on January 23, 1980, which stated that "Any

attempt by an outside force to gain control of the Persian Gulf region will be regarded as an assault on the vital interests of the United States of America, and such an assault will be repelled by any means necessary, including military force."

138　Gerd Nonneman, "The Gulf States and the Iran-Iraq War: Pattern Shifts and Continuities," in Lawrence G. Potter and Gary Sick (eds), *Iran, Iraq, and the Legacies of War* (New York: Palgrave Macmillan, 2004), p. 173.

139　Arshin Adib-Mughaddam, *The International Politics of the Persian Gulf: A Cultural Genealogy* (London: Routledge, 2006), p. 29.

140　Abdulkhaleq Abdulla, "The Gulf Cooperation Council: Nature, Origin and Process," in Michael Hudson (ed.), *Middle East Dilemma: The Politics and Economics of Arab Integration* (New York: Columbia University Press, 1999), p. 154.

141　Mai Yamani, "The Two Faces of Saudi Arabia," *Survival*, 50(1), 2008, p. 254.

142　Christopher Davidson, *The United Arab Emirates: A Study in Survival* (London: Lynne Rienner, 2006), p. 206; Karim Sadjapour, "The Battle of Dubai: The United Arab Emirates and the U.S.-Iran Cold War," Washington, DC: Carnegie Endowment for International Peace, *Carnegie Middle East Paper*, July 2011, p. 6.

143　Christin Marshall, *Iran's Persian Gulf Policy: From Khomeini to Khatami* (Abingdon: Routledge, 2003), p. 82 and p. 94.

144　Anoushiravan Ehteshami, "The Foreign Policy of Iran," in Raymond Hinnebusch and Anoushiravan Ehteshami (eds), *The Foreign Policies of Middle East States* (London: Lynne Rienner, 2002), p. 284.

145　Sadjapour, *Battle of Dubai*, p. 7.

146　John Duke Anthony, Jean-Francois Seznec, Tayyar Ari, and Wayne E. White, "War with Iran: Regional Reactions and Requirements," *Middle East Policy*, 15(3), 2008, p. 5.

147　Nader Habibi, "The Impact of Sanctions on Iran-GCC Economic Relations," Brandeis University, Crown Center for Middle East Studies, *Middle East Brief No.45*, November 2010, p. 5.

148　Ibid., p. 7.

149　Ibid.

150　"Dubai Traders Fear Sanctions Impact on Iran Business," *Reuters*, November 30, 2011.

151　"UAE Businesses to Feel Effect of Fresh US Sanctions on Iran," *The National*, July 3, 2013.

152　Jim Krane, *Dubai: The Story of the World's Fastest City* (New York: St Martin's Press, 2009), pp. 140–146.

153　Ian Jackson, "Nuclear Energy and Proliferation Risks: Myths and Realities in the Persian Gulf," *International Affairs*, 85(6), 2009, p. 1157.

154　"UAE Diplomat Mulls Hit on Iran's Nukes," *Washington Times*, July 6, 2010.

155　"A Tiny Island is Where Iran Makes a Stand," *New York Times*, April 30, 2012.

156　Kristian Coates Ulrichsen, "Iran and the Gulf: What Next?" *Houston Chronicle*, July 24, 2015.

157　Hasan al-Mustafa, "UAE, Iran Slowly Rebuild Ties," *Al-Monitor*, April 28, 2014.

158　"Dubai Eager to Capitalize on Iran Opening," *Financial Times*, January 21, 2014.

159　Kristian Coates Ulrichsen, "The Gulf States and Israeli-Palestinian Conflict Resolution," *Baker Institute Policy Report No. 61*, September 2014, p. 2.

160　"An Eye for an Eye: the Anatomy of Mossad's Dubai Operation," *Spiegel Online*, January 17, 2011.

161　Ibid.

162　"From Exile, a Divisive Figure Rattles Palestinian Politics," *Reuters*, September 16, 2015.

163　Hagar Shezaf, "Israel Eyes Improved Ties with Gulf States after 'Foothold' Gained in UAE," *Middle East Eye*, January 18, 2016.

164　"Security Expo Closes with Mega Contracts," *Emirates 24/7*, March 5, 2008.

165　"Emirates 'Has Security Links with Israel'," *UPI*, January 27, 2012.

166　Rori Donaghy, "Falcon Eye: the Israeli-installed Mass Civil Surveillance System of Abu Dhabi,"*Middle East Eye*, February 28, 2015.

167 Shezaf, *Israel Eyes Improved Ties with Gulf States.*
168 Quoted in Krane, *Dubai*, p. 174.
169 "Can Water Cooperation be a Model for Middle East Peacemaking?" *The World Post*, January 31, 2011.

7

CONCLUSION

The UAE weathered the Arab Spring upheaval that spread across much of the Middle East in 2011 and has become deeply enmeshed in regional geopolitics from Libya to Yemen by way of Egypt, as well as increasingly active in debates over the reshaping of aspects of international governance. Emirati policymakers emphasize their projection of leadership in issues of sustainable development and the Green Economy as well as the innovative and entrepreneurial potential of a young country and youthful society. Initiatives such as the 2020 World Expo in Dubai and the planned Emirates Mars Mission will ensure that the UAE remains firmly in the global spotlight as it commemorates a half-century of independence in 2021. Barely a week goes by without a new eye-catching headline from Abu Dhabi or Dubai designed to cultivate and reinforce the image of a confident and assertive actor in regional and international affairs.

Indeed, the very fact that the UAE has endured and, in myriad ways, matured as a federation is itself a mark of considerable success when set against the benchmark of other regional federal "experiments" of the 1960s and the generally low expectations of British officials at the time. The struggles of the 1970s and early 1980s over the constitutional makeup and the demarcation of emirate-level powers (and boundaries) has been gradually superseded by a degree of political consensus and a clearer and distinct notion of Emirati identity. Simultaneously, the charismatic and highly personalized structure of leadership of Sheikh Zayed bin Sultan Al Nahyan and the other "founding fathers" of 1971, based largely along tribal lines and direct access to the ruler, has been replaced by the growth of institutions and entities, many of which are today globally recognized. It is not for nothing that the UAE and, in particular, Dubai and Abu Dhabi, has become the destination of choice for aspirant young men and women from across the Arab world and further afield.

A number of questions and issues will define the next phase of domestic and international development in the UAE at both the federal and emirate levels.

Although Sheikh Zayed died in November 2004 his legacy continues to loom large throughout the UAE but an entire generation of Emiratis will soon lack any direct memory of his long and benevolent rule. The first decade of the "post-Zayed" transition was marked by the sharing of power among many of his sons and of influence with Sheikh Mohammed bin Rashid Al Maktoum in Dubai. However, developments in 2015 and 2016 appeared to indicate a coalescing of both power and influence around the Crown Prince of Abu Dhabi, Sheikh Mohammed bin Zayed Al Nahyan. This became apparent in the shakeup of federal government positions in February 2016, which generated international headlines over the appointment of Ministers of Happiness, Tolerance, and Youth and was also a cost-cutting exercise in the overall number of government ministries as the UAE, like its Gulf neighbors, responded to low oil prices and sharp falls in revenue.

However, the most significant aspect of the recent leadership changes was that, after years of exercising discreet political influence, often from behind the scenes, Sheikh Mohammed bin Zayed Al Nahyan visibly cemented his position as the de facto Head of State and became far less reticent about acting as such in the continuing absence of his older half-brother, the President of the UAE, Sheikh Khalifa bin Zayed Al Nahyan, who had remained out of the public eye since suffering a stroke in January 2014. What happened both in the federal reshuffle and in the restructuring of government and state-owned institutions, such as the Abu Dhabi National Oil Company (ADNOC) was therefore not so much a power play as the endgame in a succession process that has been at least a decade in the making but which, until 2015, occurred more in the shadows than in the spotlight of policymaking.[1]

Even though Mohammed bin Zayed had been the real "power behind the throne" in the emirate of Abu Dhabi for several years now, for a long time he trod carefully on the federal stage, mindful of the need to avoid unbalancing family dynamics within the Al Nahyan and inter-emirate relations with Dubai. What was significant about the government reshuffle in February 2016 – both in the way it was conducted and in the people appointed – was that it tallied with other developments that indicated that these constraints had now been shed. Whereas Mohammed bin Zayed previously had adopted a fairly low profile when travelling abroad, in deference to his presidential half-brother, on both his December 2015 visit to China and his February 2016 visit to India it was striking how he was treated (and acknowledged) as a Head of State – something that had not really happened before on anything like the same scale.[2]

Several of the appointments in the reshuffle suggested strongly that Mohammed bin Zayed stamped his authority over the most important aspects of federal policy. MBZ's son, Sheikh Khalid bin Mohammed Al Nahyan, became the head of the State Security Department (with ministerial rank) while a longtime ally, Mohammed Ahmed al-Bowardi, became Minister of State for Defense Affairs. Also significant was the appointment of Sultan Ahmed al-Jaber to head ADNOC, one of the few remaining entities in the UAE that had been operated by people close to the President of the UAE, Sheikh Khalifa. The Chairman of Abu Dhabi's flagship low-carbon Masdar City project, Chief Executive of Abu Dhabi's Mubadala sovereign wealth fund and a Minister of State for Foreign Affairs since 2013, al-Jaber had won plaudits for his handling of UAE–Egypt relations following the toppling of the Muslim Brotherhood government in Cairo in 2013, and immediately started to restructure the ADNOC group and play a critical role in energy policy together with Suhail Mohammed al-Mazrouei, his former deputy at Mubadala, who became the Minister of Energy in 2013.[3]

Al-Jaber rapidly set in motion a rationalization of the UAE energy sector under a new generation of leadership and may yet attempt a consolidation of the multiple sovereign wealth funds that contain energy-related portfolios, in tandem with the extensive scenario-planning that Mohammed bin Zayed reportedly has undertaken to examine options for the UAE at various oil prices down to US$25 a barrel.[4] The cost-cutting at ADNOC, which involved the shedding of 5,000 of the group's 60,000 strong workforce, was part of a broader trend throughout the UAE as oil revenues plunged from US$113.8 billion in 2014 to US$70 billion in 2015 and a forecast of US$48.2 billion for 2016.[5] Other examples of industry rationalization in 2016 occurred throughout the government sector and government-related enterprises with a 30 percent cutback in staffing at Etihad Rail that impacted primarily on expatriates rather than Emirati nationals; indeed, the demographic imbalance in the UAE, so often seen by nationals as a cause of concern, gives policymakers a cushion to impose sizeble austerity measures that hit foreign workers before they do Emiratis.[6]

Also of note was that whereas previous government reshuffles had been conducted by the Ruler of Dubai (in his capacity as Prime Minister) and rubber-stamped by the President, the latest reshuffle was accompanied by an official statement that acknowledged that the changes were undertaken in consultation with (and approval by) Mohammed bin Zayed. This was a clear signal that the Crown Prince has assumed center stage in political decision making at the federal (UAE) level in addition to the emirate (Abu Dhabi) level, and effectively was acting as President of the UAE in all but name. Given that few expected President Khalifa to recover from his ill-health and that he could pass at any point, the decision seemed to have been taken within the ruling family to remove any remaining constraints on the exercise of power by Mohammed bin Zayed mindful, perhaps, of the need to portray an image of strong and decisive leadership to avoid any lingering political uncertainty as the UAE grapples with the new era of cheap oil and the delicate economic reforms needed to cushion the transition to a more sustainable post-oil political economy.

Looking ahead, the challenge for the UAE under Mohammed bin Zayed will be one of achieving a sustainable balance on multiple issues. These include ensuring that the hawkish approach to domestic and regional security does not weaken the integrative bonds among the seven emirates, particularly if the conflict in Yemen continues and UAE casualties mount. The evolving power dynamics described above may be welcomed by policymakers looking for strong and decisive leadership at times of economic difficulty but they also risk upsetting the federal-emirate level balance should Abu Dhabi be perceived as imposing its own set of interests across the board. The consensual approach to political and economic development spearheaded by Sheikh Zayed appears very different from the security-centric focus of much of UAE policymaking since 2011. And while the UAE can continue to draw down foreign reserves and issue new debt to finance budget deficits for years to come, the speed with which budget surpluses turned into deficits after 2014 illustrated the scale of volatility in the UAE economy and its continued vulnerability to oil price swings, notwithstanding the heavy emphasis on economic diversification and innovative growth.

Similar to their counterparts in other Gulf Cooperation Council (GCC) states, officials in the UAE sought to minimize the political impact of austerity measures by cutting back on capital (rather than current) spending or by focusing on expatriate communities or corporate users. And yet, any effective transition toward a genuinely post-oil future will require deeper reforms that amount to reformulating the pillars of welfare spending and wealth redistribution that have underpinned sociopolitical stability since the 1970s and that inevitably may require policies that change the relationship of citizens with the state. Periods of profound transition in other contexts in the past often have left states and societies vulnerable to outbreaks of political violence and social conflict, and this is the worst-case scenario policymakers and their publics – as well as regional and international partners of the UAE – wish to avoid. Sheikhs Mohammed bin Zayed in Abu Dhabi and Mohammed bin Rashid in Dubai (along with, more recently, Prince Mohammed bin Salman Al Saud in Saudi Arabia) have consistently sketched out the "bigger picture" in their policy statements and will need to continue to think "outside of the box" as they pursue transformative outcomes of reform processes that will unfold in a period of accelerated change and heightened regional uncertainty, but which are necessary to become more economically sustainable over the longer-term.

Notes

1 Kristian Coates Ulrichsen, "Evolving Power Dynamics in the United Arab Emirates," *Houston Chronicle*, March 1, 2016.
2 Ibid.
3 Diane Munro, "ADNOC's CEO Institutes Seismic Shift in Corporate Strategy," *Arab Gulf States Institute in Washington blog*, June 1, 2016.
4 Author Interview, Washington, DC, February 2016.
5 Munro, *Seismic Shift*.
6 "Abu Dhabi Lays off Staff as Gulf Austerity Tightens," *Reuters*, May 22, 2016.

BIBLIOGRAPHY

Books

Abdullah, Mohammed Morsy, 1978. *The United Arab Emirates: a Modern History*. London: Croon Helm.

Adib-Mughaddam, Arshin, 2006. *The International Politics of the Persian Gulf: a Cultural Genealogy*. London: Routledge.

Al-Abed, Ibrahim and Peter Hellyer, 2001. *United Arab Emirates: A New Perspective*. London: Trident Press.

Al-Alkim, Hassan Hamdan, 1989. *The Foreign Policy of the United Arab Emirates*. London: Saqi Books.

Albaharna, Husain, 1968. *The Legal Status of the Arabian Gulf States: A Study of Their Treaty Relations and Their International Problems*. Manchester: Manchester University Press.

Al-Duraiby, Ibrahim Suleiman, 2009. *Saudi Arabia, GCC and the EU: Limitations and Possibilities for an Unequal Triangular Relationship*. Dubai: Gulf Research Center.

Al-Fahim, Mohammed, 1995. *From Rags to Riches: a Story of Abu Dhabi*. London: London Center of Arab Studies.

Ali, Syed, 2010. *Dubai: Gilded Cage*. New Haven, CT: Yale University Press.

Almezaini, Khalid, 2012. *The UAE and Foreign Policy: Foreign Aid, Identities, and Interests*. Abingdon: Routledge.

Al Qasimi, Sultan bin Mohammed, 1986. *The Myth of Arab Piracy in the Gulf*. London: Croon Helm.

Anon., 2004. *The National Commission Report: Final Report of the National Commission on Terrorist Attacks upon the United States*. New York: W.W. Norton & Company.

Anon., 2008. *The Report: Sharjah 2008*. Oxford: Oxford Business Group.

Anon., 2014a. *The Report: Abu Dhabi 2014*. Oxford: Oxford Business Group.

Anon., 2014b. *The Report: Dubai 2014*. Oxford: Oxford Business Group.

Ansari, Shahid Jamal, 1998. *Political Modernization in the Gulf*. Delhi: Northern Book Center.

Assiri, Abdul-Reda, 1990. *Kuwait's Foreign Policy: City-State in World Politics*. Boulder, CO: Westview Press.

Baker III, James A., 1995. *The Politics of Diplomacy: Revolution, War & Peace, 1989–1992*. New York: Putnam.

Balfour Paul, Glencairn, 1991. *The End of Empire in the Middle East: Britain's Relinquishment of Power in Her Last Three Arab Dependencies*. Cambridge: Cambridge University Press.

Balfour Paul, Glencairn, 2006. *Bagpipes in Babylon: A Lifetime in the Arab World and Beyond*. London: I.B. Tauris.

Bazoobandi, Sara, 2013. *The Political Economy of the Gulf Sovereign Wealth Funds: A Case Study of Iran, Kuwait, Saudi Arabia and the United Arab Emirates*. Abingdon: Routledge.

Bullock, John, 1984. *The Gulf: A Portrait of Kuwait, Qatar, Bahrain and the UAE*. London: Century Publishing.

Burdett, A.L.P., 2002. *Records of the Emirates, 1966–1971, Volume 4: 1969*. Farnham: Archive Editions.

Casey, Michael, 2007. *The History of Kuwait*. Westport, CT: Greenwood Press.

Chalabi, Fadhil, 2010. *Oil Policies, Oil Myths: Observations of an OPEC Insider*. London: I.B. Tauris.

Coates Ulrichsen, Kristian, 2014. *Qatar and the Arab Spring*. Oxford: Oxford University Press.

Coates Ulrichsen, Kristian, 2015a. *The Gulf States in International Political Economy*. London: Palgrave Macmillan.

Coates Ulrichsen, Kristian, 2015b. *Insecure Gulf: The End of Certainty and the Transition to the Post-Oil Era*. Oxford: Oxford University Press.

Coll, Steve, 2004. *Ghost Wars: The Secret History of the CIA, Afghanistan, and Bin Laden, from the Soviet Invasion to September 10, 2001*. New York: Penguin.

Commins, David, 2012. *The Gulf States: A Modern History*. London: I.B. Tauris.

Cooke, Miriam, 2014. *Tribal Modern: Branding New Nations in the Arab Gulf*, Berkeley, CA: University of California Press.

Cooper Busch, Briton, 1967. *Britain and the Persian Gulf, 1894–1914*. Berkeley, CA: University of California Press.

Cordesman, Anthony, 1997. *Kuwait: Recovery and Security after the Gulf War*. Boulder, CO: Westview Press.

Crystal, Jill, 1990. *Oil and Politics in the Gulf: Rulers and Merchants in Kuwait and Qatar*. Cambridge: Cambridge University Press.

Daly, M.W., 2014. *The Last of the Great Proconsuls: The Biography of Sir William Luce*. San Diego, CA: Nathan Berg.

Davidson, Christopher, 2006. *The United Arab Emirates: A Study in Survival*. London: Lynne Rienner.

Davidson, Christopher, 2008. *Dubai: The Vulnerability of Success*. London: Hurst & Co.

Davidson, Christopher, 2009. *Abu Dhabi: Oil and Beyond*. London: Hurst & Co.

Davidson, Christopher, 2010. *The Persian Gulf and Pacific Asia: From Indifference to Interdependence*. London: Hurst & Co.

Davies, Charles, 1997. *The Blood-Red Arab Flag: An Investigation into Qasimi Piracy, 1797–1820*. Exeter: Exeter University Press.

Dawisha, Adeed, 2013. *The Second Arab Awakening: Revolution, Democracy, and the Islamist Challenge from Tunis to Damascus*. New York: W.W. Norton & Company.

El Mallakh, Ragaei, 2001. *The Economic Development of the United Arab Emirates*. New York: Palgrave Macmillan.

Fain, W. Taylor, 2008. *American Ascendance and British Retreat in the Persian Gulf*. Basingstoke: Palgrave Macmillan.

Gilmour, David. *Curzon*. London: John Murray.

Gupte, Pranay, 2012. *Dubai: The Making of a Megalopolis*. New York: Penguin/Viking.

Halliday, Fred, 2002. *Arabia without Sultans*. London: Saqi Books.

Halliday, Fred, 2005. *The Middle East in International Relations: Power, Politics and Ideology*. Cambridge: Cambridge University Press.

Hawley, Donald, 1970. *The Trucial States*. London: Allen & Unwin.

Heard-Bey, Frauke, 2007. *From Trucial States to United Arab Emirates*. Dubai: Motivate Publishing.

Herb, Michael, 2014. *The Wages of Oil: Parliaments and Economic Development in Kuwait and the UAE*. New York: Cornell University Press.

Hey, Jeanne, 2003. *Small States in World Politics: Explaining Foreign Policy Behavior*. Boulder, CO: Lynne Rienner.

Jarman, Robert, 1998. *Political Diaries of the Arab World: The Persian Gulf. Volume 24: 1963–1965*. Chippenham: Archive Editions.

Joyce, Miriam, 1998. *Kuwait, 1945–1996: An Anglo-American Perspective*. London: Frank Cass.

Kanna, Ahmed, 2011. *Dubai: the City as Corporation*. Minneapolis, MN: University of Minnesota Press.

Kechichian, Joseph, 2008. *Power and Succession in Arab Monarchies: A Reference Guide*. Boulder, CO: Lynne Rienner.

Khalifa, Ali Mohammed, 1979. *The United Arab Emirates: Unity in Fragmentation*. London: Croon Helm.

Krane, Jim, 2009. *Dubai: The Story of the World's Fastest City*. New York: St Martin's Press.

Krause, Wanda, 2008. *Women in Civil Society*. Basingstoke: Palgrave Macmillan.

Kumetat, Dennis, 2015. *Managing the Transition: Renewable Energy and Innovation Policies in the UAE and Algeria*. Abingdon: Routledge.

Luomi, Mari, 2012. *The Gulf Monarchies and Climate Change: Abu Dhabi and Qatar in an Era of Natural Unsustainability*. London: Hurst & Co.

Macris, Jeffrey, 2010. *The Politics and Security of the Gulf: Anglo-American Hegemony and the Shaping of a Region*. London: Routledge.

Maitra, Jayanti and Afra al-Hajji, 2001. *Qasr al-Hosn: The History of the Rulers of Abu Dhabi, 1793–1966*. Abu Dhabi: Center for Documentation and Research.

Mahdavi, Pardis, 2011. *Gridlock: Labor, Migration, and Human Trafficking in Dubai*. Stanford, CA: Stanford University Press.

Marshall, Christin, 2003. *Iran's Persian Gulf Policy: From Khomeini to Khatami*. Abingdon: Routledge.

Nye, Joseph, 1990. *Bound to Lead: The Changing Nature of American Power*. New York: Basic Books.

Nye, Joseph, 2004. *Soft Power: The Means to Succeed in World Politics*. New York: PublicAffairs.

Peck, Malcolm, 1986. *The United Arab Emirates: A Venture in Unity*. Boulder, CO: Westview Press.

Pitney, Jr., John and John-Clark Levin, 2013. *Private Anti-Piracy Navies: How Warships for Hire are Changing Maritime Security*. New York: Lexington Books.

Quentin Morton, Michael, 2013. *Buraimi: The Struggle for Power, Influence and Oil in Arabia*. London: I.B. Tauris.

Ramos, Stephen, 2012. *Dubai Amplified: The Engineering of a Port Geography*. London: Ashgate.

Rugh, Andrea, 2007. *The Political Culture of Leadership in the United Arab Emirates*. New York: Palgrave Macmillan.

Said Zahlan, Rosemarie, 1978. *The Origins of the United Arab Emirates: A Political and Social History of the Trucial States*. London: Macmillan.

Said Zahlan, Rosemarie, 1998. *The Making of the Modern Gulf States: Kuwait, Bahrain, Qatar, the United Arab Emirates and Oman*. Reading: Ithaca Press.

Sampler, Jeffrey and Saeb Eigner, 2003. *Sand to Silicon: Achieving Rapid Growth Lessons from Dubai*. London: Profile Books.

Sarbu, Bianca, 2014. *Ownership and Control of Oil: Explaining Policy Choices across Producing Countries*. Abingdon: Routledge.

Simpfendorfer, Ben, 2009. *The New Silk Road: How a Rising Arab World is Turning Away from the West and Rediscovering China*. London: Palgrave Macmillan.

Smith, Simon, 2004. *Britain's Revival and Fall in the Gulf: Kuwait, Bahrain, Qatar and the Trucial States, 1950–1971*. Abingdon: Routledge.

Spraggon, Martin and Virginia Bodolica. *Managing Organizations in the United Arab Emirates: Dynamic Characteristics and Key Economic Developments*. New York: Palgrave Macmillan.

Stanley-Price, Nicholas, 2012. *Imperial Outpost in the Gulf: The Airfield at Sharjah (UAE) 1932–1952*. London: The Book Guild Ltd.

Taryam, Abdullah Omran, 1987. *The Establishment of the United Arab Emirates, 1950–1985*. London: Croon Helm.

Thesiger, William, 1991. *Arabian Sands*. London: Penguin.

Tucker, Spencer, 2014. *Persian Gulf War Encyclopedia: A Political, Social, and Military History*. Santa Barbara, CA: ABC-CLIO.

Von Bismarck, Helene, 2013. *British Policy in the Persian Gulf, 1961–1968. Conceptions of Informal Empire*. London: Palgrave Macmillan.

Vora, Neha, 2013. *Impossible Citizens: Dubai's Indian Diaspora*. Durham, NC: Duke University Press.

Young, Karen, 2014. *The Political Economy of Energy, Finance and Security in the United Arab Emirates: Between the Majlis and the Market*. New York: Palgrave Macmillan.

Chapters

Abdulla, Abdulkhaleq, 1999. "The Gulf Cooperation Council: Nature, Origin and Process." In Michael Hudson, ed. *Middle East Dilemma: The Politics and Economics of Arab Integration*. New York: Columbia University Press.

Abdulla, Abdulkhaleq, 2006. "The Impact of Globalization on Arab Gulf States." In John W. Fox, Nada Mourtada-Sabbah, and Mohammed al-Mutawa, eds, *Globalization and the Gulf*. Abingdon: Routledge.

Al-Abed, Ibrahim, 2001. "The Historical Background and Constitutional Basis to the Federation." In Ibrahim al-Abed and Peter Hellyer, eds, *United Arab Emirates: A New Perspective*. London: Trident Press.

Al-Mashat, Abdul-Monem, 2008. "Politics of Constructive Engagement: The Foreign Policy of the United Arab Emirates." In Bahgat Korany and Ali Hillal Dessouki, eds, *The Foreign Policies of Arab Gulf States: The Challenge of Globalization*. Cairo: American University of Cairo Press.

Almezaini, Khalid, 2013. "Private Sector Actors in the UAE and their Role in the Process of Economic and Political Reform." In Steffen Hertog, Giacomo Luciani and Marc Valeri, eds, *Business Politics in the Middle East*. London: Hurst & Co.

Al-Sadik, Tawfik Ali, 2001. "Evolution and Performance of the UAE Economy 1972–1998." In Ibrahim al-Abed and Peter Hellyer, eds, *United Arab Emirates: A New Perspective*. London: Trident Press.

AlShehabi, Omar, 2015. "Migration, Commodification, and the 'Right to the City'." In Abdulhadi Khalaf, Omar AlShehabi, and Adam Hanieh, eds, *Transit States: Labour, Migration & Citizenship in the Gulf*. London: Pluto Press.

Baaboud, Abdulla, 2005. "Dynamics and Determinants of the GCC States' Foreign Policy with Special Reference to the EU." In Gerd Nonneman, ed. *Analyzing Middle Eastern Foreign Policies*. London: Routledge.

Bagher Vosoughi, Mohammad, 2009. "The Kings of Hormuz: From the Beginning until the Arrival of the Portuguese." In Lawrence Potter, ed. *The Persian Gulf in History*. New York: Palgrave Macmillan.

Beeman, William, 2009. "Gulf Society: An Anthropological View of the Khalijis – Their Evolution and Way of Life." In Lawrence Potter, ed. *The Persian Gulf in History*. New York: Palgrave Macmillan.

Bristol-Rhys, Jane, 2012. "Socio-Spatial Boundaries in Abu Dhabi." In Mehran Kamrava and Zahra Babar, eds, *Migrant Labor in the Persian Gulf*. London: Hurst & Co.

Butt, Gerald, 2001. "Oil and Gas in the UAE." In Ibrahim al-Abed and Peter Hellyer, eds, *United Arab Emirates: A New Perspective*. London: Trident Press.

Coates Ulrichsen, Kristian, 2012. "Knowledge-Based Economies in GCC States." In Mehran Kamrava, ed. *The Political Economy of the Persian Gulf*. London: Hurst & Co.

Coates Ulrichsen, Kristian, 2013. "The Gulf States and the Iran-Iraq War: Cooperation and Confusion." In Nigel Ashton and Bryan Gibson, eds, *The Iran-Iraq War: New International Perspectives*. Abingdon: Routledge.

Davidson, Christopher, 2008a. "The Impact of Economic Reform on Dubai." In Anoushiravan Ehteshami and Steven Wright, eds, *Reform in the Middle East Oil Monarchies*. Reading: Ithaca Press.

Davidson, Christopher, 2008b. "Diversification in Abu Dhabi and Dubai: The Impact of National Identity and the Ruling Bargain." In Alanoud Alsharekh and Robert Springborg, eds, *Popular Culture and Political Identity in the Arab Gulf States*. London: Saqi Books.

Davidson, Christopher, 2009. "The United Arab Emirates: Economy First, Politics Second." In Joshua Teitelbaum, ed. *Political Liberalization in the Persian Gulf*. London: Hurst & Co.

Davidson, Christopher, 2012. "The Dubai Model: Diversification and Slowdown." In Mehran Kamrava, ed. *The Political Economy of the Persian Gulf*. London: Hurst & Co.

Ehteshami, Anoushiravan, 2002. "The Foreign Policy of Iran." In Raymond Hinnebusch and Anoushiravan Ehteshami, eds, *The Foreign Policies of Middle East States*. London: Lynne Rienner.

Fox, John W., Nada Mourtada-Sabbah, and Mohammed al-Mutawa, 2006. "Heritage Revivalism in Sharjah." In John W. Fox, Nada Mourtada-Sabbah, and Mohammed al-Mutawa, eds, *Globalization and the Gulf*. Abingdon: Routledge.

Gordon, Mark and Sabastian Niles, 2012. "Sovereign Wealth Funds: An Overview." In Karl Sauvant, Lisa Sachs, and Wouter Schmit Jongbloed, eds, *Sovereign Investments: Concerns and Policy Challenges*. Oxford: Oxford University Press.

Hanieh, Adam, 2015. "Migrant Rights in the Gulf: the Way Forward." In Abdulhadi Khalaf, Omar AlShehabi, and Adam Hanieh, eds, *Transit States: Labour, Migration & Citizenship in the Gulf*. London: Pluto Press.

Heard-Bey, Frauke, 1998. "The United Arab Emirates: A Quarter Century of Federation." In Michael Hudson, ed. *Middle East Dilemma: The Politics and Economics of Arab Identity*. New York: Columbia University Press.

Heard-Bey, Frauke, 2001. "The Tribal Society of the UAE and its Traditional Economy." In Ibrahim al-Abed and Peter Hellyer, eds, *United Arab Emirates: A New Perspective*. London: Trident Press.

Hellyer, Peter, 2001. "Evolution of UAE Foreign Policy." In Ibrahim al-Abed and Peter Hellyer, eds, *United Arab Emirates: A New Perspective*. London: Trident Press.

Hokayem, Emile and Becca Wasser, 2014. "The Gulf States in an Era of American Retrenchment." In Toby Dodge and Emile Hokayem, eds, *Middle Eastern Security, the US Pivot, and the Rise of ISIS*. London: Routledge.

Joffe, George, 1994. "Concepts of Sovereignty in the Gulf Region." In Richard Schofield, ed. *Territorial Foundations of the Gulf States*. New York: St Martin's Press.

Kamrava, Mehran, 2012. "The Political Economy of Rentierism in the Persian Gulf." In Mehran Kamrava, ed. *The Political Economy of the Persian Gulf*. London: Hurst & Co.

Kinninmont, Jane, 2011. "Bahrain." In Christopher Davidson, ed. *Power and Politics in the Persian Gulf*. London: Hurst & Co.

Lawson, Fred and Hasan al-Naboodah, 2008. "Heritage and Cultural Nationalism in the United Arab Emirates." In Alanoud Alsharekh and Robert Springborg, eds, *Popular Culture and Political Identity in the Arab Gulf States*. London: Saqi Books.

Luciani, Giacomo, 2005. "From Private Sector to National Bourgeoisie: Saudi Arabian Business." In Paul Aarts and Gerd Nonneman, eds, *Saudi Arabia in the Balance: Political Economy, Society, Foreign Affairs*. London: Hurst & Co.

Luciani, Giacomo, 2006. "Democracy vs. Shura in the Age of the Internet." In Abdulhadi Khalaf and Giacomo Luciani, eds, *Constitutional Reform and Political Participation in the Gulf*. Dubai: Gulf Research Center.

Luciani, Giacomo, 2007. "The GCC Refining and Petrochemical Sectors in Global Perspective." In Eckart Woertz, ed. *Gulf Geo-Economics*. Dubai: Gulf Research Center.

Martin, Susan, 2012. "Protecting Migrants' Rights in the Gulf Cooperation Council." In Mehran Kamrava and Zahra Babar, eds, *Migrant Labor in the Persian Gulf*. London: Hurst & Co.

Mednicoff, David, 2012. "The Legal Regulation of Migrant Workers, Politics and Identity in Qatar and the United Arab Emirates." In Mehran Kamrava and Zahra Babar, eds, *Migrant Labor in the Persian Gulf*. London: Hurst & Co.

Neilson, Keith, 1997. "For Diplomatic, Economic, Strategic and Telegraphic Reasons: British Imperial Defence, the Middle East and India, 1914–1918." In Greg Kennedy and Keith Neilson, eds. *Far-flung Lines: Essays on Imperial Defence in Honour of Donald Mackenzie Schurman*. London: Frank Cass.

Nonneman, Gerd, 2004. "The Gulf States and the Iran-Iraq War: Pattern Shifts and Continuities." In Lawrence Potter and Gary Sick, eds, *Iran, Iraq, and the Legacies of War*. New York: Palgrave Macmillan.

Partrick, Neil, 2012. "Nationalism in the Gulf States." In David Held and Kristian Ulrichsen, eds, *The Transformation of the Gulf: Politics, Economics and the Global Order*. Abingdon: Routledge.

Peck, Malcolm, 2001. "Formation and Evolution of the Federation and its Institutions." In Ibrahim al-Abed and Peter Hellyer, eds, *United Arab Emirates: A New Perspective*. London: Trident Press.

Peterson, J.E., 1988. "The Future of Federalism in the United Arab Emirates." In H. Richard Sindelar III and J.E. Peterson, eds, *Crosscurrents in the Gulf: Arab Regional and Global Interests*. London: Routledge.

Peterson, J.E., 2007. "Rulers, Merchants, and Shaykhs in Gulf Politics: The Function of Family Networks." In Alanoud Alsharekh, ed. *The Gulf Family: Kinship Policies and Modernity*. London: Saqi Books.

Peterson, J.E., 2009. "Britain and the Gulf: At the Periphery of Empire." In Lawrence Potter, ed. *The Persian Gulf in History*. New York: Columbia University Press.

Peterson, J.E., 2011. "Sovereignty and Boundaries in the Gulf States." In Mehran Kamrava, ed. *International Politics of the Persian Gulf*. Syracuse, NY: Syracuse University Press.

Popp, Karoline, 2012. "Regional Processes, Law and Institutional Developments on Migration." In Brian Opeskin, Richard Perruchoud, and Jillyanne Redpath-Cross, eds, *Foundations of International Migration Law*. Cambridge: Cambridge University Press.

Potts, D.T., 2001. "Before the Emirates: an Archaeological and Historical Account of Developments in the Region c.5000 BC to 676 AD." In Ibrahim al-Abed and Peter Hellyer, eds, *United Arab Emirates: A New Perspective*. London: Trident Press.

Potts, D.T., 2009. "The Archaeology and Early History of the Persian Gulf." In Lawrence Potter, ed. *The Persian Gulf in History*. New York: Columbia University Press.

Razieh Nadjmabandi, Shahnaz, 2009. "The Arab Presence on the Iranian Coast of the Persian Gulf." In Lawrence Potter, ed. *The Persian Gulf in History*. New York: Columbia University Press.

Rickli, Jean-Marc, 2016. "The Political Rationale and Implications of the United Arab Emirates' Military Involvement in Libya." In Dag Henriksen and Ann Karin Larsen, eds, *Political Rationale and International Consequences of the War in Libya*. Oxford: Oxford University Press.

Roger Louis, Wm., 2006. "The Withdrawal from the Gulf." In Wm. Roger Louis, *Ends of British Imperialism: The Scramble for Empire, Suez, and Decolonization*. London: I.B. Tauris.

Sfakianakis, John and Eckart Woertz, 2007. "Strategic Foreign Investments of GCC Countries." In Eckart Woertz, ed. *Gulf Geo-Economics*. Dubai: Gulf Research Center.

Troeller, Gary, 1976. *The Birth of Saudi Arabia: Britain and the Rise of the House of Sa'ud*. London: Frank Cass.

Valeri, Marc, 2017. "Toward the End of the Oligarchic Pact? Business and Politics in Abu Dhabi, Bahrain, and Oman." In Kristian Coates Ulrichsen, ed. *Changing Security Dynamics in the Persian Gulf*. London: Hurst & Co.

Walker, Julian, 1994. "Practical Problems of Boundary Limitation in Arabia: the Case of the United Arab Emirates." In Richard Schofield, ed. *The Territorial Foundations of the Gulf States*. New York: St Martin's Press.

Winckler, Onn, 2009. "Labor and Liberalization: The Decline of the GCC Rentier System." In Joshua Teitelbaum, ed. *Political Liberalization in the Persian Gulf*. London: Hurst & Co.

Journal Articles and Working Papers

Al-Dabbagh, May and Lana Nusseibeh, 2009. "Women in Parliament and Politics in the UAE: A Study of the First Federal National Council Elections." *Dubai School of Government/ Ministry of Federal National Council Affairs Paper*.

Al-Noqaidan, Mansour, 2012. "Muslim Brotherhood in UAE: Expansion and Decline." *Al Mesbar Center for Studies and Research*.

Al Qassemi, Fahim bin Sultan, 1999. "A Century in Thirty Years: Sheikh Zayed and the United Arab Emirates." *Middle East Policy*, 6(4).

Al-Sayegh, Fatma, 1998. "Merchants' Role in a Changing Society: The Case of Dubai, 1900–1990." *Middle Eastern Studies*, 34(1).

Al-Sayegh, Fatma, 1999. "Diversity in Unity: Political Institutions and Civil Society." *Middle East Policy*, 6(4).

Al-Shayeji, Abdullah, 1997. "Dangerous Perceptions: Gulf Views of U.S. Policy in the Region." *Middle East Policy*, 5(3).

Al Yousefi, Abdul Hafeez Yawar Khan, 2013. "50 Years in Al Ain Oasis – Memoirs of Khabeer Khan." *Liwa: Journal of the National Center for Documentation and Research*, 5(9).

Anderson, Lisa, 1991. "Absolutism and the Resilience of Monarchy in the Middle East." *Political Science Quarterly*, 106(1).

Anon., 2011. "Accidental Heroes: Britain, France and the Libya Operation: an Interim RUSI Campaign Report." Royal United Services Institute.

Armijo, Jacqueline, 2014. "DragonMart: The Mega-Souk of Today's Silk Road." Middle East Report 270.

Bahgat, Gawdat, 2011. "Sovereign Wealth Funds in the Gulf: an Assessment." LSE Kuwait Program Working Paper No. 16.

Barakat, Sultan and Steve Zyck, 2010. "Gulf State Assistance to Conflict-Affected Environments." LSE Kuwait Program Working Paper No. 10.

Baskan, Birol, 2012. "The Police Chief and the Sheikh." The Washington Review of Middle Eastern & Eurasian Affairs.

Behrendt, Sven, 2008. "Beyond Santiago: Status and Prospects." Central Banking, 19(4).

Blanchard, Christopher, 2010. "United Arab Emirates Nuclear Program and Proposed U.S. Nuclear Cooperation." Congressional Research Service Report for Congress.

Browning, Christopher, 2015. "Nation Branding, National Self-Esteem, and the Constitution of Subjectivity in Late Modernity." Foreign Policy Analysis, 11(2).

Carvalho Pinto, Vania, 2014. "From "Follower" to "Role Model": the Transformation to the UAE's International Self-Image." Journal of Arabian Studies, 4(2), 2014.

Coates Ulrichsen, Kristian, 2010. "The GCC States and the Shifting Balance of Global Power." Georgetown University School of Foreign Service in Qatar, Center for International and Regional Studies, Occasional Paper.

Coates Ulrichsen, Kristian, 2011. "Rebalancing Global Governance: Gulf States' Perspectives on the Governance of Globalization." Global Policy, 2(1).

Coates Ulrichsen, Kristian, 2013. "Foreign Policy Implications of the New Emir's Succession in Qatar." Norwegian Peacebuilding Resource Center Policy Brief.

Coates Ulrichsen, Kristian, 2014. "The Gulf States and Israeli–Palestinian Conflict Resolution." Baker Institute Policy Report No. 61.

Cordner, Lee, 2012. "Progressing Maritime Security Cooperation in the Indian Ocean." Naval War College Review, 64(4).

Dargin, Justin, 2008. "The Dolphin Project: The Development of a Gulf Gas Initiative." Oxford Institute for Energy Studies Working Paper No. 22.

Dargin, Justin, 2010. "Addressing the UAE Natural Gas Crisis: Strategies for a Rational Energy Policy." Belfer Center for Science & International Affairs, Harvard Kennedy School Dubai Initiative, Policy Brief.

Davidson, Christopher, 2006. "After Sheikh Zayed: the Politics of Succession in Abu Dhabi and the UAE." Middle East Policy, 13(1).

Davidson, Christopher, 2008. "Dubai: the Security Dimensions of the Region's Premier Free Port." Middle East Policy, 15(2).

Duke Anthony, John, Jean-Francois Seznec, Ari Tayyar, and Wayne White, 2008. "War with Iran: Regional Reactions and Requirements." Middle East Policy, 15(3).

Dutta, Soumitra, Bruno Lanvin, and Sacha Wunsch-Vincent, 2015. "The Global Innovation Index 2015: Effective Innovation Policies for Development." Cornell University, INSEAD, and the World Intellectual Property Organization (WIPO).

Habibi, Nader, 2010. "The Impact of Sanctions on Iran-GCC Economic Relations." Brandeis University, Crown Center for Middle East Studies, Middle East Brief No. 45.

Heard-Bey, Frauke, 2005. "The United Arab Emirates: Statehood and Nation-Building in a Traditional Society." Middle East Journal, 59(3).

Heard-Bey, Frauke, 2006. "Conflict Resolution and Regional Cooperation: The Role of the Gulf Cooperation Council, 1970–2002." Middle Eastern Studies, 42(2).

Henderson, Simon, 2003. "Succession Politics in the Conservative Gulf Arab States: the Weekend's Events in Ras al-Khaimah." The Washington Institute, Policywatch No. 769.

Henderson, Simon, 2010. "The Iran Angle of Ras al-Khaimah's Succession Struggle." The Washington Institute, Policywatch No. 1714.

Henderson, Simon, 2014. "Qatar Makes Peace with its Gulf Neighbors." The Washington Institute, Policy Alert.

Herb, Michael, 2009. "A Nation of Bureaucrats: Political Participation and Economic Diversification in Kuwait and the United Arab Emirates." *International Journal of Middle East Studies*, 41(3).

Herlevi, April, 2016. "China and the United Arab Emirates: Sustainable Silk Road Partnership?" *China Brief*, 16(2).

Hvidt, Martin, 2009. "The Dubai Model: An Outline of Key Development-Process Elements in Dubai." *International Journal of Middle East Studies*, 41(2).

Jackson, Ian, 2009. "Nuclear Energy and Proliferation Risks: Myths and Realities in the Persian Gulf." *International Affairs*, 85(6).

Kanna, Ahmed, 2007. "Dubai in a Jagged World." Middle East Research and Information Project Report No. 243.

Katz, Mark, 2015. "Convergent Hopes, Divergent Politics: Russia and the Gulf in a Time of Trouble." Arab Gulf States Institute in Washington Policy Paper #7.

Katzman, Kenneth, 2008. "The United Arab Emirates (UAE): Issues for U.S. Policy." Congressional Research Service Report for Congress.

Kellner, Thierry, 2012. "The GCC States of the Persian Gulf and Asia Energy Relations." IFRI Research Paper.

Keshavarzian, Arang, 2010. "Geopolitics and the Genealogy of Free Trade Zones in the Persian Gulf." *Geopolitics*, 15(2).

Khalaf, Sulayman, 2002. "Globalization and Heritage Revival in the Gulf: an Anthropological Look at Dubai Heritage Village." *Journal of Social Affairs*, 19(75).

Knights, Michael and Alexandre Mello, 2015. "The Saudi-UAE War Effort in Yemen (Part I): Operation Golden Arrow in Aden." The Washington Institute, Policywatch No. 2464.

Koch, Christian, 2012. "GCC Confronted by Disunity." Gulf Research Center Note.

Krane, Jim and Steven Wright, 2014. "Qatar "Rises Above" its Region: Geopolitics and the Rejection of the GCC Gas Market." LSE Kuwait Program Working Paper No. 35.

Lane, Jason, 2010. "International Branch Campuses, Free Zones, and Quality Assurance: Issues for Dubai and the UAE." Dubai School of Government Policy Brief No. 20.

Lawson, Fred, 2012. "Transformation of Regional Economic Governance in the Gulf Cooperation Council." Georgetown University School of Foreign Service in Qatar: Center for International and Regional Studies, Occasional Paper.

Legrenzi, Matteo, 2007. "NATO in the Gulf: Who is Doing Whom a Favor?" *Middle East Policy*, 14(1).

Luomi, Mari, 2011. "Gulf of Interest: Why Oil Still Dominates Middle Eastern Climate Politics." *Journal of Arabian Studies*, 1(2).

Matthiesen, Toby, 2014. "Mysticism, Migration and Clerical Networks: Ahmad al-Ahsa'i and the Shaykis of al-Ahsa, Kuwait and Basra." *Journal of Minority Muslim Affairs*.

Onley, James, 2006. "Britain and the Gulf Shaikhdoms, 1820–1971: The Politics of Protection." Georgetown University School of Foreign Service in Qatar: Center for International and Regional Studies, Occasional Paper.

Onley, James and Sulayman Khalaf, 2006. "Shaikhly Authority in the Pre-Oil Gulf: An Historical-Anthropological Study." *History and Anthropology*, 17(3).

Osman Salih, Kamal, 1992. "The 1938 Kuwait Legislative Council." *Middle Eastern Studies*, 28(1).

Petersen, Andrew and David Jones, 2009. "A Dubai World Debt and Nakheel Sukuk – Apocalypse Now?" K&L Gates Depressed Real Estate Alert.

Peterson, J.E., 2006. "Qatar and the World: Branding for a Micro-State." *Middle East Journal*, 60(4).

Plotkin Boghardt, Lori, 2013. "The Muslim Brotherhood on Trial in the UAE." The Washington Institute, Policywatch No. 264.

Quah, Danny, 2011. "The Global Economy's Shifting Center of Gravity." *Global Policy*, 2(1).

Quentin Morton, Michael, 2013. "The British India Line in the Arabian Gulf, 1862–1982." *Liwa: Journal of the National Center for Documentation and Research*, 5(10).

Ramos, Stephen, 2009. "The Blueprint: A History of Dubai's Spatial Development through Oil Discovery." Harvard Kennedy School's Belfer Center for Science and International Affairs/Dubai Initiative Working Paper.

Raouf, Mohammed, 2008. "Climate Change Threats, Opportunities, and the GCC Countries." Middle East Institute Policy Brief No. 12.

Raouf, Mohammed, 2009. "Water Issues in the Gulf: Time for Action." Middle East Institute Policy Brief No. 22.

Razoux, Pierre, 2010. "What Future for NATO's Istanbul Cooperation Initiative?" NATO Research Division, Research Paper No. 55.

Rossiter, Ash, 2014. "Britain and the Development of Professional Security Forces in the Gulf Arab States, 1921–1971: Local Forces and Informal Empire." Ph.D. Thesis submitted to the University of Exeter.

Sadjadpour, Karim, 2011. "The Battle of Dubai: The United Arab Emirates and the US-Iran Cold War." Carnegie Papers Middle East.

Sager, Abdulaziz, 2013. "Whither GCC-US Relations?" Gulf Research Center.

Salem, Fadi, 2007. "Enhancing Trust in e-Voting Through Knowledge Management: the Case of the UAE." Dubai School of Government Research Paper.

Sato, Shohei, 2009. "Britain's Decision to Withdraw from the Persian Gulf, 1964–1968: A Pattern and a Puzzle." *Journal of Imperial and Commonwealth History*, 37(1).

Seznec, Jean-Francois, 2008. "The Gulf Sovereign Wealth Funds: Myth and Reality." *Middle East Policy*, 15(2).

Shanahan, Rodger, 2008. "Why the Gulf Matters: Crafting an Australian Security Policy for the Arabian Gulf." Lowy Institute for International Policy, Policy Brief.

Shanahan, Rodger, 2011. "Enduring Ties and Enduring Interests? Australia's Post-Afghanistan Strategic Choices in the Gulf." Lowy Institute for International Policy, Policy Brief.

Sherbiny, Naiem, 1985. "Oil and the Internationalization of Arab Banks." Oxford Institute of Energy Studies.

Tetreault, Mary Ann, 1991. "Autonomy, Necessity, and the Small State: Ruling Kuwait in the Twentieth Century." *International Organization*, 45(4).

Thatcher, Mark, 2009. "Governing Markets in Gulf States." LSE Kuwait Program Working Paper No. 1.

Van der Meulen, Hendrik, 1997. "The Role of Tribal and Kinship Ties in the Politics of the United Arab Emirates." Ph.D. Thesis Submitted to the Fletcher School of Law and Diplomacy.

Van Ham, Peter, 2001. "The Rise of the Brand State: the Postmodern Politics of Image and Reputation." *Foreign Affairs*, 80(5).

Viramontes, Erick, 2012. "The Role of Latin America in the Foreign Policies of the GCC States." Paper Presented to the Gulf Research Meeting, University of Cambridge.

Von Bismarck, Helene, 2011. "'A Watershed in our Relations with the Trucial States': Great Britain's Policy to Prevent the Opening of an Arab League Office in the Persian Gulf in 1965." *Middle Eastern Studies*, 47(1).

Walker, Julian, 2012. "Personal Recollections of Indigenous Sources and the Rapid Growth of Archives in the Emirates." *Liwa: Journal of the National Center for Documentation and Research*, 4(8).

Wilkinson, John, 2009. "From Liwa to Abu Dhabi." *Liwa: Journal of the National Center for Documentation and Research*, 1(1).

Yamani, Mai, 2008. "The Two Faces of Saudi Arabia." *Survival*, 50(1).

Youngs, Richard, 2008. "Impasse in Euro-Gulf Relations." FRIDE Working Paper No. 80.
Zaccara, Luciano, 2015. "The Role of the Gulf Countries in the Mediterranean and the Middle East Following the Arab Spring." European Institute of the Mediterranean (IeMED), Mediterranean Yearbook.

Newspapers

Afghan Zariza
Bloomberg News
Business Standard
Business Times
Chronicle of Higher Education
Daily Mail
Financial Times
First Post India
Gulf Business
Gulf Business News and Analysis
Gulf News
Gulf States Newsletter/Gulf States News (from 2014)
Herald Sun
Houston Chronicle
International Herald Tribune
Jakarta Globe
Khaleej Times
Kuwait Times
Las Vegas Review-Journal
Le Monde Diplomatique
Mada Masr
Manchester Evening News
Newsweek
New York Times
Spiegel Online
Steady State Manchester
The Diplomat
The Economic Times
The Economist
The Globe and Mail
The Guardian
The Gulf Business News and Analysis
The Harvard Crimson
The Jerusalem Post
The National
The New Yorker
The Straits Times
The Washington Diplomat
USA Today
Washington Post
World Maritime News
Xinhua

Online and other Sources

ABC News Australia
Agence France-Presse (AFP)
Ahram Online
Al Arabiya
Al Jazeera
Al-Monitor
Al Tamimi & Co
American Shipper
ArabianBusiness.com
Arabian Industry
Arab Gulf States Institute in Washington blog
Arab Law Quarterly
BBC Magazine
BBC News
BBC Sport
Breaking Energy
Brookings Institution blog
CIA World Factbook
Clyde & Co
CNN Money
Defense News
Economist Intelligence Unit
Emirates 24/7
Emirates News
Emirates News Agency
ETFTrends.com
Forbes.com
Foreign Policy
Hansard
Human Rights Watch
Index on Censorship
Inside the Game
International Monetary Fund
IHS Global Insight
International Atomic Energy Agency
International Handball Federation
Jadaliyya
LSE Middle East Center
LSE Press Office
Middle East Economic Digest
Middle East Eye
Middle East Monitor
Mubadala
Nardello & Co
NPR
NYU Abu Dhabi
Open Democracy
Oxford Analytica

Oxford Business Group
Platts News & Analysis
Public Library of US Diplomacy
Reuters
SeaTrade
The Arab Weekly
The Atlantic
The National Archives (United Kingdom)
Senate Print (United States)
Sovereign Wealth Fund Institute
United Nations Conference on Trade and Development (UNCTAD) Country Fact Sheet:
    United Arab Emirates
UPI
US Energy and Information Administration
Vanity Fair
Variety
War on the Rocks
Washington Times

INDEX